P9-DTY-428

DATE DUE

MR 3 95			
AP 2 00			
JE 9 00			
JE 2 3 00			

Managing Indonesia

Studies of the East Asian Institute
Columbia University

MANAGING INDONESIA

The Modern Political Economy

JOHN BRESNAN

Columbia University Press • New York

Columbia University Press

New York   Chichester, West Sussex

Copyright © 1993 Columbia University Press

All rights reserved

Library of Congress Cataloging-in-Publication Data

Bresnan, John, 1927–

Managing Indonesia : the modern political economy / John Bresnan.

p.   cm.

Includes bibliographical references and index.

ISBN 0-231-07990-7

ISBN 0-231-07991-5(pbk.)

1. Indonesia—Economic conditions—1945–   2. Indonesia—Politics
and government—1966–   I. Title.

HC447.5.B74. 1993

338.9598—dc20   92–23598

⊗

Casebound editions of Columbia University Press books
are printed on permanent and durable acid-free paper.

Printed in the United States of America

c 10 9 8 7 6 5 4 3 2 1
p 10 9 8 7 6 5 4 3 2

To Barbara

THE EAST ASIAN INSTITUTE
OF COLUMBIA UNIVERSITY

The East Asian Institute is Columbia University's center for research, education, and publication on modern East Asia. The Studies of the East Asian Institute were inaugurated in 1962 to bring to a wider public the results of significant new research on modern and contemporary East Asia.

Contents

Preface

I am grateful to many people for their contributions to this study. I am indebted to a number of individuals associated with the Ford Foundation for making possible my extended residence in Indonesia and my acquaintance with a wide range of its national elite. I wish to thank three by name. Frank J. Miller was the representative of the foundation in Indonesia under whom I served as assistant representative from November 1961 to June 1965. David E. Bell and McGeorge Bundy were, respectively, the executive vice president and president of the foundation under whom I served as representative in Indonesia from July 1969 to June 1973. They also were responsible for my subsequent appointment as head of the office for Asia and the Pacific, which made possible my continuing close acquaintance with Indonesia from 1973 to 1981. Much of what I have learned about Indonesia is a result of the confidence these three demonstrated in me over a period that spanned more than two decades.

I also wish to express my gratitude to two colleagues at the East Asian Institute of Columbia University, James W. Morley and Gerald L. Curtis—both long-time professors of the university and directors of the East Asian Institute—for the friendship, encouragement, and support that made my work on this study possible since 1982. To the latter I am also indebted for his having first suggested the general structure this study has taken.

My principal thanks are directed to the scores of members of the Indonesian elite who granted me interviews, in some cases repeatedly, over a period of years. They were unfailingly generous in their efforts to enlighten me, even on matters they had reason to find personally painful. It is a source of great regret to me that I have not felt able to quote any of them by name. No interviewee ever asked my intention on this point. Many had known me for years; others had been introduced to me by individuals who had known me for years. Consequently, all or almost all had every reason to expect me to honor the confidentiality of their remarks. At the same time, even individuals I was meeting for the first time sometimes surprised me by the directness of their comments, especially those aimed at the president. Because it is against the law in Indonesia for citizens to criticize their head of state, I was in a quandary. I had no wish to place any individual at risk. Yet I could not possibly know when a source could be named without possible danger to the individual. Torn between my duty to sources and readers, I concluded that I must protect the former.

Several individuals read and commented on portions of the manuscript in draft form: Malcolm Gillis, Sidney Jones, Dorodjatun Kuntjoro-Jakti, J. A. C. Mackie, Leon Mears, Muthiah Alagappa, Widjojo Nitisastro, Mohammad Sadli, the late Soedjatmoko, Hadi Soesastro, and Harry Tjan. I am deeply grateful for their critiques of my interpretation of events. I hasten to add that none is in any way responsible for the final manuscript; all errors of judgment that remain are my own.

The staff of the Ford Foundation in Jakarta performed valuable services during my many visits in connection with this study; I am particularly indebted to Utje Lekatompessy, Adnan Madewa, Lucy Sundjaja, and Nani Supolo. In addition, William Fuller and Jennifer Beckett made several of my visits to Jakarta immeasurably more pleasant by taking me in as a guest in their home. Several graduate students of Columbia University—Jeff Benz, Henry Carey, Lorien French, David Kim, Timothy O'Shea, Sara Robertson, and Jonathan Stromseth—assisted me in my research. So did Jeffry Maskovsky and my daughter, Joan Bresnan. Takeshi Kokubu translated the Japanese press for chapter 6. Aysha Pande assisted in word processing. Rita Bernhard was my copyeditor at Columbia University Press. Financial support for my research and writing came from a variety of sources, notably the Rockefeller Brothers Fund and the Henry Luce Foundation; I wish to thank in particular Russell Philips and Terrence Lautz of their respective staffs for their encouragement and support.

Finally, I wish to thank my elder children, Patricia, Mark, and Peter, for the sacrifices they made during my residence in Indonesia from 1969 to 1973, without which this study would not have been possible.

I have made every effort to make the text and its sources accessible to readers not acquainted with the Indonesian language. Indonesian words and phrases have been held to a minimum and have been defined when their use has been unavoidable. English language sources have been preferred when they have been available.

All names of Indonesians follow the spellings found in *Apa & Siapa*. Spellings otherwise conform to current usage, with the exception that titles of published materials conform to the usage of the time of publication. Translations from the Indonesian are by the author unless otherwise indicated.

Managing Indonesia

Studies of the East Asian Institute
Columbia University

Introduction

In 1965 Indonesia experienced political violence on a scale without parallel in its history and of a kind unknown elsewhere in the late twentieth century. Hundreds of thousands of people, most of them rural supporters of the Communist party, lost their lives. No other nation has experienced a more violent and broadly based reaction to the political Left in our time. The accompanying destruction of the party, then the third largest Communist party in the world, marked a turning point in the history of communism globally. The meaning for Indonesia itself was profound.

In the same year the economic and social deprivation of the Indonesian population reached unprecedented levels. Indonesia was already among the poorer countries of Asia at the time it achieved its independence in 1949. Subsequent civil war and foreign adventure left it poorer still. Amid the chaos of 1965, gross national product fell to only $30 per capita per year, and the food supply to only 1,800 calories per capita per day. These were among the lowest levels in the entire world at the time. Every other country in Asia, including China, India, and what is now Bangladesh, was better off.[1]

More than twenty-five years later Indonesia presented a greatly altered political, economic, and social aspect. Power resided exclusively in a strong central executive; a single army general had filled the office of president uninterruptedly since 1966. Many other government offices were also filled by armed forces personnel, and criticism of official conduct was sternly and sometimes severely repressed. At the same time the population was considerably better off in other respects than it had been a generation earlier. Average life expectancy had risen from forty-five years to a remarkable sixty years. Primary education was virtually universal. The average Indonesian was better fed than the average person in China, Indochina, India, or the rest of South Asia. Many of Indonesia's economic and social development indicators were approaching those of the Philippines, long its wealthier neighbor in island Southeast Asia.[2]

What is one to make of these developments? How is one to explain and assess them? Was the violence of 1965 in some sense inevitable for its time and place? Was the authoritarianism and militarization that followed a necessary eventuality? Why has opposition not been more effective over the quarter century since? And how is it that such great economic and social changes have occurred? How significant have external factors been, such as foreign aid and the international price of oil? How significant have domestic factors been, including institutions and individual leaders? Most important, how significant have policies been? And how significant to the policies has been the character of the regime? Was authoritarianism necessary for Indonesia's economic and social development over the past generation? Is it still? Or is Indonesia, at the beginning of the 1990s, like so much of the rest of the world, moving toward a more open political future?

These are the principal questions with which this study is concerned. They are seldom answered with regard to Indonesia. Indeed, it is among the least known of the populous nations of the earth.

Indonesia is particularly remote—for reasons of geography, culture, history, and policy—from the English-speaking world. Lying midway between the Asian land mass and Australia, the Indonesian archipelago is almost as far away from the North Atlantic nations as it could be. Culturally, the Indonesian people are related principally to the other Malay peoples of peninsular Malaysia and the islands of the Philippines, to the ancient Hindu/Buddhist world of the subcontinent of India and of mainland Southeast Asia, and, as a result of more recent contact, to the Islamic thought and devotion centered in and around the Arabian peninsula. The colonial period of Dutch domination did little to bring the Indonesian people into a significant cultural relationship with the West, and the rejection of that domination, achieved by force of arms and diplomacy at the end of World War II, set the seal on a disposition by the nation's elite to make their own way, so far as possible, on their own terms. Policies adopted at one time or another over the years of independence with regard to language, education, religion, agriculture, industry, trade, and foreign relations have tended to reinforce the disposition to be a nation apart.

Indonesia is little known even to itself. Its population, estimated at 186 million in mid-1991, is the fourth largest in the world after China, India, and the United States, and is distributed among several thousand islands and among dozens of ethnic groups that have their own identities, speak their own languages, and are large enough to dominate one or another of the nation's administrative units. Unified administratively in modern times by the Dutch, the Indonesians themselves have only begun the process of exploring the great diversity of history and culture within their own society. This process has been delayed by indigenous traditions that are more oral than literary; by the limited modern education made available to the native population during the colonial period; by fears among national leaders since independence of dangers, both real and imagined, to the integrity of the state; and by a resulting political orientation that has given greater emphasis to the unity that is desired than to the diversity that is ever-present.

An analyst of the Indonesian political economy faces two problems as a result of these circumstances. One is the limited quality of available data. A large volume of quantitative data has been made public by various government authorities, and a large body of reportage has been published by the Indonesian periodical press. At the same time, given the deference traditional to much of Indonesian society and the repression of expression endemic to a military-led regime, little qualitative data are available from Indonesian sources on many issues of political and economic consequence. As a result, one is in constant danger of being overwhelmed by information and at the same time starved for authoritative expressions of what has been thought and felt about major national events, even by those who have participated most directly in them.

A solution to this problem has been sought through confidential interviews with more than a hundred members of the Indonesian elite, beginning in 1983 and repeated, in some cases annually, up to and including 1991. The interviews were conducted with members of the Indonesian cabinet from 1965 on; others who reported directly at one time or another during the same period to General, later President, Soeharto; military officers of flag rank; Muslim religious leaders; heads of state enterprises; leaders of the private business community; leaders of student and other dissident groups; and intellectuals with positions in the major universities, the research institutes of the capital, and the mass media.

The elite thus described has much in common with that already functioning in the 1920s and 1930s.[3] Only the category of military officers is entirely new. Two other significant differences should be noted, however. Many more private business firms of some scale existed by the early 1990s than had existed even in the 1950s and early 1960s. And intellectuals, who before independence were largely employed in the civil service, were now employed in a variety of institutions with varying degrees of independence from the political authorities. The elite has thus been undergoing a long-term process of privatization, increasing the heterogeneity of experience, creating an economic base for a middle class outside the bureaucracy, and encouraging an increasing independence of thought, if not yet of expression.

The interviews provided new information about events since 1965, as well as much commentary on the large volume of materials already published domestically and abroad. The interviews also led to copies of numerous unpublished papers, reports, and other documents. Indonesians have been seriously underrepresented among the writers of their own history, but they are by no means lacking in interest in how it is done.

The analyst of Indonesia's political economy faces a second problem: conveying one's findings to a readership unfamiliar with the country. The problem is particularly acute since few books dealing with Indonesia are published in the English language. Few readers can come to a new work with prior knowledge of the subject, as is the case with China or India. One thus runs the danger either of overwhelming readers with more information than they can absorb, or of traversing the ground so quickly that they have no opportunity to weigh the evidence and draw their own conclusions.

With this problem in mind, I decided to limit the present work to a manageable series of chapters concerned with major political and economic events. The study begins with an account of the failed leftist coup of October 1, 1965, the most significant political event in Indonesia since the declaration of its independence on August 17, 1945.

Each of the nine chapters that follows is a case study of a major event that occurred in the ensuing twenty-five years. These events are taken up in chronological order, but they have been selected for the light they shed on leading personalities and their ideas; key elements of the political structure, including the presidency, the army, the civil bureaucracy, students, and Islam; and central factors of the economy, including rice, oil, manufacturing, and foreign aid, trade, and investment. The chapters also explore issues that recur during the period, including corruption, foreign influence, the state's role in the economy, and the distribution of power and wealth in the society. Each case is described in sufficient detail to convey a firm sense of the immediate environment in which the event took place, its proximate causes, the personalities and ideas most centrally involved, and the group interests at issue as seen by participants themselves. Earlier history is recounted only to the extent it is essential to an understanding of the particular event under discussion.

An epilogue, in which the questions posed in this introduction are recalled and some answers are advanced, follows the case studies.

ONE

The Coup That Failed

During the last months of 1965 the Indonesian nation was gripped in a great and tragic madness. It was one of those times in human affairs when the assumptions on which civic life depends are swept away in a flood of hate and violence. In the capital city of Jakarta the children of the elite took to the streets, and public buildings were sacked. In the countryside of Java and Bali, villagers attacked their neighbors with knives and machetes. The dead were too numerous to count; estimates ran into the hundreds of thousands. By the time the killing came to an end, the third largest Communist party in the world lay destroyed.

It is in the nature of such events that controversy should surround the central questions they present.[1] Much of the controversy has concerned the role the Communist party of Indonesia played in the violent coup attempt that set so many other bloody events in motion. Another controversial subject has been the extent to which Sukarno himself might have known in advance about the attempted coup by dissident army officers. Still other questions have concerned the role of Soeharto, the army general who succeeded to power in the aftermath of the killings, and the role of the Chinese and the Americans in the affair. Yet, by far the most disturbing question has been how so many people could die, not anonymously as in modern warfare, but at the hands of their neighbors.

Wholly satisfactory answers to these questions will probably continue to elude us. Too many participants are dead, too many survivors silent. The trauma remains one from which the society can hardly be said to have recovered.

7

1. The Coup That Failed

Nevertheless, it is important to search out as best one can the true nature of what happened. For these violent events, and the perceptions of those who survived them, contain the origins of much of what followed.

The Immediate Background to the Coup

The story begins in Jakarta in August 1965. It was a time of great discord in Indonesia's national government. President Sukarno seemed nominally supreme in his command of state affairs, but this was far from the actual case. He had presided over the banishment from public life of a growing number of nationally prominent personalities and their parties, until his government no longer represented a large portion of the nation's elite. As his political base narrowed, his role was increasingly reduced to that of balancing the interests and ambitions of the two powerful groups that remained, the Communist party and the army. The party leaders and the army had been deeply divided over a number of issues for many years. Neither side doubted that some kind of showdown would eventually occur between them. At the time, however, both had reason to feel unprepared for such a test of strength.

The Communist Party of Indonesia (Partai Komunis Indonesia, or PKI) had suffered a serious setback during the previous year. Breaking with its own long-term strategy of working in concert with other major groups in the national front, the party had struck out on its own in urging tenant farmers in Central and East Java to take "unilateral action" against their landlords, to make the land they tilled their own. But the campaign was disastrously ill conceived and considerable violence occurred; in the end the party's rural forces were bested. Meanwhile, the party was progressing in its efforts to infiltrate the army officer corps, but the number of officers it could rely on in a physical showdown was small.

The leadership of the Indonesian National Army (Tentara Nasional Indonesia, or TNI) had meanwhile been shaken by evidence of significant disunity in its own senior ranks. A seminar that had been called earlier in the year to draw the army's regional commanders together in a unified stand on matters of national policy had degenerated into polemics. It was the first such meeting since the regional rebellions of the late 1950s had been put down. In the political environment of 1965, army unity in ideological matters had become a high priority. According to participants, a significant minority of commanders held out in support of Sukarno's increasingly leftist domestic and international priorities.

In the background lay Indonesia's "confrontation" against neighboring Malaysia. The decision to "confront" the founding of Malaysia in late 1963 may well have been the result of happenstance as much as studied Indonesian intent. In any case, the time could not have been worse from the Indonesian point of view. The country was in the midst of a prolonged drought; rice production was down, and food was in short supply. In addition, the confrontation campaign disrupted Indonesia's exports and this, in turn, reduced not only the country's earnings of foreign exchange, but also the government's revenues, the bulk of which came from taxes on foreign trade. Thus the government was increasingly obliged to finance its own operations by printing paper money. Inflation spiraled. Among the urban population, many of whom depended on civil servants' incomes, the conditions of daily life became harsh indeed.

The campaign against Malaysia created serious problems for the Indonesian armed forces. The army was organized and trained for territorial defense; most of its units had no experience outside their native provinces. The air and naval arms necessary for invasion had proven hopelessly inadequate in the West Irian campaign. The army leadership also mistrusted both the air and naval services; they had been equipped and trained in recent years by the Russians, and their leaders were on good terms with the local Communist party leaders. Moreover, army intelligence had little knowledge of what awaited invading forces on their arrival on the Malayan peninsula; the first small units sent ashore on intelligence and sabotage missions had been quickly rounded up. But the balance of military forces on either side of the Straits of Malacca was not what weighed most heavily on the army commanders. Their main concern was the domestic political situation. From the outset they had to avoid the Communist party outflanking them on an issue of such strong nationalist appeal. As plans for the invasion of Malaysia advanced, they also had to avoid having their best and most loyal officers and their units removed from Java. The recent Communist party campaign in the countryside of Java left army commanders deeply concerned about their own rear defenses. From late 1964 on, Indonesian army intelligence officers were in secret communication with their opposite numbers in Kuala Lumpur, with a view to limiting the scale and costs of engagement.[2]

The anti-Malaysia campaign presented the Communist party, on the other hand, with an opportunity to strengthen its standing with Sukarno and to isolate Indonesia still further from the Western powers. Sukarno was deeply committed personally to the anti-Malaysia policy but, after almost two years, little had happened beyond the war of propaganda; the army was obviously dragging its feet. By the beginning of 1965 the Communist party was pressing for a full role in the cabinet, and under the ground rules Sukarno himself had laid down, the party could not be denied indefinitely. In the early months of the year the party had further unnerved the generals by making two even more threatening proposals: (1) that the commanders of the armed forces, at every level, should be advised by a "troika" of political commissars, one of whom would represent the Communist party; and (2) that "workers and peasants" should be armed in a "fifth force" for the "safeguarding of the revolution." By March 1965 Sukarno was receiving intelligence reports that some army commanders were making plans to overthrow him. In May he began to support the "troika" idea.

These developments thoroughly alarmed the army leadership, as well as many in the civilian elite. Lt. Gen. Achmad Yani, the army commander-in-chief, was now meeting regularly with a "brain trust" of his closest associates to discuss the army's deteriorating political position. He protested the party proposals. He denied reports of an army plot against the president. But the party initiatives had placed him and his colleagues thoroughly on the defensive, and civilian friends wondered how long the army could stave off the PKI's accession to formal power.

All this fed into the tension that was mounting in the background when, on August 3, Sukarno suddenly fell ill. The precise nature of his illness was never clear. He had had a long-term kidney condition and periodically sought treatment in Vienna. On this occasion, however, a team of Chinese doctors was flown in from Beijing, and Sukarno's personal staff was totally mute about his condition. The impact this development had on both the party and army leaders is not difficult to imagine. Indeed, both were soon engaged in planning their moves should Sukarno suddenly die. Within a few days, Sukarno was said to be recovering; soon he was said to be preparing his annual address for Independence Day on August 17. But leaders of the party and the army were now receiving reports that the other was on the verge of a coup. By early September the Jakarta press was referring to rumors of a possible coup by either the army or the party. As things turned out, it was the army's most senior officers who were caught unprepared.

The Coup and Its Aftermath

In the early hours of October 1 General Yani and five of his closest army associates, all general officers, were routed from their beds by units of the presidential security guard and told the president wished to see them immediately. Three resisted and were shot and killed on the spot; the other three were bundled into trucks and taken away, along with the bodies of the three dead. The most senior general of all, Abdul Haris Nasution, the celebrated former army commander and now Minister of Defense, also was sought at his home that night but escaped, although an aide was killed and Nasution's young daughter mortally wounded. (Nasution had gone over a garden wall to the grounds of the Iraqi ambassador's neighboring residence, but broke his leg in the fall and remained hidden there until well after dawn.)

The following morning Radio Indonesia announced that army units under the leadership of Lieutenant Colonel Untung, the commander of a battalion of the presidential guard, had forestalled a coup that was planned by a Council of Generals. The statement declared, inter alia: "Power-mad generals and officers who have neglected the lot of their men and who above the accumulated sufferings of their men have lived in luxury, led a gay life, insulted our women and wasted government funds, must be kicked out of the army and punished accordingly. The army is not for generals, but is the possession of all the soldiers of the army who are loyal to the ideals of the Revolution of August 1945."[3] A later broadcast reported that a Revolutionary Council would be named as the "source of all authority in the Republic of Indonesia."[4] President Sukarno was said to be safe, but his whereabouts were not disclosed.

In a matter of hours, amid continued uncertainty about where either Sukarno or the missing generals were, the uprising was brought under control by Major General Soeharto, commander of the Army Strategic Reserve, without a shot being fired. Sukarno was found to have gone to a nearby air base, as had D. N. Aidit, the leader of the Communist party. The army occupied the air base during the night of October 1, after Sukarno had been advised to leave and the Communist party chairman had fled. The bodies of all six missing generals were found a few days later in a well on the edge of the base. Nasution's daughter died of her wounds soon thereafter. The violence of these deaths, coupled with the breach of Guided Democracy convention, infuriated the army leadership that remained and deeply shocked many of the civilian elite.

Meanwhile, the leaders of several army units in Central Java declared their support for the Revolutionary Council. The mayors of several towns did the same. There were a few mass demonstrations of support by local communist organizations. Otherwise, the province remained in a state of suspended animation until mid-October, when a battalion of paratroopers arrived from Jakarta to bring the rebel units to heel. The arrival of this battalion seems to have spurred the local Left to action. Roadblocks were set up; telephone lines were cut. The paratroopers made a show of strength in one town after another, and by the end of the month the rebel army units agreed to follow orders and leave the province.

By this time, however, attacks were beginning on Communist party offices and on Chinese property in several cities of Central Java, anti-communist demonstrators had been fired on, and reports were circulating that religious and nationalist leaders had been killed. By early November, still able to control only a single town at a time, the paratroopers began arming youths from religious and nationalist organizations. The affair was soon thoroughly one-sided, and killings occurred on a massive scale.

A short story written by Umar Kayyam in 1966 provides a fictional account, based on an eyewitness interview, of an army "sweep" through a rural communist stronghold:

> Suddenly people were running through the streets screaming that the army had taken the village of B. The army had moved in quickly and silently, passing through barricades the people had thought impenetrable, attacking without warning. What kind of force were they dealing with? Some kind of spirit? The army was everywhere.
>
> The farmers, drilled by Hassan and their own leaders, fought relentlessly. They took up guns, Molotov cocktails, sharpened bamboo poles, any available weapon. The reactionary army was their enemy. It had come and it would kill them and rob them of their land unless they destroyed it first.
>
> But one by one the villages of the Subdistrict fell. Resistance was soon crushed, and the outcome of the fighting was horrible. Insufficiently

trained, the farmers resisted blindly and in a single day the whole (of) T. had fallen and was occupied by the army. The farmers in their frenzy set fire to their own homes and granaries. Those who didn't surrender were cut down mercilessly. Corpses lay sprawled on the dikes of the rice fields, along the banks of the rivers, and on the footpaths throughout the countryside. One quarter of the inhabitants of the Subdistrict were dead and nearly half of the surviving men taken captive.[5]

In East Java no army units declared support for the Revolutionary Council. The commander of the naval base at Surabaya did so, however, on October 1, and the following day the communist labor union began a previously announced program of taking over the state enterprises in the province. On October 13 the Islamic youth organization, Ansor, held rallies in several towns, which were followed by attacks on Communist party offices; at one such rally, eleven party supporters were hacked to death. On October 18 a clash between communist and Ansor youth left ninety-seven dead. In the next few days several thousand Communist party supporters were reported massacred. Army units seemed to have been directly involved in the killing by the end of October, but chiefly in the towns. In the villages religious leaders seemed to have been given their head. By mid-November killings had taken place throughout the province.[6]

In Bali rumors were soon circulating about what was happening in Central and East Java. On November 11 a clash between communist and Nationalist Party youths left seven dead. By the first week of December the killing was widespread.

Fictional accounts tell of youths interrogating their friends and former teachers, even their family doctors. Brutal beatings took place. Groups were taken to a river bank and shot. Others were made to sit at the edge of their graves, and then shot.[7]

Satyagraha Hoerip, in "The Climax," describes a district in which hundreds were killed in a three-week period. "Even those with only minimal connections [with the Communist party] had been killed. Others were given to the authorities, then taken back at night and taken out of town."[8] The story's narrator describes his efforts, eventually successful, to avoid killing his brother-in-law.

In each province, after several weeks of this mass butchery, local army leaders appeared to have decided that the violence had gone far enough. By late November military authorities in Central Java had prohibited unauthorized arrests and were warning against "excesses." By the end of

December those in East Java were doing the same. In Bali paratroopers had to be rushed from Central Java to bring the situation under control. But violence continued in all three provinces well into 1966.

Equally fierce action was taken against Communist party members and supporters in several other parts of Indonesia. In Aceh, in the far north of Sumatra, the population was, as it is now, overwhelmingly Islamic, and Communist party followers were few in number, perhaps totaling only several thousand; attacks on them were sufficient for the military commander to announce in December that the province had been "entirely purged in a physical sense of PKI elements."[9] In the adjoining province of North Sumatra, members of an army-supported labor union attacked members of the Communist party's union, many of them migrants from Java working on state plantations; members of Muslim and Christian youth groups attacked other known Communist party followers in the vicinity of Siantar, again with the loss of several thousand lives. In West Java, where the Communist party was not particularly strong, the army might have forestalled wider killing by its quick arrest of more than ten thousand party activists; close to ten thousand others were estimated to have been killed there nevertheless. In these and other parts of Indonesia, however, the scale of violence did not approach that of the densely populated provinces of Central and East Java and Bali.

Who Was Responsible?

Much later, men close to the army leadership of the time would deny that any central command ever authorized army units to carry out mass executions. They have argued that initially the army was not at all in control of the situation in much of Java. Some of the army's most trusted commanders and their units had already been removed from Java and were in North Sumatra and West Kalimantan, committed to the campaign against Malaysia. The army has also claimed that it was in fact the army itself that eventually brought the killings to an end. Nevertheless, the army certainly played an active role in the deaths of countless numbers of people, not only through the paratroopers sent to Central Java under the command of Gen. Sarwo Edhie Wibowo, who made no attempt to disguise the role his men played, but also through the many civilian youths whom these and other units organized, armed, and transported. At no time did General Nasution, General Soeharto, or any other figure in the army leadership publicly condemn these actions of army units, or call publicly for an end to the violence. The army leadership knew more or less what was happening and, by its action and inaction, sanctioned it.

Yet, it is also true that much of the killing, with and without army involvement, was carried out by civilians. In Central Java these were principally members of the conservative wing of the National Party, the once-dominant party in the region, commanding the loyalties of the traditional elite down to the leaders of the villages. The Nationalists had seen their position steadily eroded as Communist party strength grew, challenging their heritage as the major party of the national revolution, the party of Sukarno, the rightful heir to the positions and perquisites of the former colonial regime. They also had witnessed a deep split in their party over whether to enter into an alliance with the Communist party or stand apart from it. The same was true in Bali. In East Java, on the other hand, the killing was done principally by followers of the Nahdatul Ulama, the region's major Islamic party, led by its youth wing, Ansor.

Evidence also indicates that some of the worst of the killing was centered in areas that had previously seen violence between Communists and anti-Communists. In September 1948, when the republican government was confronted by superior Dutch forces in Java, its own military and paramilitary units experienced great dissension. A group of procommunist officers took control of the town of Madiun, declared a revolutionary government, and touched off an ill-coordinated and poorly executed revolt. Communist party leaders, apparently caught unprepared, nevertheless gave the revolt their support. Loyal army units, among which the Siliwangi Division was most prominent, recaptured the town of Madiun in two weeks and put down the entire rebellion in two months. Armed rebel units, however, killed scores of civilians in the surrounding district in the course of the rebellion, and Islamic teachers and civil servants seemed to have been singled out for execution. In the aftermath a few party leaders fled, but most were captured and executed. Some thirty-five thousand of their armed followers were held under arrest for a time. Retribution also was exacted by the Muslim community in a wave of violent attacks on party followers in the Madiun area.[10]

At the time of the attempted coup in 1965 conflict had been raging between the two groups for almost two years. The violence was touched off by a Communist party campaign in support of land reform, which inspired violent incidents across the whole of rural Central and East Java. What began with knifings and kidnappings escalated to group battles, with as many as two thousand on each side using clubs, knives, and machetes. According to one authority, it was the largest outbreak of violence in the recorded history of rural Java up to this time.[11]

The Land Situation

The land situation in Java was indeed critical. Some 54 percent of rural households on Java owned less than half a hectare (or less than 1.1 acres); another 13 percent were landless. Although in certain localities a small rural elite held sizable portions of land, a large landlord class simply did not exist in Java. Rather, Java's population growth had led to the progressive fragmentation of all landholdings. In addition, the increasing demand for land led to a constant increase in the value of land. Both these processes were driving an increasing number of poor farmers into daily wage labor, and obliging tenants and sharecroppers to accept less and less equitable terms in order to remain in farming.

The national government paid little attention to this problem until radical unionists in the late 1950s forcibly took over foreign-owned plantations. Up to this time land ownership had been regulated by an agrarian law promulgated by the Dutch colonial authorities in 1870. But a legal basis had to be provided for the expropriations in order to assure the security of plantation exports. So long as the plantations were legally the property of foreign owners, their products faced seizure by court order in foreign ports.

Nevertheless, the national political consensus was that a limit should be placed on the amount of land any one family could hold, and the surplus should be distributed to the landless. When Parliament passed the new land law in September 1960, it limited the amount of land any family might own or control through mortgages or leases. In the case of irrigated rice land in densely populated areas the limit was 8 hectares, or approximately 17.6 acres. The excess was to be registered with government officials who would then distribute it to landless peasants; owners were to be compensated over a period of years. The Department of Agrarian Affairs initially estimated that 1 million hectares would be available for distribution. By 1963, however, this had been scaled down to about one-third that amount. By the end of 1963 the government was reporting that only one-tenth of the latter figure, or some 35,000 hectares, had so far been distributed. Communist critics claimed the true figure was less than 20,000 hectares.

Wolf Ladejinsky, writing in early 1964 and using official data, concluded that not more than 6 percent of the four to five million sharecroppers on Java could possibly ever receive any land under the law. Few landlords with any sizable holdings were on this island, where two-thirds of Indonesia's population lived, and some districts had no land to redistribute at all. A more important question, in Ladejinsky's view, was the terms of tenancy. The law required that all agreements between landowners and tenants were to be in writing and registered with local authorities, but by 1964 this was honored chiefly in the breach; of several million probable agreements in all of Java and Bali, only twenty thousand had been recorded.[12] The law also required that landlord and tenant should each receive 50 percent of the crop, but the law failed to specify the sharing of expenses, such as the cost of fertilizers. Moreover, landlords frequently loaned money to their tenants for various purposes. Rural economic relations were far more complicated than the new agrarian law had taken into account. Ladejinsky concluded, in a private report to the government, that although the new law was on the books, "All else appears to be as of old."[13]

The Communists' Rural Strategy

About the time the new land law was enacted, the Communist party was beginning to work vigorously to build a rural base, particularly in Java. The party had obtained only 16.4 percent of the total vote in the national parliamentary elections of 1955. But 88.6 percent of its vote was in Java, and much of this support was believed to be concentrated among *abangan* peasants in Central and East Java. *Abangan* are largely peasants and lower-class townsmen in Java whose religious tradition consists of animistic, Hinduistic, and Islamic elements, with emphasis on the former two.[14] In the local elections of 1957 the Communist party supplanted the National Party as the leading party in Central Java. This was attributed, in part, to the party's appearance as an energetic and effective champion of *abangan* values against the interests of the *santri* community. *Santri* are largely traders and richer peasants in Java whose religious tradition consists of "a careful and regular execution of the basic rituals of Islam."[15]

3 3

Party leaders might well have seen a need for a new and stronger rural base. The mass base the party had developed by the late 1950s was largely made up of organized workers of firms and plantations formerly owned by the Dutch and other foreigners. In many cases, these workers had taken control of the enterprises that employed them in 1957, but they became increasingly vulnerable following the introduction of martial law later the same year. Army officers were put in charge of the enterprises, and some did not shrink from using force to establish their authority. Party leaders may also have been responding to critics within the party who were unhappy about the leadership's accommodation to some of the authoritarian features of Sukarno's Guided Democracy. In any event, party leaders decided to enlarge and tighten up their organization among the general rural population. In 1958 preparations were begun for a first National Peasants Conference to launch a concerted drive to organize the rural population.

The main feature of this drive was a "go down" movement, a campaign to encourage party cadres in cities and towns to go to the villages, become familiar with conditions there, and educate the peasants about the policies and programs of the party. The "go down" movement was needed because party cadres were mostly townsmen unaccustomed to the physical conditions of rural life, and reluctant to spend long periods in the villages. They also faced obstacles there from village authorities, the well-to-do, and traditionalist advocates of village harmony. In some villages, divided among hostile factions, party support tended to come from unemployed youth and other radicalized elements, but these were mostly illiterate, accustomed to showing deference to people of higher status, and unversed in the ways of modern organization. So it was decided to introduce organizers from outside the villages, and to put the authority and prestige of the party's leadership behind the effort.

The National Peasants Conference of April 1959 resolved that the most important aspect of party work in the villages was to bridge the gap between urban party cadres and villagers through the "three togethers"—living together, eating together, and working together. The official position was that this would be a gradual process, both to educate the cadres and to win the peasants' confidence. Nevertheless, the party chairman, D. N. Aidit, on the occasion of the Conference, authorized an attack on landlord interests and, on the party's behalf, demanded that the traditional division of crops be changed from 60:40 in favor of landowners to the same ratio in favor of their tenants.[16]

1. The Coup That Failed

The Communists' Rural Offensive

There the matter rested until December 1963. At that time, having given scant attention to the subject for several years, Aidit called on the party to undertake a "rural offensive" in support of land reform. The peasants, he said, had to take "unilateral action"—to "take the law into their own hands."[17] This marked a radical break with the past: the long-term party strategy of maintaining a united front with other parties was put aside; for the first time the theme of a struggle between the haves and have-nots was introduced into the villages in a direct and organized way; and, finally, the established social and political allegiances and traditional values of social harmony and deference were challenged.[18]

The timing of this initiative was well chosen; it so happened that in the last months of 1963 and the first months of 1964 parts of Java and Bali were experiencing the worst drought in living memory. Without any rain the irrigation channels stood dry, and rats infested the villages in search of food. Village stores of rice were ravaged; even trees around people's homes were shorn of their leaves. Reuters reported in February 1964 that a million people were starving in Central Java. Antara, the official Indonesian news agency, reported that thousands were starving in Bali. D. N. Aidit himself was quoted as saying, "People are now eating virtually anything edible."[19]

Serious conflicts were soon occurring in Central and East Java as a result of unilateral peasant action. By April 1964 the press was reporting serious outbreaks of violence over peasant actions throughout Central Java. By June the incidents had spread to East Java and were being reported daily in the Surabaya newspapers. The clashes were marked from the outset by knifings and kidnappings, and soon large-scale confrontations were taking place. Factions took to burning down the houses of hostile elements and destroying their crops in the field. Groups of between three hundred and four hundred, and even as many as two thousand, were reportedly involved in some incidents. In a number of places, police intervention led to serious loss of life.

These developments created considerable alarm among leaders of the National and Nahdatul Ulama parties. The Islamic party leaders were particularly incensed, because the Communist party appeared to be engaged in a broad offensive against Islamic interests. Many of the holders of sizable plots, especially in East Java, were *santri* family heads. Often the owners of extensive tracts of land were Islamic religious institutions. The Communist party had only recently tried to have Sukarno declare the leading Muslim student organization illegal. Islamic leaders, feeling increasingly threatened by the direction Guided Democracy was taking, viewed the attack on Muslim land rights as the last straw.

The uproar was muted in the controlled Jakarta press, and Sukarno sought at first to put the weight of his authority behind the land reform program. In July 1964 a special session of the Supreme Advisory Council resolved that implementation of the program should be speeded up. In August, in his annual Independence Day address, Sukarno criticized the slow pace of the program. But by early December Aidit was acknowledging that the party's opponents were getting the better of his cadres. Then Chaerul Saleh of the Murba Party claimed he had documents showing that the Communist party planned a coup. On December 12, in an atmosphere of great tension, Sukarno called a meeting of the heads of the ten then-legal political parties. After thirteen hours the meeting ended in a unanimous call for a truce in interparty conflict. But the violence continued well into 1965.

In May 1965, at a meeting of the Central Committee of the Communist party, Aidit blamed the situation on party cadres who had acted impetuously and without regard to party guidelines. But it is difficult to avoid the opinion that he and the other party leaders had misjudged the situation. In breaking the line on their own long-term "national front" strategy, the party leaders had succeeded chiefly in isolating themselves from the other national groups in the Sukarno coalition. By attempting to instigate confrontation along class lines, the party leaders also had revealed the weakness of class-consciousness, as well as the enduring strength of traditional attachments to party and religion among the rural population.

In August and September 1965 reports in the local press of Central and East Java indicated a resurgence of conflicts in these provinces, particularly of incidents in which youth groups—attached to the Communist party, on the one hand, and the Nationalist Party and Nahdatul Ulama, on the other—engaged in violent attacks on each other.

Longer-Term Contributions to the Violence

Sartono Kartodirdjo, who has documented the history of unrest in Indonesia's rural society over several centuries, has argued that the

1. The Coup That Failed

events of 1965–66 were part of a long-established pattern of political competition that was at least as intense in the countryside as in the towns. Radical social movements arose with some regularity among the lower social strata, the oppressed, and the underprivileged. These movements did not, however, arise only from conditions of economic deprivation and oppression. A strong element of millenarianism also emerged in the late colonial period. "The severe threat to the Javanese sense of identity posed by an increasingly heavy foreign political and cultural hegemony produced a powerful reaction in peasant society, expressed in an intense longing for a restoration of an idealized traditional order."[20] If the Communist party thus drew on utopian hopes that were important in Javanese culture from very early times, the reaction to the party's intrusion from early 1964 on also had a basis in a powerful tradition.

Of the intensity of relations between party politics and religion in rural Java, Clifford Geertz, writing in the late 1950s, had this to say:

> Because the same symbols are used in both political and religious contexts, people often regard party struggle as involving not merely the usual ebb and flow of parliamentary maneuver, the necessary factional give-and-take of democratic government, but involving as well decisions on basic values and ultimates. Kampong (village) people in particular tend to see the open struggle for power explicitly institutionalized in the new republican forms of government as a struggle for the right to establish different brands of essentially religious principles as official: "If the abangans get in, the koranic teachers will be forbidden to hold classes"; "If the santris get in, we shall all have to pray five times a day." The normal conflict involved in electoral striving for office is heightened by the idea that literally everything is at stake: the "If we win, it is our country" idea that the group which gains power has a right, as one man said, "to put his own foundation under the state." Politics thus takes on a kind of sacralized bitterness.[21]

The bloodshed in the countryside was further influenced by popular ideas of political history, learned by every Javanese peasant from the stories of the *wayang*. Benedict Anderson has argued that power has generally been regarded in traditional Javanese thought as highly concentrated—in the capital city, in the palace, and in the person of the ruler, "who personifies the unity of society."[22] Sukarno had demonstrated this concern for unity time and again in his attempts to create by rhetorical invention—of which *Nasakom,* the union of nationalism, religion, and communism, was an example—symbols of a unity that did not exist in

1. The Coup That Failed

the society. The same concern was seen in the dogged refusal of the largely Javanese elite to recognize the claims of the "outer islands" for a larger measure of autonomy in the 1950s. In this tradition, in which a diffusion of power is seen as weakness, Anderson argued that as "Power begins to ebb away from the center, the reigning dynasty loses its claim to rule, and disorder appears."[23] And "a ruler who has once permitted natural and social disorders to appear finds it particularly difficult to reconstitute his authority. Javanese would tend to believe that, if he still had the Power, the disorders would never have arisen."[24]

Those Javanese who were taking their cues from what was occurring in the capital city in October 1965 were presented with ample evidence that anticommunism was in the ascendancy. The same government radio station that had carried the leaders' announcements of the attempted coup, and thus encouraged the uprisings that followed for a short time in Central Java, was now reporting widening popular demonstrations, and army arrests, directed against the Communist party and its subsidiary organizations. Many of those involved in the demonstrations and arrests in Jakarta were thoroughly convinced that the Communist party had been behind the coup, and they were using the situation to wreak vengeance on the party and its people. They did so not only because of the deaths of the generals and the attempt to take control of the government, but also in return for all the intimidations they had suffered themselves at the hands of party activists in the past. Thus, reactions to the coup on the part of the capital's elite provided a further sanction to the rural anticommunist pogrom.

One is left, then, with a partial answer to the principal question with which this discussion began. The deep divisions within Indonesian society, divisions of religion, economic interest, social class, and political party, appear to have been at the root of the violence. These divisions were exacerbated by the procommunist revolt of 1948, by the national and local elections of 1955 and 1957, and, most recently and deeply, by the campaign of the Communist party to change the traditional rules that governed the use of land. The failure of the attempted coup provided an impetus to anticommunists in the countryside to wreak vengeance on those who had been attacking and intimidating them for almost two years. Moreover, traditional political thinking that placed a high value on the direction of events in the capital city could only have provided further encouragement to anticommunists in the provinces.

1. The Coup That Failed

Finally, the army's own actions contributed directly to the scale of the violence, and sanctioned the violence of others.

Some Remaining Issues

The number of dead was never determined. Official and unofficial estimates ran from 78,500 to 500,000. Whatever the number, one has to assume that many others died as an indirect result of the violence and the breakdown of family and community relations. Prominent among these would have been such vulnerable groups as infants, children, and the elderly, especially those from the poorest families who must have been on the edge of survival in the drought years of 1963 and 1964. Routine registrations of births and deaths, which had been unreliable even in normal times, were useless for this period. Data from the census of 1961 were not sufficiently analyzed to provide a basis for later comparison. And when preparations for the 1971 census were being made, it was found that all the 1961 data had been thrown away. So reliable estimates of mortality for the districts in which the violence occurred could never be made.

Among other issues, the role of the Communist party in the attempted coup has been a matter of considerable controversy. The coup itself did not involve any known members of the party directly. That the party was involved in planning the coup—as much as that seemed a foregone conclusion to many anticommunists in the elite—is not grounded in conclusive evidence. It is known from their own testimony at their later trials, and from criticisms by surviving remnants of the party both in Indonesia and abroad, that some party leaders knew the coup was going to take place. It is possible that Aidit had a larger hand in the affair than this. But we have no proof and it is possible we never shall.

What Sukarno knew, and when he knew it, is also uncertain. The most damaging evidence was circumstantial. On the morning of October 1, Sukarno fled to the same air base to which Aidit fled, and at which the bodies of the six generals were later found. He met during the day with some cabinet ministers, the heads of the other armed services, and one army general representing the coup leaders. He was later reported to have told the general that he wanted no more bloodshed, that the movement should be stopped. When he prepared a public statement late in the day, however, he announced only that he was taking over the temporary leadership of the army. He did not denounce the attempted coup, or express regret at the deaths of the generals, until October 6. These circumstances were enough to arouse grave suspicions about his role, and he was to be dogged by them in the months that followed.

Several years later speculation arose outside Indonesia as to whether Soeharto himself might have had some advance knowledge of the coup.[25] Soon after the night of September 30 the story was put out to journalists that Soeharto had gone fishing that evening with a son. In 1968, in an interview with a foreign journalist, Soeharto corrected this account to reveal that he had gone that evening to a military hospital to visit a sick son and, while he was there, Colonel A. Latief, a central figure among the plotters of the coup, came and spoke to him briefly. The colonel was well known to Soeharto, who had been his commanding officer. Critics have inferred that Latief came to inform him of what was about to happen and to ensure that Soeharto would not intervene. Soeharto has suggested that Latief must simply have been checking on his whereabouts. It seems probable that the plotters would indeed want to satisfy themselves that Soeharto, who was next in command to succeed to army leadership, had not been alerted to any untoward events that might occur later that night. That he was not on the list to be kidnapped was probably because many of the plotters had served under his command in the Irian campaign, and he was close enough to the plot leader, Untung, to have attended his wedding. In addition, the plotters might well have calculated that they could "handle" Soeharto; it was well known that Yani did not take him seriously. In any event, Soeharto was awakened at about five the next morning by Mashuri, a prominent lawyer and secretary of the local neighborhood administration, who had reports that shots had been heard in the vicinity of Nasution's house. Mashuri later said that the surprise with which Soeharto greeted his early morning report was undoubtedly genuine. Nevertheless, the meeting with Latief remains a curious event, as does the long delay in reporting it.

The Chinese role is also a matter of speculation. That the Chinese leadership in Beijing enjoyed a warm relationship with D. N. Aidit and the other leaders of the Indonesian Communist Party is beyond question. Chinese leaders had encouraged the newly aggressive stance of the Indonesian party leaders, to the point of having first suggested the idea of an armed "fifth force." Chinese officials in Beijing also initially greeted the news of the coup with much satisfaction, congratulating the members of the Indonesian delegation who were in the Chinese capital for the annual October 1 celebrations. There is no evidence, however, that Chinese leaders either knew of the plot in advance or were party to it. Many Indonesians were nevertheless convinced that the Chinese had known, and were involved. Among them were the leaders of the anticommunist student demonstrators, who were soon attacking official Chinese property in Jakarta, and Soeharto himself, who was to remain personally opposed to official recognition of the Chinese government for almost twenty-five years.

The most curious misunderstanding of the whole tragic affair, however, is the continuing belief in the West that primarily Chinese and Indonesians of Chinese descent died in the killings.[26] Both groups have long been objects of attack in periods of social unrest in Indonesia, and 1965 was no exception. Their schools were closed, and their shops and even homes were ransacked in many towns. But Chinese-Indonesians were not prominent among the members of the Indonesian Communist Party, unlike the situation in neighboring Malaysia. Chinese also were not present in any large number in the countryside after 1959, when a presidential decree ordered resident aliens out of the villages as part of a program to reduce their role as middlemen in the economy. Later efforts to calculate the number of Chinese victims have yielded estimates as low as two thousand.[27] Alien Chinese and Chinese-Indonesians undoubtedly lived in great fear for many months, and close to 10,000 opted to leave the country in 1966–67. But the violence was largely to property, and the number who left Indonesia was not to be compared with the estimated 100,000 who left in 1959–60.[28]

The impression abroad might have resulted from press reports of the ransacking of the embassy and other property of the People's Republic of China (PRC) in Jakarta. The press also reported the anti-Chinese action in Aceh, where an overzealous army commander ordered the entire community of several thousand Chinese-Indonesians out of the province. These hapless people were stranded in the port city of Medan for several years, refugees in their own country. The Chinese government carried two shiploads of them to China before official relations collapsed and it became impossible to continue the rescue effort. Christian churches looked after the rest until the matter was finally taken up by higher authorities. The army commander's order was reversed, at least in practice, and the people were permitted to return to Aceh.

Controversy has also surrounded the issue of possible American involvement in the coup. Colonel Untung, in his first radio announcement, claimed that his action was intended to forestall a government takeover by a Council of Generals sponsored by the Central Intelligence Agency (CIA). The charge of CIA complicity has been repeated from time to time, but the evidence is highly circumstantial. The CIA did take the unusual step of making public a 1968 report concluding that the coup was directed by the leaders of the Communist Party of Indonesia.[29] Much later it was revealed that, following the failure of the coup, a political officer of the U.S. embassy in Jakarta turned over the names of several thousand communists to Indonesian army headquarters and kept track of those killed or captured.[30] As to American complicity in the coup attempt itself, however, there is no more support than in the case of the PRC.

Ramifications of the Coup

The horror of the events of 1965 in Java and Bali had few comparisons in the contemporary world. Gunnar Myrdal, searching for a way to describe the killings, compared them with the partition of India and the continuing war in Vietnam.[31] The comparisons had some foundation, for the Indonesian violence did erupt in part out of deep religious intolerance, as the partition of the subcontinent had, and also emerged out of a life-and-death struggle over political ideology, as had the war in Vietnam. But there was a third element, which linked the events in Indonesia to the Great Leap Forward occurring in China in the mid-1960s, and that was the intrusion into rural society of a radical national political program. Like those other tragedies, what occurred in Indonesia must be seen, in the end, as the result of monumental political failure.

The failure was not that of any one individual, although a few individuals mattered disproportionately. Yani had indeed been corrupted by his experience as a member of Sukarno's palace circle, was open to the charge of neglecting the welfare of the army rank and file, and was in no sense a leader of the political Right, a deficiency which left a large part of the political spectrum without a national spokesman. Aidit failed to appreciate the vulnerability of his position, and permitted himself to be caught up in a rebellious adventure for which he was quite unprepared. Over a longer period of time, he had aimed to come to power as the leader of a revolutionary party, but by parliamentary means, without a revolutionary army. The imbalance between these ends and means seems, in retrospect, to have been fatal to his enterprise.

Yet Yani and Aidit had come to play the roles they did in 1965 principally because the Indonesian government had by this time come to represent so little of the body politic. Indeed, one might seriously question whether the Indonesian government ever did, from the declaration of independence in 1945 on, represent the bulk of the Indonesian people in a meaningful way. It was frustration of this magnitude that had led the "outer islands" to rebel against the Jakarta government in the late 1950s. And it was the same intense frustration that had led to the reaction against the communist ascendancy in the political heartland of Java in 1965.

Sukarno may well be remembered by future generations of Indonesians for his contributions to their independence and national unity. It was argued at one time that he lacked only the skills to administer the independent and unitary state he helped to found. But the events of late 1965 raised a much larger question: Had Sukarno led the nation in creating a political order it could live with? Not only he, but a large part of the national elite as well, had participated in the creation of a state in which all power was lodged at the center, and had then acquiesced in his pronouncement of a one-man dictatorship over the whole. It was this investment of all authority over a large and varied society in a single person that invited rebellion. And it was the effort of Sukarno and his ministers to exercise authority with increasingly limited means that led to resistance and reaction.

The social impact of so many deaths, whatever the number, as well as the arrests that occurred—official reports put these at 106,000 in 1966, at 200,000 in 1967, and, later, it was estimated that as many as 500,000 had been arrested at some time or other, although most were quickly released—remains largely a matter of speculation. After 1965 the number of religious conversions grew dramatically, particularly in Central Java; increasing numbers of people turned to mystical Javanese cults and to Christianity. Many village families migrated—to the towns or the "outer islands"—to escape the stigma of having been on the losing side. The wives of some of those arrested divorced them. But of the widows and orphans, and the men who survived and were eventually, after many years, released, next to nothing is known.

A political outcome of the deaths, arrests, and intimidation of the remainder of the political Left was to leave the Indonesian elite even more conservative than it had been before. Most members of the elite at the time were civil servants or members of the armed forces. The remainder were, for the most part, politicians who, in the spirit of Guided Democracy, were similarly appointed to their posts and dependent on their government salaries for a living. The Communists, never numerous in these circles, nevertheless loomed large because of the aggressiveness of their representatives in the national front and the mass media. The elimination of radical voices from these arenas in the last months of 1965 permitted the conservative majority in the elite to express their traditional political values without effective opposition.

It was probably inevitable that as the political life of the capital city became increasingly chaotic the urban economy should worsen. Later estimates placed the per capita income of Indonesia in 1965 at the lowest level in all of Asia. Food availability was low, and life expectancy short. These conditions greatly exacerbated the political situation. With so much of the capital city dependent on government employment, it was not long before student protests, which initially had been targeted at the Communist party, began to take aim at the government itself.

The virtual destruction of the Communist party by the end of 1965 facilitated this redirection of attention. So long as there was a stand-off between the party and the army, Sukarno had room to maneuver, to play one side against the other. Now only the army and the president remained. It was just a matter of time until one or the other would emerge as the sole holder of power and authority in the nation.

TWO

Sukarno Yields to Soeharto

In the center of the government quarter of Jakarta in the mid-1960s lay one of the largest open squares within the precincts of a modern city, nearly a full kilometer long on every side. From the early nineteenth century, this square was known as Koningsplein, or King's Square, and on its northern side the Dutch colonial government built a palace to serve its governors-general. On December 27, 1949, the Dutch flag in front of the palace was taken down for the last time, and the flag of the new Republic of Indonesia was raised in a simple ceremony before a crowd of several hundred people. The square was subsequently named Medan Merdeka, or Freedom Square. The palace was known in early republican days as the Presidency, but by the 1960s, in the spirit of Guided Democracy, the building was again a palace, officially, and was named Istana Merdeka, or Freedom Palace.

The first raising of the Indonesian flag before the palace was reenacted each year on August 17, the anniversary of the proclamation of Indonesia's independence in 1945. By the early 1960s the event was attended by throngs of people who stretched across the great square almost as far as the eye could see, while in demarcated ranks in front stood groups representing the armed services, the government departments, the boy scouts and girl scouts, the political parties and their affiliated youth and student groups, labor groups, farmers' organizations, women's associations, and all the rest, wearing uniforms or carrying banners that identified their attachments. Before such an assembly Sukarno was a spectacular orator, stirring the feelings of the great masses of people to a high pitch, until tens of thousands chanted with him, roared in response to him, exhibiting, as nothing else could, the power of his claim that a mystic union existed between himself and the Indonesian people. Resounding with his phrases, the palace and the square before it were filled with an emotional charge of very high voltage in the political imagination.

By March 11, 1966, however, when a morning meeting of the cabinet was to take place in the palace, opinion in the capital had turned against Sukarno. His purpose in calling the meeting was to obtain a statement from the cabinet denouncing the student demonstrations that had been creating an uproar in the city. Even as the day began, students were amassing in front of the palace. The atmosphere was tense. Two weeks earlier, presidential guards had shot and killed two students. But on this day, the forces that had been building up against the president would prevail.

Events Leading to March 11

Mass violence of the kind that swept the towns and villages of Central and East Java did not occur in Jakarta. Army units based in the capital city and its vicinity had come quickly to the support of General Soeharto, as had the Siliwangi Division responsible for the province of West Java, which constituted the capital's immediate hinterland. The army units available to Soeharto were, however, countered for some time by units of the other services on which Soeharto could not rely, including the navy, the air force, and the police. In addition, army leaders did not arm civilian youths in the capital in any significant number; on the contrary, they attempted to keep what control they could over civilian demonstrators. The result was that, although violence did occur, it was directed principally against property, not persons, and was highly selective, not indiscriminate.

What was significant in Jakarta, as a result, was not violence so much as the threat of it, and the growing estrangement that developed in this environment between activist army officers and students on the one hand, and Sukarno and the political figures long associated with him on the other. The issue was initially the Communist party, but as Sukarno remained unyielding, and the economy neared collapse, the issue became the president himself.

Some sense of the spiraling of feelings on either side can be gained from a brief review of the larger events that followed the failure of the September 30 Movement.

On October 1 Sukarno declared that he was taking personal command of the armed forces. On the following day, after a tense meeting, General Soeharto was given responsibility for "the restoration of security and order."[1]

Late on the night of October 3, after the bodies of the generals were discovered at the air force base, Sukarno made a radio broadcast in which he denied accusations that the air force had been involved in the affair.

On October 4 the bodies were removed from the well in the presence of a large assemblage of journalists, photographers, and television crew. Soeharto, who was present, spoke briefly for radio and television, suggesting that the president's assessment was not acceptable to the army. It was not possible, he said, that the incident was unconnected to certain members of the air force. He also suggested that the Communist party had been involved.[2]

On October 5 a massive funeral was held for the slain officers. The funeral was attended by almost everyone who mattered in the noncommunist elite—except Sukarno, who sent an aide.

On October 6 Sukarno presided at a meeting of the entire cabinet at the "summer palace" in Bogor, about an hour's drive from the capital. He now condemned the killing of the generals, said he had not approved of the formation of the Revolutionary Council, and appealed for calm. Two members of the Central Committee of the Communist party attended the meeting and read a statement dissociating the party from what they termed "an internal army affair."[3]

On October 8 a rally organized by anticommunist students was attended by tens of thousands. Speakers called on the government to ban the Communist party. Posters read: "Crush the PKI! Hang Aidit!" One group of youths went from the rally to Communist party headquarters and set the building on fire.

On October 11 Sjarif Thajeb, an army medical doctor and Minister of Higher Education, ordered the closure of fourteen leftist institutions of higher education, including Res Publica University, which was owned and operated by a Chinese-dominated organization, and ordered the Communist party's student organization to halt its activities. On October 15 Res Publica was gutted by fire.

On October 16, presumably in a move to moderate the situation,

Sukarno dismissed Omar Dhani as head of the air force, and appointed Soeharto commander of the army. At the ceremony installing Soeharto, the president spoke of the coup attempt as "a ripple in the ocean of revolution."[4]

On October 21 Sukarno issued a number of decrees, which in the rhetoric of the time were described as "commands," one of which prohibited unauthorized demonstrations.

In late October a new and larger anticommunist student organization was formed at a meeting at Sjarif Thajeb's home. This was the Indonesian Student Action Front (Kesatuan Aksi Mahasiswa Indonesia, or KAMI) (*Kami* also is the Indonesian word for "we").[5]

By early November the army was rounding up leading figures in the Communist party and its affiliated organizations in Jakarta. Three members of the party Central Committee were arrested, and a fourth was shot. Aidit himself was captured and summarily executed in Central Java on November 22.[6]

The deepening political divisions reflected in these events worked their way quickly through the economy. Commodities were already in short supply, and prices were rising rapidly. In November rice mills were placed under government supervision, and in December all foreign trade was placed under government control. By mid-December the government also decided to grant a large New Year's bonus to government employees. There were an estimated four million government employees of one kind or another at the time, and further inflation was bound to follow the government action. The problem was confounded even further when the government hastily announced a "currency reform," called in all the currency in circulation, and introduced one new rupiah note for every thousand old ones.

The timing could not have been worse. At this season of the year, about nine months from the last rice harvest and three months before the next one, rice supplies were traditionally low and prices were pressing upward; the approaching year-end holidays added further to the pressure on prices. A buying panic followed the announcement on the currency, and the price of rice rose by two-thirds in a single day. By the end of December foreign exchange reserves were exhausted, and prices had reached a record growth of 500 percent for the year. Nor was any end in sight. On January 3 the price of gasoline was increased by 400 percent, and fares on Jakarta buses by 500 percent.[7]

These economic developments produced a rapidly widening reaction among the anticommunist students in Jakarta. On January 10 the Indonesian Students Action Front opened a seminar at the University of Indonesia on the state of the economy. On the same day the Action Front also sponsored a rally that adopted a statement entitled "Three Demands of the People," calling for the banning of the Communist party, a halt to inflation, and the purging of leftists and incompetents from the cabinet. On January 15 the cabinet again met in Bogor, and Sukarno invited all the leading student organizations to send representatives. The Student Action Front mobilized thousands of anticommunist students in Jakarta and Bandung, and trucked and bussed them to Bogor. When they were outside the spacious Bogor palace grounds, some of the students tried to climb the high iron fencing, and warning shots were fired by the presidential guard.[8]

Sukarno on this occasion compared himself to Martin Luther and proclaimed, "I will not move a millimeter."[9] He called on those who believed as he did to organize a Sukarno Front in his support. Leaders of numerous organizations made statements in support of Sukarno in the next few days, among them the leaders of the National Party and the Nahdatul Ulama, the nation's foremost political parties, other than the Communist party, that were still legal. Soeharto followed suit, issuing a statement that the army "stands behind the President/Great Leader of the Revolution and awaits his further commands."[10]

At this point, perhaps buoyed by this show of support, Sukarno overplayed his hand. On February 21 he announced a new cabinet of a hundred members. Notably missing from the long list was Nasution, at this stage the most prominent military figure in the nation and the army's most prominent anticommunist. On February 24, the day the new cabinet was to be installed, a huge outpouring of students surrounded the Jakarta palace starting early in the morning. The army also had troops in place, separating the students from the presidential guard. Frustrated, students halted traffic and let air out of the tires of scores of vehicles, blocking the roads to the palace, and obliging Sukarno to order helicopters to bring some of his cabinet officers to the ceremony. As the cabinet, having been sworn in, was having tea, shots were heard. Students had broken through the army buffer, and presidential guards had fired, this time into the crowd. Two students were shot dead.[11]

Events now moved swiftly. A massive procession marked the funeral on February 25 of one of the students, a rightist activist from the medical faculty of the University of Indonesia. In a lengthy meeting with

Soeharto that same day and into the night, Sukarno insisted that the students be stopped, and again Soeharto gave in. The Student Action Front was declared "dissolved" and demonstrations were banned. At the same time, on the advice of army officers, student leaders moved out of the University of Indonesia campus—and into the intelligence headquarters of Colonel Ali Moertopo, a long-time aide to Soeharto.[12]

On February 28 Subandrio—a vice premier, the foreign minister who was seen as the architect of Indonesia's increasingly warm official relations with Communist China, and a focus and symbol of the entire conflict—told a crowd of Sukarno supporters that terror on the part of the government's enemies would be met with terror. A new anticommunist organization, nominally of high school students, held a rally at the University of Indonesia, and Subandrio was hanged in effigy. Leimena, another vice premier, ordered the University closed. Army guards were posted but ignored Leimena's order, and the Women's Action Front, joined by Yani's widow, brought food to feed the large number of students who were now occupying the campus around the clock.[13]

By early March Soeharto was under increasing pressure from some of his officers to take aggressive action. According to an official army history, he met with Sukarno on March 6 and warned, "I would not be responsible if some officers permit their troops to violate discipline and join the people's action."[14] That evening he met with the principal anti-Sukarno officers: Ahmad Kemal Idris, chief of staff of the Strategic Reserve, Soeharto's own former unit, and Sarwo Edhie Wibowo, commander of the Paracommando Regiment.

Sukarno now evidently feared that a showdown was imminent. On March 8 he issued an Order of the Day reminding members of the armed forces that it was their duty to be loyal to him as president of the republic. Nationalist supporters of Sukarno attacked the United States embassy. Anti-Sukarno students, now under yet another name and led by a militant Muslim student leader, occupied the foreign ministry and ransacked the building; occupied a Ministry of Education building; and attacked the New China News Agency office, a People's Republic of China (PRC) consular building, and a PRC cultural center.

On March 10 Sukarno met with party leaders and demanded they sign a statement condemning the student demonstrations. After discussions that lasted five hours, language was agreed on and all signed.

Thus, for almost six months, the Indonesian state was increasingly divided between two poles of power. At issue by now was not only the legality of the Communist party, the foreign policy tilt toward Beijing, the mismanagement of the economy, and the whole cast of policy in the direction of revolutionary change. Among an elite that had all along been largely traditional in its orientation, at issue now was the duality in government, the lack of unity, and the prolonged absence of any kind of stability in the nation's affairs.

The Events of March 11

On March 11 the cabinet met at the palace on the square. The topic was again the student demonstrations. Again the students were in the streets in the vicinity of the palace, letting air out of the tires of vehicles, and bringing traffic to a halt. Notably absent was Soeharto, pleading a sore throat. The atmosphere in the room was said to be tense. Sukarno began by calling on his ministers to resign if they were not prepared to follow his leadership. At this point an aide rushed to his side with a message: large numbers of unidentified troops were in the square and were advancing on the palace. Alarmed, Sukarno rushed from the room, followed by Subandrio and Chaerul Saleh, and fled the palace grounds by helicopter.

By early afternoon it was established that Sukarno was at the palace in Bogor. Three major generals of the army—Amir Machmud, Basuki Rachmat, and Andi Muhammad Jusuf—went to Bogor by helicopter to see him. They found Sukarno in the company of Subandrio, Leimena, Chaerul Saleh, and one of Sukarno's wives, Hartini. Discussions among them went on for some hours. When the talks ended, the generals returned to Jakarta, carrying a short letter signed by Sukarno and addressed to General Soeharto, instructing him "to take all measures considered necessary to guarantee security, calm, and stability of the government and the revolution, and to guarantee the personal safety and authority of the President/Supreme Commander/Great Leader of the Revolution/Mandatory of the MPRS in the interests of the unity of the Republic of Indonesia and to carry out all teaching of the Great Leader of the Revolution."[15]

Soeharto acted promptly. On March 12, on the president's behalf, he signed a decree banning the Communist Party of Indonesia. On March 18, having failed to persuade Sukarno to dismiss them, he ordered the arrest of Subandrio and other leftist cabinet members. Soeharto aides were soon referring to the March 11 letter as the *Surat Perintah Sebelas Maret* (Letter of Instruction of March Eleven) from which was coined the acronym *Super-Semar.* The acronym gave the letter, and Soeharto, a symbolic tie to one of the most mystical and powerful figures in the Javanese *wayang.*

For all their ambiguity, the events of the day were powerfully evocative of the forces operating in Jakarta at the time. They also were revealing of the personality of the new chief executive.

The Student Movement

The mass mobilization of anticommunist students, some of whom by January were demanding that Sukarno be arrested and tried for complicity in the attempted coup, was a new element in Indonesian political life. Students had played a significant role in the country's political history before. Indonesian students in Europe were the leading advocates of national independence in the 1920s. On August 16, 1945, youth leaders had kidnapped Sukarno and Hatta and prevailed on them to issue an immediate declaration of national independence. Indonesian youths also fought in the revolution; in a battle recounted in schoolbooks for every Indonesian child to read, armed youths held off more than a division of British and Indian troops in Surabaya for ten days in November 1945—a battle that marked a turning point in the independence struggle. But university students—even secondary school students—had been few in number in 1945, the children of middle-ranking officials in the prewar colonial government. By 1965, with the rapid growth of the civil service after independence, some nine thousand students attended universities in Jakarta, and tens of thousands were in the city's secondary schools.[16]

The initial decision to organize Jakarta's students to take political action after October 1 was made by two youthful Muslim and Catholic leaders: Subchan Z. E., vice chairman of the Nahdatul Ulama, and Harry Tjan, secretary general of the Catholic Party. Mar'ie Muhamad, secretary general of the large nonparty Islamic Student Association (Himpunan Mahasiswa Islam, or HMI) was present as well. The three had found common cause during the previous year in trying to counter the increasingly aggressive initiatives of the Communist youth and student organizations. A principal battleground had been the national youth federation, which was part of the national front. Another was the campus of the University of Indonesia, which was the scene of continuing demonstrations and counterdemonstrations from early 1965 on. Learning that the air force was training young communist activists in the use of small arms, one of the three young men met with General Nasution to arrange the same training for anticommunist youth. The date was September 28.[17]

When the Revolutionary Council was announced on the state radio on the morning of October 1, the young men had no doubt that the Communist party was behind the event. Their first thought was to flee the city and seek the protection of the Siliwangi Division. But one of the group, Catholic activist Lim Bian Kie (who later changed his name to Jusuf Wanandi), had a position with the Supreme Advisory Council and a government jeep with palace plates, and it was decided to send him in search of information; Lim drove through the square, saw the army units in formation there, and found the palace staff in a state of confusion: no one knew where Sukarno was. As time passed without further news, the youth leaders waited. When the state radio announced in the evening of October 1 that army units under the command of General Soeharto were in control of the city, they saw as well as anyone the significance of the event.[18]

After their big rally of October 8, the religious youth leaders had paid their first call on General Soeharto. The student movement now grew in size and complexity. While most of the city's students were Javanese, much of the organizing was done by activists of other ethnic origins— students from the more aggressive cultures of Sumatra and Sulawesi, and a handful who were of Chinese descent. Also, although most of the demonstrators were Muslims of varying persuasions—the Islamic Student Association had provided the bulk of the manpower to counter the Communists on the campus of the University of Indonesia—some of the leaders were Christians. The leadership group also acquired members who were democratic socialists in orientation, who identified with the old Socialist Party (Partai Sosialis Indonesia, or PSI), and who were soon publishing a daily newspaper and operating a string of radio stations in the name of the student movement. It was a loosely knit phenomenon, and it held together marvelously well—so long as its purposes were few and simple.

The student leaders were in touch with Soeharto and his associates on a more or less daily basis from early October on. The students had to deal with the army. They needed permission to travel at night in spite of a curfew. They needed funds to organize and transport their demonstrators. They needed to be sure their demonstrations would not be stopped. And they needed small arms to defend themselves. So student leaders consulted regularly with officers of the Strategic Reserve, notably its two principal commanders, Ahmad Kemal Idris and Sarwo Edhie Wibowo, and with the Strategic Reserve's principal intelligence officers, Ali Moertopo and Yoga Sugama. The students also needed physical protection as the atmosphere grew increasingly heated. It was out of fear that their lives were in danger from pro-Sukarno military units—chiefly members of the presidential guard, and, after January, the marines—that they agreed to move in with Ali Moertopo's intelligence staff. It was the first intimate contact between student leaders and members of the army who were close associates of Soeharto.[19]

Relations between the student leaders and these army men were antagonistic almost from the beginning. The students wanted to get rid of Sukarno while their own movement had momentum, and before he could build a countermovement of his own. As far as the students were concerned, Soeharto and his associates were overly cautious, wanting to be sure of every step before it was taken. Ali Moertopo and his fellow intelligence officers, on the other hand, viewed the students as young hotheads who could bring the government down but could not put a new one in its place. More immediately, Soeharto and his associates did not want any more student martyrs; one more student martyr of either the Left or the Right, they feared, could plunge the city into a level of violence they could not hope to control.[20]

The Army Activists

The students gained considerable strength from their open alliance with anti-Sukarno activists among the army officer corps. These officers also lent a good deal of credence to Soeharto's warning to Sukarno that they might take action against him.

The senior figure was Brig. Gen. Ahmad Kemal Idris. His father was a Minangkabau from West Sumatra, a region that has produced an inordinate share of the intellectuals, politicians, and businessmen of modern Indonesia. Kemal Idris had a sizable reputation for speaking his mind in plain language—and for taking direct action. In 1952, as a young cavalry officer of the Siliwangi Division, he had made the dramatic gesture of placing an armored unit in front of the Presidency with its cannons aimed at the building; this was at the height of an army protest over a cabinet decision to sack Nasution, as well as other accumulated grievances, an incident that set in train a series of events that eventually led to the fall of the cabinet. In 1956 Kemal Idris was implicated in another plot by Siliwangi officers, this one touched off by allegations of corruption against Roeslan Abdulgani, the Nationalist foreign minister; Abdulgani was eventually charged and convicted, but not before Kemal Idris and others had been relieved of their commands.

Sukarno refused to approve any further appointments of Kemal Idris for several years; Kemal Idris managed to be reinstated only by offering to serve in the Congo with the Indonesian detachment that was part of the United Nations forces there. On his return to Indonesia he served under Soeharto in the Strategic Reserve and, in an extraordinary show of defiance of the president by army commander Yani, was designated to lead Sukarno's pet project, the invasion of Malaysia. Kemal Idris is thought to have been against the proposed invasion, and was later said to have done what he could to delay it.[21]

Certainly no love was lost between Kemal Idris and Sukarno. And by March 1966 Kemal Idris was in effective command of the army's crack units in Jakarta.

The other principal activist officer was Colonel Sarwo Edhie Wibowo, commander of the elite Paracommando Regiment, which was at the core of Kemal Idris's reserve forces. Sarwo Edhie was born in Central Java and had his early career in the Diponegoro Division. He stood in the *jago* or "fighting cock" tradition of the region and was early drawn to more adventurous pursuits. He was trained as a paratrooper and, in 1957, led a daring raid on a rebel-held airfield in Sulawesi. On October 1, 1965, by his own account, he had asked permission of Nasution and Soeharto to lead the predawn raid on the air base to which Sukarno and the Communist party leaders had fled. He also personally led one of his battalions in putting down the army rebellion in Central Java in late 1965, and trained and armed the youth groups responsible for much of the killing there. Later, he captured headlines in Jakarta when he went to the University of Indonesia, addressed a student rally, and, in a further show of support, registered himself as a student.[22]

Both men said later that, along with Maj. Gen. Hartono Rekso Dharsono, the commander of the Siliwangi Division, they had wanted to depose Sukarno as a prelude to a thorough reform of the political system. Kemal Idris said that the main purpose of the troops in the square was to frighten the president. Both men said they also thought they might be able to arrest a few cabinet officers as the men came out of the cabinet meeting; Soeharto had told them to arrest certain Sukarno cabinet officers when they had the opportunity, but had left it to them as to how to proceed. The two officers also claimed they had not been ordered to put the troops in front of the palace on March 11; both said they had decided it on their own. They also said they did not give details to Soeharto beforehand.[23] It is inconceivable, however, that Soeharto did not know what was afoot. Both Ali Moertopo and Yoga Sugama, intelligence officers who were reporting to Kemal Idris at Strategic Reserve headquarters, were Soeharto aides from Diponegoro days, and undoubtedly were keeping him fully informed.

The principal aim of the anti-Sukarno officers, then, was to follow up Soeharto's warning to Sukarno five days earlier, and to make the point more strongly that his personal security could not be guaranteed by his own security guard, but only by the leadership of the army itself. That accomplished, talks would no doubt ensue. Soeharto would be able to say that the troops were not there on his orders, that some of his hotheaded officers were threatening to take action against the president, and that he could not predict what they might do next unless the president were to demonstrate greater confidence in him and give him a wider mandate. And there was a good deal of truth to this view of the situation.

The Letter of Instruction

The message the three generals took to Bogor, then, was that Sukarno had to give Soeharto increased executive authority if he was to keep the army in line. If not, Soeharto would not accept responsibility for what might happen.

The three do not seem to have been especially qualified to serve as "king makers." What seems to have led to their selection was their presence at the palace that morning when Sukarno had fled. The three also were on good terms with Sukarno.

Amir Machmud was the Jakarta area commander at the time. He was a Sundanese from West Java, where he had helped put down a rebellion that had aimed to establish an Islamic state, and later served under

Soeharto in the West Irian campaign. He had the reputation of being equidistant between Sukarno and the hard-line Nasution camp. When Sukarno had complained to him back in January about the increasingly aggressive student demonstrations, Amir Machmud issued orders that in the future they were to be "chanelled through the proper authorities in an orderly and proper way."[24]

Basuki Rachmat was a politically experienced man who had helped to run the martial law authority under Nasution's direction after 1959, and was the commander of the Brawijaya Division of East Java on October 1. Visiting in Jakarta at the time, he had quickly come to Soeharto's support. He was named Minister of Veterans Affairs in the Sukarno cabinet of a hundred, from which Nasution had been excluded. He was seen as a moderate reformer who was probably willing to see Sukarno remain as head of state, but with some curtailment of his decision-making powers. He also had a reputation for keeping his own counsel. He was the senior member of the group and, according to Amir Machmud, Soeharto initially thought of sending him to Bogor alone.[25]

Andi Muhammad Jusuf was a titled aristocrat from Bone in Sulawesi, a man long experienced in politics. When his own former superior officer in Sulawesi had gone into rebellion in the 1950s, Jusuf supported the army leadership in Jakarta and tried unsuccessfully to negotiate a truce. When the Communist party launched a verbal attack on General Nasution and others in 1960, and the army had rounded up the entire Central Committee "for interrogation," Jusuf was one of the commanders in the "outer islands" who used the occasion to ban the party in his area. He was in 1966 the Minister of Basic Industry in Sukarno's cabinet. In addition, he had a brother-in-law who was a member of the palace staff, and for this reason it was thought that his going to Bogor would "ease the way" for the group.[26]

Only Amir Machmud has spoken for the public record on the origin of the "letter of instruction." According to his accounts, Soeharto had asked the three generals to assure Sukarno that the army commander could bring the security situation under control if the president would place full confidence in him. Sukarno is said to have been extremely angry at the start of the discussion. He accused the army leaders of failing to follow his orders to control the students and their own troops. Moreover, he asked, what more did he need to do to show his confidence in Soeharto? According to Amir Machmud, the letter was his own idea. Basuki Rachmat wrote out a draft. Sukarno met with Subandrio, Leimena, and Saleh, heard their opinions, then retired to his study for an hour before sending the draft back with proposed changes. Basuki Rachmat wrote out a final draft. What changes were involved in these several drafts is unknown. Sukarno then met in a reception room with all six men, asked to have the letter typed on his letterhead, and signed it.[27]

General Nasution later remarked that the three generals realized only on the trip back to Jakarta that the letter constituted a transfer of power. It is highly unlikely, however, that either Sukarno or Soeharto failed to realize the import of what was involved. Sukarno and his advisers might have seen the letter as assuring their personal safety and buying time to rebuild their political forces. The letter was brought from Bogor directly to Soeharto's home. Soeharto then went to Strategic Reserve headquarters, where his staff assembled and the letter was read. It was quickly decided that the letter was enough to enable Soeharto to ban the Communist party.

Sukarno soon made it clear that he did not construe his letter as having given Soeharto authority to act independently. He issued a statement that he was responsible only to the Assembly that had elected him president for life and to Almighty God. He issued "commands" and in other ways attempted to exercise the powers and prerogatives of the presidency. But he did not rescind the letter. And his efforts to restore his position were met with a slowly diminishing response from his supporters in the army, the other armed services, and the political parties. Trials of coup plotters, Communist party leaders, and former cabinet officers reflected badly on Sukarno. And Soeharto was no longer to be outmaneuvered. The letter gave him only a thread of legitimacy, but with patience and persistence he slowly reined the president in.

On June 21, 1966, a Provisional Consultative People's Assembly confirmed the transfer of authority of March 11, making it impossible for Sukarno to revoke it, and called on Sukarno for an explanation of his actions in connection with the September 30 Movement. On March 12, 1967, the Assembly revoked Sukarno's title and powers and appointed Soeharto acting president. On February 28, 1968, the Assembly appointed Soeharto president pending elections.

Thus the long history of Indonesian army contention with the country's civilian leadership reached an end. That history had included kidnappings and arrests of cabinet officers, and at least one kidnapping of a prime minister. The motives were sometimes personal. But the central theme was corporate. Army commanders, not the least of them Nasution, had stood for an army role in national policy-making ever since 1945.

Yet the army leaders were not much different from the civilian leaders with whom they had contended. By the 1960s, even a sympathetic observer concluded that army officers, being involved in current politics as they were, had acquired the political habit of settling for small gains and individual rewards. They had failed to close ranks, just as the political party leaders had, and failed to use their collective strength to create a strong and effective government. Material corruption and moral deterioration were as widespread within their own ranks as among the rest of the elite.[28] Now they were left to decide the future course of the government.

The Question of Succession

It was not clear at the beginning of these events that Sukarno would be removed from the presidency. There was a good deal of indirect evidence to link him with the September 30 coup attempt, and many members of the elite later concluded that he must at least have known that something of the kind was going to occur. On the other hand, his position was almost sacrosanct, and the constitutional situation was delicate. If Sukarno were found guilty of having broken the laws of the nation the previous September, the validity of his delegation to Soeharto in March 1966 would be open to question. Also, having forestalled an unconstitutional military push, most of whose leaders had previously served under his own command, Soeharto had to avoid even the appearance of unconstitutional action on his own part. Soeharto seems to have entertained for some time the possibility of Sukarno's remaining as titular head of state. The man continued to enjoy strong support among the population, especially in Java, and among some elements of the armed forces. When the Parliament adopted a resolution early in 1967 calling for Sukarno's trial, Soeharto opposed it on the grounds that the evidence was not sufficient to charge him. But it was not in Sukarno's character to accept a ceremonial role, and as the months passed he made that abundantly clear.

A further consideration was that the only likely candidates to succeed to the presidency in the early months were General Nasution and the

Sultan of Jogjakarta, and neither showed any serious taste for the prospect.

Nasution has been seen by many commentators as indecisive, especially at times of crisis. He had given important political support to Soeharto by coming to his headquarters on the afternoon of October 1, his leg in a cast, and indicating his approval of Soeharto's actions of the day. Some felt this merely reflected Nasution's reputation as a stickler for regulations: Soeharto was the officer in line to act for Yani in his absence. But it was well known in army circles that the two men were not close—that Nasution had relieved Soeharto of his divisional command over charges of corruption. Nasution also was vastly more experienced on the national political scene, and had a much clearer sense of direction than Soeharto did at this point; he had put some stiffening into Soeharto's position more than once before March 11. But because he was experienced, he must also have known that as a Sumatran he would not be acceptable to the Javanese commanders who dominated the army, or the Javanese politicians who dominated the civilian elite. As a confirmed Muslim, he also knew he would be viewed with some suspicion by the *abangan* element among these same men.[29] So Nasution, outmaneuvered by events, chaired the Congress that stripped Sukarno of his titles and installed Soeharto in his place.

The Sultan had been a national hero from the time he declared for the revolution against the Dutch and gave sanctuary to the revolutionary leaders in his capital, the city of Jogjakarta, in Central Java. He was briefly active in national politics in the early 1950s; as Minister of Defense, he had supported Nasution's plan to demobilize large numbers of soldiers and use scarce resources to build a modern army—a plan rejected by politicians who stood to lose constituencies of military groups with ties to themselves. The Sultan then retreated to private life, except for the ceremonial tasks of his inherited office. His strength in 1966 was that he had the aura of royalty about him, had been neutral in the political wars of the previous decade, and was revered by many of the common people of Java. The Sultan told one supporter that although he knew Sukarno had to go for the good of the country, he simply could not bring himself to take part in his downfall.[30] He also observed to an aide that the army generals were not the people pressing him to take the presidency.[31] So the Sultan also hung back, served for a time with Soeharto as a member of a short-lived triumvirate, and later served as his vice president.

2. Sukarno Yields to Soeharto

Soeharto also had reason to hesitate. Aside from the constitutional element, he might well have shared the Sultan's scruples, and indeed close associates were to say much later that Soeharto eventually did feel a burden of guilt over his role in Sukarno's fall.[32] Also, having had no previous role in national politics, he was almost unknown outside army circles, and it was some months before people prominent in the political life of the capital concluded that Soeharto was the man to succeed to the presidency. Nor was much known about him. A naturally reticent man, he kept his opinions largely to himself. When he finally consented to the writing of a biography, his biographer had to inquire how he preferred to spell his name.[33]

Clearly the country was going to have to get used to a very different kind of leader.

Soeharto and the Army

The first insight into Soeharto that was made clear on March 11 was that the army had been more than his career. It had been his family—or, more accurately, it had given him the warmth and security his family never did.

Soeharto was born the son of a village official in Central Java in 1921. His father was responsible for the village irrigation system; not a small thing, as the position gave its holder the right of use of two hectares of village-owned rice land, enough to provide considerable economic security and social position in village society. But Soeharto had an unsettled childhood. His parents separated when he was only forty days old, and he lived with one, then the other, and later with a series of relatives and family friends. One of these, with whom Soeharto went to live at age fifteen, was a *dukun*, a traditional healer and seer, as well as an irrigation official like his father. Soeharto also managed to get a junior high school education.

Soeharto served briefly as a policeman toward the end of the Dutch period, reaching the rank of sergeant. He later enlisted in the Japanese-sponsored army of Indonesia, where he reached the rank of lieutenant. Not long after the Japanese surrender, he was a young officer in the new Indonesian revolutionary army that was to be his home. Here he performed well, reportedly led a famous attack on the city of Jogjakarta while it was occupied by the Dutch, and was a lieutenant colonel by the time independence arrived. He married well in the meantime, into the family of a *wedana,* a rather high official in the traditional administrative hierarchy of Java, with ties to the royal family of Solo. He thereafter spent the bulk of his peacetime career in the ranks of the Diponegoro Division.

The Diponegoro Division in which Soeharto spent his early adult years was widely regarded as the most traditional of the major divisions of the Indonesian army. Responsible for the territorial defense of Central Java, its officers and staff were exclusively natives of the region. Noted particularly for its loyalty to Sukarno and other Javanese nationalists, the Diponegoro provided the troops that put down rebellions in Sulawesi and Aceh in the early 1950s and those that occupied West Sumatra after the rebellion of 1958. In 1956, at the age of thirty-five, Soeharto became the division's commanding officer.

Commanders of Indonesia's territorial divisions were not far removed from local political and economic affairs. At the end of 1957 the nation was already under martial law when radical unionists took over Dutch-owned enterprises throughout the country. Nasution, as martial law administrator, ordered the army to bring them under government control. Army involvement in economic activity was now enormously extended. Soeharto oversaw the confiscated enterprises in Central Java, and controlled the trade that passed through the port city of Semarang, where his headquarters were located. Soeharto also began at this time to work together with local Chinese businessmen, among them Liem Sioe Liong, protecting the smuggling of scrap metal to Singapore and the import of cloves for the local *kretek* or "spiced cigarette" industry. From such sources, Soeharto obtained funds to supplement his official budget and assure the minimal welfare and loyalty of his troops; it was a pattern widely followed among regional commanders at the time. During this same period he also watched the rapid growth of the Communist party in Central Java, and established close relations with men in the conservative wing of the National Party there, including Hadisubeno, the mayor of Semarang.

Soeharto was abruptly relieved of his command by General Nasution, then the army chief of staff, in 1959. A former aide to Nasution, who was carrying on an anticorruption campaign at the time, has said Nasution was concerned that Soeharto was engaging in too much fund-raising and was setting a bad example for others.[34] A former aide to Soeharto has said the issue was not the fund-raising itself but how much was being passed on to army headquarters in Jakarta.[35] A senior officer who was a liaison between the two men in 1966–68 was inclined to dismiss the incident as unimportant. The significant difference between the two, he said, was in their personalities and their political philosophies, and while Soeharto was leading the executive branch of government and Nasution was chairing the Consultative Assembly, he and several others had been obliged to work unceasingly to bridge the constant gaps in perception and style between the two men.[36]

Whatever the truth of the matter, the break in Soeharto's career had two significant outcomes. One was that he spent a year-and-a-half at the Staff and Command School in Bandung, where he became acquainted with fellow officers from other divisions around the country who were to stand by him in 1965–66. (One member of the class was Sutojo Siswomihardjo, who was one of the six generals killed on the night of the attempted coup.) The other outcome was that Soeharto was subsequently available for staff assignments in Jakarta.

From here on, Soeharto was largely the recipient of good fortune. He was first placed in command of the 1961–63 campaign to obtain control of West Irian, or Western New Guinea, from the Dutch. The forces available to him were appallingly ill prepared, his initial losses were high, and he was saved from having to launch the invasion Sukarno wanted by the intervention of the United States. John F. Kennedy was determined to deny Sukarno's Indonesia to "the international communist camp" and put considerable pressure on both parties to agree to a negotiated settlement.[37] Soeharto did gain significant experience from the West Irian episode, however. He learned that the navy and air force were not up to supporting an invasion, such as was later proposed across the Straits of Malacca into neighboring Malaysia. He also learned that the international environment was strategic in shaping the framework within which large domestic decisions had to be assessed—decisions such as those he later faced in setting about to rehabilitate the economy.

By the middle of 1964, as head of the army's Strategic Reserve Command, Soeharto was already advising the army commander, General Yani, against the transfer of loyal units from Java for the invasion of Malaysia. Before the year was out, Ali Moertopo, Soeharto's intelligence officer, was in secret contact with the Malaysian army leadership.[38]

So Soeharto was no ordinary soldier when he made the most important decision in his life on the morning of October 1, 1965. But that he was an army man through and through was made clear on the following March 11. No civilian played any role whatever in his actions on that day. It was an army exercise from beginning to end.

Soeharto and Javanese Culture

Yet, the army leadership was hardly of a piece. It was equally significant that Soeharto was a product of the Dipenogoro Division, and Javanese to the core. Consider the following: Soeharto never differed with Sukarno in public, with the one exception of his speech at the exhumation of the bodies of his colleagues. He accomplished the transfer of executive authority without any direct orders to his officers to station troops in the square. He extracted from Sukarno a written document, signed by Sukarno and addressed to himself, that gave him the authority he sought. It was a masterful display of power as it was understood in the political culture of Soeharto's native region.

Soedjatmoko, the most prominent Indonesian intellectual of recent decades, has written of this culture:

> A central concept in the Javanese traditional view of life is the direct relationship between the state of a person's inner self and his capacity to control the environment. Inner perfection, reached through detachment and the control of one's emotions and reactions, radiates, through the inner stillness thus acquired, to the world and influences it. And as social hierarchy is seen as a reflection of the cosmic order, one's place in the hierarchy reflects the degree of inner perfection and power one has achieved. At the apex of this hierarchy stands the ruler, who rules by divine sanction and whose state of inner development is reflected in the condition of his realm.[39]

This intense focus of attention on the psychic state of the ruler inevitably cast Soeharto's contest with Sukarno in terms of his own inner harmony with the cosmos. Thus, soon after he received the March 11 letter from Sukarno, Soeharto submitted himself to a ritual purification by bathing to prepare himself for the final confrontation. The ritual was arranged by Soedjono Humardani, Soeharto's long-time army aide, and a man immersed in the pre-Islamic religious beliefs and practices of central Java. The ritual was conducted by a mystic teacher known to Soeharto from his Semarang days. As word of the event circulated, friends and acquaintances of Soeharto concluded that he was ready to seek the presidency.[40]

This personal preparation aside, Soeharto also had to adopt a public persona that could help explain, especially to long-time Sukarno supporters in central Java, who Soeharto was and what he stood for. The decision of Soeharto aides to label the March 11 letter from Sukarno as *Super-Semar* was designed to identify Soeharto with one of the most revered figures in the Javanese *wayang*.

The principal stories of this musical drama are drawn from the Ramayana and Mahabarata epics. Semar does not appear in the Indian originals of these epics; he must have been added after the arrival of the stories in Java, and thus is a legitimate, and possibly ancient, folk figure. He is not much to look at: short, fat, flat-nosed, old, with an enormous rear end and a bulging paunch—at first glance, a grotesque clown. But Semar wears a checkered hipcloth that is a visible sign of sacredness.

Claire Holt wrote of Semar in the 1960s:

> Semar is not only loved, but revered and regarded by some as the most sacred figure of the whole *kotak,* or *wayang* set. He appears on the screen precisely at midnight, preceded by *gara-gara,* (signs of) 'ominous manifestation,' when danger is greatest, the distress of his master deepest, and when help is essential.

She went on to say that he and his sons are regarded by some as

> the voice of the simple village folk, with all their strength, misery, and wisdom. Without them a princely master is unthinkable; without their support, advice, and succor, he may be lost. Semar, who is never in the wrong, is particularly powerful. Of all the *wayang* heroes he alone dares . . . to remonstrate with the gods . . . and may even force them to act or desist.[41]

Semar was thus an idiom for the role Soeharto saw for himself and asked both the elite and the common people to accept: Semar as the voice of the common man, the peasant, the realist, concerned about the here and now; Semar as the loyal servant of a kingly master, observant of his own lowly status, yet able to bend even the gods to his will; Semar, the mystic restorer of peace to a divided land.

If there was an element of manipulation in the choice of Semar as a political idiom, one nevertheless should not suppose that Soeharto himself was motivated by a cynical disregard for the source of his own power. On the contrary, he was genuinely coming to believe that fate had selected him to lead the nation. Why else had he been spared on the night of the coup? Why had he succeeded in putting down the attempt without firing a shot? Why had he obtained a grant of authority from Sukarno with only a threatening show of troops? Something of the sort seems to have been at work as he faced the task of rebuilding the economy, for he now exhibited unusual self-confidence. With no more than nine years of indifferent rural schooling, Soeharto set about to surround himself with some of the best-educated minds in Indonesian society.

THREE

The Rise of the Technocrats

Indonesia's economic and social crises were significant factors in bringing about Sukarno's fall. The extraordinary rise in prices, which doubled every few months during 1965, and the financial panic created by the government's mishandling of the currency in December added greatly to the president's vulnerability; moreover, the impact of inflation on the population of the capital city contributed to the turn in the student demonstrations against the government. When the Communist party was banned in March 1966, Soeharto came under considerable pressure to take action to improve the economy. With the arrest of a number of cabinet officers, including the head of the central bank, he had the means to reshape the government and to give its policies a new direction.

Following the arrest of cabinet ministers, officials in many departments of the government, as well as in some provinces and towns, were dismissed or suspended. Several hundred air force officers were arrested, as were lesser numbers of naval officers and police. But Soeharto was in no position to alienate the many Sukarnoists within the army and other branches of the armed forces; the possibility of another coup attempt could not be ruled out. As a result the purge was limited, and the new cabinet included many members from the previous one. The principal change was in the cabinet "presidium"or "super-cabinet." For some months the main policy lines were to be shared by members of a triumvirate: Soeharto was chairman and also responsible for security; Adam Malik, the nimble Sumatran who had survived the rough and tumble of party politics ever since the 1930s, who had served as ambassador in Moscow, and who was the foremost anticommunist in the previous Sukarno cabinet, was now responsible for international affairs; and the Sultan of Yogyakarta, bringing the aura of long-term legitimacy, was in charge of economic affairs.

Economic deprivation was now widespread in the society, and for many had reached a severity unknown since the years of wartime occupation. The situation called for action across a wide front. Yet Gunnar Myrdal's dictum, written at about this very time, seemed unassailable. Indonesia and the other states of South and Southeast Asia were, he said, "soft states." Hard economic decisions could not be taken or, if taken, could not be implemented. The fundamental problem was the lack of effective governments. Myrdal acknowledged that, reluctantly, he had reached the conclusion that political democracy no longer seemed a fundamental requirement of modernization. The situation had reached a point, he believed, when some measure of "compulsion" had become "strategic."[1]

Herbert Feith, a close student of the Indonesian case, had described policy-making under Guided Democracy in similar terms:

> This is not a government which can easily exert much weight of power. Many of its decrees are effectively ignored by those who are charged with their implementation. This is sometimes attributed to the ineffectiveness of its administrative machinery. But it is more accurately described in terms of the weakness of the political elite's cohesion, the heavy dependence of this elite on the bureaucracy as a social class, and the great importance of intra-bureaucratic politics as a force for immobilization of the government.[2]

Soeharto and the Sultan were thus in great need of new and large ideas. They also faced a substantial task in building a consensus behind any economic program that would be responsive to the circumstances. Indeed, if much was going to change, the entire national elite had to be reeducated.

That substantial changes actually occurred, and within the space of several months, was owing principally to a series of catalytic events that placed a handful of young economists of the University of Indonesia at the center of the discussion of what the government should do, and led to their rapid rise to power as the key members of Soeharto's "economic team."

3. The Rise of the Technocrats

Perceptions of the Economy

Much romanticism had surrounded the economic wealth of Indonesia. This was not wholly a matter of invention, nor entirely a native perspective; the islands were indeed rich in a wide range of natural resources, and many Dutch politicians and colonial officials had built their careers on the promise of this wealth. But after independence the romance took on a characteristically Indonesian element. A number of Indonesians, and particularly many Javanese, believed that because the country was rich in natural resources the government could make people rich simply by making wise decisions or, as it was frequently put, by issuing the right commands. Sukarno had reflected this view—as well as his impatience with the entire subject of economics—in his Independence Day address of August 17, 1963:

> The economic question demands our full attention. Is not food and clothing one of the points of the Government's Three Point Program? And is not the economy one of the "points" of our Revolution?
>
> As the Great Leader of the Revolution, I devote very great attention to this economic "point." But let me be frank: I am not an economist. I am not an expert in economic techniques. I am not an expert in the techniques of trade. I am a revolutionary, and I am just a revolutionary in economic matters.
>
> My feelings and ideas about the economic question are simple, very simple indeed. They can be formulated as follows: If nations who live in a dry and barren desert can solve the problems of their economy, why can't we? . . .
>
> What more can I say other than to ask you to be patient for a while longer? I have already issued the Economic Declaration known as Dekon, and fourteen Government Regulations are also out. Now I say only: be patient a while longer, be patient, wait and see![3]

Sukarno's view of what needed to be done was in striking contrast to the views expressed that same month in two lectures delivered at the Faculty of Economics of the University of Indonesia. Widjojo Nitisastro, in his inaugural lecture as professor of economics at the university on August 10, 1963, defended the role of economic analysis in development planning, and argued that if the country was to break out of its stagnant economic situation a process of planning and policy-making was required in which efficiency, rationality, consistency, clear choices among alternatives, and attention to prices and material incentives all played a central role. Mohammad Sadli, in a lecture later the same month, made a theoretical defense of the stabilization program and a major assault on the causes and costs of inflation. These were political events in the life of the capital city, attended by cabinet ministers and other prominent figures, and it seems fair to say that many of those present shared the views expressed on these two occasions.[4]

Sukarno showed no deeper understanding of the situation as it worsened. In his speech of August 17, 1965, he was still acknowledging shortages of food and clothing and asking for patience, for more time, although he now blamed the shortages on others rather than himself. It seems inescapable that whatever the other problems that stood in the way of the government's getting a grip on the economy—and they were considerable—a central problem was that Sukarno simply did not understand the roots of the economic deterioration that was eroding the people's welfare, the government's credibility, and his own hold on the presidency.

Even so, the psychological and political obstacles to breaking with the president were enormous. The process began within weeks of the currency fiasco when, on January 10, 1966, the students of the Faculty of Economics opened a conference at the University of Indonesia on the state of the economy. The event was notable chiefly for an address by Mohammad Sadli. Sadli used the occasion to make a wide-ranging attack on the problems of inflation, on imbalances in price relationships ("Where else in the world can a person ride a train for 500 or 1,000 kilometers with a ticket that costs the same as a few dozen eggs?"), on the size of the government bureaucracy, and on the decline in exports. But the basic problem, he said, was "the state of mind." It was no longer enough for the country to rely on "tension management." A "day of reckoning" had arrived. The economy no longer had any savings. The "only way out" was to restore the good will of the international community and seek new credits abroad.[5]

It was still something of a leap from the language of this pronouncement on the university campus to the unvarnished terms the Sultan used in his first formal statement as triumvir on April 12, 1966. One had to go back to the annual reports of Sjarifuddin Prawiranegara, head of the central bank in the early 1950s, to encounter in an official Indonesian document anything like the frank tenor and realistic detail of the Sultan's statement. The statement was drafted by Selo Soe-mardjan, secretary to the Sultan and professor of sociology at the University of Indonesia; the university economists, all close associates of Soemardjan, were deeply involved in its preparation. The statement said in part:

> In 1965 prices in general rose by more than 500 percent; in fact the price of rice soared by more than 900 percent. Unless swift and correct steps are taken, it may sky-rocket by more than 1,000 percent in 1966.
>
> In the 1950s the State budget sustained deficits of 10 to 30 percent of receipts and in the 1960s . . . soared to more than 100 percent. In 1965 (the deficit) reached 300 percent. The most serious (increase) of all took place in January, February and March of 1966. Within the first quarter of this year (the deficit) amounted to almost the whole government expenditure in 1965.
>
> For years to come Indonesia's economy is saddled with foreign debts totalling $2.4 billion. This year we have to begin to pay our long-term debts. If we fulfill all our obligations, we (will) have no foreign exchange left to spend for our routine needs. . . . For years we have been import-ing our daily necessities through short-term loans on conditions detri-mental to us.
>
> There must be an austerity programme, a programme of retrench-ment covering all facets of government.
>
> All State enterprises, whether commercial or otherwise, have to oper-ate on truly economic norms.
>
> In the agricultural sector, food yield and farmers' income must be improved appreciably. . . . Irrigation, fertilizer, pesticides and imple-ments to boost output are essential.
>
> Rehabilitation of highways, maintenance and expansion of the net-work of roads in economically important areas are a necessary condition for our economic recovery and stability.
>
> We need port facilities, particularly dock facilities to render fast ser-vice to ocean-going vessels . . .
>
> What are the prerequisites . . . to economic rehabilitation? Every official, whether in the government or the private sector . . . should ren-der the greatest contribution within his ability in the interest of the State and nation, not merely for personal gain. . . . The Government delib-erately restricts its programme within the limit of its capacity and the prevailing atmosphere in the conviction that it will not reach its goal without public support and aid.
>
> We decline to make promises which may arouse unrealistic hopes among the people. They may become disappointed if improvements fail

to come up to their expectations. The only promise we give is that we will do our best honestly to meet the challenge.[6]

The picture this statement revealed, Heinz Arndt noted, had "few parallels in a great nation in modern times except in the immediate aftermath of war or revolution."[7]

The Great Inflation and Its Causes

The inflation that marked the decline of the Indonesian economy to this sad state, and that played a central role in mobilizing opinion against the Sukarno government, had been a feature of economic life since 1961, doubling every year from 1961 to 1964, increasing sevenfold in 1965, and continuing at the same rate in the early part of 1966. An inflation of such magnitude was by this time reflected in every aspect of economic and social life.[8]

One of the causes of the inflation was the persistent and growing deficit in the government budget. The deficit was related, in part, to the impact of important political events. The deficit jumped in 1958, reflecting the "outer island" rebellion; again in 1961, reflecting the West Irian campaign; and again in 1964, reflecting "confrontation." On each of these occasions, the increase in the deficit was greater than it had been the time before.

It was believed at the time that expenditures also grew because of increasing government bureaucracy. By early 1966 it was estimated that employees of the government, members of the armed forces, and employees of state enterprises numbered 4 million; when their family members were taken into account, it was estimated that at least 10 million people, or 10 percent of the population, were directly dependent on the government for their incomes. Data that became available later put these estimates in doubt, however.

In any case, the deficit was caused by declines in revenue, as well as by increases in expenditures. From 1960 on, total government revenues were less each year than the budget for even routine expenditures, such as salaries, and the gap grew larger annually. A principal reason was that government revenues were raised mainly by direct or indirect taxes on international trade, and trade was falling steadily from the late 1950s.

Credit expansion also was a factor. From 1950 on, the money supply often increased more rapidly than the government budget did. During

1965 alone the money supply increased almost fivefold, and not much more than half of this could be attributed to the budget deficit. Credit expanded mainly through the state banks, going to state enterprises, private enterprises, and for various extrabudgetary projects. The governor of the central bank later testified at his trial that he had extended numerous unsecured loans to official agencies and to private individuals on either his own or the president's approval.

While the money supply was thus growing rapidly, the supply of goods was declining, and an important reason was the decline in export earnings. Indonesia was historically an exporter of tropical agricultural products and of minerals, principally tin and oil. As a percentage of all domestic production, exports between 1958 and 1962 averaged each year only about a third of prewar levels, and in the period from 1963 to 1965 were even lower still. Factors behind this downward trend included the takeover of Dutch-owned plantations and tin and oil companies during the West Irian campaign, the loss of Singapore as a processing center because of "confrontation," the mounting cost of doing business as a result of inflation, and the continuing deterioration of roads, ports, trucks, ships, and power supply. Still another factor was the lack of control over state enterprises; agencies responsible for significant percentages of rubber and oil exports, for example, retained substantial portions of their earnings, ostensibly to pay for imported spare parts and materials for their own operations, rather than pay them over to the Ministry of Finance.

The decline in exports threatened the country's ability to import, and imports were essential; the country was not self-sufficient in food or in textiles, let alone in machinery and other capital goods. Through 1957 the government drew heavily on its foreign exchange reserves, virtually liquidating its gold reserves in the process, in order to sustain imports, the largest portion of which consisted of consumer goods. During 1962 to 1964 a third of the country's total imports was paid with foreign loans and credits, including Japanese reparations. Most of the loans were theoretically tied to specific projects, but in fact an average of 26 percent was used for raw materials and another 18 percent for consumer goods. As early as 1961 Indonesia was unable to meet all the payments due on its foreign debt, and the arrearages grew annually. In 1965 the accumulated payments due amounted to 77 percent of the total value of exports during the year.

3. The Rise of the Technocrats

How the deteriorating trade situation fed the domestic inflation can be seen in the case of rice. Between 1954 and 1961 rice production increased annually at a rate about equal to population growth. By importing supplemental supplies from abroad, the government was able to increase the availability of rice on a per capita basis. In 1962, which was a good year in terms of domestic production, imported rice amounted to about 10 percent of the total rice available. The imported rice was used to supplement the cash wages of civil servants and soldiers, and to "inject" supplies into urban markets to stabilize prices and prevent unrest. After 1962, however, the volume of rice produced domestically ceased to grow, and the government was at this point less able to finance imports. The amount of rice available in the country steadily declined on a per capita basis. Hence Sukarno's appeals from August 1963 on for patience in regard to food supplies. Moreover, because rice was the principal item of expense in urban household budgets, the price of rice tended to pull the prices of other goods along with it. Hence, the uncontrollable rise in prices.

The great inflation, then, resulted from declines in productivity of all the country's key producers—its rice farms, rubber plantations, tin mines, and oil wells; it reflected the withering decline of foreign trade and, with it, a massive decline in government revenues; it reflected a pattern of expenditure of public funds that showed a disregard of economic cost; and, finally, it was accompanied by a decline of discipline in the banking system, eventually leading to that system's virtual collapse.

Consequences of the Great Inflation

The social and political consequences of inflation were equally wide-ranging. Perhaps most significant was the decline in the government's ability to command the resources it once had at its disposal. Government expenditure in real terms declined by more than two-thirds over the brief three-year period from 1962 to 1964. Thus, even before 1965 began, the government had already lost much of its ability to take any significant action whatsoever—except perhaps for the symbolic action that the president still commanded, or, one might say, to which he was reduced.

Another result of inflation was ever-widening economic control in the hands of the government bureaucracy. The multiple exchange rates made available to exporters and importers were continually changing.

When importers nevertheless experienced windfall profits, price controls were established for imported materials. When importers evaded the price controls, the government took over the importing of key industrial materials—yarn, some textiles, wheat, and cloves (for the spiced cigarettes widely popular in Java)—and sold them to domestic industrial enterprises at official prices. When consumers also demanded protection from the inflation, the government went a step further and regulated the prices of finished goods produced by domestic industry. When a black market continued to flourish despite this last step, the government went even further and, by 1965, took to distributing food and clothing through state-owned retail shops.

A further result of the inflation was abandonment of the commitment to social justice. Again rice was a prime example. The government did not control enough of the total rice supply to be able to ration the rice at fixed prices for all. Those protected by the government's distribution system comprised only a small portion of the total consuming public—government employees, members of the armed forces, employees of state enterprises, and some inhabitants of the larger cities. In addition, government subsidies to lower public utilities rates also benefited only a fraction of the population; even electricity and piped water were enjoyed only by the upper classes in the cities. Possibly most serious was the gap that inflation created in rural communities between those who had access to land and those who did not, although an absence of data made it impossible to assess how far this extended.

Because of inflation, the traditional respect people had for bureaucratic office declined. One analyst observed that a middle-grade civil servant would have seen his cash salary increase twelve times from 1957 to 1964, while prices were increasing thirty times. Another noted that a senior civil servant with a salary of 200,000 rupiah a month would have needed 750,000 a month for household expenses at the end of December 1965, and 2.5 million by May 1966. Most government employees by this time were working for the perquisites of office, including housing, transport, and rations of rice and textiles, compared to which their cash salaries were negligible.

Civil servants turned to various devices in order to survive. Wives went to work in the private sector and earned more than the "head of the family," straining family relations. Many civil servants appeared in their government offices for only a few hours a day, and often for only a few days a week. The pervasive government involvement in the economy also encouraged rampant bribery, both because the opportunities were presented to bureaucrats who had the power to distribute scarce goods, and because little moral authority or practical sense was attributed to many of the controls in the first place. The arrests of ministers and dismissals of other senior officials that began in March 1966 left government employees thoroughly demoralized. The bureaucracy was ripe for attack.

Educating the Elite

Within a few weeks of the Sultan's statement on the economy, from May 6 to May 9, 1966, a second symposium was held at the University of Indonesia. The sponsors this time were the University's rector and deans, the national Indonesian Students Action Front, and the more recently formed Indonesian University Graduates Action Front, a federation of anticommunist university alumni. Ali Wardhana of the economics faculty was chairman of the event, and Emil Salim of the same faculty was rapporteur. The entire cabinet was invited. The agenda was the full range of economic, political, social, and cultural problems confronting the country.

The high point of the conference was an address by Subroto, an economics lecturer at the University, who made a slashing attack on the policies of Guided Democracy. The country's economic interests had fallen victim to the government's political ambitions, he said. Almost half the country's foreign debt had been entered into for military purposes, and a large part of the government's spending since 1960 had gone into its pursuit of West Irian and then into the anti-Malaysia campaign. Although the government planned that a large part of its income would come from state enterprises, the fact was that the government depended on import taxes, and these were declining. Maintaining the government apparatus, which was already too large, was using up so much government income that little was left for development. Even the share of foreign credits available for nonmilitary purposes did not go to projects that would directly benefit the people or rehabilitate production, but went to projects selected for political purposes, like the Asian Games. It was time, Subroto said, for Parliament to approve the government budget before the fiscal year began; to use government funds to rehabilitate the economy instead of spending funds on helicopters, airplanes, and other "luxuries"; and to expend every effort to bring into balance the entire array of monetary and fiscal policy, foreign trade, prices, the salaries of civil servants, and production.[9]

Another speaker, Sumiskum, a leading figure in national legal circles, and later a speaker of parliament, said that "confrontation" as a strategy had failed to take into account the balance of power between Indonesia and its opponents. The opinion was now encountered on all sides, he said, no matter with whom one spoke, that the "strategy of struggle" that Indonesia was pursuing had been calculated inadvisably. But people were afraid to say so, for fear of being branded "agents of imperialism, subversion, or the CIA."[10]

In June the Provisional People's Consultative Assembly met for the first time since the political crisis began nine months earlier. The Assembly was now lacking its former members from the Communist party, as well as some other Sukarno supporters; nevertheless, the majority had been members several years before when the body had unanimously elected Sukarno to the presidency for life. So it was not at all a foregone conclusion that Soeharto would gain the Assembly's complete support. Sukarno might even have agreed to the session somewhat hopeful that he would recover lost ground. In the event, the Assembly elected Nasution as its chairman and produced a series of decisions that represented a considerable victory for Soeharto. The Assembly confirmed Soeharto's position as chief executive, and made this irrevocable by the president; it confirmed Soeharto's outlawing of the Communist party; and it instructed Sukarno to submit a full explanation of his role in the events of the previous October 1, and forbade him to issue any further decrees. The Assembly further instructed Sukarno and Soeharto jointly to form a new government, the main objectives of which were to be political stabilization, economic rehabilitation, preservation of an independent foreign policy, and preparations for general elections.

The Assembly failed to resolve the question of the future of the political parties, but it did approve a lengthy statement on the economy, finance, and development. The statement was drafted not by the government, but by five members of the economics faculty—Sadli, Salim, Subroto, Wardhana, and Widjojo. They were careful to provide early copies to Soeharto and his personal staff; they also lobbied every Assembly member they knew. According to several of the drafters, the statement was virtually unchanged as it was discussed and approved, first by the Economic Commission chaired by General Jusuf, and then by the full Assembly. The statement rejected both "free fight liberalism," which it said led only to exploitation, and "etatism," which killed all initiative outside the state sector. In the short term, the statement said, the priorities were to bring inflation under control, revitalize production, meet the people's needs for food and clothing, and increase exports. In the longer term the economy needed to be developed, with agriculture given the first priority. The government was to play the central role in guiding the course of development, but private businessmen were to be encouraged to play an active role. The government was to adopt a drastic austerity program at once, which would affect both civil and military expenditures. Foreign borrowing was approved, provided the funds were used for the essential purposes of the government's stabilization and rehabilitation plan. Because of the country's limited capital resources, legislation was to be prepared promptly to provide for foreign private investment as well.[11]

But the chief member of the elite whom the university economists had to win over to their way of thinking was Soeharto, and up to this point they had not even met him. That occurred only in August when a second army seminar was held at the Staff and Command School in Bandung in order to establish a consensus among the army's commanders, now shorn of the leftists among them, on their future course of action. The seminar is best remembered because it reaffirmed and extended earlier doctrine about the army's nonmilitary role. Now, it was claimed, the people were looking to the army above all to provide the nation with leadership and stability. But Colonel Suwarto, who was the organizer, arranged for several of the University of Indonesia economists to meet with the army commanders and argue in person for their ideas. Soeharto evidently was impressed. He was soon calling the economists in for discussions, and before long he appointed them his official "expert advisers."

One of the economists recalled that initial experience:

> The whole purpose was to give Soeharto a concept and the beginning of a program. After all, he had just come from nothing. The need was to give him some ideas and some rudimentary programs. . . . After *Super Semar*, Soeharto had to have a program. There was really nothing else available, and the seminar was sponsored by the army, so he took it over "skin and hair," as the Dutch say—the program and the people who proposed it.[12]

To another of the economists, it was not that simple: "It was a step by step process. The Assembly statement was clear, but it needed to be worked out, to be made more operational. It had to be accepted by the army leadership as a whole, not just Soeharto. And he, of course, was not a vacuum into which we could just put our ideas."[13]

Indeed, the task was even larger. The entire national elite had to understand what was proposed. A man who had served in Sukarno's cabinet and later became a prominent critic of Soeharto's leadership explained:

> The great achievement of this government has been to teach us to think economically. . . . Even I saw the banks as alien to me. Money was just for buying things, and if you didn't have any, you bartered for what you wanted. We were still basically agrarian in our thinking in 1965. Water? Oil? Why pay for them? Weren't they God's gift out of our own ground? So the government had to move slowly. There had to be a period of education, of forming a public mentality, where the costs of things, and choices, were taken into account."[14]

The New Economic Policies of 1966

The new economic policies were first outlined at a conference of representatives of the Indonesian government and its major noncommunist creditors in Tokyo on September 19. Seven creditor nations were represented: the United States, Japan, Britain, France, West Germany, Italy, and the Netherlands. The International Monetary Fund (IMF) and Australia also were represented, while Canada, New Zealand, and Switzerland sent observers. The largest single creditor, the Soviet Union, was not invited. The Sultan led the Indonesian delegation, and the principal Indonesian statement was presented over the name of General Soeharto as chairman of the Cabinet Presidium. The statement said in part:

> For some months now a reshaping of our political structure has taken place. A new order has emerged with a pragmatic rather than doctrinaire approach in solving our nation's problems.
>
> Specifically, the (Consultative Assembly) ordered the Indonesian Government to formulate and to carry out an economic stabilization programme, to be preceded by an immediate rescue programme. In this respect the control of inflation receives first priority, while the rehabilitation programme is primarily concerned with the following sectors: food, infrastructure, exports and clothing.

3. The Rise of the Technocrats

The creation of the right social and monetary condition being upper-most in our mind, the Government has planned to introduce to this end measures which in broad outline are as follows:

(a) by rendering a more proper role to market forces, create a wider and equal opportunity for participation in the development of our econ-omy by all creative efforts, state and private, domestic and foreign alike;

(b) the achievement of a balanced State Budget;

(c) pursuance of a rigid yet well-directed credit policy of the banking system;

(d) establishment of a proper link between the domestic and the inter-national economy through a realistic exchange rate, and thus creat-ing stimuli to reverse the downward trend of the balance of pay-ments.[15]

The major significance of the Tokyo meeting was in the fact that Soeharto had put his own name behind these general objectives. The donors did not react positively as a group until a later meeting in Paris in December—and not until the general objectives laid out in the September statement had been translated into policies and programs within the domestic system of rules and regulations that had grown up during the Guided Democracy years. This was accomplished quickly, however, as the process was already well advanced. On October 3, Soeharto announced a sweeping program of economic policy reforms. The aim was to decontrol the economy, balance the budget, begin to get inflation under control, and pave the way for foreign aid. Taken togeth-er, the measures constituted the single most significant statement of eco-nomic policy of what was to become the long Soeharto presidency. The form and language of the reforms were as notable as their substance. In place of "commands," the office of the president now issued detailed decrees. In place of revolutionary rhetoric, the language of government was now, if anything, given to understatement. The measures of October 3 reflected a change in the whole way of thinking about the government's role in the economy.

Decontrolling the Economy

With the October 3 decrees the government took a series of steps to decontrol the economy: it eliminated the existing system of multiple exchange rates and import-export licensing controls from a large por-tion of the country's international trade. The central bank announced it would sell foreign exchange at a rate to be fixed from week to week. On the same day, import licensing restrictions were greatly liberalized. In practice, importers were free to import what they wished, with the exception of certain specified luxury goods. Government departments and enterprises lost the privilege of importing at special exchange rates, with the exception of certain key commodities. At the same time export procedures were simplified, and most central and regional government authorities were expressly precluded from interfering in the export trade. The effect of these actions was to remove numerous distortions from the domestic price structure and to eliminate a major source of bureaucratic and political corruption.

The exceptions were significant. Selected government departments and enterprises were permitted to continue to import directly from foreign suppliers a number of "essential" commodities: in fact, they were assigned as sole importers of rice, fertilizer, newsprint, and diesel oil needed for electric power generation. The government faced a dilemma with regard to these "essential" commodities imported on its own account. If the import of these commodities were opened to the market and prices were set by market forces, the government would have had to increase substantially either their prices to the public or their subsidies in the state budget. If it exercised the first of these options, a further inflation of urban prices, and no doubt of student protests, would have followed. The government also would have faced a major problem in keeping the armed forces and the bureaucracy under control. In addition, it would have lost its leverage over the publishing industry, the only aspect of the mass media not under direct government management. On the other hand, if the government were to show the real cost of these subsidies in its budget, its pledge to the international community to balance its budget could not have been met. The decision was therefore made to avoid this dilemma by applying an artificial exchange rate to these selected imports, thus "hiding" their real cost in the public accounts. The decision reflected the government's continuing weakness at the time, as well as its caution. The panic of the previous December, when the government had taken radical action in regard to the currency, was not to be repeated.

Balancing the Budget

The Soeharto statement to the Tokyo meeting reported that between

1960 and 1965 the share of the net national product accruing to the government as revenue fell from 13 percent to 1.5 percent. This was an even more dramatic illustration of the collapse of the government's financial capacity than the decline through 1964, noted earlier. The extremity of the situation encouraged some government advisers to propose radical action. Even moderates among them believed that the government's only remaining choice was to withdraw, to get out of the economy as far as it could, at least for a time, and let market forces work their way. The government did not control enough of the economy to enable it to make much difference. As J. A. C. Mackie observed, the Indonesian economy by this time was, in reality, a thoroughly laissez-faire system anyway, despite all the talk to the contrary.[16]

On the revenue side, hopes frankly had to rest on a considerable increase from import duties. In the first quarter of 1966, 65 percent of tax revenue came from indirect taxes, mainly on imports. Some consideration was given to reforming tax administration, to collecting the substantial arrears that had accumulated, and to collecting more of the taxes that were falling due, mainly income and sales taxes from individuals and corporations. It was also believed that the rural sector had substantial unused taxable capacity, because inflation had reduced the land tax to nominal amounts. The political and administrative obstacles in the way of all such schemes were, however, formidable. The prospect for increased revenues from import duties rested on the hope of a larger volume of imports, and from much higher landed values at the new exchange rate. But an increase in the volume of imports depended on an increase of exports or of foreign aid, and both of these depended on ending the confrontation with Malaysia.

The Sultan had made clear in his April 12 statement that the government intended to inaugurate a program of austerity with regard to expenditures. Proposals had been made at seminars at the University of Indonesia for massive retrenchment of the civil service. In January the suggestion was that one out of every four government employees could be dismissed with no loss in efficiency; in May it was proposed that half of all government employees should be dismissed and all nonessential agencies abolished. Some agencies found that when all employees did show up for work, as they were now obliged to do, not enough chairs were available for all of them to sit on. But no alternate employment was available either; government employment, both civil and military, constituted a vast system of unemployment relief. Most secondary school graduates assumed, with some reason, that they would be employed by the government. Putting a cap on hiring would be difficult enough. Some agencies did reduce some costs by ordering excess employees not to report for work, thus saving at least on transport, and urging them to try to turn their secondary jobs into primary ones. All in all, however, given the political obstacles, large savings were not likely to be found in this direction.[17]

Work on the president's Special Projects was brought to a halt, and work was also suspended on most other development projects pending the formulation of a program of priority public works. Budget control was restored to the Ministry of Finance, and the Cabinet Presidium issued a decree restricting expenditures on the purchase of official vehicles and the like. But without cuts in subsidies or in government employment, the prospect of balancing the budget was nil—in the absence of foreign aid.

The government did rein in credit expansion sharply, which was politically easier to do as the business community was relatively small and unorganized for political action. The October policies included highly restrictive controls on bank credit: no credit was to be extended for imports except in special cases, credit for exports was placed under stricter control, no long-term loans were to be made, no overdrafts were permitted, no credit could be advanced to finance debts to the government, and no preference was to be given to state enterprises. These strictures were reinforced by high interest rates (6–9 percent per month) and requirements that banks maintain larger reserves.[18]

Foreign Debt and Foreign Aid

Balancing the state budget was clearly essential to bringing inflation under control. But most economists in Jakarta at the time did not believe this could be accomplished in less than several years. In fact, the inflation of 1966 was actually worse than that of 1965 and, although several budgets were formulated, each was rapidly overtaken by the continuing advance of prices. Meanwhile, the real economic situation, that is, the supply of food and clothing, had become critical.

Indonesia's foreign debt as of December 31, 1965, totaled $2.3 billion. Sixty percent of the total was owed to communist countries, and 70 percent of this, in turn, was owed to the Soviet Union. Most of this portion of the debt was for material that had been sought, principally for use by the air force and navy, for the West Irian campaign and, subsequently, for the campaign against Malaysia.

Much has been made of the role the International Monetary Fund played during the months that followed, and of the roles played by the U.S. and Japanese governments. Some Western academics, politicized by the American prosecution of the Vietnam War, were not prepared to think kindly of these institutions. One early study accused them of leading Indonesia into "debt slavery" by their actions in the latter part of 1966.[19] Another contended that the events of this period resulted from a long-term American plot.[20] But such explanations gave too much credit to foreign agencies, failed to give adequate attention to the development of thinking within Indonesia itself, and ignored the Indonesians' capacity for autonomous decision making.

Most Indonesian economists saw no alternative to seeking foreign assistance. Mohammed Sadli had argued as early as January 1966 that Indonesia was obliged to seek foreign help. Export earnings in 1966 were not expected to equal even the payments due that year on Sukarno's debts, he said, and inflation, as he had been arguing since 1963, had destroyed the whole fabric of domestic savings. Nor did anyone see an alternative to the country's looking to the West for the needed assistance. Neither Russia nor China was a potential source of emergency food supplies, and even in 1965 the communist states had provided only 25 percent of Indonesia's economic aid. In addition, relations with the Chinese were at this point all but broken, and the Russians, having been allied with the Indonesian air force and navy, were deeply distressed by the army's accession to power.

Still another consideration was that the United States, Japan, and the noncommunist nations of Western Europe were the principal markets for Indonesia's exports. If the Indonesian economy were ever to pay its way again, it would have to expand its trade ties with these markets. Even a major effort to direct exports to the communist countries in the early 1960s had met with little success, except for sales of rubber to China and the Soviet Union, and most of what the Chinese bought was resold on the world market. These sales were dwarfed not only by the sale of rubber but of other commodities as well to the United States, the Netherlands, West Germany, and Japan, and by exports of crude oil to Japan, Australia, and the United States.

The banning of the Communist party in March 1966 set the seal on a course of action from which Indonesia could not turn back; it had no place else to go but to the industrial democracies. The United States and Japan, for their part, were expected to rally to the assistance of an anti-communist Indonesian regime. In addition, the IMF was a natural ally. It had participated in working out the aborted stabilization plan of 1963. Many of the same officials were still in place in both the Indonesian government and the Fund, and quick action was anticipated. Things did not work out as quickly as the Indonesians expected.

The U.S. government was, by all accounts, pleased with the turn of events in Indonesia, but several factors inhibited a quick response. The upper echelons of the U.S. government were at the time heavily preoccupied with the course of events in Vietnam. Moreover, with the cost of American support to Vietnam rising sharply, Washington was of a strong disposition to avoid acquiring a large financial commitment to yet another Southeast Asian state. In addition, Indonesia was by now in default on its debts, and until this obstacle was removed U.S. law barred the country from receiving most forms of official American assistance.

The Japanese government found it equally difficult to take action. The Japanese had developed a close working relationship with Sukarno, involving Japanese veterans of the occupation of Indonesia, and Japanese business interests that had played a role in introducing Sukarno to his most recent wife, Ratna Dewi Sari, a former Japanese cabaret hostess. For some months after October 1, 1965, Dewi played an active role in trying to heal the breach between Sukarno and the army generals, and the Japanese ambassador in Jakarta continued to report that Sukarno was likely to survive the crisis. In addition, the Japanese government suffered the further limitation that it had had relatively few dealings with the Indonesian military. Yet Japan, more than any other external power, depended on Indonesia's natural resources. Japan was therefore among the first countries to recognize the Soeharto government, and the first to propose a consortium of Indonesia's international creditors. At the same time the Japanese were concerned to see the new government act on its promises, and might also have been reluctant to accept the American proposal to provide a third of the aid Indonesia needed. According to the testimony of Indonesian participants, they found the Japanese the most difficult to deal with of all their foreign creditors, and were uncertain right up to the last minute whether the Japanese would fall into line with the rest in Paris in December.[21]

The IMF, meanwhile, was not ideally suited to the task of providing a rapid or broad response to developments in Indonesia. Many outside the Fund saw it as rigid and slow-moving at the time. Also, while it could play a role in the rescheduling of Indonesia's debt, it was not in the business of providing economic aid. That was the domain of the World Bank, and Indonesia had lost its membership in the Bank when it pulled out of the United Nations. On the other hand, the IMF had helped work out the monetary stabilization program with the Indonesians as recently as 1963. The head of the Asia department of the IMF, the highly regarded Burmese economist Tun Tin, had become acquainted with Sumitro at the Asia-Africa Conference in Bandung in 1955, and he was disposed to think well of Sumitro's former students who populated the economic agencies of the government, as well as the economics faculty at the university. The individual he chose to represent the IMF in Jakarta was Kemal Sieber, a Turkish economist who was one of the Fund's ablest men in the field, and a man who was to champion the Indonesian case within his own organization and among officials of the creditor governments through the next several years.

It was this constellation of forces, then, that led to the ensuing events. In April Adam Malik went to New York to announce that Indonesia would resume its seat in the United Nations General Assembly. Shortly thereafter, the United States offered an emergency credit of $8.2 million for the purchase of rice, one of the few actions it was in a legal position to take. In May the Sultan went to Tokyo and obtained an emergency credit of $30 million from the Japanese. That same month Adam Malik met in Bangkok with Tun Abdul Razak of Malaysia and announced that Indonesia's "confrontation" would be brought to an end. In September the creditor nations, meeting in Tokyo, gave Indonesia an eighteen-month moratorium on debt payments. And in early October the Indonesian government announced a sweeping set of new economic policies and regulations designed to give force to its earlier general pronouncements.

In December the Western creditors met again with Indonesian representatives, this time in Paris, and now they were prepared to act more positively. The creditors agreed to a moratorium until 1971 on payments of interest and principal on long-term Indonesian debts incurred before June 1966. They also set a target of $200 million in new assistance for 1967. Their assistance to Indonesia was to rise steadily from this point on; in the three years from 1967 through 1969 foreign aid accounted for 28 percent of the Indonesian government's total spending, including all its development spending and, at first, even a portion of its routine expenditures. In the same period, although domestic tax efforts almost doubled the share of taxes in gross domestic product (GDP), the level remained well below the share in 1960. Inflation was brought under control by the end of 1968, and over the subsequent three years was never greater than 10 percent.[22]

It was hardly surprising that any of the principal actors in these events behaved as they did. Even in Jakarta there was a lack of effective opposition. The 1963 stabilization program had been extremely unpopular, and given the alignment of political forces in the Indonesian capital at the time, it is unlikely that the program would have endured for long even without the confrontation campaign and the resulting loss of Western support. Most Indonesian political leaders in 1963 were not willing to give up the patronage that growing government budgets made possible. Nor did they believe that monetary austerity would lead to economic recovery; many feared it would lead the country into deeper recession, and continued to hope that government spending would promote a return to increased productivity. But their confidence was greatly shaken by mid-1966, and their voices were muted.

Many members of the elite, interviewed in the late 1960s, expressed unhappiness with the country's position of international dependency. Many felt the independence of Indonesia's foreign policy was unduly circumscribed by the need to maintain the good will of the United States, Japan, and the West European states. A small number took issue with specific policy positions, especially with the depth and duration of the austerity program. But there was no widespread rejection of the government economic program as a whole. A large majority supported it.[23]

The reservations were, however, a harbinger of the storm to come. Soedjatmoko explained the problem:

> There is in Indonesia . . . a continuing and deep suspicion towards outside interference, infiltration, and subversion directed both towards East and West, reinforcing a xenophobic tendency already inherent in it, with the result that political change—even desired change—is rejected if the process of bringing about such change involves overt or covert foreign participation.
>
> There is also another set of attitudes, not generally shared but sufficiently widespread to warrant our attention, namely the feeling that, "even now after the communists have been removed as an effective polit-

ical force, the imperialists are not really willing to help us to develop our economy because of their fear of eventual competition from the new nations." Linked with this is the feeling that "we will remain poor as long as imperialism exists. We will therefore have to fight imperialism before we can properly tackle our problem of poverty."

The prevalence of these attitudes suggests profound fears and suspicions, as well as the deep-seated need for self-assurance and self-assertion. . . . It would be denying some essential characteristics of Indonesian nationalism to say that Sukarno's foreign policy until its last few years was not widely supported in the country.[24]

The University Economists

The university economists' involvement in national policy was not unique to Indonesia. To some extent it was a global phenomenon, encouraged in part by the demands of dealing with foreign assistance agencies, including those of the United States, Japan, and the West European states, and such intergovernmental institutions as the IMF, the World Bank, and the Asian Development Bank. But this deference to technical expertise in the governments of the new states also reflected a change in leadership within them: the solidarity-makers of the independence period had given way to a successor generation of leaders who sought legitimacy in their ability to promote economic development.

The change was particularly marked among the noncommunist states of Southeast Asia. Gunnar Myrdal, in decrying the political incapacity of the governments of the region in the mid-1960s, had witnessed the last years of an era. By the late 1960s or early 1970s, every government of Southeast Asia was authoritarian to some degree, and economic planning agencies were playing significant roles in most of them. Individuals with technical expertise also were found in increasing numbers in agencies of these same governments before the decade was out. The number of Western doctorates even among cabinet officers became striking, often far surpassing their presence in the cabinets of the Western countries themselves. The new breed spawned a new word, *technocrat,* and the word entered several of the national languages of the region.[25]

The Indonesian case was remarkable, nevertheless, for two elements that tended to set it apart from the rest. First, the highly trained elite of

3. The Rise of the Technocrats

Indonesia represented a much smaller proportion of the population than did its counterparts in the other countries of the region in 1966. This meant that their skills could not be distributed as widely in the political system, but could be made available only in a few select locations—inevitably at the very top. This circumstance reinforced the centralizing tendencies already inherent in the political culture, and was even more significant in a still largely illiterate society in which men of knowledge were shown great deference. (That Soeharto was able to surround himself with men of modern science not only increased his ability to control the surrounding environment from a technical point of view, but also added symbols of power to his person that carried considerable weight in the society.) Their small number also set the technocrats apart from the bulk of the bureaucracy, which continued to adhere to the same values it had held before the technocrats moved into the top of the system—"parachuted" in, as the phrase went. Thus, while the Indonesian technocrats could have a significant impact on broad policies—in the economic case, on monetary policies and on major allocations of resources—they could have little influence on the processes responsible for policy implementation—on contracts, licenses, promotions, profits, payoffs, and all those other events of microeconomy that are the stuff of daily economic life.[26]

The Indonesian economists also remained in public office far longer than their counterparts elsewhere in the region. This was partly a function of Soeharto's own long tenure. Yet, the stability of his relations with his initial five economic advisers—Sadli, Salim, Subroto, Wardhana, and Widjojo—was exceptional. All were to remain his personal advisers or members of his cabinet for many years. Widjojo was Minister of Planning and later Coordinating Minister for all economic affairs until 1983. Wardhana was Minister of Finance and replaced Widjojo as Coordinating Minister until 1988. Both were still full-time advisers to the government into the 1990s. Salim was still in the cabinet as Minister of State for Population and the Environment. Subroto filled several cabinet posts, including that of Minister of Mining until he became secretary general of OPEC in 1988. Sadli was head of foreign investment and then Minister of Mining until, in the wake of the Pertamina crisis in 1975, he took a post at the Chamber of Commerce and Industry. In addition, numerous other economists from the University of Indonesia followed the initial five into government over time, and while factions developed as their numbers grew, the cohesion of the group was, on the whole, remarkable.

If Soeharto and his army associates initially found common cause with the university economists in their shared sense of the need to break with the recent past, the relationship in fact went deeper. They also shared the view that the principal threat to the nation lay in its delayed economic and social development. And if foreign aid were to help make development possible, Soeharto needed the help of men such as these. He was quite innocent of international economic affairs at the time; according to one U.S. embassy official in 1966, it was doubtful that Soeharto even knew what the IMF was.[27] Given the disparity in their backgrounds, it took considerable self-confidence on Soeharto's part to put himself in the hands of the university men as he did.

Over the longer term, the stability of the relationship between Soeharto and the economists appears to have been founded chiefly on the fact that they worked well together. Soeharto immersed himself in the details of economic management, seemed to have a good head for the work, and learned quickly. Over the years he seldom met with his cabinet as a whole, but many years, when resources were tight and choices were difficult, he met as often as weekly with his economic ministers, chairing the sessions himself, hearing the alternatives, taking copious notes, and summarizing the consensus at the end. From the economists' point of view, Soeharto exhibited those very qualities of rationality and consistency that Widjojo had described in 1963 as essential to the task of economic policy-making.

Relations between Soeharto and his economic advisers over time also owed something to the traditional political culture of Java. One of the economists, pressed to describe the working environment with Soeharto, recommended a reading of Benedict Anderson's essay on kingship in precolonial Java.[28] Here the central government of Java is seen as an extension of the ruler's personal household; officials are granted their positions and the perquisites that go with them as personal favors; and tension invariably exists between the ruler's family and his officials of common origin who have risen to power on the basis of their ability and loyalty. At the same time, the traditional ethics applying to officials require them to work hard for the good of the state, to refrain from indulging personal motives, and to behave in a refined manner, meaning, among other things, to use polite and indirect language. Thus, one of the economists attributes Widjojo's long influence with Soeharto to his policy of avoiding public exposure; Widjojo's public statements since 1965 could probably be counted on the fingers of one hand.[29] Thus, too, the publisher of one of the nation's leading news media suggested that Widjojo enjoyed elite support not so much for the rationality of his policies as for the "purity" of his language.[30]

By such means did the Indonesian economists, Widjojo and his associates, as much as any comparable group in the contemporary world, place the stamp of their ideas on a large national economy. The origins of the Indonesian economists, and their ideological orientations, are thus of unusual interest.

Professional Origins

The University of Indonesia was founded only in 1950 after independence was achieved. At the time, although Indonesia was then a nation of some 77 million people, only a relative handful of Indonesians had completed any study beyond secondary school. J. S. Furnivall, reviewing the educational situation in Southeast Asia in the last years before World War II, found there were 1,101 individuals in institutions of higher education in the Netherlands Indies in 1938 out of a population of 68.4 million. By comparison, there were 759 in Malaya out of a population of 3.4 million; 872 in Thailand out of a population of 14.9 million; and 10,340 in the Philippines out of a population of 16.2 million.[31] The poverty of the Indonesians in terms of formal education stood in stark contrast to the relative wealth of their neighbors.

The Dutch colonial system had not reckoned with the needs of independence in the postcolonial era; indeed, independence was not foreseen at all.[32] The tiny educated Indonesian elite provided much of the leadership, however, of the national independence movement and of the national government of Indonesia in its early years. Their small numbers assured influence to the individuals among them, but also contributed to their separation as a group from the bulk of the population.[33]

The few trained economists in this small elite were at odds with Sukarno almost from the beginning. Mohammad Hatta, who had studied economics at Rotterdam in the late 1920s, and who was the first vice president of Indonesia, resigned in 1956 because of his unbridgeable differences with the president. Sumitro Djojohadikusumo, who studied at

Rotterdam in the 1930s, and was minister of trade and of finance in some of the first postindependence cabinets, joined the "outer island" rebellion in 1958. More than any others, these two—they were not alone, all the major parties had prominent intellectuals in their leadership—but they were among the few trained economists to serve in an Indonesian cabinet prior to 1966—represented the clash of the rationalist-administrative minds in the elite with the solidarity-makers of whom Sukarno was the unquestioned leader.

Hatta and Sumitro also were of major consequence in shaping the economic thought of Indonesia.[34] Hatta is credited with being the author of Article 33 of the 1945 Constitution, which reads:

> The economy shall be organized as a common endeavour based on the principle of the family.
>
> Branches of production which are important for the state and which control the lives of large numbers of the people shall be controlled by the state.
>
> The land and water and the natural resources contained therein shall be controlled by the state and utilized for the maximum prosperity of the people.[35]

Hatta saw socialism as being rooted in Islamic thought, he told George Kahim in 1949. He believed that a mixed economy was best suited to Indonesia, and for him that meant a large state-run sector, a substantial cooperative sector, primarily operating among the farming population, and a limited capitalist sector comprised of small business.[36] He did not believe that more than a few hundred Indonesians had the education and experience to set up a firm, a limited liability company, or a trade association the way Europeans and Chinese did. The only way the people could become economically strong was through the cooperative movement.[37] The background to this view of cooperatives was the picture he had formed of Indonesia's economy when he was a student in Europe: "At the top the economy was entirely in the hands of the whites. The economy in the middle was 90% in the hands of the Chinese. What was in the hands of the Indonesians was the small part. Everything that was small! It was obvious that all those small concerns could not possibly become strong by their own powers."[38]

Hatta was much influenced by the growth of the cooperative movement in Britain and Scandinavia. But he also reflected the values of the Islamic trading community of West Sumatra from which he came. He had no time for communism. And while he favored a strong government role in the economy, he also favored efforts to promote small-scale enterprises owned and operated by Indonesians—specifically, as he made clear, by non-Chinese Indonesians.

Sumitro was the son of a senior official in the rural administration of Java, and he wrote his own doctoral dissertation on problems of rural credit in Java. Politically he was a Social Democrat, and when he published an economics text in 1955 he argued that the underdeveloped nations were obliged to plan and manage their economic development. Entrepreneurs with capital and skills were too few within the societies themselves. Unless development was to be left to foreign economic interests altogether, the state had to take the lead in creating the necessary capital and skills. This did not mean, however, that the government had to be involved directly in the ownership and management of enterprises, although that might be desirable in some cases, such as public utilities. A government could stimulate the economy in many other ways for it to develop as the government desired.[39]

Indeed, as early as 1951, Sumitro had sponsored plans for extensive government intervention to strengthen indigenous industries. The aim was to make it possible for small Indonesian firms to produce substitutes for manufactured goods that were being imported, by giving them capital assistance and by restricting certain markets from foreign competition. (The program was undertaken after Sumitro was out of the cabinet, and the import-licensing element of the program was a disastrous failure. A later minister issued import licenses primarily as a means of financing the National Party, and the indigenous business community—rather than being helped—was seriously discredited.)[40]

If Hatta was a man of ideas, grounded in the socialist thinking of Europe in the 1920s, and somewhat romantic for the circumstances of postindependence Indonesia, Sumitro was a man of policy, well attuned to the prevailing sentiments of his profession in the wider world of the 1950s and 1960s, and with a sharp eye to the needs and possibilities of the moment. And Sumitro was to become the dominant ideological force for a later generation of Indonesian economists. He was not only more "modern," more pragmatic, than Hatta. He also was Javanese, and in a position to speak from the dominant center of Indonesian politics. In addition, he had an electric personality that attracted a large following of younger men.

3. The Rise of the Technocrats

The Faculty of Economics

Sumitro was early named to the leadership of a faculty, or school, of economics in Jakarta, and this was to be a powerful instrument for the development of Indonesian economic thought and policy. Sumitro's own ambition was to create an Asian version of the London School of Economics. It would conduct research, train students, and advise government and business; in short, it was to be a major influence in national affairs. Sumitro quickly attracted a number of unusually able students, and put together a makeshift teaching staff that included two visiting UN experts from the United States, Benjamin Higgins and Nathan Keyfitz, and a number of Dutch lecturers. Almost from the outset, however, he began to look for means to replace the Dutch in order to build the school on Anglo-American lines.[41]

Most of Sumitro's first students came from the families of officials in the former colonial administration. Most had attended Dutch-language secondary schools before the Japanese occupation. Many served in student military detachments during the anti-Dutch actions following the Japanese surrender. They joined the new Faculty of Economics with every expectation of playing significant national roles in the new era of independence. Indeed, many of them, while still pursuing their studies, were soon working in the national planning agency, under the leadership of Djuanda and Ali Boediardjo, two of the most prominent members of the country's central administration.[42]

Sumitro found support for the Faculty in 1955 with the arrival in Jakarta of Michael Harris as the resident representative of the Ford Foundation. Harris had had no formal education beyond high school. He began work as a CIO organizer, rose quickly in union ranks, acquired a wide circle of acquaintances among figures in the New Deal, and served in wartime economic posts in Washington. At the end of the war he was appointed director of the U.S. aid program in Sweden, and later was a senior member of the economic staff of John McCloy, U.S. high commissioner in Germany. In between these latter two appointments, he had been sent on a brief assignment to Indonesia. Harris and Sumitro apparently were already acquainted, either as a result of Sumitro's assignment in 1949 to Indonesia's unofficial republican "embassy" in Washington, or as a result of Harris's later brief assignment to Jakarta. In any case, they were kindred spirits. In a matter of months the University of California was drawn into the discussions, in part because students at Berkeley, since as early as 1950, had been raising funds to help the new universities of Indonesia, and in part because some members of the Berkeley faculty, such as Thomas Blaisdell, were well known to Harris from the war years in Washington. The Dutch contingent in the teaching staff of the Faculty of Economics was supplemented by the first visiting professors from the University of California in the middle of 1956. It was none too soon. In April of the following year, fleeing arrest, Sumitro joined the dissidents gathering in Sumatra. In December communist-affiliated labor unions "took over" all Dutch banks, plantations, and other enterprises, and in a matter of months most Dutch nationals left the country.

In 1958 the long-simmering discontent in the "outer islands" erupted in a full-fledged rebellion, and Sumitro accepted the position of Minister of Finance in the rebel government. When the rebellion collapsed, as it quickly did, Sumitro became a hunted man, not only as he fled through the jungles of Sumatra, but in the ensuing years across half a dozen countries. His former students in Jakarta were left vulnerable to attack from several quarters in the increasingly radical environment of Jakarta after 1958.

Yet, the young economists, most of whom at the time were in their late twenties and early thirties, were not without protection. Some of the most prestigious professors of the university, notably Djokosutono and Djuned Pusponegoro, who led the law and medical faculties, and who enjoyed the personal confidence of Sukarno, were resolute in their defense of their younger colleagues. Had it not been for these elder academic statesmen, the economics faculty may well have been disbanded before it even began to function as a corporate body. As it was, the dangers in the external environment caused the group to develop intense internal loyalties. One foreign visitor, writing in late 1964, described the young leadership group in the Faculty of Economics as "proud, resourceful, and self-reliant."[43]

The Heir Apparent

The heir apparent to Sumitro on his sudden departure from the scene was Widjojo Nitisastro, who was thirty years of age at the time and about to start his doctoral studies at the University of California. Widjojo came from a family of teachers, on both his father's and his mother's sides, and grew up in several district capitals in East Java. At the age of twenty he was commanding a student army unit in the fighting against the British in Surabaya. In the eyes of his commander of the time, he was a brave young man who was mindless of risk to himself.[44] The leader of the student army, Mas Isman, later founded and led a politically powerful organization of student army veterans, Kosgoro, and appointed Widjojo its economic adviser.

In 1955, the year he graduated from the University of Indonesia, Widjojo engaged in a notable debate with a former prime minister, Wilopo, on the structure of the Indonesian economy. Wilopo was an intellectual among the leaders of the National Party; someone interested in the cooperative movement conceived the event, and Wilopo, as expected, argued the case for cooperatives. Widjojo, asked to respond, found this approach unduly concerned with the redistribution of income. If economic development was to be successful, he said, redistributing income could not be separated from increasing it. These were complementary aims; they were integrally related, and they had to be pursued concurrently. He also argued that the constitution did not have to be interpreted to mean that any particular form of ownership was to be preferred. The point of the constitution, he said, was that it established a clear role for the state in the economy. Thus, as Widjojo saw it, the constitution called for "an economic system based on the joint efforts of the entire community, with the objective of achieving a higher level of per capita income and an equitable distribution of income, with the state playing an active role in guiding and implementing economic development." In such a system, private enterprise was not at all incompatible.[45]

Widjojo and the other university economists also acquired a circle of acquaintances among the officer corps of the Indonesian army as a result of two training programs in which they were engaged as part-time teaching staff. Djokosutono, who doubled as dean of the economics faculty when Sumitro fled, had persuaded the army leadership of the desirability of training some of its younger officers in law and economics; he was the first director of the Academy of Military Law when it was established, and, in turn, named several economists of the university among its first faculty members. Graduates of the academy quickly found their way into senior staff positions; among them was Sudharmono, who later served as secretary to Soeharto's early cabinets, by the mid-1980s was head of the government's political party, and in 1988 was elected vice president.

3. The Rise of the Technocrats

Meanwhile, the economists also were engaged as part-time lecturers at the Army Staff and Command School in Bandung. The principal figure in the school from the late 1950s on was an officer by the name of Suwarto, who came from a middle-class family of officials, had been educated in a Dutch secondary school in Central Java, and had pronounced intellectual leanings. In 1958 Suwarto was charged with organizing the first year-long course at the school; he envisioned the "long course" as a vehicle for providing a wide-ranging education to the general officers of the future. Half the curriculum was to be concerned with nonmilitary subjects, and to teach them he arranged for the school to enter into formal agreements with the leading universities. Suwarto had gone to secondary school with Sadli, and so the tie with the Faculty of Economics was quickly established. Because transportation was poor, the Jakarta economists usually went to the school for several days at a time, staying over with the young colonels who were their students, and spending the evenings in long talks about the state of the country and its future.

As the early 1960s wore on the university economists were placed increasingly on the defensive by initiatives from the political Left. An effort was made by leftists to take over the national economic association. The Faculty leadership was pressured to add known leftists to the teaching staff. Students of the Faculty were recruited by the communist student organization to serve as campus provocateurs. By early 1965 junior members of the Faculty staff were scanning the communist press every day to alert Widjojo and the other senior members to any change in tactics that might affect them. By this same time the campus also had become a battleground of competing demonstrators as the principal student organizations, the Islamic Student Association, which was affiliated with the Islamic social organization Muhammadiyah, and the Indonesian Student Movement Center, an offshoot of the Communist party, organized shows of strength and disrupted each other's rallies.

Widjojo traveled to China and Eastern Europe in 1964 and 1965. He was not favorably impressed. A colleague later recalled:

> What was going on in China was extremely important. China was in the midst of the "great leap forward," and authoritarianism was very strong. As far as we could see, development had come to a complete halt there. But remember that the whole orientation here at the time was toward Peking. There was a constant flow of delegations going there; it was a "must." Widjojo went to China with Djuned Poesponegoro in

1964, and he returned full of concern about the nature of the Chinese regime and the implications that had for us. This was the source of the references in our 1966 documents to "etatism."[46]

But if the university economists were not impressed with the regimes of China and Eastern Europe, neither were they adherents of a liberal ideology. Indeed, capitalism had no defenders whatsoever among the Indonesian political elite. One of the economists later reflected on this predisposition of his countrymen: "Nineteenth century images are strong. The United States is thought to be a libertarian economy in the nineteenth century sense, when of course it is highly regulated. People don't understand that competition is a means of promoting efficiency."[47]

Further Intellectual Orientations

What mattered principally in almost any discussion of the economy was the recent experience of Indonesia itself. Social solidarity was a major element in the national independence movement, and Sukarno had added the power of his personality to the ideal of equality. The economic policy statement drafted by Widjojo and his colleagues, and passed by the Provisional Consultative Assembly in July 1966, reflected these influences in rejecting "free-fight liberalism" on the grounds that it would lead inevitably to "the exploitation of man by man." What many Indonesians mainly had in mind, however, was not abstract theory but that Dutch capital had dominated the heights of their economy until only eight years earlier; and that much of the private sector that remained, other than agriculture, was still dominated by the Chinese.

One of the leading economists later recalled that ideology had had little to do with his and his colleagues' thinking in 1966: "The problem was: how to start the damn thing moving? . . . Ideological calculations just weren't there. The numbers were on the table."[48]

Indeed, the economists' political ideas were poorly developed. Like many other members of the Indonesian elite, they were deeply concerned about the growing strength of the Communist party. Moreover, the army contained men whom they knew and with whom they could talk. As choices narrowed, they worked more and more with the army. They were concerned about authoritarian government, but they seem to have given little thought about how it could be avoided. Political issues, properly speaking, seemed not to have a place in their thinking at all.

The economists also did not share the Indonesian nationalists' dis-

3. The Rise of the Technocrats

comfort with foreign aid or foreign investment. Of course, they had more experience in living in Western countries than all but a handful of their fellow countrymen. In addition, their dealings with the West were conducted through the good offices of men trained in economics and finance like themselves, men who talked the same language they did. When Harvard University was recruited to provide economic advisers, the Indonesians invited the Harvard economists to share their government offices. When the World Bank appointed an unprecedented resident mission, and named Bernard Bell, a former Djuanda adviser, to head it, Bell and his group also were housed in the offices of the Planning Agency. Further, Bell followed Sieber in becoming an advocate for Indonesian interests and policies, and was all the more powerful because of his direct line of communication to Robert MacNamara, the Bank president.

The young Indonesian economists had, as this suggests, considerable confidence that mainstream Western economic thinking could be applied to Indonesia. Their years at Berkeley and other (largely) American universities also gave them great confidence in their professional ability to set the nation on the path to economic growth; this alone tended to set them apart from others, to bind them closely together as a kind of secular brotherhood, earning them the sobriquet "Berkeley mafia." They fully shared Sumitro's view of government as the source of plans, guidance, and direction for economic growth. They were much influenced by India's experience with community development, had done village studies themselves for the Indonesian planning agency in the 1950s, were in agreement that the government had to see agriculture as the base for growth in other sectors, and believed that greater incentives had to be given to agricultural producers. They were committed to population control; Widjojo's dissertation, in fact, was a demographic study that is now a classic in the field.[49] The economists also were confident that other sectors of the population and economy could be more productive. This certainly included the export-producing populations of the "outer islands." It also included the Java-based community of manufacturers.

This last element set the Indonesian economists apart from some theorists. An influential element in Western thinking had been the "Orientalist" cast of mind of such scholars as J. H. Boeke, who had begun his own economic study of the Netherlands Indies in the late 1930s and completed the bulk of it in a German concentration camp in

83

the early 1940s. Boeke adopted, with some modification, the view that the Indonesian economy was doomed to be indefinitely a "dual" economy, one in which a relatively small number of producers were "modern" or "Western" in their values, capitalist and entrepreneurial in their behavior, and part of a larger international system, while the great majority were trapped in a domestic system that was "traditional" or "oriental" in its values, precapitalist or "stagnant" in behavior, and operating within a domestic system that had no significant contact with the wider world.[50] J. S. Furnivall, at work at the same time, argued that Western economic theory was of limited application in a tropical dependency such as the Netherlands Indies precisely because it did not address political and social aspects of the colonial situation. The basic problem, he argued, was that, in a colonial society, there was "no community as a whole." The purpose of policy thus should be "to integrate society and to organize social demand."[51] Sadli, in a long critique published in 1957, rejected the Boeke view as one that seemed designed to justify the perpetuation of the colonial relationship. It might take more than one generation, Sadli said, but there was no reason why Indonesia could not develop an industrial sector in its economy, a larger middle class in its cities, and, along the lines suggested by Furnivall, provide greater linkages between the social elite and the mass of rural society.[52]

One aspect of this debate often went unstated, that the bulk of the larger urban traders and the small-scale private manufacturers were of Chinese or of mixed Chinese-Indonesian descent. All along Indonesian economic nationalism had had a strong element of racism, and in 1966 anti-Chinese sentiment was widespread. The university economists appear not to have shared this sentiment. The University of Indonesia was one of the few institutions of the postindependence establishment that provided an honored place for Chinese-Indonesians; the economics faculty, like the medical and law faculties, numbered Chinese-Indonesians among its leading figures, and in the conditions of the time these were not only professional colleagues, but also personal friends and political allies. One should not overstate the case, however. Few Chinese-Indonesian economists would follow their colleagues into government; even the economic agencies were largely the preserve of indigenous Indonesians. It was assumed, however, that Chinese-Indonesians would play a significant role in the private sector, in the new industrial sector that was to come, and in the middle class that was to grow in the cities. Exactly how this was to lead to greater social cohesion, however, was not clear.

These, then, were the strengths and weaknesses with which the economists entered the government. When the need for their economic expertise was great, as it was in the late 1960s and in other periods to come, they would be relatively immune from criticism. But when criticism did come, it would focus on those views that set them apart from others in the elite—views about foreigners, about the Chinese, and about the place of both in the economy.

FOUR

Creating a Political Machine

Eventually Soeharto had to obtain an electoral mandate to govern. That was clear as early as July 1966 when the Consultative Assembly confirmed his executive authority. The Assembly did so only pro tem, pending elections.

The prospect of an election raised many questions. The country's only experience with national elections in 1955 had not been a positive one. How another round of elections could be held without increasing the divisions in the society, already the cause of so much bloodshed, was indeed questionable. In addition, how could a Parliament be produced that would have a majority capable of governing? The Parliament that resulted from the earlier elections had been unable to deal effectively with any of the country's problems, and had lasted less than eighteen months before collapsing in the face of regional rebellions and Sukarno's call for a "Guided Democracy."

The constitutional situation in 1966 was highly favorable to executive action. In the wake of the rebellions, Sukarno had had broad support among the Java-based parties for his reinstatement of the 1945 constitution as a key element of Guided Democracy. This constitution, written at the start of the independence revolution, provided for a strong central executive. The president was free to select his cabinet members solely on his own authority. The legislature had no power of initiative, but it did have two residual sources of power. Members of Parliament were *ex officio* members of the Consultative Assembly, which was charged with selecting the president and vice president and with approving the broad lines of government policy. Further, a minority of legislators could forestall a government measure by refusing to go along with the majority—Sukarno's innovation and a central feature of Guided Democracy.

If elections were to be held, many questions had to be dealt with, however. The Consultative Assembly that confirmed Soeharto's executive authority was composed of both elected and appointed members; how seats were to be shared between the two was bound to be controversial. In addition, the electoral law in place in 1955 was based on the principle of proportional representation; now the "action fronts" expressed strong sentiment in favor of single-member constituencies. Moreover, an election meant parties; many were in favor of legalizing the parties Sukarno had banned, and Soeharto faced the decision of whether to launch a party of his own. Finally, the question remained as to the army's role in the elections and in the government that would result.

This was a substantial agenda, and in the wake of Sukarno's fall from power, the general expectation was that the government would now be chosen more democratically. Electoral reform was in the air.

The Experience with Elections

The idea of election to public office was not well grounded in the political ethos of Indonesia. The first Parliament sat for five years, from August 1950 until September 1955, without having any elections other than intraparty elections for party leadership. No one knew how much popular support any of the parties actually had; distribution of seats in the early Parliaments was largely determined by vague considerations of maintaining a balance among ideological, geographic, ethnic, religious, and economic interests. Sukarno himself held the presidency with no more expression of the popular will than the rest.

On September 29, 1955, the first national elections took place for seats in the national Parliament.[1] Several reasons seem to account for why these elections were considered necessary or desirable. One was a sense of national pride; holding elections would demonstrate that Indonesia was worthy of being the independent nation it had insisted on becoming. Another was the more practical belief or hope that elections would bring about a more stable and authoritative government.

Coalition cabinets had come and gone with some rapidity, and none had shown itself able to deal with the country's problems, which only continued to grow. The initial Parliament was thought to lack cohesion, in part because it was temporary, and to lack moral authority because it was not truly representative. But the purpose of the elections, or the terms on which they would take place, were at no time debated on a grand scale. Elections had been talked about for years, and in 1955 the country more or less backed into them.

When the time came, the elections took place in conditions of considerable uncertainty. The idea of "one man, one vote" was wholly new to the population, and voting was widely seen as more of a duty than a right. Strenuous appeals were made on religious and ideological grounds, intimidation was widespread, and the electioneering greatly aggravated ideological cleavages within the society on the very purposes of the state. Some members of the elite, judging the election by Western standards, concluded that Indonesia was not ready for democracy.

The new Parliament also did not fulfill the hopes that had been lodged in the electoral process. The cabinet, again a coalition, seemed to have the same problems in reaching decisions as before. The parties themselves lacked cohesion, and ethnic and regional protests soon took the center of the political stage. Groups in Sulawesi and Sumatra, with the public support of local civil and military authorities, defied Jakarta in opening their own foreign trade relations. The cabinet came under increasing criticism for ignoring or protecting high-level corruption. Nasution, the armed forces chief of staff, deplored what he called the selfishness of political leaders and noted the existence of proposals for a junta of military officers or veterans of the revolution. Sukarno took up the cry, announcing that it had been a mistake in 1945 to have urged the establishment of parties. Some new form of government was needed, he said. Not a dictatorship, but democracy with leadership, a "Guided Democracy."

Sensing a power vacuum in Jakarta, military groups expressed their resentment against Nasution, and regional groups demanded autonomy. Hatta resigned the vice presidency, heightening feelings of antagonism against Sukarno and the whole Jakarta establishment in the regions outside Java. Coups followed in several provinces of Sumatra and Sulawesi, where local army officers announced a temporary severance of relations with the central government. The national cabinet resigned. Sukarno proclaimed a nationwide state of war. It was March 1957, not eighteen months since the national elections.

A decade later, this experience remained very much alive in the minds of the elite as the country again faced the need to reconstitute the national government. Yet, there seems to have been no significant opposition to the idea of turning to national elections in order to establish the nation's rightful leadership. Anti-Sukarnoists among the army generals, and leaders of the "action fronts," were concerned to avoid a return to the authoritarian features of Guided Democracy. They also had little confidence in the remaining political parties and their leaders. Attention in these circles focused quickly on how to reform the electoral system.

Proposals for Electoral Reform

The high point of the reform movement was the seminar of military commanders that took place at the Staff and Command School in Bandung in August 1966. Suwarto was now a major general and commandant of the School. In addition to arranging the discussion of the economy that led to the new economic policies, he placed on the agenda a discussion of the electoral system.[2]

The antiparty sentiment among senior army officers assembled at the seminar was strong. They acknowledged that elections would have to be held in accordance with the Assembly decision of the previous month. They also recommended rehabilitation of the Socialist and Masyumi parties, which Sukarno had banned because of their leaders' involvement in the "outer island" rebellions. At the same time, the group concluded, "it is very clear that the Panca Sila forces must be victorious in the General Elections."[3]

The means selected to assure this victory was a proposed change in the electoral laws. The 1955 Parliament had been elected by proportional representation among provincewide constituencies. This meant that voters were not given the opportunity to select an individual to represent them in the Parliament, but were presented with a choice among parties. The share of the total vote a party received in a province determined the share of the seats allotted to the province that would be filled by that party. Seats were filled according to rank in a party list that party leaders prepared in advance of the election. The system placed considerable power in the hands of party leaders. It also tended to favor a multiplicity of parties and to lead to coalition governments. In the circumstances of 1966, this system would assure that the remaining legal parties would win an overwhelming majority of seats in the Parliament, that the large number of voters in Java would place many Sukarnoists among the winners, and that the army's civilian allies among the urban "action fronts" would attract only a small minority of the votes among the largely rural electorate.

The seminar concluded that the next elections should be conducted on the basis of single-member constituencies, and that an eligible candidate should have lived in the constituency for at least one year. The result would be to reduce the power of party leaders, and open up the prospect that popular local personalities, not allied with any party, would win some seats, further reducing the role of parties in the legislature. The plan followed the lines of a presentation made to the seminar by Sarbini Sumawinata, an economist of the University of Indonesia, who had long been identified with the banned Socialist Party, and who was a long-time friend of Major General Suwarto.

Soeharto took no position on these plans. According to one man involved in the process, he simply let the idea go forward. A general elections bill providing for single-member constituencies was drawn up and presented to the Parliament early in 1967. Another bill provided that all representative institutions—the Consultative Assembly, the Parliament, and local bodies—would be composed of members only half of whom would represent political parties. The other half would represent "functional groups," and half of these, in turn, would be appointed to represent the armed forces, whose members would have no vote in the elections. A third bill established conditions for the recognition of political parties and functional groups, and was seen as an effort to reduce the number of parties.

The bills ran into a storm of criticism in the Parliament, and Soeharto decided to negotiate. On July 27, 1967, a compromise was announced. Soeharto agreed that the system of proportional representation would remain. The parties agreed that the government would have the right to appoint one-third of the members of the Consultative Assembly, and 100 members, or 22 percent, of the 460-member Parliament. The Assembly was of central interest to Soeharto, because under the prevailing 1945 constitution it was the body that would decide the future of the presidency. But unless he was to attempt to rule by decree, as Sukarno had done, he also had to take seriously the composition of the Parliament. One senior political aide later said it would have been "easy" for Soeharto to have assumed dictatorial powers, even before March 11, 1966, but it is doubtful that Soeharto was strong enough to do so at that point. Nor did he seem inclined by nature to face down harsh critics a year later when compromise was an available alternative.

The compromise disappointed a good many New Order figures, including at least three senior army generals. Nasution, Kemal Idris, and Dharsono had all argued strongly for the single-member constituency. In Bandung, General Dharsono, commander of the Siliwangi Division, was not ready to concede the fight. He had wanted a two-party system, and he was determined to get it. Putting pressure on local party leaders, he forced the formation of two groups in the district boards of the province, one representing the government, the other the opposition. But by this time Soeharto was committed to cooperation with the parties. When party leaders protested, Dharsono was ordered to stop. Dharsono was then sent off to Bangkok as ambassador, and Kemal Idris was assigned to the East Indonesia command headquartered in distant Makassar.

In retrospect, it seems doubtful that Soeharto was ever committed to this effort to reform the system essentially along Western legal lines. The supporters of reform were all prominent figures in or alumni of the Siliwangi Division, and included no one with long experience in Central Java such as himself. In addition, the reform would have meant a large step in an uncharted direction, with possible outcomes no one could foresee—not the sort of action with which Soeharto usually associated himself. It also remains an open question as to whether the plan would have given the country a more coherent parliamentary system than what had gone before. The parties, including those that had been banned, remained a social reality in the minds of many of their followers. In addition, in the Consultative Assembly, which had confirmed Soeharto's executive authority and was the only body that could settle the succession to the presidency under the constitution, the remaining legal parties were a political reality. It is difficult to see how Soeharto could have ignored the parties at this point unless he were prepared to declare himself president, and this he was wise enough not to do.

4. Creating a Political Machine

Old Parties in the New Order

The compromise reached on the electoral system did not carry with it any intended departure from the basic principle agreed on at the army seminar in Bandung. When elections were held, it was intended that Soeharto's forces would win. That did not rule out a working relationship with the parties and their leaders.

This did not seem to Soeharto and his advisers too much to expect. The political parties had already lost much of their independence and prestige after the institution of Guided Democracy in 1959. They had come to look to Sukarno for approval of their plans, and to depend even more than before on government subsidies and licenses. The subsidies and licenses continued after 1966, or, where they had been halted, were soon resumed.

There were three parties of consequence. Two of these, the National Party and the Nahdatul Ulama, were parties that had their strength in Java, had been willing participants in Sukarno's Guided Democracy, and included among their leaders some who seemed likely to accept an accommodation with the new regime. The third case was more problematical. This was the Masyumi, the large Islamic grouping that had its principal strength in the "outer islands," had been banned as a result of some of its leaders' involvement in the 1958 rebellion, and represented a stream of Indonesian society and of political thinking with which Soeharto and his associates were much less familiar.[4]

The National Party (*Partai Nasional Indonesia,* or *PNI*) was of the greatest interest to Soeharto. It had a large following in Central and East Java, provided the only major balance to Muslim interests, and also was a possible link with followers of the banned Communist party. The National Party had divided into two factions even before the attempted coup over the issue of cooperation with the Communists under Sukarno's Nasakom formula. The anticommunist faction held a party congress as early as April 1966, which opened with an address by Soeharto and voted out of party office all the leaders of the "progressive" faction. Army regional commanders reinforced this direction of the party's affairs by taking a wide range of actions against provincial branches that remained strongly pro-Sukarno. By the time the party held a preelection congress in 1970, and under a good deal of pressure from Soeharto's personal assistant, Ali Moertopo, the party elected an old Soeharto acquaintance as its leader. He was Hadisubeno, who had

been mayor of Semarang in the late 1950s when Soeharto was the commander of the Diponegoro Division and had his headquarters in the
same city.[5]

The Nahdatul Ulama was not a political party in the same sense as
the others. It was led by traditional religious teachers, chiefly the heads
of significant Islamic schools in rural Java. It had the reputation of
accommodating itself to the national political leadership of the day.
Although there was some interest among Soeharto associates in seeing a
change in the party's leadership—Subchan, the staunch anticommunist,
was a favorite in these circles—the old guard under Idham Chalid seems
to have had no great difficulty in fending off outside intervention. At
the same time, Idham Chalid and his associates had no problem in making peace with Soeharto and his staff.

The former leaders of the Masyumi had welcomed Sukarno's fall and
at first expected to regain their former positions of national prominence.
Their followers were too numerous to be ignored, and the army seminar had recommended that the ban on the party should be lifted.
Soeharto refused to act, however, on the grounds that army officers and
men had died in putting down the rebellion, and that he owed it to their
memory to see that their deaths were not in vain. A long series of negotiations took place, first to determine how the Masyumi might be
replaced by a new party, and then over whether its former leaders could
hold office in the new grouping. Soeharto refused to budge on the latter issue. When the new Indonesian Muslim Party was finally recognized, and leaders amenable to the government were in place, again with
the active involvement of Ali Moertopo, the result satisfied no one. The
new party did not attract much of the old Masyumi following, and this
large and influential group remained unintegrated into the new regime.[6]

Thus, well before elections took place, the political parties had been
considerably domesticated by the Soeharto administration. If the government needed partners after elections, partners would be available.
And if decisions were to be reached by consensus, the parties would,
within broad limits, be amenable.

Election Versus Appointment

Initially some of Soeharto's civilian supporters suggested that a new
party be organized to run progovernment candidates for election to the
Parliament. This "independent group" included a number of prominent

intellectuals, most of them former leaders of the "action fronts," now holding appointments to Parliament or, in a few cases, to high posts in the new administration.[7] Why they failed to persuade Soeharto is not entirely clear. One member of the group has suggested that Soeharto found the idea too Western, and some of those behind it too Western in their orientation.[8] But the principal reason seems to have been that the notion was too abstract and its proponents had no proven record. The existing parties had their roots in identifiable sections of the Indonesian population. Exactly how this new party would relate to these multiple divisions of Indonesian society was not clear. So Soeharto held off giving his personal endorsement to the "independent group" and their plans.

Another possible move was to enter into a partnership with one of the existing parties, such as the National Party or the new Muslim Party, either before or after elections. The possible need for a coalition with one of the parties acted as a brake on army militants, who were taking action against the parties in various parts of the country and urging action against them at the national level. The same concern led the Soeharto group to carry on extended negotiations, initially in the Parliament, and subsequently outside it, over the allocation of elective and appointive seats. However the government might campaign in an election, it did not know how it would fare. It might need appointed members of the legislature to enable it to build a majority to govern, with or without a party as partner.

As these negotiations dragged on into late 1969, Soeharto's political advisers were urging him to postpone the elections, now scheduled for July 1971. They told Soeharto they were not ready for elections. But Soeharto already had gained valuable time. His economic program was showing results: inflation had been halted and a new five-year development program was under way, inaugurated on his insistence a year or two before his economic team was entirely ready. By this time domestic stability had also greatly improved; Soeharto had the armed forces under control, the parties were cooperating, and the "action fronts" had fallen away considerably. In addition, the UN-supervised voting in West Irian had just been successfully completed. Thus Soeharto had reason to feel that the time was as good as it was likely to be. He told his political advisers that people would soon be calling him a dictator if he did not go ahead with the elections as planned.

In October 1969, apparently against his staff's advice, Soeharto met with the leaders of the nine legal parties and suggested they formalize the 1967 agreement on the issue of elective versus appointive seats and proceed with the elections on schedule. On November 22, the Parliament unanimously passed revised bills on the elections and on the structure of both the Consultative Assembly and the Parliament. Functional groups were allotted appointed seats throughout the structure: 307, or one-third, of the 920 seats of the Consultative Assembly; 100, or 22 percent, of the 460 seats of the Parliament; and 22 percent of the seats in local representative bodies at the provincial, city, and district levels.[9]

At about this same time Ali Moertopo began to develop a capacity, within the army's organization of allied "functional groups," to wage an electoral campaign on behalf of the government. Characteristically, no documentation appears to exist, and no elaborate instructions seem to have been given. According to at least one associate who claims to have been present, Soeharto simply asked Moertopo to see what he could do.

The Idea of Functional Groups

The idea of providing a role for "functional groups" in Indonesia's political system was one that had some history. The term itself might have originated with Sukarno. As early as the 1920s Sukarno's vision of Indonesian unity had led him to see the desirability of a single, all-encompassing political party, "a state within a state." He had initially seen the National Party as providing the basis for such a single state party, in which representatives would be drawn from groups that were defined in terms of social or economic functions, rather than religion or ideology. Hatta and others had refused to accept this proposal in the early days after independence was declared.[10]

The constitution of 1945 nevertheless provided for the representation of groups other than political parties in the highest organ of the state. The constitution provided that the People's Consultative Assembly, which would elect the president and set the main lines of state policy, would be composed of the members of the Council of People's Representatives, which was the Parliament, plus "delegates of the regions and of groups." An elucidation of the constitution explained that the term *groups* referred to workers' groups, cooperatives, and other collective organizations.

In 1958, after Sukarno had made his "bury the political parties" speech and had introduced his concept of Guided Democracy, an agreement was reached to give functional groups half the seats in the Parliament. The candidates of these groups were to be nominated through a National Front that Sukarno would lead. A long list of functional groups was agreed on: workers, employers, farmers, religious teachers, members of the professions, regional representatives, youth, women—and members of the armed forces.

The inclusion of the armed forces in the 1958 list of officially recognized functional groups gave the army its first legally sanctioned role in national politics. The role suited Nasution's ideas about the army's place in politics. In addition, the army had already been developing friendly organizations in a variety of fields as part of its developing contest with the Communist party. The core group was an army-sponsored labor federation, composed of twenty-five organizations of workers and officials of government-run firms and plantations. A coordinating secretariat was formed in 1964. The groups themselves were now officially known as "Functional Groups," or *Golongan Karya,* which in common usage was shortened to "Golkar."

When the transfer of authority to Soeharto took place, the Parliament included a large number of "functional group" representatives. Although many were representatives of groups affiliated with the political parties, Soeharto was able to appoint his own in filling vacancies from 1966 on. In addition, by the time Soeharto had decided to make an electoral machine of such groups, some senior army officers had been at work developing these organizations for up to a dozen years. Soeharto himself had urged the armed services as early as 1966 to provide all possible facilities for the development of these groups. A report by the Golkar secretariat announced that its affiliated organizations had increased from 64 in 1965 to 128 in 1966, and to 252 in 1967.

The secretariat was firmly under army control; six of its seven divisions were headed by military officers. Nevertheless, the prospect of turning this unwieldy federation into a machine capable of winning an election was awesome. According to his associates, Ali Moertopo had no respect for the official leadership of Golkar at this point, and went about his task by leaving the formal structure in place and creating a new organization within it to manage the election campaign. Moertopo's aim was to create a new kind of party, committed to modernization and led by civilian intellectuals, such as those now holding appointive positions in the Parliament and leading the prodevelopment forces there. The weapons of victory, however, were to be the army, the civil service, and the state corporations.

Winning the Election

On December 4, 1969, Amir Machmud, now Minister of the Interior and presiding over all provincial and local governments, issued a regulation prohibiting all functional group members in local councils from retaining membership in political parties. This prohibition did not extend to Golkar; by the government's definition, Golkar was not a political party. In effect, the new regulation meant that all seats allocated to functional groups would henceforth be filled by representatives of Golkar functional groups.[11]

On February 11, 1970, Machmud prohibited all civil servants from engaging in political activities that might "damage their positions as civil servants," and barred all top-ranking civil servants from belonging to "political organizations." Machmud soon took the further step of requiring all officials in his own department to sever their ties with any party except Golkar; in addition, he encouraged them to join two new organizations under his control, the Home Affairs Department Employees Association for men, and a parallel association for their wives and female officials. All government agencies were soon pressured to follow this example, and by the time elections took place practically all government agencies and institutions had organized similar associations, from the public schools to the state corporations.

The election machinery was in the hands of a General Elections Institute attached to the Ministry of the Interior and chaired by its minister. Committees at all lower levels—province, city, district, subdistrict, and village—were chaired by the senior government executive of the area. In the words of Masashi Nishihara: "In effect, the General Elections Institute assumed the character of a military command with local chief executives as local commanders and election committees as their staffs."[12]

Many of the executives involved were, in fact, military officers on temporary assignment to civil government positions. Of the 26 provincial governors, 20 were military men, as were 26 of the 53 city mayors and 116 of the 228 district heads. In addition, a military security organization was given responsibility to screen the qualifications of candidates, as a result of which an initial total of 3,789 candidates was reduced to 3,021; the largest numbers of disqualifications were among candidates of the National Party and the new Muslim Party. The central intelligence agency, also under army leadership, took regular soundings of Golkar's prospects.

Election committees were buttressed on election day by substantial security forces. Not only were all four armed services mobilized for the purpose; some two million members of the civil defense corps and similar groups, responsible for village security under army territorial commanders, were mobilized as well.

Golkar also fielded the largest number of candidates, at or close to the legal maximum in every constituency. Its candidates also included the highest percentage of college graduates. Golkar rallies were large and well organized. They obviously were also well financed, reportedly with substantial help from Pertamina, the state oil company.

So strenuously did Ali Moertopo pursue his mission that in the opinion of Nishihara: "By the time the formal campaign period began, Golkar had finished its essential electioneering effort."[13]

Still another factor influencing the outcome of the popular vote was the concept of the "floating mass." The essential element underlying this concept was the concern that the rural population, especially that of Central and East Java and of Bali, was in serious danger of being divided on ideological grounds as it had been in 1955 and again in 1965. The view among a number of civilian intellectuals and army officers surrounding Soeharto was that this had to be avoided at all costs.[14] It did not require a sophisticated analyst to see that a Golkar slate would face the same potential difficulties that had been seen in the idea of the "action fronts" for a new party. A new party might carry some cities and towns. But how would any new party, including Golkar, fare in the countryside where the vast majority of votes was to be found? The answer was to deny the old-line parties the advantage of representation in rural areas, and to reduce the period for electioneering in rural areas to a minimum—in short, to assure the government the rural vote in advance.

In the event, in 25 provinces, where 351 seats were contested in direct elections, Golkar won 227 seats, or 65 percent of the total. In the one remaining province, West Irian, where seats were contested by an indirect method, Golkar won all 9. With 100 additional seats to be filled by presidential appointment, the government's position in the Parliament was overwhelming.

The Fruits of Victory

What did the elections signify? Probably they reflected a consensus in support of the Soeharto government's priorities of political stability and economic development. Other evidence, including public criticism from the Left and the Right, indicated that opinion within the elite supported these broad aims. Some thought the government might even have won a majority of the contested seats in a fair vote. But manipulation was so pervasive that even the government was denied the satisfaction of knowing.

The government's heavy-handed manner of victory also led to outcomes that might not have been anticipated. Elections were now viewed as symbolic. The government intended to win, and it had done so overwhelmingly. Thus the role of elections was changed from what it had been, at least on the one occasion of 1955; from now on elections would not be seen as conferring authority on the government, but rather as merely acknowledging the power the government already had accumulated. As grounds for authority, the government would need to look elsewhere—particularly to its pledge to bring about higher economic growth and a wider distribution of the benefits.

The elections also marked the end of political parties as central to the governance of the country. The elections confirmed that the legally recognized political parties were without strong roots in the society; their leaders could be manipulated at will; and the parties themselves could be safely ignored as significant participants in the political process. The government subsequently forced the parties to merge into two "factions" in the Parliament, in order to "simplify the administration" of that institution, and the Parliament itself ceased to perform any significant function. The government also banned political activity between elections in the villages, depriving the rural population of its rights to permanent membership in a political party. In every meaning of the word, politics was now dead.

The election deprived even the government of a political party, and this was a more serious matter. While arguably Golkar did resemble, on paper, the homogenized party of functional groups Sukarno had visualized, it was no more a political party than the newly minted Muslim

Party was, and was even less of a party than the National Party had become. Until fairly late in the Soeharto era, Golkar did not even have individual members; in its formal structure it remained a federation of associations, and in actual function an election machine that was cranked up once every five years. Thus the opportunity was missed to create a vehicle for participation and information, and public affairs remained every bit as Jakarta-centered as they had ever been. Equally serious, the opportunity to create a means of managing leadership transition was also missed, and the problem of presidential succession remained so sizable that confronting it was continually postponed.

The election also created a coalition of mutual dependency on the part of Soeharto, the army, the civil service, the state corporations, and the technocrats. While Soeharto and the army were clearly more powerful than the rest, none of these elements of the regime was able to function with complete independence from the others. Each had its own interests, and pursuing them depended on the cooperation of one or more of the others. In addition, none was monolithic internally. Factions within Soeharto's personal staff and cabinet rose in prominence over time. Factions within the army continued to be significant for quite some years. Some departments of the government, which came to be dominated by one army group or another, proved equally difficult to bring or keep under central direction. A few state corporations became so large and wealthy that many saw them functioning as states within the state. Technocrats also became more variegated over time. Managing relations among all these groups occupied an increasing portion of the president's time.

Given his penchant for negotiation and compromise, Soeharto himself tended to reinforce the strengths and weaknesses of this thoroughly bureaucratic regime. What he lacked in the way of Sukarno's personal vivacity and rhetorical skill, he more than made up for with organization and money. While some complained that Soeharto lacked charisma or that he had no vision of the country's future, many more found the new government, and the style of the man who led it, comfortably predictable.

Controlling the Civil Service

Not many months after the elections, the government moved to place the civil service on permanent basis as a political arm of the regime. The various groups that had sprung up in government departments and enterprises in the first half of 1971, and that had campaigned for the government in the elections, were abolished in December. In their place a single, all-embracing organization was established for all government employees. This was the *Korps Karyawan Pegawai Republic Indonesia*—the Corps of Civil Servants of the Republic of Indonesia, commonly known as *Korpri*. The Corps was organized along the same lines as Golkar, with a leadership council chaired by the Minister of the Interior, Amir Machmud, and identical structures all the way down the line to every village. Included were not only the members of administrative services, but every public school teacher and state corporation employee as well. Overnight the Corps became the ultimate "functional group."

A parallel organization of women, the *Dharma Wanita*, also was formed for the wives of civil servants. Rank in the organization was determined by one's husband's rank in the government. Thus, women worked in the organization under the direction of the wives of their husbands' superiors. Some confusion and tension arose when wives themselves were government employees. In government offices, however, men predominated in the more senior positions. In all the higher civil service ranks, less than 10 percent were female. In the very highest ranks, held by 160 individuals in 1981, only 9 were female.[15] So the senior civil service remained very much a male preserve, and the impact of *Dharma Wanita* was to bureaucratize the social life of civil service families.

Perhaps the ultimate expression of the bureaucratization of social life was a presidential regulation of 1983 regarding the marriage and divorce of civil servants at all levels down to village heads and their staffs. The regulation required all such personnel to report their marriage in writing "through hierarchical channels," to obtain a senior official's approval in advance of a divorce, and to obtain similar approval of a marriage to a second, third, or fourth wife.[16] The regulation also included procedures designed to protect the rights of spouses, which was evidently its principal purpose.

The campaign to win the 1971 elections also marked the beginning of a renaissance in government employment as a prominent element in the Indonesian social system. As a core group of the new regime, the civil service was no longer railed against, but cultivated. Now that its loyalty was assured, it received attention and investment. Yet, within its strictly hierarchical structure, the civil service also had to be modernized. At the same time that the ethos of the bureaucracy spread further into the social life of the families associated with it, the bureaucracy had to be made more efficient, or at least more effective.

The Colonial Civil Service

The delayed modernization of the Indonesian civil service was a heritage of its own distant past and of the country's more recent history as a Dutch colony. Of traditional government in Java, Sir Stamford Raffles had written in 1817:

> The government is in principle a pure unmixed despotism; but there are customs of the country of which the people are very tenacious, and which the sovereign seldom invades. His subjects have no rights of liberty of person or property: his breath can raise the humblest individual from the dust to the highest distinction, or wither the honours of the most exalted. There is no hereditary rank, nothing to oppose his will. Not only honours, posts, and distinctions, depend upon his pleasure, but all the landed property of his dominions remains at his disposal, and may, together with its cultivators, be parcelled out by his order among the officers of his household, the members of his family, the ministers of his pleasures, or the useful servants of the state. Every officer is paid by grants of land, or by a power to receive from the peasantry a certain proportion of the produce of certain villages or districts.[17]

The Dutch did little to disturb this system until late in the colonial era. Militarily weak and financially parsimonious, they held to a theory of "like over like." When the first detailed colonial regulations were approved in 1854, they provided that the native population was to continue to be supervised by its own governing aristocracy. The native rulers were given the grand title of *Pangreh Praja,* or Rulers of the Realm, and, to the rural population of Java, were a feared and admired ruling class. But to the Dutch they were the *inlandsch bestuur,* the "native administration," the lower level of local government. Toward the end of the century, they lost their ex-officio right to land and to the personal service of the local population. Slowly, in the words of Heather Sutherland, "Javanese warrior-chiefs, living off the tribute of their people, were becoming salaried Malay-writing clerks, agricultural overseers and colonial policemen."[18]

The modernization of this local government apparatus began only in the twentieth century. Salaried clerkships were created only in 1910.

4. Creating a Political Machine

General government administration was separated in the same year from specialized economic functions, such as the salt and opium monopolies, coffee warehouses, pawnshops, and irrigation services. In 1913 the first requirements other than high birth were established for new district heads, including some formal education and an ability to speak and understand Dutch. In 1917 all sixty-five district heads of Java and Madura came from highborn families; almost all had inherited their office from a father or other close relative; only ten had attended secondary school.[19]

These late and hesitant steps to modernize the native administration represented the high point of progressive Dutch policy. Communist uprisings in the 1920s and the depression of the 1930s provided ample grounds for the colony's managers to halt the process of decentralization and devolution. In 1936 Governor-General B. C. de Jonge was able to say in an interview that considering the limited progress the Dutch had been able to make in three hundred years in the Indies, probably another three hundred would be needed before they were "ready for some kind of autonomy."[20]

By this time, however, the whole archaic system was under pressure—from the Dutch, who saw the local administrators as ineffective and inefficient, and from the increasing ranks of Indonesian nationalists, who saw them as agents of an alien regime.[21]

Independence and the Civil Service

Following independence, these previous views of the civil service persisted. Most people saw government employment as a sign of superior social status; moreover, the prestige that accompanied a government position, however menial, was shared by all the relatives, friends, and neighbors of the individual fortunate enough to obtain an appointment. The political elite, largely government employees themselves, tended to see their rank as justified by their birth, education, and connections. Many of the same individuals saw the civil service as an object of manipulation, or as an obstacle to modernization, and frequently as both. As a result, the bureaucracy expanded rapidly in the early years of independence, while political party leaders played a major role in public management, and also faced a whole range of critics—army officers, student leaders, technocrats—in the new atmosphere of the late 1960s.

In 1951 it was acknowledged that "at the present time the government does not know how many public servants it actually has working in its agencies."[22] At the end of 1953 the Central Bureau of Statistics put the number at 1.7 million, not counting members of the armed services. The total included 270,000 civilian employees of the central government; 229,000 employees of provinces, cities, and rural districts; 462,000 village officials; an additional 469,000 regular daily workers without civil service status, including 200,000 in the forest service alone; and 195,000 others employed by various government enterprises, among them the railways, the postal service, agricultural estates, and tin and coal mines.[23]

There is a paucity of data on the size of the armed forces at this time. The police numbered 100,000, and one estimate put the army at about 200,000. There seems no question that, in the first years of national independence, the armed services, including the police, employed more personnel than all the civil departments of the central government put together.

These numbers in the civil departments increased annually and more or less across the board until 1958, and then, reflecting the regional rebellion and the economic depression that followed, declined to well below their 1953 levels by the early 1960s.[24] This was not the case with the armed forces, however, which continued to grow under the impetus of the demands placed on them—putting down the "outer island" rebellion, then the West Irian campaign, and, finally, the anti-Malaysia confrontation—so that their uniformed personnel numbered nearly 600,000 by the mid-1960s.[25] The sheer physical presence of these men in uniform among the personnel working directly for the central government was now vastly greater than ever before.

In addition, the civil service was demoralized by the inflation that occurred from the early 1960s through 1966, and by the arrests and dismissals of known or suspected leftists after the attempted coup. How many were dismissed is unknown. One report said twenty-three thousand were dismissed between 1965 and 1967, or about 1.5 percent of the payroll, which hardly constitutes much of a purge.[26] Nevertheless, the civil service suffered a considerable loss in its ability to perform even routine tasks. During the first several years of the First Five-Year Plan, which began in 1969, most development projects were three to nine months late in starting, and this in turn created massive confusion when budgets terminated at the end of each fiscal year. The government raised salaries gradually, but no improvement in performance was apparent.[27]

4. Creating a Political Machine

Changing the Civil Service

Over the course of the 1970s and 1980s the civil service was to change markedly. First, its size in total numbers expanded rapidly. Members of the civil service proper at all levels of administration had declined from 855,000 in 1953 to 608,000 in 1963. At this time, even the statistical services of the central government broke down, and no data were ever published for 1964, 1965, or 1966. By 1967 the numbers began to rise again, and rapidly—to 1.6 million in 1974, and to 2.7 million in 1984.[28] Thus during only two decades, from 1963 to 1984, the civil service increased in size more than four times. This growth rate far exceeded that of the population increase and was about equal to the rate of increase in the Gross National Product. The numbers of civil servants have continued to grow since. By 1986 the total well exceeded 3.0 million.

Meanwhile, the composition of the civil service changed in two significant respects. As late as 1974, at the end of the First Five-Year Plan, the civil service was still shaped like a pyramid with the largest number of personnel in the lowest ranks, which required little or no education. But employees in these ranks declined in number in the years that followed. Employees in the middle and higher ranks increased from three to five times within the decade to 1984. Inasmuch as the middle ranks required some secondary school education, and the higher ranks a college degree, a massive change was brought about in the educational level of the civil service as a whole in the short span of ten years. Since most positions in the higher ranks were in the upper reaches of departmental headquarters and specialized agencies in Jakarta, a side effect was to bleed the provinces of skills and talent.

The changes in the civil service were made possible by an equally massive change in the educational system. The department of education experienced a fortyfold increase in personnel from the number it employed in 1953, making it far and away the largest employer in the country, with a total of 1.7 million employees by March 31, 1986. This dramatic expansion was made possible principally by the windfall profits from high oil prices from 1974 on. Most of the increase in employment took place in elementary schools and junior secondary schools. This reflected not only the severely limited educational opportunities that had been available to children of the poor prior to this time, but was also the result of a policy that made universal primary education the government's first educational priority.

Thus a government that had come into office with highly negative views of the civil service, and amid much talk of reductions in its scale, not only did not act on these initial ideas but, in fact, moved in the opposite direction. Political stability and economic development—in about equal measure—provided the incentives. Foreign aid, beginning in 1967, and oil money, beginning in 1973, provided the means.

The marriage of the civil service and the government party, Golkar, was to prove enduring. In the 1982 parliamentary elections, about 62 percent of Golkar's candidates came from the government bureaucracy.[29]

These features of Indonesia's civil service—its size, social prestige, and political role—are not unique to that country. On all these counts, the Indonesian civil service conforms to a general pattern, elements of which are evident elsewhere in Southeast Asia. What mainly distinguishes the Indonesian case is the degree to which the civil service has been penetrated and led by officers of the armed forces.[30]

Scaling Back the Armed Forces

It is one of the ironies of Indonesian history that Soeharto succeeded in accomplishing Nasution's long-term aims with respect to the country's armed forces. He reduced the size of all four services and turned them into more professional institutions. He also introduced officers of each service, and particularly army officers, into every aspect of government.

Nasution had failed to obtain cabinet approval of his plans for a major "rationalization" of the armed forces in 1953. Soeharto brought this about. According to one standard source, Indonesia's armed forces numbered 358,000 men in 1970, and declined to 250,000 in 1978. As a percentage of Indonesia's population, the armed forces numbered about the same as those of India in 1970 and were smaller most years thereafter. On the same scale, they were already smaller in number than those of any other Southeast Asian country in 1970, with the sole exception of the Philippines, and, by 1974, were smaller than those of the Philippines as well.[31]

Undoubtedly, cost was a factor. Official data show military spending declining as a percentage of central government expenditures—from 24.5 percent in 1970 to 15.0 percent in 1978 (and 8.4 percent in 1988).[32] Official reports of military expenditures are notoriously unreliable, however, and those of Indonesia have been widely assumed to be highly incomplete, especially for the early Soeharto years. Public statements by official and semiofficial sources in 1969 and 1970 indicated that only a third to a half of the armed forces' operating requirements were being met by the government budget in those years.[33] It is assumed that most of the remainder came from the profits of state enterprises, particularly from the largest and most powerful among them, the state oil company, Pertamina, whose chief executive reported directly to the president; the accounts of this and other state enterprises have never been made public. Additional funds came to the armed forces, at least for a period of years, from a number of corporations, cooperatives, and foundations established for the purpose, although not all were successful business ventures.

The retirement of armed services personnel, particularly the most senior among them, also was facilitated by widespread use of government connections to obtain licenses, contracts, bank loans, and import credits for private firms established by individual officers, often in partnership with local Chinese businessmen. A few cases involved elements of fraud that led to financial collapse and major public scandals. Other avenues of fund-raising ran from smuggling to overpricing equipment imports for the military. The problem was sufficiently widespread as early as 1968 that a group of Western businessmen, in a confidential report to Soeharto, warned him: "The chief threat to long-term stability . . . is abuse of power by military officers and the expansion of their vested interests, particularly in the economic realm, which could give rise to resentment and rebellion should the economic situation deteriorate."[34]

What the foreign businessmen were reflecting was the common opinion of prominent civilians whom they knew or met in the course of their brief visit. The civilian elite of Jakarta and other cities was still living in extremely modest circumstances at the time. The sudden emergence of army officers as patrons of the country's leading hotels, restaurants, and resorts was widely remarked on. Army personnel usually wore combat uniforms of dark green even when not on duty, following the style of Soeharto in this period. In addition, their official vehicles were utility models painted a distinctive dark green. There was no mistaking an army officer who was using his official vehicle for a private outing during off-duty hours. "Green shirts" became a way of referring to the army in private conversation that had a definite edge to it.

From the beginning the elite tended to see only the most grievous cases of army corruption as "excesses." The implication was that a certain amount of corruption was to be expected. The pattern was certainly well established. The benefices granted by the kings and sultans of Java to their friends and relatives were continued, in effect, by a series of later extractive rulers, from the officers of the Dutch East Indies Company to the leaders of the political parties of independence. Martial law, and particularly the years of Guided Democracy and economic depression that followed, provided army officers with the opportunity, and the need, to do as others had done before them. Many members of the elite were prepared to accept a certain amount of this behavior as something to be expected of those in power. Eventually, however, as it became known that financial corruption was occurring on a grand scale, student critics elevated the problem to a moral issue, and, as the foreign businessmen had predicted, it led to the regime's first political crisis.[35]

Militarizing the Government

At the same time that armed forces personnel were gradually eased into retirement, still others were placed on temporary assignment in the civil administration and the state corporations. Nasution had called for such a military role as early as 1958. Given his strong opinion that the armed forces were too large to be made a credible modern fighting force, and his equally strong opinion that politicians were self-seeking and incapable of giving the country an effective government, it is not surprising that he also believed the armed forces should be put to work in the government. He was aware, however, of the limitations of military dictatorships, particularly as they had functioned in Latin America. His "middle way" was an alternative to either a wholly civilian or wholly military government; it was to be a shared partnership between the two.[36]

The establishment of Guided Democracy introduced representatives of the armed forces by appointment into the Parliament and Consultative Assembly, and into civil administrative positions. By 1965 many of Sukarno's cabinet members, and half the provincial governors, were military men. The assignment of military personnel to positions in civil administration appears not to have become a generalized phenomenon in this period, however. Nasution himself was removed as army commander in 1962, and his successor, Yani, was much less forceful a personality. The Nasution program also was set back by the death in 1963 of the first minister, Djuanda, who had managed the executive machinery of government and whose relations with the army leadership were well established.[37]

After March 1966 Soeharto resumed the program of assigning military personnel to previously civilian posts, and did so with vigor. Official data have never been made public, and the full picture remains unknown. From a number of studies of appointments at senior levels, however, it is clear that military penetration of the civil apparatus has been massive.

The army was already in a strong minority position in the cabinet by the end of the Sukarno period. No military officer had been at the head of a civil government department until 1957. Thereafter, the percentage increased almost annually, reaching 41 percent in 1964–65. After Soeharto became acting president in 1967, military officers at the head of civilian departments rose to 44 percent, and fifteen years later, in 1982, reached 47 percent.[38]

A brief experiment was tried with cabinets that were predominantly civilian in their membership. After 1967 and up to 1973, military appointments to the cabinet declined steeply to 18 percent. Civilians who held academic degrees, and most of whom had no party affiliation, increased in the same period from 38 percent to 77 percent.[39] This was to be the peak period of technocratic influence in the government of Indonesia. The enhancement of the civilian role probably reflected army confidence following the 1971 victory at the polls, and the crucial role that foreign economic aid was playing in the government's development program. The return to a larger military role probably was a result of the 1974 student riots, and the sharp increase in the price of oil in world markets the same year.

Data on the army's role in subcabinet positions prior to 1967 appear not to be available. It has been reported that in 1967 more than half the secretaries general of central government departments were military personnel, as were almost half the directors general and inspectors general as well.[40] As occurred at the cabinet level, military men in these posts also dropped in or after 1971, from 55 percent to 41 percent, and then increased again dramatically to 89 percent in 1982. The levels in other senior positions also rose or held more or less as they had been.[41]

In addition, as we have seen, military officers were early in gaining appointments to governorships in the wake of the regional rebellion. Several were in place in the early 1960s, and the percentage rose quickly thereafter to 48 percent in 1965, 68 percent in 1968, and all but a small fraction by the 1970s. The ubiquity of army officers in these posts was reflected in a private joke that circulated in the early 1970s: "Under colonialism, we had a governor-general; now that we're independent, we have general-governors."[42]

Much scattered evidence indicates that the presence of military personnel at other key levels of territorial administration also was increasing steadily in this period. Data collected by several analysts showed that military men filled about 20 percent of the offices of town mayors and district heads in provinces studied in 1965, a figure that reached 54 percent nationwide in 1969, and climbed as high as 59–84 percent in provinces studied in the early 1970s.[43]

In addition, in areas seen as politically unstable or insecure, military penetration was even deeper. In Central and East Java, for example, in the wake of the mass violence of late 1965, Soeharto ordered the creation of an army structure parallel to the civilian administration all the way down to every village. At the subdistrict level, a command post was established with three senior noncommissioned officers. No villager could travel without its approval.[44]

By the late 1980s the practice of appointment of military personnel to civil office was highly institutionalized. An assistant chief of staff was fully occupied with the program. Numerous positions at home and abroad came to be regarded as armed forces preserves. All indications were that the army expected the program to continue indefinitely. The average rank of officers assigned to senior civil service posts rose. Officers selected for appointment to the Parliament were given public assurances that they would not suffer any unfavorable discrimination in terms of promotions. Many of those in high administrative posts stayed on through retirement.

This militarization of the government was, predictably, not widely popular in civilian circles. Even civilian cabinet officers did not hesitate to express their concern about the phenomenon in private conversation. But no one was prepared to make it a public issue. The official explanation was that experienced managers were in short supply among the civilian population. It also was suggested that military men were looked to in the early Soeharto years as a means of stiffening the spine of the bureaucracy, to assure that policy decisions were implemented down the line. But such thinking was not supported by the historical record. On the contrary, the rapid increase of civilians in high office after the 1971 elections suggests that personnel policy changed principally as a result of political events. The 1971 elections, despite all the heavy-handedness, were seen as a victory for civilian elements within the regime. The 1974 riots, however, overrode the prior civilian contributions. When the youth of the capital were in the streets, the armed forces were the ultimate political resource. Soeharto understood this as well as anyone. Militarization of the government had little to do with management experience. It was the outcome of the government's failure to assure its future by other means.

Nevertheless, one problem with this "solution" would have to be faced eventually. The retired officers in civil posts were aging, with long experience in political and economic affairs. The men commanding the major field units and filling the major staff positions of the army and other services were all much younger men, who had considerably more professional military training, and who also had much less experience in political and economic affairs. How long this younger generation would be content to see the senior posts in government continue in the hands of older retired officers, while they were by implication left to deal with strictly military matters, was uncertain. A series of confidential surveys was said to show that younger officers were becoming impatient to see the looming generational change discussed and planned for. At the same time, as the armed forces declined in numbers and as military tasks became more demanding of technical skills, the cost of deputation to civil posts was growing in terms of the operations of the armed forces as military institutions. Eventually the "recivilianization" of the government, on some significant scale, had to be faced.

Achieving Rice Self-Sufficiency

R ice was at the center of Indonesian politics. The shortage of rice was by far the most serious of all the food and clothing shortages that contributed to Sukarno's fall. As domestic production stagnated and foreign exchange ran out, daily life in Jakarta and the other cities became increasingly intolerable, and the balance of opinion had turned against the president. The new government gave top priority to its requests for emergency rice supplies as it opened talks with the Americans and the Japanese. Further, it took measures to boost domestic rice production even before deciding on the broader aspects of an economic program.

Within months of Soeharto's having assumed executive authority, a scientific event occurred in the neighboring Philippine islands that was to alter profoundly the political economy of rice. A new rice hybrid was developed that had the potential of increasing severalfold the traditional yields of irrigated land in tropical Asia. This new hybrid, the first in a series, was the beginning of what would soon become known as "the green revolution."

The new variety of rice presented an extraordinary opportunity to the Soeharto government. Since independence, Indonesian governments had been trying to make the country self-sufficient in rice. Rice was the nation's principal staple food and was the main product of the villages of Java. The need to spend foreign exchange to import rice was a serious drain on the national economy. And the need to ask foreign governments for gifts of rice was a national embarrassment. Yet, supplemental supplies from abroad were essential to feed the armed forces, the civil service, and the population of the cities, as well as to bring the runaway inflation of prices under control. The new rice variety thus held out multiple possibilities: new levels of productivity for the farmers of Java, greater self-respect for the nation in its foreign dealings, and an essential contribution to economic stability at home.

Indonesia was ill prepared to manage the new technology, however. The new varieties of rice were untested outside the locale of the rice institute in the Philippines, and Indonesia had virtually no scientific personnel to test them in Indonesian environments. The new varieties were designed for irrigated rice land in the tropics, and, although Java was one of the most highly irrigated regions in Asia, its irrigation canals were in serious disrepair and droughts and floods were a common experience. Finally, the new varieties required massive applications of nitrogen fertilizer in order to be productive, but Indonesia had no fertilizer industry. Information about the new technology had to be spread among the farmers, but the mass media did not reach them. Farmers would need credit to buy the new seeds and fertilizer, but the former system of rural credit had collapsed with the removal of the Chinese from the countryside in 1959. In short, Indonesia lacked everything that was required to take advantage of the new technology.

The Colonial Economy of Rice

Rice has been grown in what are now the Indonesian islands since about sixteen hundred years before the Christian era. It did not become the predominant staple food of the islands, however, until comparatively recently. Boeke described the important food crops of Java in the 1930s as including rice, maize (corn), cassava (tapioca), sweet potatoes, peanuts, and soya beans. The poor of Java, and even larger portions of the populations of the eastern islands of Indonesia, continued to depend on indigenous root crops, such as sago, or, more often, on maize and cassava, which were introduced from the New World by the Portuguese in the sixteenth century.[1]

The Dutch altered the self-sufficient economy of Java, and later that of the "outer islands," by the promotion of agricultural crops for export to Europe. Tea, which had reached the islands from China or India some centuries before, was being carried by Dutch ships to Europe by the seventeenth century. Coffee from Yemen, sisal from the Yucatan, and oil palm from West Africa were introduced by the Dutch for export to Europe. Sugar, which had reached the islands much earlier, was the single most valuable export of Java in the 1920s and 1930s.[2]

The Dutch invested heavily in irrigation, principally in order to promote sugar, although rice flourished in somewhat similar soil and water conditions. At the turn of the century, Java was almost as heavily irrigated as Japan. No other part of tropical Asia was so well irrigated at the time. The Dutch continued to expand the island's irrigation system in the early part of the twentieth century, with the result that Java was a major participant in the worldwide "sugar boom" that came to an end only with the Great Depression.[3]

The Dutch also invested heavily in agricultural research. The first research priority was the export crops; a sugar research institute in Java, along with one in South India, developed hybrid varieties that were in use throughout the sugar-growing world in the 1930s. Nevertheless, varieties of rice were brought to Java from elsewhere in Asia in the early part of the century, and several experiment stations were established exclusively to search out varieties of rice with a shorter growing period. A number of newly bred varieties was released by Dutch scientists on the eve of World War II, one of which, named Peta, came into widespread use in Indonesia and the Philippines after the war ended. The Dutch have been credited, more than any other colonial power, with contributing to the early scientific development of rice in tropical Asia. But the war and the national independence that followed led to the virtual collapse of the scientific enterprise, not only in Indonesia but throughout South and Southeast Asia.[4]

The Dutch colonial government also took an interest in the price of rice. Rice was needed to feed the workers on the rubber and other plantations, and because cheap labor was a major factor in the plantation economy, cheap rice was a major policy objective. Beginning as early as the late nineteenth century, the Dutch authorities intervened from time to time to stabilize the price of rice at low levels, chiefly by controlling imports and exports at times of shortage and surplus. The depression of the 1930s plunged the government deeply into the rice economy on a continuing basis. Beginning with the placement of controls on rice movements in and out of the colony, the government became involved in the shipping of rice among the islands, set the price to be paid by the mills for paddy (unmilled rice), and then put inspectors in the mills to see that the price regulations were observed. In 1939 a government agency was created to buy and sell rice for the purpose of stabilizing its price at low levels to consumers.[5]

When the Japanese occupied the Indies in early 1942, it was in order to gain access to its raw materials. Their primary interest was in petroleum and rubber, the two ingredients essential to transportation and thus to the prosecution of the war that now extended across the entire Western Pacific and its East Asian littoral. But the Japanese also needed rice to feed their troops in the Southwest Pacific, and all of Southeast Asia was pressed to provide it. Forced rice deliveries were imposed on the rice-growing villages of Java, as well as on the rice-surplus river deltas of the Southeast Asian mainland.[6]

Early Indonesian Programs

These, then, were the models that Indonesian leaders had to draw on as they organized their first government after independence. Rice was seen as a central governmental concern; it was an established government function to buy rice from the peasantry, sell it in the cities, and have a concern for the price to consumers. The prewar rice procurement agency was re-created. Then, as inflation began to impinge on policy, the government decided to pay a portion of the salary of the armed forces, and subsequently of the civil service as well, in rice instead of cash.[7]

Because rice played such a central role in public affairs, it was decided to make the new nation self-sufficient in rice as soon as possible. This was difficult to accomplish, because the national economy was structured at the time much as it had been before the war. The plantation crops of rubber, sugar, coffee, tea, and the rest still had to be produced at a low cost in order to compete in international markets. And the government program of using rice in lieu of currency to pay its own personnel reinforced the bias. The government therefore tried to hold rice prices down, returns to farmers were not considered, and, in these circumstances, the self-sufficiency programs failed. The first program aimed to make the nation self-sufficient in rice by 1956, but in that year Indonesia imported almost 800,000 tons. Another program was begun to achieve self-sufficiency by 1962; in that year, Indonesia imported more than a million tons.[8]

This second failure was complete. As reports of rice shortages and hunger circulated, Sukarno canceled a long-planned visit to Great Britain and made a radio address to the nation. All elements in the national front were to be mobilized in a new economic command under Sukarno's personal leadership. Committees were to be established in every province, district, and village to fix rice targets and set rice prices. The presidential speech was followed by a flurry of instructions, tours of inspection by cabinet ministers, and a highly publicized investigation of harbor congestion. But as time passed, and rice production did not increase, talk of self-sufficiency faded.[9]

Sukarno himself launched a personal campaign in 1963 to urge the population to eat maize and other foods in place of rice. He also directed that the rice allowance being paid to the armed and civil services be paid in part in maize. But the outcry was so great that the idea was dropped. In 1965 rice production in Java was not much higher than it had been before World War II. Because the population had increased greatly during the same period, the availability of rice on a per capita basis was dangerously low.[10]

Early Soeharto Efforts

Within months of its establishment, the Soeharto government took direct action. In addition to arranging emergency rice deliveries from Japan and the United States, the new administration decreed that fertilizer, which was in short supply, should be distributed to village headmen in rice-growing districts. The headmen would be responsible for distributing the fertilizer to the farmers in their villages and for collecting a portion of the rice harvest for payment back to the government. Despite the disorder in rural administration, the effort proved successful. Although repayments fell short of expectations, the government procured a record volume of domestic rice. Soeharto took advantage of the opportunity to increase rice rations for government employees in order to solidify his political support, particularly among the armed services. Little was left for "injection" into the market, however, with the result that rice prices increased by 300 percent in 1966, contributing to the record inflation of that year.[11]

The new rice varieties discovered in the Philippines, the first late in 1966 and the second in 1967, seemed tailor-made for Indonesia. One of the "parents" of the new varieties was Peta, developed at Bogor in the late 1930s. As noted above, the new varieties were particularly well suited to irrigated land, and this gave a prospective advantage to irrigated regions such as Java, Malaysia, and Sri Lanka, which up to this time were far behind the surplus river basins of Burma, Thailand, and Indochina in their yields. Because the new varieties also required heavy applications of nitrogen fertilizer, countries with domestic sources of petroleum and natural gas had an added advantage; in Asia these were notably Indonesia and Malaysia.[12]

Seeds of the first new varieties, named IR 8 and IR 5, found their way into Indonesia almost immediately. Having no capacity to subject the new varieties to serious testing, the Indonesian government simply approved both varieties in 1967.[13]

As the political crisis over succession eased in 1967, Soeharto reorganized the rice procurement agency and placed it in new hands. The head of the agency was henceforth to report directly to Soeharto. General Achmad Tirtosudiro, who had been managing the army's own procurement operations, was put in charge of the new agency. Initially the agency was directed to purchase rice for the provisioning of the armed forces, the civil service, and state corporation employees. That it might later be given broader powers, however, was suggested by its new name, the National Logistics Agency, or *Badan Urusan Logistik,* commonly known as *Bulog.*[14]

Eager to capitalize on the new rice technology, but lacking institutions that enabled it to do so, and with army officers playing key roles in the office of the president, the government was initially drawn to a "command" approach. Beginning in 1968, "blocks" of rice-growing villages were identified, fertilizers and pesticides were delivered on credit by foreign suppliers, farmers were directed to use these in conjunction with the new "miracle" seeds, and village headmen were directed to manage repayment to the government with a portion of the harvest. But farmers resisted the government pressure. Many farmers took the fertilizer, used it on other crops or sold it for cash, and minimized their payments in return. In 1970, with little to show for its effort, the government acknowledged defeat and canceled the program.[15]

From this point on, greater economic rationality was observed. The government concentrated on three lines of action. Fertilizer was distributed at subsidized prices by a state trading corporation. A government bank was mobilized to extend rural credit. And Bulog was assigned to maintain a floor price to farmers. None of these agencies was able to manage the task adequately; the demand for credit far outran the bank's ability to provide it, much of the fertilizer arrived too late to be of any use, and it took Bulog several years to control the floor price. Nevertheless, seeds of the new IR 5 variety swept the country; by 1970 it was the most widely planted variety of rice in Indonesia, in use on a fourth of all the rice land in the nation. With fertilizer and capital both being pumped into the countryside at subsidized rates, and with floor prices beginning to hold firm, the farmers of Java were responding. Rice yields increased, and in 1970 and 1971 Indonesia experienced the highest levels of rice production in its history.[16]

Even so, extremely serious deficiencies remained. The nutritional level in Indonesia in 1970 was still among the lowest in Asia. The average supply of calories was only 80 percent of the basic requirement, about on a par with that of Afghanistan and Bangladesh. In addition, despite the price support program, overall terms of trade were still to the rural population's disadvantage. While a minority of urban consumers was considerably better off as a result of the government's new development spending, it was thought that rural incomes had probably declined.[17]

The Rice Crisis of 1972

It took a genuine crisis in the world supply of food grains to galvanize the Indonesian government to a full-scale commitment to rice self-sufficiency. The rice outlook was promising as 1972 began. The government was approaching the midpoint of its First Five-Year Plan for the economy, rice production was up by 20 percent over 1969, and the aim of increasing production by 50 percent by 1974—enough to make the country self-sufficient in rice—appeared within reach. Bulog held reserves of 300,000 tons, and the Minister of Agriculture confidently predicted another record output.

The vagaries of nature were to intervene, however, and they were compounded by human failure. The major crop of rice was planted in Java largely in the month of December as the monsoon rains began in earnest and moved from west to east across the island. If the government was to influence planting, its purchase price for rice had to be announced before that time. It was not until May 1972, however, when the harvest was being brought in from the fields, that the government acted. By July the results were already evident. Rice procurement was only a third of that of the previous year.[18]

The months of June to September are dry months in Java, and at that time of year farmers with well-irrigated land can produce a second rice crop. With the spread of irrigation, the new varieties, and fertilizers, this second crop was coming to occupy an increasingly significant place in national food supplies. In 1972 the dry season was unusually dry, and not only in Indonesia. The drought extended across the entire rice-growing belt of tropical Asia. In Indonesia the shortfall in production did not become clear until September when the second crop was coming into the market. The weather conditions were known to be poor, but, with no system for close monitoring of crops, Indonesian authorities were not alerted to the severity of the situation until prices began to rise in the marketplace.[19]

By the time the government realized the seriousness of the situation, it was too late. Bulog officials appealed for help to their traditional foreign suppliers, and cabinet ministers were sent to foreign capitals to underline the urgency of the situation. But adequate supplies could not be found at any price. Japan agreed to increase its rice shipments from 250,000 tons to 400,000 tons, but total imports for 1972 reached only 730,000 tons. In some parts of Indonesia, rice prices doubled. In early November alone the cost of living index in Jakarta rose by 16 percent.[20]

The crisis was so severe that its impact extended throughout 1973. In the Bangkok market no rice prices were quoted at all from the months of April through December of that year. The international price of rice, which had fallen to a low of $125 per ton in 1971, rose to a high of $630 per ton before the crisis eased. In March 1973 the governments of the United States and Japan, the principal donors of rice to Indonesia, informed the Soeharto government that their shipments would total only 450,000 tons. The rest had to be bought on less favorable terms. Between mid-1972 and mid-1973 one million tons of very expensive rice were imported into Indonesia.[21]

The economic crisis had its inevitable political consequences. In Jakarta, as prices rose in late 1972, Soeharto had the unpleasant experience of seeing the students of the capital, his one-time allies in bringing about Sukarno's removal from office, demonstrating in the streets against inflation, corruption, foreign capital, and the entire direction of economic policy. The demonstrations were to erupt into violence in January 1974.[22]

Internationally, the rice shortage reinforced concerns about the world supply of food grains. The United Nations sponsored a world food conference, which took place in late 1974, to review the situation. An effort was made on this occasion to gain international agreement to create an international grain reserve. But the effort failed; the wealthy nations were not prepared to finance the international stockpiling of food grains, and the grain-surplus nations were not prepared to give away their market leverage to an international authority.[23] The lesson for importing countries such as Indonesia was clear: they would have to take responsibility for their own food security.

The Indonesian Reaction to the Crisis

How the Indonesian government might have responded to the rice crisis had its resources remained as they were in late 1972 when the crisis broke is uncertain. It is possible at least that the government, driven back on its domestic resources, might have been somewhat more open to private initiative and to farmer opinion. As events unfolded, however, its resources did not remain as they had been. Just as the government was bringing the crisis in rice supplies under temporary control, and was settling into what it now recognized was a long-term undertaking, the international environment created a new window of opportunity.

Between September 1973 and January 1974 the Six-Day War in the Middle East, and the oil embargo it spawned, increased the price of Indonesia's crude oil by 200 percent in international markets. The Soeharto government was suddenly released from the financial constraints under which it had labored, and was given new scope to deal with the rice problem as its policymakers thought best. It would be a mistake to read the later history of oil prices into the government's behavior at the time. The initial view in international oil markets was that the development was only temporary, and much of the Indonesian government behavior at the time reflected this opinion. Nevertheless, for what was initially seen as probably a short period of time, and only as the months and years passed came to be viewed as a more or less permanent condition, the Indonesian government was given a freedom of action across the entire range of economic policy that was unimaginable before.

5. Achieving Rice Self-Sufficiency

The first result of the rice crisis was to increase the authority of the civilians whom Soeharto had appointed to his cabinet after the electoral victory of 1971. As he had done in 1966, when the economy was experiencing runaway inflation, Soeharto opted for competence. Another outcome was to impress on the senior technocrats in the cabinet that it was not enough to apply their minds to policy; it would be necessary to give detailed attention to how the policies they designed were carried out. One economic official described the weekly meetings that now took place among the government's impromptu "rice team" as seminars in which everyone was under considerable pressure to be able to answer the questions put to them by Widjojo Nitisastro, head of the planning agency. Widjojo's own office became a workshop where his rice policy staff worked to track every new piece of information as it was received, and to plan the next round of responses. Perhaps the most important outcome, however, which held more or less until oil prices were to rise again in 1979, was to solidify the government's economic apparatus at the very top. With the international community now seen as unable to protect them with rice supplies when needed, and with the students demonstrating against them in the streets, senior figures in the government began to work together to protect the reputation of the regime—and their positions in it.[24]

The new oil money also gave the government planners an economic license to attack the rice problem across a broad front. This circumstance, added to the genuine fear engendered by previous failures, tended to set the Indonesian experience somewhat apart from that of other South and Southeast Asian nations. Most of the governments of Asia controlled the import and export of rice, and many also purchased on the order of 10 percent of the domestic production. All promoted the production of fertilizer, and many subsidized its price. Indonesia was alone, however, among the rice-importing nations of South and Southeast Asia, in the extent to which it invested its political and economic capital in the drive for self-sufficiency. The result was to make the industry a heavily regulated and protected one that had more in common with the rice industries of Japan, Korea, and Taiwan than with those of the rest of tropical Asia. The World Bank reported in 1987 that rice production was subject to seventeen central government regulations and many more at provincial and local levels. The Bank also calculated that subsidies to agriculture in 1986 alone had cost the government more than $700 million.[25]

5. Achieving Rice Self-Sufficiency

The New Varieties

The first high-yielding varieties of rice that swept Indonesia in the late 1960s were developed by the International Rice Research Institute at Los Baños in the Philippines. Indonesia had only one rice breeder of any note at the time, and in 1966, frustrated by the lack of funds, facilities, and staff, he had retired to his native North Sumatra. When the National Food Research Institute was made semiautonomous in 1974, only twenty members of its staff had been trained to the level of the doctorate, and only one of these was working on rice full-time. Rice research expenditure in 1974 was the lowest per 100,000 hectares in irrigated South and Southeast Asia: less than half that of the Philippines, for example. Building an indigenous scientific capacity was a long-term task involving extensive international cooperation. The new rice varieties experienced continuing problems with pests and diseases and caused serious losses to farmers in some districts in some years. The accomplishment of Indonesian scientists in developing resistant varieties and reducing dependence on chemical pesticides in the 1980s was justifiably celebrated by international organizations.[26]

Fertilizer Production

One of the early government successes was in fertilizer production. At the time of the rice crisis of 1972, all the fertilizers in use in Indonesian agriculture were imported. The first domestic plant, financed by the World Bank and Japan, went into production in 1975. A new plant followed each year thereafter until, in 1982, the country had seven fertilizer plants in operation and domestic production met domestic demand. The state oil corporation, Pertamina, and the state fertilizer corporation, Pupuk Sriwijaya, or Pusri, became major distributors. The price was highly subsidized—the World Bank in 1987 indicated that the price was the lowest reported in Asia—and price margins were a source of bureaucratic competition. It was believed, however, that the bulk of retail trade was in private hands.[27]

Local Public Works

The government made substantial investments in rural infrastructure that contributed to rice production. In addition to its own programs to improve and expand primary irrigation canals and major highways, and mainly using World Bank loans, the government contributed to the improvement of small canals, roads, and bridges through a large program of grants to local governments. The program was believed to have played a major role in improving the reliability of the water supply, speeding the distribution of fertilizer, and reducing the cost of transporting rice to the towns. The initial program was followed by others for primary schools, health centers, markets, and reforestation. By 1977–78 these local programs amounted to 12 percent of the national development budget, with the result that large amounts of money were spent in small towns and villages, and casual employment opportunities were greatly expanded.[28]

Mass Guidance

It was assumed from the outset in government circles that the rice farmers of Java would need to be "guided" by the government to use the new technology. The principal vehicle was a program known as "mass guidance." The core of the program was a standardized "package" of seeds, fertilizer, and pesticides, made available on easy credit terms. The agricultural extension service was expected to promote the program, but it appears that only village officials and other leading villagers were reached directly, and the program worked through them. "Mass guidance" played a role in spreading the new technology, as the Masagana 99 program had in the Philippines, but most farmers, after some initial experience, dropped out. The standardized "package" did not make allowances for the varied environments with which farmers had to deal. As seeds and fertilizer became widely available, and as local sources of credit recovered, farmers preferred to be guided by their own experience.[29]

Village Cooperatives

The government also attempted to encourage organizations of the farmers themselves, a key element in the early rice modernization of Japan, Korea, and Taiwan. In the early 1970s the government undertook to create "village economic units," which it was hoped would eventually evolve into genuine cooperatives. The initial function of the new units was to purchase rice for Bulog at the floor price set by the government; in the first year it was projected that the new organizations would be responsible for meeting half the government's domestic procurement target. So the prospective cooperatives were cast in the mold of government agents from the very outset. In addition, many local officials did not understand the new policy of price supports; when rice prices rose, and farmers did not sell to the new units at the floor price, some officials tried to force them to do so in order to meet their "targets." The number of "village economic units" increased until they numbered more than five thousand, but reports of nonrepayment of credit and allegations of other irregularities were widespread. The most serious allegation held that many of these organizations had fallen into the control of local village officials and prosperous farmers who ran them in the name of local farmers and pocketed the government subsidies for themselves. By the late 1980s many were said to be defunct.[30]

Price Supports

In spite of these serious institutional deficiencies, the price support program succeeded in maintaining stability in the price of rice, and Bulog became the government's principal agent in the rice field. The floor price was raised every year throughout the 1970s, although, relative to other basic commodities, the price peaked in 1977. As the floor price increased, and the subsidy of fertilizer prices continued, the yields on Java became the highest in tropical Asia, and national production registered annual records. In the decade of the 1970s, nationwide production increased from 12 million tons to 22 million tons. Senior economists later considered this the Soeharto government's most significant achievement. And they credited Bulog with having made it possible.[31]

Even with the record rice production, however, self-sufficiency eluded the government. As oil money financed an ever-growing range of programs and projects, more and more of the population could afford to buy rice. As they were able to do so, families stopped eating maize and cassava. The result was that Indonesia continued to import rice. As late as 1980 Indonesia was the largest importer of rice in the world, buying 2 million tons of rice, almost 20 percent of the rice that was traded internationally.[32]

Finally, in the 1980s Indonesia did achieve self-sufficiency in rice in the sense that the trend lines of domestic production and consumption converged during the decade. How solid the claim was depended on how one took account of losses and of carry-over stocks from prior years. When domestic production was up, as in 1984–85, the volume of rice stocks the government held became so large as to seriously burden its financing and warehousing capabilities. When domestic production was off, as in 1987–88, the volume of rice stocks fell short of sufficiency. It was, in any case, a major achievement. In the decade from 1974–75 to 1984–85 Indonesia's growth in cereal production per capita was the second highest after Burma, and well above China and India. This was all the more remarkable since Indonesia's growth in agricultural production in the 1950s and early 1960s was the slowest of any major Asian country.[33]

The Rise of Bulog as a Power Center

The agency credited with contributing most to the government's achievement in rice production and price stabilization was the National Logistics Agency, or Bulog. As mentioned above, Bulog was established as an autonomous government agency in 1967. Its head sat in the National Stabilization Council, a cabinet-level body, and reported directly to the president.[34]

Bulog was initially given a monopoly over all purchases of rice on behalf of the government, both at home and abroad. These functions required Bulog to manage large amounts of credit advanced to the agency by state banks, and, within a year or two of its founding, reports of financial scandals involving its officials began to appear in the public press. A panel of prominent national figures appointed to look into official corruption in 1970 reported to Soeharto that Bulog was managing "billions" of rupiah with staff officers who were newly hired and had no prior financial experience. It said Bulog was in need of "strict internal control" and "skilled and honest employees."[35] It also recommended that Bulog's branches be closed and that Bulog itself be moved out of the president's office and into the Ministry of Agriculture.[36]

Soeharto reportedly never discussed the panel's recommendations with the economic ministers of his cabinet, and, so far as was evident to the public, never took any action himself. On the contrary, Bulog's functions were broadened in 1970; its principal function was henceforth to be "the control of prices of rice, paddy, wheat flour and other basic commodities with a view to safeguarding price stability both in the interest of producers as well as consumers in accordance with the Government general policy."[37] Only in mid-1973, after the rice crisis had revealed how costly Bulog's management deficiencies were to the nation and to his government, did Soeharto finally retire Gen. Achmad Tirtosudiro as head of the agency. The presumption was that Soeharto had delayed this action out of a sense of obligation to Achmad for his loyalty and support, including the provision of funds for any number of special projects important to the president—for example, the Golkar electoral campaign of 1971.

This presumption was reinforced by Soeharto's choice of Bustanil Arifin to succeed Achmad. Arifin had been a long-time figure in the army procurement agency, had been part of the effort to locate rice supplies abroad in the early months of the Soeharto government in 1966, and had been deputy head of the agency before going off to serve as consul general in New York. He was, in addition, a dynamic Minangkabau from West Sumatra, and he was to turn Bulog into a much more competent organization, possibly the most powerful food agency in Asia. Even critics gave Arifin high marks for putting the public need ahead of personal and bureaucratic interest.[38]

An undoubted element in Bulog's success was that it was heavily subsidized by the government. At the outset this was accomplished principally through the pricing of Bulog's management of rice imports. Much of the rice imported in the early years came by way of foreign aid programs sponsored by the United States and Japan. U.S. rice shipments under the aid program were sold at prices well below the world market price, leaving a substantial mark-up available to the Indonesian government. The government, in turn, charged Bulog for the rice according to a complicated formula that protected it from any loss. By the early 1980s, when most imported rice was being acquired from commercial sources, Bulog was subsidized by a line of credit provided by the Central Bank at highly favorable interest rates; the volume of credit was limited only by Bulog's stocks of rice to serve as collateral.[39]

Bulog did not become powerful through money alone. It acquired power because it developed a reliable system of information to guide policymakers, developed the capability of managing the physical movement and storage of large quantities of commodities, and demonstrated the capacity to protect price stability. In the absence of a smoothly functioning market for rice among the widely separated islands, Bulog developed a market information service that provided daily reports by radio and telex on prices in every district of the country. In the absence of adequate warehouses—Bulog initially leased warehouses from private owners, but most were old, poorly managed, and a source of significant losses—Bulog built a chain of more than three hundred modern warehouses spread throughout the country, capable of holding more than 1.5 million tons. Daily reports of movements in and out of these warehouses provided a close watch on the national rice reserve and its internal distribution.[40]

Bulog also developed a modern staff that was lean by Indonesian standards—five thousand in the early 1980s. Bulog officers were among the vanguard of the new elite in Indonesia's civil service, the well-trained and well-paid employees of the state corporate sector, at work in modern facilities, and well provided with housing, recreational facilities, child care facilities, and all the other perquisites of bureaucratic success in Indonesia. In Jakarta, Bulog officials were ardent joggers and participants in other exercise programs to guard against heart disease, a national campaign that Bustanil Arifin founded and promoted as assiduously as he did everything he turned his hand to. In the small towns that served as the centers of rural districts in distant islands, Bulog facilities were spanking new, standing out from the colonial architecture of older government offices, and even further removed from the seedy appearance of most private commercial establishments. Bulog officials in the provinces were university men, the sort who knew important people in the capital, and who played tennis in the afternoons with the local civil and military leadership.[41]

As Bulog's capacity grew, the scale and scope of its transactions grew as well. In fiscal year 1982–83, it was operating on a scale that was three times that of 1967, managing an estimated 8.3 million tons of commodities with a value of $4.2 billion. By this time it was involved not only in the marketing of rice, wheat, and wheat flour, but had expanded to sugar, soybeans and soybean meal, peanuts, mungbeans, and poultry. The wheat Bulog imported was milled into flour by three mills: two of these were controlled by the private Salim group, led by Liem Sioe Liong, Soeharto's business partner from Semarang days, and the other was sold by Singapore interests in the early 1980s, reportedly under Bulog pressure, to PT Berdikari, a government-controlled corporation led by Arifin himself. A World Bank report in 1987 said that the profit margin of the flour millers was 25 percent, which it described as "high by international standards" and "difficult to justify."[42]

Criticism of Bulog

The most serious criticism of Bulog had to do with its entry into the sugar industry. In 1975 the government launched a major program to restructure the industry, which was by this time in serious disrepair;

domestic consumption was running well ahead of production, and large quantities of sugar were being imported. The sugar mills that remained from the 1930s were much reduced in number and technically outdated. They were, in addition, since the takeovers of 1957–58, owned by the government, yet they were still dealing with the cane farmers as in the colonial period. The mills rented land from the farmers in surrounding villages and cultivated it with hired labor. Beginning in 1975 the government undertook to modernize the mills with World Bank financing, and, at the same time, to take cane production out of their hands and leave it to the land-owning farmers themselves. On the face of it, the plan made excellent sense; small-holders had demonstrated they were more efficient than the nationalized plantations producing rubber, coffee, tobacco, and other cash crops.[43]

In practice the program achieved its main aim: the production of sugar increased significantly. But, as in the case of rice, the cost was high. Sugar cane was in competition with rice for the most cultivatable land in Java, and with the new varieties of rice making it possible to grow two to three crops a year, farmers preferred to plant rice. The new program therefore required "administrative guidance" from the beginning. Local district heads and other local officials had to set targets for each lower level of administration; at the bottom of the system, village heads were obliged to parcel out among local villagers the acreage to be planted in cane. Considerable coercion was sometimes needed to accomplish this, particularly as contiguous parcels of land were highly desirable for cane production. After 1981 the "village cooperative units" were given extensive powers to manage the whole process of production, harvest, and delivery to the mills; in practice, however, this simply permitted small groups of government officials, mill managers, and leading villagers to control the process in the name of the farmer-members of the local groups.

Bulog's involvement had to do mainly with the wholesale trade in sugar. The government set the price that cane farmers were to be paid at harvest; Bulog bought the cane, contracted with the mills to do the milling, and managed the wholesale trade of the refined product; it also held a monopoly on the importation of sugar from abroad. Farmers might have been expected to welcome this development, but, in fact, many thought the price was too low, and by 1983 their angry protests surfaced in an official report.[44] By 1987 the World Bank criticized the entire management of the industry. Prices were stabilized, and imports were reduced to zero, but this had been achieved, the Bank said, "at substantial costs in terms of efficiency foregone and high consumer prices." Critics added that no one knew what Bulog was doing with the profits.[45] The criticism of Bulog seemed reasonable. As a multibillion dollar organization responsible directly to the president, Bulog was largely unsupervised in its management of very substantial funds and massive quantities of goods. Bulog never issued a public financial report up to the time of this writing. Bustanil Arifin reported only to Soeharto. Reflecting on this pattern, which extended to other major economic agencies as well, one of Indonesia's leading business analysts observed that there was nothing modern about this style of accountability. "It's the way a king governs," he said.[46] The system did have its benefits. "It used to be that the political parties always got a profit out of rice, whoever was in control at the time," a senior Bulog figure said in 1983. "But no party gets a piece of the pie anymore, and that includes Golkar. No generals come in here to tell me what to do either, not anybody."[47]

For the circumstances of the 1970s, that might have been all that could have been accomplished. At least Bulog was effective with regard to rice. In the more straightened financial circumstances of the 1980s, however, costs also mattered. The World Bank recommended that the agency be pared back to its initial function of ensuring a secure supply of rice. Trade in wheat, corn, and soybeans, it said, should be left to the private sector. And the government should ease the whole pattern of control of the production and marketing of agricultural commodities.[48] But Bulog was now a center of power in its own right, and bringing it to heel would not be easy.

The New Rice Economy in the Villages of Java

The massive increases in rice production, of which Bulog was the paramount symbol, did not result only from decisions at the national level, and did not have their impact only there. The increases also reflected the decisions of millions of rice farmers in Java who moved quickly to use the new varieties, invest in fertilizer, and respond to the incentive of the floor price. These decisions, and the increasing land productivity that resulted, suggested that a complex process of rapid change was taking place in rural society. The precise nature of this process, and its meaning for the poorer families in the villages of Java, continues to be a matter of uncertainty and the subject of much debate.

5. Achieving Rice Self-Sufficiency

An influential view of the village society of Java has been that of Clifford Geertz, whose writings since the late 1950s have been the most extensive on the subject. Geertz saw wet rice cultivation as having the peculiar ability to absorb almost unlimited amounts of labor. As the population of Java grew, and more hands were available to tend the rice fields, production increased. But it increased only in proportion to the increase in the labor supply. The village was able to sustain its larger populations, but remained as poor as before. This process of growth without expansion he called "agricultural involution."[49]

According to Geertz, this special characteristic of rice cultivation was associated with a complex village social system in which land was divided and work opportunities shared, practices that also sustained the village community. In the face of problems posed by a growing population, increasing monetization, greater dependence on the market, more intimate contact with bureaucratic government, and the like, village society proved highly resistant. Although the basic pattern of village life was maintained, that life grew ever more elaborate in the arrangements it required to survive. While Geertz believed that this "shared poverty" was "ultimately self defeating," his vision of the self-sufficient, self-contained village of Java, resistant to all pressures from outside, had a powerful influence.

The idea that Java's rural society had great internal strength was shaken by the mass violence of 1965, but the notion was not abandoned among the Indonesian elite. The proposal to make rural society into a "floating mass," disengaged from party politics, owed much to the belief that village life was fundamentally well ordered, that it mainly had to be protected from the intrusion of ideologies from the cities and towns. The emphasis in government rice policies of the village community as an undifferentiated whole was largely the result of Geertz's optimism regarding the distribution of economic benefits in the village. At the same time, the government did not share Geertz's pessimism about the possibility of economic growth. Some scholars did argue that significant economic cleavages had existed in rural Java all along.[50] Others argued that these difference were in large part responsible for the 1965 violence.[51] The discussion was substantially broadened, both in its scope and participation, by reports that began to appear by 1970 of innovations, mechanical and social in nature, that were displacing human labor in various aspects of the rice industry. Inasmuch as large numbers of villagers depended on the work being displaced, the reports immediately generated concern and debate.

One innovation that seemed to come quickly into the widest use was a small machine, powered by electricity, that removed the coarse hulls from the rice grain. The rice huller did not polish the rice as milling machines could do, but villagers were not accustomed to cooking and eating polished rice. Most rice consumed in the villages was merely hulled, and until the arrival of the hulling machines, the hulling was accomplished by hand-pounding. This was a traditional occupation of village women, especially those of poorer families. The new hulling machines were invariably owned by one or a few of the wealthier village families. The machines were capable of hulling the rice quickly and at lower cost than hand labor. As use of the machines spread, millions of village women were losing a source of part-time employment that was significant to their family income.[52]

Other mechanical improvements also were reported in the early 1970s: power tillers (hand tractors) to prepare larger tracts of land for planting; mechanical weeders; scales to measure harvest shares; and mechanical threshers to separate the grain from the stalks. The most controversial innovation, however, had to do with the harvesting of rice. It was the custom in much of Java for village women to help in the rice harvest and share in the crop. The custom was so ingrained that even women from neighboring villages, in times of need, would not be turned away. In her work the harvester used a small knife, called the *ani ani*, with which she would cut one stalk at a time, enabling her to collect the grain with minimal loss. But in the early 1970s reports began to appear of a wholly new harvesting system. A landowner would sell the crop as it stood in the field to a broker from a neighboring town. The broker would then bring in a team of hired men to collect the harvest. They worked with sickles rather than the *ani ani* knife, and were paid in cash. Thus only the landowner received any benefit from the harvest.[53]

All these developments raised questions about the state of rural economic welfare and village social solidarity. It was possible that certain of the practices only appeared to be new; some evidence suggested, for example, that sickles had come into use in some areas before World War II. It also was possible that still other practices had been present as early as in the 1950s and simply had gone unreported by the few scholars in the field. Exactly when the new harvesting arrangements appeared, for example, was difficult to establish, and, because the practices seemed to vary from place to place, their impact was difficult to assess. But there was no question about the emergence of the mechanical rice hullers, and these were seen as part of a wider pattern of development that was pushing many villagers out of the rice industry. The question was what effect these changes were having on the distribution of land, employment opportunities, income, and welfare.[54]

How many villagers owned rice land, and how much land they owned, was difficult to establish. The population census of 1980 indicated that 53 percent of all household heads in Java operated agricultural land at their own risk—as owners, lessees, or sharecroppers. Almost half operated less than 0.25 hectare, or little more than half an acre, and these were thought unlikely to be full-time farmers. Another 31 percent of household heads worked as agricultural laborers, and most of these also were thought unlikely to be engaged in farming full-time. The picture that emerged was of a rural society in which approximately a fourth of household heads were full-time farmers, half were part-time farmers and farm laborers, and another fourth were not employed in farming at all. Official data showed that the distribution of holdings by size was stable. Yet, the productivity of irrigated rice land was rising rapidly, land values were increasing, and long-time observers believed that a lot of land was changing hands. It seemed reasonable to conclude that a new land-owning elite was emerging in rural Java, composed of village Golkar officials, leaders of village cooperatives, retired civil servants and military personnel, and households with family ties to individuals earning incomes in urban areas.[55]

Employment data were ambiguous in their implications. It was clear that some innovations that came along with the new rice varieties— especially the sickle and the mechanical huller—reduced employment opportunities in the rice industry. Yet, the widespread rural unemployment that had been feared did not eventuate. Perhaps some changes occurred more slowly than expected. Also, rice was not the only important crop; it was found that many poor villagers earned the largest share of their income from the intensive cultivation of small garden plots surrounding their homes. In addition, many rural families earned large portions of their income from a multiplicity of occupations outside farming, including food processing, other home and village industries, construction, transportation, and petty trading. For many rural dwellers, such job opportunities appear to have been sharply on the rise in the late 1970s and early 1980s.[56]

The impact on the distribution of income was less clear. It was commonly agreed that government policy tended to favor urban consumers all through the 1970s, and to favor the minority of larger rice farmers in the villages. In the early years of the Soeharto administration, up to 1970, it was believed overall that real incomes in rural areas actually declined. Later data indicated that from 1970 to 1976 per capita income in the villages of Java increased by 3.4 percent per year—more slowly than per capita income in Jakarta and the other cities of Java, but faster than in the rest of the country. Soeharto, in his State of the Nation Report of 1977, said that, according to World Bank standards, an increasing share of the population was moving above the poverty line. A World Bank report of 1990 found a decline in poverty in the population—from 35 million people, or 22 percent, in 1984 to 30 million people, or 17 percent, in 1987—with evidence that the benefits of growth favored rural areas. Village studies throughout the period tended to find the gap in consumption patterns continuously growing, however, with the poorest villagers only slightly less poor than before, and others far richer, able to own motorbikes and even automobiles and to send their children to secondary school and even to the university.[57]

By the late 1980s it was clear that rural Java was becoming more and more a part of the larger national economy. As rice production increased, more of the village production was sold in the towns. As wealthier villagers experienced increased incomes, more of the village's income was spent in the towns. As the "old" village elite gave way to the "new" elite of government-appointed officials, even the source of funds for village religious festivals was said to be changing. As village men migrated to work in the cities, Islamic preachers were said to follow them. And in the cities, these rural migrants found the gap in living standards vastly wider than at home.

It seemed a potent combination, and the implications for policy seemed clear. The government had brought about a revolution in the economy of rice in the villages of Java. Not only had national production set records, but many village families had grown wealthy as well. The achievement was accomplished at some cost, however. Those who had benefited most were among the government's strongest supporters in the villages; the government was as dependent on the continued regulation and subsidy of the rice industry as the better-off villagers were. Meanwhile, funds were urgently needed to generate continued employment opportunities outside agriculture on Java, and at the same time to provide some form of social security for the poorest of the population. As to the first of these needs, the new rural credit program of the People's Bank (*Bank Rakyat*) was most promising, generating a total of U.S. $500 million in loans to 1.6 million borrowers by the end of 1989. As to security for the very poor, that remained a task that the government and the elite had barely begun to address.

SIX

The January 15 "Disaster"

The rice crisis that began in 1972 and extended through 1973 left the government highly vulnerable to its critics. These included such national figures as former Vice President Hatta and former Defense Minister Nasution. But the most vociferous critics were students of the major universities, notably the University of Indonesia. And their voices were amplified by the press in the capital city. Foreign aid and investment were benefiting only a few, the critics complained. The Japanese were exploiting the Indonesian economy. Local Chinese businessmen were profiting. The government itself was riddled with corruption. These criticisms came to a violent focus on the visit of Japan's Prime Minister Kakuei Tanaka in January 1974.

Tanaka arrived in Jakarta during a tour of Southeast Asia that already had generated hostile student reactions in the capital cities of Thailand and Malaysia. In Bangkok he was burned in effigy, and in Kuala Lumpur was found guilty in a mock trial on the university campus.[1] The reception in Indonesia's capital was to prove the most hostile of all.

Arriving after nightfall, Tanaka and his party were met by eight hundred students and a powerful array of police and troops in battle dress. Some students had broken through the security cordon and were on the airfield itself just before Tanaka's arrival. Others attempted to block his party from the roadway to the city. A decoy convoy provided distraction, and, as troops cleared the way, the official group sped through the crowd.[2]

The following morning, students of three universities in the city, rejecting army appeals to call off their plans, held a large protest march. While this was in progress, bands of youths, many in their teens, began to form in various parts of the city. On major thoroughfares, they halted Japanese-made vehicles, deflating their tires and setting the cars on fire. At the Astra Toyota showrooms, windows were smashed and the entire stock of new cars set ablaze. At the President Hotel, which was operated by Japan Air Lines and was housing the Japanese press corps accompanying the prime minister, security forces stood off several waves of demonstrators attempting to storm the building. In the main square, near the state guest house on the palace grounds where Tanaka was staying, a crowd variously estimated at 20,000 to 100,000 was dispersed by troops in armored cars.[3]

For the most part, according to reporters on the scene, police and soldiers did not attempt to stop the rioters. Adam Malik, the foreign minister, said the security forces could not control the crowds because President Soeharto had ordered them not to shoot. At one point during the day, Malik himself, a one-time youth leader, and General Soemitro, the deputy commander of the armed forces, addressed crowds of young people in the streets, urging them to go home. By late afternoon warning shots were fired over the crowds, and as night fell a curfew was imposed on the city.[4]

The scale of the protests was much reduced the following day, but one particularly violent incident occurred. At Pasar Senen, a major shopping center, thousands of youths smashed and looted shops and set them on fire. At least eight youths were shot dead. The entire shopping complex went up in a spectacular blaze.[5]

At dawn on January 17 Tanaka was whisked to the airport by helicopter from the palace grounds, where he had remained since his arrival.[6]

Later in the day the government issued its first official statement on the affair to the press. The demonstrations in the streets, the statement said, had threatened to lead to anarchy; they would no longer be tolerated. The government would "put in order" the life of the universities and schools so they could not be used for political purposes. The government also would "put in order" the reporting of news in the press. The same day troops occupied the campus of the University of Indonesia.[7]

In the days that followed, intellectuals and student leaders were arrested. Six daily newspapers and four weekly magazines, among them the country's leading news journals, were charged with publishing material that tended to incite public unrest and were ordered closed. Meetings of five or more persons were banned. It was subsequently announced that eleven youths had been killed and more than a hundred injured during the two days of demonstrations and rioting. Almost 1,000 vehicles had been damaged or destroyed, and 144 buildings had been burned or otherwise damaged. Some 820 individuals were arrested. One group, numbering 472, were "caught in the act" on January 15 and 16; they included 14 university students, 83 high school students, 41 youths, 250 laborers, 28 peddlers, two *becak* (pedicab) drivers, 1 unemployed person, and 26 loiterers. A second group of 330 were arrested for taking radios, television sets, and the like from shops. A third group included four members of parliament and several officers of the armed forces.[8]

Before the end of the month, reflecting the widespread support his student critics had obviously attracted, Soeharto acted on three student demands. He abolished the posts held by four senior army officers in his personal staff, including Ali Moertopo; he announced a series of measures to protect indigenous enterprise; and, finally, he issued orders designed to moderate the extravagant life-styles of senior military officers and civil servants. He also removed General Soemitro from his post as head of public security and dismissed General Sutopo Juwono as head of central intelligence. In March Admiral Sudomo, chief of staff of the public security command, announced to the press that several individuals detained in the aftermath of the riots would be tried for subversion under a 1963 law. He charged that the riots were part of a plot by "radical socialists" to overthrow the government. The "intellectual brains" behind the plot, he said, were former members of "banned political parties." The conspirators had questioned basic tenets of the regime, such as the "dual function" of the armed forces, had tried to create the impression of division within the armed forces, and had launched issues designed to obstruct the government's development strategy. The Tanaka visit was only the "spark" the plotters had used in their attempt to create a revolutionary situation.[9] These, then, were the issues in what came to be known as *Malari*, the acronym coined from the Indonesian for "the January 15 disaster." The "disaster" was a watershed in Indonesian public life. The government had been shocked to its very roots by its inability to maintain law and order during the visit of an extremely important foreign guest. The reverberations were to run through the political and economic life of the country for many years. The affair raised a host of questions, beginning with why the rioting had occurred. That was to prove the most difficult question of all.

Events Leading up to January 15

The Tanaka visit came at a time of considerable ferment in Indonesia. The economy had suffered a serious setback as a result of the rice crisis of the previous months, inflation was the most serious it had been in years, and the government's whole economic development strategy was coming under increasing fire. Racial and religious feelings were in a heightened state. On the previous August 5 a traffic accident had occurred in Bandung in West Java between the Indonesian driver of a *becak* (pedicab) and the Chinese driver of an automobile. The story quickly spread that the *becak* driver had been killed. Although this was not in fact the case, thousands of young people were only too ready to believe it and went on a rampage through the main business district of the city, a district of largely Chinese-owned shops. Within several hours, one Chinese was killed and twenty-three hospitalized, and damage to property was estimated at $3 million. Two senior Siliwangi officers were relieved of their commands, and nineteen officers and men were arrested. It was suggested that the division's leaders had delayed ordering their troops into action because they knew that many junior officers and their men were sympathetic to the rioters.[10]

Meanwhile Islamic leaders, already offended by the recent proliferation of bars, night clubs, and massage parlors in the capital city, were angered by a government marriage bill they viewed as secularist. Hundreds of Muslim students stormed the floor of Parliament when the Minister of Religion spoke in support of the bill on September 27.

The chief catalyst of the January events, however, might well have been the fall of the military government of Thailand in October. The first in a series of massive student demonstrations occurred in Bangkok on October 14; many other members of the middle class joined in as the demonstrations continued. The army was divided in its support of the government, and on October 20 Field Marshal Thanom Kittikachorn, prime minister for almost a dozen years, was forced into exile.

6. The January 15 "Disaster"

This event reverberated almost immediately in Jakarta. On October 24 the student council of the University of Indonesia, in a ceremony at the national heroes' cemetery, announced a resolution protesting corruption, abuse of power, rising prices, unemployment, extralegal activities by the president's assistants, and a lack of political institutions through which the people's views could be expressed.[11]

By November students were picketing and distributing leaflets at the National Planning Agency, the Bank of Indonesia, the Miss Indonesia contest, and assorted night clubs.[12]

In mid-November J. J. Pronk, the Minister for Development in the government of the Netherlands and chairman of the Intergovernmental Group on Indonesia (IGGI), the consortium of governments providing economic aid to Indonesia, arrived on an official visit. He was greeted by student demonstrators who handed him a statement that declared: "We do not take pride in the results of foreign aid and foreign capital in the form of tall buildings and hotels, Coca Cola, nightclubs, etc. In the meantime more people are without jobs, homes, and land, our small textile industry has died, our forests have become barren, and our oil fields depleted."[13]

At about the same time General Soemitro, then both deputy commander of the armed forces and head of the public security agency, began a series of visits to major university campuses. His general theme was the need for "two-way communications" between the government and the people. In Jogjakarta he told students that "hide-and-seek leadership" was to be replaced by "social leadership and social communication." This initiative was received with cynicism. An editorial in *Kompas,* a leading Jakarta daily, said it was "naive" to think that "our problems can be solved by public officials patiently and amicably listening and giving answers."[14]

On November 30, at a meeting in Jakarta, a manifesto critical of foreign capital was signed by a group of prominent dissidents, including former Vice President Hatta.

In December, after the Tanaka visit was announced, students began appearing at the Japanese embassy and at outlets for Japanese-manufactured goods, carrying placards accusing the Japanese of exploiting the Indonesian economy. On December 31, at a "Night of Concern" sponsored by the student councils of the major universities of Jakarta, Bogor, and Bandung, Hariman Siregar, chairman of the student council of the

University of Indonesia, declared that economic development had become "a new political myth." Economic development, he said, "means the expropriation of land, forced sales of rice to the government, and increasingly difficult life in the villages." For a "small group in power," he said, the economic strategy of the government was providing "the means to accumulate wealth and satisfy passions for luxury commodities."[15]

On January 2 Soeharto held a meeting with General Soemitro and his personal political adviser, General Ali Moertopo. Afterward, Soemitro met with the press. He had no personal ambitions in speaking of a new type of national leadership, he said. It was, moreover, not accurate to suggest, as some had, that he was opposed in any way to Ali Moertopo. All this talk was "strange and cruel."[16]

Also early in January students in Jakarta issued a further statement, entitled "Three Demands of the People," echoing the student protest of January 1966, and now demanding that Soeharto dismiss his presidential assistants, bring down prices, and bring an end to corruption.[17]

On January 12, just two days before Tanaka's scheduled arrival and after some days of student pressure to do so, Soeharto met for two hours with a hundred student leaders representing thirty-one Indonesian universities. The meeting ended with no specific promises, but Soeharto did pledge to take the students' views into account in the future.

Thus the students had taken considerable initiative in expressing their grievances, and they had been relatively free to do so. Their complaints were broadly political, as well as economic, and were focused increasingly on the presidential office. Yet, they had been able to meet, hold demonstrations (although these were illegal), and have their views reflected in the daily press. The government had responded with patience, given the students their head, and gone to rather unusual lengths to give the young people a hearing. Soeharto and other senior figures in the government seem to have believed that this should have been enough. Yet, the students rejected their appeals for patience. In a political system that was plainly authoritarian, and a society in which deference to persons in authority was expected, the students' aggressive behavior created consternation in official circles. And the scale of the rioting was totally unexpected. With the recent events in Bangkok in the background, questions about the students' intentions and their possible support among army officers quickly surfaced.

6. The January 15 "Disaster"

The Question of a Plot

The official view that a plot had existed to overthrow the government was laid out in some detail in an editorial that appeared in the *Monthly Review*, published by the Centre for Strategic and International Studies, a think tank which had been founded by Gen. Ali Moertopo, and which itself had been surrounded by hostile demonstrators on January 15. The *Review* was scornful of statements made by the student councils of many universities, including the University of Indonesia, deploring the violence. The student demonstrations were undisciplined, the *Review* said, unlike the student actions of 1966 against Sukarno, in which there was no burning of cars or destruction of buildings. The students "did not seem to have a good organization (or) good leaders with high motivation and orientation to the national interest."[18]

But not only students were involved:

> Surely not only the students, who had created a lot of agitation by their discussions, petitions, statements, dispatch of delegations, and demonstrations, before all these reached their culmination on 15 and 16 January, but also a large part of the press, which had generally given support and encouragement to the students' actions by their distorted and biased reporting and writing without being critical[,] thereby fomenting the situation, and certain individuals, particularly a number of intellectuals and former members of the PSI and the Masyumi party, who had instigated the students and taken part in their various activities, thereby exploiting the students and their issues and obscuring the genuine issues and grievances of the students to criticize and oppose the government for their own political ends, should be held responsible for what happened and for the consequences thereof.[19]

The problem went even deeper than the press and former party leaders, however:

> A mention is to be made of the State apparatus for the maintenance of security and order, which should also share the responsibility for the actions of the mobs that got out of hand. . . . It would seem hard to tell whether or not they were actually prepared to face the eventuality of a riot on those two days. At any rate, for some unknown reasons, neither the police nor the soldiers on guard took any meaningful action to prevent the burning and destruction of cars, shops, and other buildings and properties. Still it is not as yet clear whether or not there has been an organized movement involving the students and certain former members

of the outlawed PSI and Masyumi backed by a number of Army officers to topple the government. This has been the issue of the day in the country since the affair.[20]

So there it was all laid out. The students had grievances. A large part of the press had supported them. Individuals associated with banned political parties had encouraged them. The question was whether all these had been part of an organized movement, backed by army officers, to bring down the government.

For their part, student leaders later claimed to have been completely surprised by the violence. Without informing their student followers, they had privately alerted security authorities of exactly what they aimed to do; they did not want any clash with the military. What they had genuinely feared was that they would be set upon by thugs in the hire of domestic security agencies. They had had that experience on one previous occasion. But no such violence occurred during their demonstration on January 15. The march had gone off without incident, and the rioting had taken place elsewhere in the city.[21]

The students and other young intellectuals did believe they had the moral support and perhaps the protection of like-minded military officers. Many ties between the two groups had persisted since 1966. Army officers, from generals to majors, had come to the meetings of the student discussion groups that were proliferating on the campuses, and while some officers were angry and berated the students, others were sympathetic and offered help. According to leaders of the "discussion group" movement, these offers were rejected. Later, when students were interrogated, they were pressed particularly about their sources of funds. But times had changed. Students now had funds, the movement collected dues, and the student leaders had money of their own for travel and communication. Their error, one leader later suggested, was their failure to analyze correctly the forces arrayed behind them and against them. Or, as another put it, they had a sense of invincibility arising from the moral force of their ideas. They also were impelled by a sense of urgency, by the conviction that time was running out, that the country was heading for autocracy. Undoubtedly they hoped to spark a series of events that, if not capable of bringing down the government altogether, would at least put a brake on the growth of presidential power.[22]

The principal targets of government ire among the press were three of the capital's leading daily newspapers. Others the government had shut down were permitted to resume publication after their editors promised to be more careful in the future, but these three did not appear again. One of these was *KAMI*, the sometimes irreverent student daily, which had survived the demise of the student action front of the same name. The two other papers were even more serious losses. *Pedoman* and *Indonesia Raya* were edited by two of the most widely respected figures in Indonesian journalism, Rosihan Anwar and Mochtar Lubis. Both natives of West Sumatra, they had already seen their papers closed down once before, by Sukarno, and had spent more than half of the 1960s in prison. When they resumed publication in the late 1960s, *Pedoman* and *Indonesia Raya* were the most forthright of the Jakarta papers in their reporting of political developments. A fellow Sumatran in government acknowledged his respect for one of these editors: "You have to give him credit; he called a spade a spade."[23] In the circle of Javanese generals around Soeharto, however, that was at the very least impolite, and at its worst, subversive. It seems likely that more than one member of the presidential circle had been looking for an opportunity to silence these critics for some time. From the point of view of the press also, antagonism was deepening. Many journalists were former student activists, intellectuals in their own right, and their sympathies were clear. It did not require a plot for many journalists to share the students' criticisms of the government and to support their demands.

The principal suspect cast in the role of "mastermind" of the alleged plot was apparently Soedjatmoko.[24] He was certainly an intellectual, and he had been a leading figure in the Socialist Party. But he also had impeccable social and political credentials. Soedjatmoko was the son of a medical doctor who had attended the household of the royal family of Solo; was a member of Sjahrir's underground during the Japanese occupation; and, while still in his early twenties, had been sent to the United Nations in New York to seek support for Indonesian independence. Thus, while Rosihan Anwar and Mochtar Lubis spent the later Sukarno years in prison, far from their families in the capital, Soedjatmoko had remained at home in Jakarta, with only restrictions on his travel. Soeharto appointed him in 1968 as ambassador to the United States, where he was much admired. In January 1974 Soedjatmoko was engaged as a consultant on social and cultural affairs to Widjojo at the National Planning Agency. This record was not enough to save him from some months of house arrest and interrogation. He was told that his name had surfaced early in the interrogation of student leaders; asked where they had gotten their critical ideas, they had readily named him as a prominent source. Soedjatmoko had made no secret of his opinion that development was failing in Indonesia for lack of the people's involvement, especially in the villages, and for lack of rapport with the country's youth, many of whom were unemployed or underemployed—the result of government policies, he believed. Much sought after by students, Soedjatmoko was a frequent visitor to the nation's campuses. And he was increasingly apocalyptic in his views: "We may be sitting on a time bomb," he told a visitor at the time, "or maybe, more accurately, a volcano."[25] No charges were ever brought against him, and eventually the restrictions on his travel were removed.

The principal army victim of the affair was General Soemitro, a rotund, affable man, popularly known as "fat Soemitro." Born in East Java, he had climbed the ranks of the Brawidjaja Division there, was serving in East Kalimantan at the time of the attempted coup in 1965, and from shortly thereafter held a series of posts in Jakarta. He was, in the opinion of many, the second most powerful person in Indonesia when the riots occurred. A man who liked to theorize about the larger meaning of events, he was attracted to officers with an intellectual turn of mind, officers of the sort often labeled "PSI." He counted himself a friend of Suwarto of staff college fame, for example, and of Guy Pauker of the Rand Corporation in the United States. His public security assignments brought him in touch with others in this circle, such as Sutopo Juwono, who had taught at the staff college and was head of the intelligence agency at the time of the riots. Soemitro had a reputation for being blunt, self-confident, and politically ambitious. So he was well removed by background and style from the long-serving Central Javanese aides to Soeharto, and his ambitions set him against them as well.

Many thought at the time that Soemitro's highly publicized visits to the campuses represented an independent move to challenge the members of Soeharto's inner circle. Soemitro has said this was not so, that the campus visits were Soeharto's idea. But Soemitro does appear to have been committed to a moderate approach. He might have shared the students' concerns to some extent. And he had feared that a large demonstration against Tanaka would lead to violence, as had occurred in Bandung. Student leaders have said that he called them in and urged them to cancel their plans to demonstrate on these very grounds. Had he succeeded in stopping them, he might well have enjoyed the political career he seemed to be aiming for. When he failed, Soeharto removed him as head of public security, taking on the job himself for a time, and Soemitro resigned from the armed forces.[26]

Soemitro's principal army rival was Gen. Ali Moertopo, one of Soeharto's four personal assistants at the time of the riots, Soeharto's principal political adviser, and deputy head of central intelligence. Moertopo was born in Central Java, had his early army experience in the Diponegoro Division, was Soeharto's intelligence officer there, and followed him to Jakarta. Moertopo carried out secret operations during the confrontation against Malaysia; provided liaison with student leaders in 1965–66; managed the successful UN-supervised vote in West Irian that completed West Irian's formal integration into Indonesia; and organized Golkar's successful campaign in the 1971 elections. As his record suggests, he was a man of considerable intellectual capacity. But his principal asset was his proximity to the president. He was thus Soeharto's political adviser and agent par excellence. Moertopo had recently renewed his contacts with students out of an interest in providing them with a nonparty association, one organized along professional lines that ran parallel to Golkar; it was an interest shared by many ex-KAMI intellectuals who were concerned to find a structure through which they could continue to be engaged in the political process. But Moertopo's new student "clubs" were meeting increasing competition from the independent "discussion groups" that also were appearing on the campuses. These latter groups were attracting prominent people to their meetings, people such as former Vice President Mohammad Hatta, former Prime Minister Ali Sastroamidjojo, General Nasution, Soedjatmoko, and intellectually minded army officers such as Sutopo Juwono. Students active in the "discussion groups" were much attracted to the "dependencia" literature coming out of Latin America at the time; they saw Japan as coming to play the dominant economic role in Southeast Asia, and this was a prospect they believed should be resisted. Students sharing these views were beginning to dominate the student senates on the major campuses across the island of Java and were even moving into Moertopo's "clubs." Considering the speed with which the "discussion group" movement was growing, and the prominence of the people who were attracted to it, Moertopo had some reason to suspect that the students might not be acting entirely on their own. Moertopo was later accused of having instigated some of the initial rioting in order to discredit the student radicals and, perhaps in the process, General

Soemitro and other moderates. According to a student leader arrested after the Malari riots, he met young toughs in jail who claimed they had been working for Moertopo at the time, had started the burning, and had been picked up along with other rioters. A senior intelligence officer friendly to Soemitro said later that he believed this was indeed the case.[27]

A variant view at the time was that Americans might have been involved in encouraging the dissidents. The possibility was pursued for a time by army interrogators. University teachers were largely American-trained, and visiting American academics had sat in on some of the student meetings. Moreover, Soedjatmoko was by this time a trustee of the Ford Foundation in New York. According to one figure at the center of the "discussion group" movement, "The interrogation actually went so far as to try to establish the truth of David Ransom's thesis—that is, that there was a long-term American plan to dominate us through Ford Foundation financial support of the Faculty of Economics—though I don't think it ever got anywhere."[28]

Other leads were never pursued at all. The students had meetings in the weeks before January 15 with a number of army officers. But student leaders have said they were never asked about the army contacts, although the authorities must have known about the meetings. Possibly the interrogators themselves were divided in their loyalties.

Whatever the facts of the case, the interrogations slowed over a period of months, and then ceased altogether. Several of General Soemitro's army associates were transferred, and he eventually went into private business. Three young intellectuals were tried in court: Hariman Siregar, leader of the student council of the University of Indonesia, who was sentenced to six years; Aini Chalid, a student leader at Gadjah Mada University in Yogyakarta, who was sentenced to four years; and Sjahrir, a young economics lecturer at the University of Indonesia, who was sentenced to six-and-a-half years. All three were released before serving their full sentences. Siregar returned to his studies and became a medical doctor; Sjahrir completed a doctorate at Harvard. Rosihan Anwar and Mochtar Lubis turned to writing and editing books. Soedjatmoko became rector of the United Nations University. Ali Moertopo and Soedjono Humardhani remained close associates of the president, and Ali went on to become a cabinet minister. No official report on the affair ever appeared. One prominent participant, himself among the detainees, reflected on the history with more regret than anger. "The result," he said, "is that people on all sides of the affair feel that they never got to the bottom of it."[29]

If there was a "bottom" to the affair, it was not in a plot by any civilian members of the elite. The government might not have believed the charge even when it was made; no evidence to support it was ever made public, and the inference has been drawn that none was ever found. There was ample evidence of miscalculation—by the students, by Soemitro, by Moertopo, and by army officers aligned with one or the other. The indications of division within the armed forces were only a sign of the times, however. What was principally made evident by the events of January 15 and 16 was that Soedjatmoko had been right, that the elite was sitting on a volcano, and that the ordinary youth of the capital were deeply disenchanted with the regime. There was thus substance to the student protests, to the misgivings of army officers, and to the popular disenchantment. The issues had to do mainly with the growing presence of the Japanese in the Indonesian economy, with the position of the local Chinese in the economy, and with alleged corruption on the part of people close to the president. In the view of many, these issues were of a piece.

The Japanese Presence

Indonesia was the principal country on Tanaka's itinerary, according to an aide, although he visited all five ASEAN countries. The reason was that Indonesia was the principal supplier in Asia of resources to the Japanese economy. At the time, 13.7 percent of Japan's oil imports was coming from Indonesia; in the wake of events in the Middle East, Tanaka had gone to Jakarta to protect the stability of Indonesian oil supplies to Japan and to promote the development of supplies of liquified natural gas.[30]

Oil also figured in the student plans for demonstrations in Jakarta against the visit. Some time before the visit was announced, information was leaked to student leaders that Pertamina, the Indonesian state oil company, had provided "kickbacks" to two Japanese oil companies authorized to buy Indonesian oil, in order to provide funds to finance the ruling Liberal Democratic Party. Where the story originated is not known; some believe it might have come from the faction of the LDP headed by Tanaka's archrival Fukuda. In any event, the story seemed to the Indonesian students to be a revival of the Sukarno-Dewi connection, and when the Tanaka visit was announced, they began to organize demonstrations against the Japanese. It was only in the last days, however, after students had demonstrated against Tanaka in Bangkok, that the student leaders of several other universities in Jakarta decided to join forces with those of the University of Indonesia, thus considerably enlarging the scale of the march.

Japan was at the time providing one-third of Indonesia's foreign economic assistance, matching that of the United States, as it had been doing from 1967 on. In May 1973 the Intergovernmental Group pledged $876.6 million in aid to Indonesia for fiscal year 1973–74. Japanese aid was thus large and visible, and that much of it was tied to the purchase of goods manufactured in Japan was widely known and criticized. It was assumed, not only in Jakarta, that the principal aim of the aid was to develop markets for Japanese products.[31]

Japanese private investment was a relatively new phenomenon. Japan had not been a factor at all in the Indonesian leadership's thinking when the new law on foreign investment was put in place at the beginning of 1967. Japan still faced a balance of payments problem, and private investment abroad was under tight government control. The Indonesians expected most private investment to come from the United States, and indeed the United States was initially the major source, primarily in the fields of oil and hard minerals. Through the late 1960s, however, Japan experienced a series of annual trade surpluses and, with these, rising reserves of foreign exchange. To avoid a drastic revaluation of the yen, which would have worked against exports, the Japanese government began in 1969 to grant automatic approval of investments abroad by private Japanese corporations, at first of small-scale investments, and from 1971 on without regard to size. At the same time rising land and labor prices in Japan were causing Japanese manufacturers to encounter increasing price competition in foreign markets, and they began to take a growing interest in moving some of their production abroad.[32]

Another consideration was the continuing Japanese search for markets for parts and semifinished goods; a Ministry of International Trade and Industry survey in 1974 showed that Japanese affiliates engaged in manufacturing in Indonesia depended on their parent companies for 46 percent of their inputs, the highest ratio in Southeast Asia. Within a few years of Indonesia's opening its economy to foreign investment, the Japanese had multiple reasons to respond to the opportunity.[33]

6. The January 15 "Disaster"

Although Japanese investment had a late start in Indonesia, it grew with great rapidity. During the 1971 fiscal year $30 million was invested in Indonesia, and the total by the end of that year exceeded all Japanese investment in Thailand, even though the latter had a history of more than a decade. In the following two years Japanese investment in Indonesia continued to increase, coming close to $100 million in 1973 alone. By the end of that year total Japanese investment stood at about $185 million, about twice the total in Thailand and about nine times that in the Philippines.[34]

Japanese investors were in an extremely strong bargaining position in Indonesia during these years. The foreign investment law obliged them to enter into a joint venture with a local partner, but the partnership was often more nominal than real. The Japanese partner often provided the equity capital, the management, the technology, and the operating capital. It was not uncommon that the only contribution the Indonesian partner made was the land on which the factory was to be built; foreign nationals could not own land in Indonesia. As the value of the land was usually not sufficient to provide the Indonesian share of equity capital required by law, it was common practice for the Japanese partner to provide the Indonesian partner with a loan; all the Indonesian-held shares were then pledged as collateral.

Panglaykim, a prominent Indonesian business economist, described the situation that resulted in these terms: The Indonesian partner usually "had no choice but to surrender all the managerial and organizational power to the Japanese partner." The Japanese partner imported equipment and materials from Japan at "their own set prices . . . which were probably considerably higher [than] those of other suppliers." Other services, including factory design and layout, and insurance coverage, also were provided by Japanese companies affiliated with the Japanese partner. "It would not be unfair to say that in many cases, the Japanese partner had already calculated his risk . . . and had . . . taken his profits in advance."[35]

The Case of Textiles

The Japanese investment in Indonesia was, in addition, highly concentrated. Of the $185 million of Japanese investment by the end of 1973, $122 million, or about two-thirds, was invested in textile production, and 94 percent of this latter amount was concentrated in the production of synthetic fibers and in integrated textile mills. Numerous reasons have been advanced to explain the phenomenon. Japan had a long history in the textile field, and Indonesia was the last country with a large population and a potentially large market available for penetration. In addition, the production of man-made fibers was highly concentrated within Japan itself; in 1972, the five top producers accounted for 90 percent of Japan's production of nylon, 85 percent of its polyester, and 93 percent of its acrylic. As opportunity beckoned, these firms were unusually well positioned to respond with vigor in a sector of the industry that depended on high technology and large amounts of capital.[36] Major Japanese trading companies were active participants in the effort to establish Japanese firms in the textile industry throughout the region, including such houses as Mitsui & Co., C. Itoh, and Marubeni. Two major Japanese producers of synthetic fibers, Toray Industries and Teijin, by early 1974 accounted for 83 percent of the total investment in synthetic fiber production in Southeast Asia.[37]

The existing textile industry in Indonesia was in no condition to withstand the onslaught of the big Japanese firms. Centered in Bandung and the towns and villages of West Java, the industry had been only partially modernized before World War II; while some six thousand looms were power-operated in 1940, almost sixty thousand were operated by hand. The subsequent Japanese occupation and national revolution inflicted enormous damage on the textile industry; only 25 percent of the prewar looms survived to 1950. Textile self-sufficiency was therefore put on a par with rice self-sufficiency in the early years of the republic, and a series of government subsidies and regulations followed. Despite much inconstancy in government policy, the industry prospered and by the early 1960s was supplying 44 percent of the country's total textile consumption. By 1966, however, many and perhaps most textile enterprises were suffering serious shortages of capital, materials, parts, electricity, and even labor.[38]

Under the pressure of adverse press reports and student demonstrations, Indonesian policymakers had begun in 1968 to develop a program to promote domestic industry. Medium- and long-term loans were made available to Indonesian citizens for up to 75 percent of the capital requirements of new investments. In 1971 a further step was taken with the creation of a government corporation that insured up to 75 percent of bank loans to small and medium-scale enterprises engaged in a wide range of fields. In 1972 a new financial institution was created to specialize in financing medium-sized and small-scale industry. In 1973 yet another specialized institution was established to provide up to 12.5 percent of the equity financing of new local enterprises, along with managerial assistance when it was needed. In December 1973 the government announced a long-awaited program of further "credit indigenization," which provided small amounts of fixed investment and working capital to new local enterprises on liberal terms, including a waiver of minimum collateral.

Given time, these programs of incentives might have worked. But time was not on their side. Obliged to compete with the powerful new foreign producers, many existing Indonesian textile firms went bankrupt. Out of a desire to open the economy to foreign capital and technology in the interest of modernization, and a determination to focus on financial incentives rather than bureaucratic controls, Indonesia's economic policymakers had permitted the destruction of one of the few modern industries the country already had. By the time the government did act, the political crisis required dramatic action. With the wide range of restrictions imposed on foreign investment in early 1974, the rush to invest in Indonesia came to a rapid end.[39] In the decade that followed, the bulk of investment flowed instead into neighboring Thailand, Malaysia, and Singapore.[40] And while the Indonesian restrictions applied to all foreigners, regardless of national origin, the Malari riots contributed to a particularly sharp retreat by the Japanese. The number of Japanese firms doing business in Indonesia peaked at forty-five companies in 1973, at least into the latter years of the decade.[41]

Why Indonesian policymakers held so firmly to their open-economy position regarding textiles is not clear; as we have seen, they had compromised that position in regard to rice from the very beginning. One possible reason is that the textile industry was in a weak political position after 1966, composed largely of firms that had been favored by Sukarno or by one of the political parties of the Sukarno period. Indonesian officials probably also were eager to avoid a quarrel with the Japanese because of the value of Japanese aid, which in volume was much larger than private investment. In Thailand, which was much less dependent on the Japanese for economic assistance, government officials appear to have modulated the pace of Japanese investment more effectively.

Additional differences between the Indonesian and Thai cases also help explain the difference in behavior and outcomes. In January 1974, at the time of the Tanaka visit, Thailand was in the early stages of a new "democratic period," and the students who were demonstrating against the Japanese were strongly progovernment. In Indonesia, on the other hand, the students were critical not only of the Japanese, but were deeply critical of the regime as well.

Still another difference was the position of the Chinese in the two countries. In Thailand, anti-Chinese feeling was very much a thing of the past. It had been a significant element in the events that had led to the end of the absolute monarchy in 1932, but considerable assimilation had occurred by 1974. If most of the Japanese partners in Thailand were Sino-Thais, that did not figure in the student protests there. In Indonesia, the racial element was crucial.

The Role of the Chinese

The bulk of the local partners of Japanese investors in Indonesia were unquestionably Chinese. A Japanese embassy official put the figure at 70 percent. It was not only the Japanese, however, who found the Indonesian Chinese more attractive partners than indigenous business-men; American and European investors were thought to have selected their local partners in about the same proportions. Moreover, many of the non-Chinese partners were not private citizens but state enterprises or other quasi-public entities. The result was that indigenous In-donesian businessmen tended to be excluded from the principal oppor-tunities that government policies were making available.

Senior officers of the Department of Defense and Security were known to view the growing gap between the Chinese and indigenous business communities as a potential threat to political stability. The Chinese issue troubled Soemitro and other security officials concerned with the Tanaka visit; the racial incident in Bandung was still fresh in their minds. Moreover, anti-Chinese sentiment was strongly implied in the student protests on behalf of "Indonesian" industry. As events demonstrated, security officials had had reason to be concerned; the damage in Jakarta on January 15 was chiefly to Japanese-made goods, but the goods were largely Chinese-owned. As the government moved to respond to the substance of the student protests, therefore, it faced not only the question of the Japanese role in the economy, but that of the Chinese as well.

The Chinese had become well established in Indonesian industry in colonial times. The textile industry offered an example that was not unrepresentative. Chinese merchants in the towns controlled a large portion of the hand-weavers in the villages by contracting work to them. More than half of all the looms in the organized part of the industry also were owned by Chinese, both before and after the war. As fashions changed and village people stopped wearing sarongs and other garments of coarse fabrics, the Chinese influence grew still stronger. Of all the broad power-looms suitable for modern textiles, the share owned by Chinese was 75 percent.[42]

A fundamental problem that the government programs of the late 1960s and early 1970s confronted was the relatively small number of indigenous entrepreneurs with some experience. A senior economist who had much to do with foreign investment in this period said the problem was too basic to be resolved within a few years. Simply too few genuine entrepreneurs existed among the indigenous population, and most of these were over sixty years of age. "Most got their start as small traders before the Japanese occupation," he said. "Some were already in textiles, but that was a handful. Most of them were deal-makers, looking to make a killing." Younger businessmen had started out after independence. "So they started with some political support. But their history was largely one of instability; when their political support was lost, their fortunes declined." There were a few exceptions, but generally no well-known houses existed, only individuals. "The Chamber of Commerce and Industry is full of rich Indonesian businessmen," the former official said, "but there has been almost no institutionalization. . . . All the bigger groups are Chinese, and they have all grown up since the New Order began."[43]

An added disability indigenous businessmen suffered was that they had no financial networks of their own. Most indigenous businessmen seem to have been unable to mobilize even the 25 percent of capital required by the new government credit programs, and so were precluded from taking advantage of them. The Chinese, on the other hand, had well-established systems of self-financing that extended along family, clan, and regional lines. Although no records were made of the race of loan recipients, it was widely believed that the bulk of state investment credits were going to Chinese-Indonesians.[44]

In the immediate aftermath of the Malari riots, as the government moved to protect local interests, it also acted to protect indigenous Indonesians. During the month of January 1974 the government issued a series of decrees and regulations. Regulations requiring the hiring of local personnel by foreign firms were tightened. Foreign investors in the future would be obliged to select "indigenous" Indonesians as the partners in their joint ventures, and the controlling interest in these firms was to be turned over in stages to the local partner. Furthermore, medium-term investment credits would henceforth be given only to "indigenous" enterprises, which were defined as those in which 75 percent of the shares were held by "indigenous" shareholders, or in which "indigenous" personnel had a controlling managerial interest. These policies presumably were followed for a time. But as later developments were to demonstrate, the role of the Chinese in the economy was not going to be altered by decree.

The Issue of Corruption

Student criticism of corruption in government surfaced early in the Soeharto presidency. In March 1967 the government was already faced with a barrage of criticism regarding the state of the economy. Although no data existed on the point, press accounts gave the impression that domestic industry was slowing down or shutting down completely in the face of the government's austere monetary and fiscal policies. In April anti-Chinese demonstrations in Jakarta brought business to a standstill for several days. By May the demonstrations had spread to the issue of corruption. The government responded to these disturbances with a series of concessions to its critics. It agreed to begin a relaxation of its tight-money policies. It created a state committee to examine and report on the recent anti-Chinese violence. And finally, in December, it announced the creation of a special team, headed by the attorney general, to combat corruption. Thus, the pattern was set that tied criticism of economic policy to complaints against the Chinese, and these, in turn, to charges of official corruption. Also set was a pattern of government failure to respond to the substance of public criticism until demonstrators were in the streets.

Corruption was a fact of daily life; everyone was familiar with the problem of government salaries, and small gratuities for the simplest public service were familiar to all. Even collecting one's paltry government salary usually required leaving something behind for the paymaster and his staff. But this was not the corruption that critics had in mind. As the young intellectual leader, Arief Budiman, wrote in an article after meeting the president in August 1970:

> Corruption has its limits if they want to survive. The limit is that cor-
> ruption should not be so great as to obstruct economic development. If
> it obstructs development to the point, for example, where peasants can
> no longer grow rice because corruption has made the price of fertilizer
> extremely high, then it will no longer be only the youth in the cities
> [who] will take action but also the youth in the villages. This means a
> people's revolt, a social revolution. Thus, if the corruptors are clever (and
> in Indonesia they are indeed clever enough), I think they will not violate
> this "code of ethics." Clever corruptors will not destroy the nation, they
> will keep the nation alive, although very thin.[45]

Clearly the youthful critics were concerned about corruption on a
large scale, and that meant corruption at or near the very top of the
regime. That inevitably included the top of the armed forces.

Corruption and the Armed Forces

The army itself owned a number of business enterprises. These already
had some history before they were reorganized in 1969 as registered private companies and coordinated by a registered private holding company, PT Tri Usaha Bhakti. Firms in the group included an automobile
assembly plant, a battery factory, clothing and shoe factories, rice mills,
a bank, an airline, and several joint forestry ventures with foreign
investors.[46]

Independent of this headquarters group of firms was another operated by Soeharto's former command, the strategic reserve, which Soeharto
had begun as a foundation in 1964. The Yayasan Dharma Putra Kostrad
had joined with Liem Sioe Liong, Soeharto's Chinese businessman
friend, to establish a bank, Bank Windhu Kencana, and with credit
from the bank established two airlines and operated a number of other
subsidiaries in film distribution, building construction, and other
fields.[47]

This pattern was repeated by the navy, air force, and police, by the
territorial divisions of the army, and by local units. In the late 1960s and
early 1970s, local military commanders were reported to be raising funds
by way of a wide range of legal and illegal activities. Smuggling was common in the early years of the new government, along with the use of military vehicles and naval vessels to transport passengers and freight. But
military units also engaged in the operation of legitimate businesses,

including bus lines, construction companies, rice mills, movie theaters, and banks. Most of these enterprises were said to be operated by Chinese businessmen on behalf of the military authorities.[48]

As accounts of these ventures circulated in Jakarta, an effort was made to justify them in terms of the armed forces' need to meet their budgets. In late 1969 and early 1970 official spokesmen said that the army was receiving only enough from the government to meet 40 percent of the army's budget, and the navy only 30 to 40 percent. An army newspaper said that the armed forces as a whole were receiving only slightly more than 50 percent of their budget from the government.[49]

Such fund-raising on behalf of the armed forces themselves might have been tolerated by civilian elements had it not been for the public scandals that implicated senior military figures. Several of these involved the rice agency, Bulog. In the latter part of 1967 a series of private banks crashed; it later developed that Bulog funds had been deposited in one or more of these banks, although Bulog was required by law to deposit its funds only in state banks. Following yet another bank crash in December 1968 Bulog's loss of funds reportedly contributed to a major failure in domestic procurement during the following year.[50] At this point Bulog lacked the organization to buy or sell rice on any terms other than a wholesale basis; it bought rice, and sold it, through middlemen, most of whom were Chinese. Bulog's scale of operations and its continuing performance failures inevitably earned it the reputation of being a center of corruption, as well as incompetence.[51]

Press accounts also suggested that government favors were being extended to firms that involved members of the president's family and his long-time Chinese friend, Liem Sioe Liong. A trading firm, CV Waringin, which included among its directors both Liem and the president's foster brother, Sudwikatmono, was reported in 1967 to have obtained approval to export large amounts of coffee beyond its quota, and in 1968 to have obtained large credits to expand its operations. Mrs. Tien Soeharto, the president's wife, established a foundation, Yayasan Harapan Kita, that was reported to own several companies and, in association with Liem Sioe Liong, established PT Bogosari, which set up the first of several flour mills in 1970. In the same year firms controlled by Liem Sioe Liong and the president's younger brother, Probosutedjo, were given exclusive rights to the importation of cloves, an essential ingredient in the manufacture of *kretek,* the spiced cigarettes widely popular in Java.[52]

6. The January 15 "Disaster"

The biggest scandal of the period involved outright fraud in the use of foreign exchange that foreign governments had made available as aid. In 1968, with foreign exchange still in short supply, the government attempted to reduce controls by selling foreign exchange at a price set by the daily market. At the same time, for the import of goods on an official priority list, it sold a portion of its holdings of foreign exchange at a preferential rate. Predictably, a number of importers bought foreign exchange under this latter system and then used some or all of it for other purposes, doctoring purchase orders and shipping documents to hide the illegal transactions. In August the practice came to the attention of Sumitro Djojohadikusumo, the founder of the Faculty of Economics at the University of Indonesia, who had been invited back from exile and, as a measure to reassure the business community, had recently been appointed Minister of Trade. On learning that fraud was widely practiced in dealings with his new department, Soemitro called in the attorney general. It was reported soon thereafter that $35 million had been misused in a three-month period, or one-third of all the foreign exchange used for imports during that time; the total amount misused during the year might have been as high as $100 million. It was later reported that some thirty-four importers, apparently Chinese, had fled the country; one importer was detained, along with several government officials. But no one was ever charged, and it was widely supposed that senior military men figured in the background. The case was eventually settled out of court.

A year later similar transactions by a Bulog affiliate in Japan led to the arrest of two men by the Japanese government on charges of violating Japanese currency regulations. The detainees were important enough that one of Soeharto's personal assistants, Soedjono Humardhani, was dispatched to Tokyo, met the finance minister, Takeo Fukuda, and obtained the release of the pair.[53]

The Commission of Four

Reports of these developments appeared in the Jakarta press, and in the wake of the foreign exchange scandal, and further student demonstrations in January 1970, Soeharto felt obliged to clear the air. On January 31 he appointed a four-man commission to inquire into corruption and advise on ways to eliminate it. The chairman was Wilopo, the former prime minister and National Party leader. The other members were I. J.

157

Kasim, the long-time leader of the Catholic party; Johannes, a physicist and former rector of Gadjah Mada University; and Anwar Tjokroaminoto, leader of a splinter Islamic party. General Sutopo Juwono was appointed secretary of the commission, and former Vice President Hatta was appointed an adviser to both the commission and Soeharto.

At the end of June, after the commission was known to have submitted a series of reports to the government, and as the government continued to give no indication of when the information would be made public, the reports were leaked to Aristides Katoppo, editor of the daily *Sinar Harapan,* which published the commission's findings in a series of front-page installments in July. The reports revealed that the commission had told Soeharto that the situation was "critical," that corruption was "running unchecked," and that efforts to control it were falling far behind, to the point where corruption had become "a social evil" that was slowing development "in all fields."[54] The commission urged "priority attention" to a number of prominent cases, including the foreign exchange scandals, the Department of Religion, the forestry directorate, and CV Waringin.[55] In addition, the commission submitted two highly detailed and uncomplimentary reports on Pertamina and another on Bulog.[56]

In its final report, which sounded a warning of "moral decline"—"people no longer know what is corrupt and what is not"—the commission told Soeharto pointedly that the clean-up "must begin at the top." It urged that "open management" replace the secret use of extrabudgetary funds in the office of the president—"no matter what the excuse."[57]

Two cases involving telecommunications and official management of hadj (Islamic pilgrimage) affairs did go to court on the commission's urging. In his address to the nation on the eve of the twenty-fifth anniversary of Independence Day, Soeharto said there was insufficient evidence in the remaining cases. He did order all high-ranking government officials and military officers to prepare statements of their personal wealth. As the commission had urged, he also created a board to oversee the state oil company. And he announced that he was taking personal command of efforts to eradicate corruption.

That was, for all practical purposes, the end of the matter so far as the government was concerned. And so the problem continued to fester. No issue was more central to the growth of the "discussion groups" on the campuses, and none was more powerful in convincing the students that they constituted an essential moral force, that it was their inevitable responsibility to clean the government up.

The Lessons of the Affair

Numerous lessons were drawn from the "January 15 disaster." The Japanese were well aware of the antigovernment and anti-Chinese elements in the event. They also were familiar with the history of the textile industry. The largest newspapers in Japan urged change in the way Japanese aid was being used.[58] A government official was quoted as saying that aid had to be made available through government channels, rather than disbursed through private companies, as was the practice at the time.[59] Saburo Okita echoed this view, saying that Japan had to give up profit as the principal aim of its aid.[60] And indeed, later in the year, the Japan Economic Cooperation Fund was created, and Okita was appointed to the new cabinet-level post of Minister for International Economic Affairs.

One line of thinking in Jakarta had to do with how to deal with the Japanese from a position of greater strength. Daud Jusuf of the Center for Strategic and International Studies, in an article published in 1974, saw the problem in terms of the interface between the national and international economies. Autarchy would lead the country into economic decline; it could not cut itself off from the rest of the world. But the danger in dealing with the global economy was that the colonial experience would simply be repeated, that small Indonesian firms would find themselves dealing with giant foreign firms, and that "the Indonesian partners . . . would serve as a mere 'extension' of the foreign companies." To avoid such a repetition of history, Daud proposed "a pattern of close cooperation between the government, bureaucrats, technocrats and businessmen so as to facilitate the development of a power entity on a national scale which can serve as a countervailing power against both multinational corporations and foreign national (read Chinese) enterprises." To be effective, the effort would have to be based on "large-scale national participation" through "national integrated units in the industrial, managerial, commercial and financial fields." These "big business units" would help enterprises that were small and medium in scale by relying on them to supply raw materials and to market finished products. The heart of the plan was a national financial consortium that would "make the maximum use of the creditworthiness that our national financial institutions as a whole actually have among international circles." Foreign banks might then be prohibited from channeling funds into Indonesia except through this national consortium. Daud acknowledged that he was proposing an "Indonesia Incorporated," modeled after the Japanese.[61]

The proposal was timely, for it responded to the nationalist and racist sentiments that the riots had expressed. It was immediately criticized by other intellectuals, however, on the grounds that Japanese society had a set of values and a century of experience that were lacking in the Indonesian case.[62] The proposal also ran head-on against the antibureaucratic convictions of Widjojo, who was Minister of Planning, and of Ali Wardhana, who was Minister of Finance. So "Indonesia Incorporated" never became official strategy. Nevertheless, Daud's ideas were highly influential. They provided an intellectual justification for the expansion of state conglomerates such as Bulog, Pertamina, and others that were to follow. And as oil revenues enriched the state treasury, the idea of using the national weight more fully in international economic transactions became increasingly attractive.

A different lesson was drawn from the Malari affair by Dorodjatun Kuntjoro Jakti, who was a young lecturer at the Faculty of Economics, a central figure in the campus "discussion groups," and one of the planners of the January 15 march. He was detained for two years, and then denied permission to travel for some years more, before he was able to return to the University of California at Berkeley. In a doctoral dissertation finally completed there, Dorodjatun argued that Daud's "Indonesia Incorporated" came close to describing the reality of the situation in 1974. Industrial and commercial conglomerates, whether publicly or privately owned, and involving military officers, Chinese businessmen, and others close to the president, already dominated the heights of the economy. He went on to argue that the power and influence of these groups was causing serious imbalances in the nation's development. One of these imbalances was regional; the centralization of power was reflected in a heavy concentration of modern industry in the Jakarta metropolitan area, while other regions of the country were allowed to languish. Another imbalance was social; the new conglomerates were in the hands of a small number of individuals who were becoming immensely wealthy, while the great bulk of the population saw its fortunes improving only incrementally. As he saw it, development in Indonesia had gone seriously awry because of the very centralization of the political process.[63]

It was acknowledged by some of Dorodjatun's former teachers, now the leading economic strategists of the regime, that his concerns had some foundation. But they also thought that the social situation was not nearly so polarized as he pictured it, and that the political process was more complex. Not only was wealth being accumulated by a few, but a middle class also was coming into existence, and that was essential to any long-term hope of greater political pluralism. Moreover, as they saw it, economic decision making was becoming less centralized, not more; as the economy grew in a mixed system of public and private ownership, decision making increased in complexity, and this was desirable. In the late 1960s, when foreign aid was at a premium, the economists' expertise was at a premium as well. By the mid-1970s oil exports were worth twice what they had been a few years earlier, the government was meeting a larger portion of its budget from its own resources, foreign private investment had been growing rapidly, and foreign private lending was entering the picture as well. These changes in the sources of finance led to a reduction in the economists' influence, and to an increase in the influence of others. Even the appointment of several economists to the cabinet after the 1971 elections contributed to a shift in influence within the government, as the economists became caught up in administering their agencies. It was readily acknowledged by more than one of the cabinet-level economists that they were often in competition in these years with the generals around the president. But that was why they were needed. The overriding task was to keep the economy growing, to get the policies right and see that they were implemented. In the absence of that, the bulk of the population would never enjoy a better life. Public approval was to be desired, but in competition with these other priorities, it had to come last. The lesson of Malari, the economic strategists concluded, was that they had to stay the course and, so far as possible, hold the government to their views.

At the same time many of those around Soeharto believed he had performed well in dealing with the political crisis created by the riots. The analogy that was chiefly in the minds of Soeharto's aides was the downfall, only three months before, of the regime of General Thanom in Thailand. As they saw it, Thanom had been unresponsive in the face of criticism, had relied on a divided army to defend him, and had been forced to leave the country as a result. In comparable circumstances, Soeharto had acted in a spirit of compromise. He had seriously tried to hold a dialogue with the students, and when that failed he had defused the crisis quickly by giving in to many of the students' demands. To the way of thinking of Soeharto's aides, this was not the behavior of a weak man; it was a prudent performance by a wise one. With a minimum use of force, he had taken the steam out of a tense situation.

Soeharto himself appears to have drawn three lessons from the affair. The most important was that factionalism within the army was a danger to the stability of the entire political system he had spent years constructing. Over the succeeding years, mainly under General Jusuf's leadership, a major reorganization of the army was put in train, ending the practice of long-time service of junior officers in a single territorial division, and making the army a more truly national institution.

Public dissidence was an equally serious matter from Soeharto's point of view. The young intellectuals, driven by the logic of their critique, had come to question not only foreign capital and corrupt behavior, but the very structure of the regime. Beginning with policy concerns, they had come to believe that the country's economic and social problems would not be resolved without a change in the way policy was made. The constitutional institutions other than the presidency were not functioning as they were intended. The parties were cut off from the rural population and from the young people in the cities, and they were not providing any alternatives to the government's development strategy. The legislature was not channeling the views of the public into policy-making, and it was not serving as an instrument of social control over the performance of the executive. They could talk all they liked, young people said, but nothing was going to change as a result.

Like Sukarno before him, Soeharto was in fundamental disagreement with the entire way of thinking that lay behind these views. Debate and division were the very problems that the 1945 constitution was designed to avoid. Public disputation had only led to bloodshed, twice threatening the very fabric of the nation. The governing principles of the Indonesian state were not to be found in such foreign values. They were to be found in the Pancasila: unity and harmony were rooted in the philosophy of the Indonesian people, and they were the supreme values of the Indonesian state. It was the function of the state's institutions to reflect these values in their structure and to serve them in their actions. As this seemed not to be understood by young people who had not experienced the country's earlier political history, it was necessary that they should learn. And so a program of indoctrination was undertaken in the principles of Pancasila. Much like Sukarno's program of indoctrination in Nasakom, this one was eventually extended to a large part of the citizenry.

Finally, there was the matter of extraconstitutional means of expression. To his youthful critics Soeharto had left no recourse except the streets and the press. After Malari these, too, were brought under control. It was an outcome costly to all sides. The student councils and the national press had been more of a nuisance than a danger to Soeharto; no one seriously believed that they could bring about a change in the government unless they were supported by military elements. At the same time they had been a valuable source of information that helped the government to track the outcomes of its policies and to know when and where correctives were needed. Moreover, the student councils and the national press were consequential institutions; they articulated and projected elite opinion during a period in which no other institutions were doing so. The repression of the students and the press thus removed significant elements from what was already a highly attenuated political process. The government was no safer without them; it was, rather, less well informed and more isolated.

SEVEN

The Pertamina Crisis

If the supply of rice and the role of foreign investment were at the center of Indonesia's policy concerns in the early 1970s, they were soon replaced as the price of oil rose dramatically in the international market. Even as the students were demonstrating against the Japanese in January 1974, the price of oil was altering Indonesia's terms of trade, raising its national income, and enriching its public treasury. For more than a decade oil was to be the engine of Indonesian development. This did not occur, however, without an early crisis that was to absorb the energies of senior officials for several years, divert resources from major projects in the government plans, and leave a substantial foreign debt to be serviced for years to come.

Oil was a principal export of independent Indonesia. By the time of the attempted coup on the night of September 30, 1965, however, oil production was in decline, and the new Soeharto administration, eager to get the economy moving, opened the country to exploration by a large number of foreign firms. At the center of this activity, from 1968 on, was a single state oil company, Pertamina. As exploration led to new finds, oil production mounted. And as international oil prices rose following the Arab embargo in 1973, Pertamina became the center of enormous financial resources, its annual budget reaching half that of the national government. With the money came a growing system of political patronage and widening charges of corruption. But Pertamina and its free-wheeling president-director, Lt. Gen. Ibnu Sutowo, were impervious to attack—until, that is, the general's management of the enterprise provoked an international financial crisis.

7. The Pertamina Crisis

At the heart of the crisis was a battle for control of oil revenues. Many saw this battle as a contest between civilian "technocrats," who were trying to enforce a central economic strategy on the nation, and army "entrepreneurs," who controlled the state enterprises and were determined to strike out on their own. But the conflict was larger than this suggests. It involved making choices as to how public funds were to be dispersed—at bottom, deciding on the development strategy the government was to pursue. The division within the regime was deep, with Soeharto himself uncertain, and army officers lined up on either side. Powerful foreign interests also were involved, both in the events that led to the crisis and in the steps needed to resolve it. For many members of the Indonesian elite, the Pertamina crisis was a dramatic example of the dilemmas the nation faced in its search for an appropriate governmental role in the economy, and in its search for economic independence in the wider world.

The Pertamina Collapse

On February 18, 1975, Jakarta time, it was reported that Pertamina had failed to repay a short-term loan of $40 million owed to a group of U.S. banks led by Republic National Bank of Dallas.

Ali Wardhana, the Minister of Finance, informed the president. Soeharto is said to have asked him to consult Widjojo Nitisastro, who was at a conference in Algiers, and Rachmat Saleh, the governor of Bank Indonesia (the central bank), about what action the government should take.[1]

The three economists were of the opinion that the government would have to stand behind the Pertamina debt. Rachmat Saleh was later reported as saying: "The overwhelming consideration on our part was how to preserve Indonesia's creditworthiness. If a big state enterprise like Pertamina turns out to be unable to pay its debts, that means the Indonesian government is out of the market."[2]

The scale of the problem was unknown. Pertamina had several separate systems of accounts, and Pertamina officials were unable to provide the government with reliable data on the scale of its borrowings. Rachmat Saleh is said to have sent cables to some two hundred banks around the world, requesting information on their loans to Pertamina; it seemed the only way to get the information quickly.[3]

In addition, there was disagreement about the terms of a bail-out. Rachmat Saleh has acknowledged that "not everyone was equally enthusiastic about the government stepping in."[4] The economic ministers believed the government could restore confidence only if Pertamina were barred from further independent borrowing. But the economic "technocrats" had been trying to put a rein on Ibnu Sutowo for some years; Sutowo believed they were blowing the problem out of all proportion.

With the international banking community besieging the government with inquiries about its intentions, Ali Wardhana prepared a two- or three-page memorandum and took it to the president. Soeharto read the memorandum and signed his approval.[5] It was none too soon.

On March 10 it was reported that Pertamina had defaulted on a second foreign loan, this one for $60 million from a Canadian bank group led by Toronto Dominion Bank.

On March 14 Bank Indonesia sent a circular to all known creditors of Pertamina stating that the central bank was prepared to meet Pertamina's foreign currency obligations and that $650 million had been earmarked for this purpose. The circular also stated that Pertamina would not be borrowing funds on the international market in the foreseeable future.[6]

By March 31 representatives of three international investment houses—S. G. Warburg of London, Lazard Freres of Paris, and Kuhn Loeb of New York, the so-called troika initially appointed to advise the Indonesian government on the management of its foreign reserves— were working with the government on the refinancing of Pertamina's short-term obligations.[7]

In April Bank Indonesia halted publication of its weekly and monthly statistical reports, presumably out of concern over Indonesia's precarious foreign exchange holdings.

On May 15 Minister of State J. B. Sumarlin announced that American and Japanese banks had agreed to raise funds to replenish Indonesia's foreign exchange reserves, in effect enabling the government to pay off Pertamina's short-term foreign debt with medium-term credits.[8]

On May 20 Sadli, the Minister of Mining and chairman of the Pertamina board, made a detailed statement on the case before Parliament, charging that Pertamina had taken on large financial obligations without the government's approval or knowledge. He put the total debt of Pertamina at more than $10.5 billion, including $2.5 billion for civil works and commercial credits; $1.9 billion for certain large projects involving liquified natural gas (LNG), fertilizer, a gas pipeline, and other exploration and production projects; $2.1 billion for completing construction of a steel plant; $156 million for telecommunications; $3.3 billion for the hire/purchase of "an armada" of oceangoing and domestic tankers; and other contracts totaling $700 million. "A large part of these activities," Sadli said, "were not economical and lacked any direct relation with the basic function of Pertamina."[9]

At the end of May it was reported that Maj. Gen. Piet Harjono, budget director in the Ministry of Finance, had been appointed director of Pertamina's financial affairs. It was said that he had presidential authority to overrule Ibnu Sutowo in all financial matters.[10]

On July 25 Widjojo, in his capacity as State Minister for Economic, Financial, and Industrial Affairs, appeared before Parliament to give an account of the government's handling of the affair. To bring the situation under control, he said, and to prevent a repetition, all Pertamina's international transactions were now being made through Bank Indonesia, and all state-owned enterprises had been banned from seeking foreign loans on their own accord. A team comprised of Lt. Gen. Hasnan Habib, Maj. Gen. Piet Harjono, and Brig. Gen. Ismail Saleh would review Pertamina as an organization. State Minister Sumarlin would review all aspects of the steel mill project. Supervisory teams would examine the physical and financial plans for other projects, including those concerned with liquified natural gas production, oil refining, and fertilizer production.[11]

In October auditors from the international accounting firm of Arthur Young & Co. were reported to have discovered that Ibnu Sutowo, on behalf of Pertamina, had been chartering oil tankers worldwide and that, with shipping fees plummeting, the business was costing Pertamina tens of millions of dollars a day.[12]

In his annual budget message the following January, Soeharto said that the amount of funds needed to pay Pertamina's domestic debts alone was "enormous."[13]

Varying assessments of these startling developments were made at the time. Pertamina was, for many members of the Indonesian elite, the symbol of either the best or the worst of the nation's drive for modernization: "high-tech" and rich to some, big and corrupt to others. On one point those on either side of the case seemed to agree. Ibnu Sutowo was a central element in the affair.

7. The Pertamina Crisis

The Rise of Ibnu Sutowo

Ibnu Sutowo was so closely identified with Pertamina and its extraordinary rise as a center of power that it is difficult to recount the history of one without the other. To his supporters, Ibnu epitomized the modern Indonesian, educated as a medical doctor, honed in the revolution as a leader of men; a nationalist who had succeeded in bending the powerful Western oil companies to his will; and, in an era that otherwise seemed dominated by foreign aid and investment, the one Indonesian who was finally gaining economic independence for Indonesia to match the political freedom it had won three decades earlier.

Ibnu was born into a family of rural gentry in Central Java. He attended medical school in Surabaya, was posted to South Sumatra, became head of the youth wing of the National Party there, and, by 1947, was chief of staff of the revolutionary army. After independence Ibnu returned to medicine, and stayed on in South Sumatra where he had married. The family was "in rubber" and wealthy. He retained his army status, and, in 1957, with rebellion spreading in Sumatra and other "outer" islands, Nasution asked Ibnu to come to Jakarta to help in the new martial law administration. According to an army officer close to General Nasution:

> He was in Palembang at the time of the . . . rebellion, and he had been running a barter trade with Singapore, just like a lot of others at the time. In fact, one of the reasons for bringing him to Jakarta was to cut down on the smuggling. His first assignment was as deputy chief of staff for administration, and in that position he supervised the staff responsible for logistics. The most valuable asset taken over from the Dutch was the oil fields, which included all the fields operating at the time, except for Caltex and Stanvac. He was put in charge of a team to oversee their operations, and when Permina was formed, he was made the first president-director. And that was the beginning of a whole series of things that gave the army, and the whole armed forces, a bad name.[14]

As head of Permina, known at the time as "the army company," Ibnu enlisted the help of an independent American oil man in 1958. With the American's funds and expertise, abandoned Shell fields in North Sumatra, now in army hands, were restored to marginal production; a small Japanese coastal tanker took the first exported product to Japan in that year. The Japanese themselves had a survey team visiting these same fields in 1958, and in 1960 they reached an agreement with Permina, providing $53 million in credits for equipment and technical assistance, to be repaid in crude oil. Meanwhile, Permina also bought its first river tankers.[15] Although this activity was conducted on an extremely small scale by the oil industry's standards, all the essential ingredients of Ibnu's later, large-scale operations were already present in this early experience: enlisting an independent American operator with technical expertise, borrowing capital from the Japanese, repaying the debt with crude oil, and getting into the tanker business on the side.

According to a long-time friend and associate:

> Ibnu was accountable only to the army leadership in the way he ran Permina. It was then one of two sources of foreign exchange for the army. The other was Colonel Jusuf in Makassar. . . . Jusuf controlled the rice exports from South Sulawesi; even when Java was in deficit, South Sulawesi rice was sold in Hong Kong for foreign exchange. These funds kept army troops loyal to their commanders for the next five years.[16]

The amounts must have been small at first; Permina was repaying the Japanese with 40 percent of its production.[17]

In any event, the principal oil fields were elsewhere, and dealing with the major foreign firms that held concessions to exploit them was high politics. The Indonesian constitution had provided that the nation's mineral resources were the property of the state, but a series of cabinets had been ambivalent about how to treat the concessions. The foreign oil firms—Royal Dutch Shell, Caltex, and Standard Vacuum—were a critical line to foreign exchange, and no Indonesian government could afford to risk that. A "let alone" policy prevailed all through the 1950s; even when all the other Dutch enterprises were taken over in 1958–59, Sukarno had not touched Shell. Nationalist sentiment had to be satisfied, however, and in 1960 Sukarno signed into law a decree providing that "the mining of oil and gas shall only be undertaken by the State" and that "mining undertakings of mineral oil and gas are exclusively carried out by State Enterprises." The foreign companies were dealt with in a further provision to the effect that: "The Minister may appoint other parties as contractors for the State Enterprises, if required for the execution of operations which can not or can not yet be executed by the State Enterprises involved as holders of the authority to mine themselves."[18]

The state enterprises that were to perform these functions did not exist at the time; even Permina was legally incorporated as a private company. This gap was filled in due course, however, and as nationalist feeling was rising over the founding of neighboring Malaysia, the foreign firms came under increasing pressure to come to terms with the government. In June 1963, after all-night negotiations in Tokyo in which U.S. government representatives participated, the three "majors" relinquished their concessions, and in return became contractors to what were now three small Indonesian state enterprises. The agreement also provided for the sale of their refineries and domestic distribution and marketing facilities.[19]

In 1965, with radical unionists staging walkouts and the Communist party calling for nationalization, Royal Dutch Shell had had enough. The coup attempt that occurred on September 30, 1965, did not appear to be altering things very much, and on December 31 Shell signed a contract of sale. This event soon provided Ibnu with another opportunity. On February 21, 1966, when Sukarno named his last 100-member cabinet, Ibnu was made minister for oil and gas. He retained the presidency of Permina. Before March was out, Ibnu had ordered the transfer of all oil exploration and production activities then in Indonesian hands to his own firm.

The final, seemingly inevitable step was taken the following year by a new minister of mining, Sumantri Brodjonegoro, a one-time aide to Nasution, a chemical engineer, and, at the time of his appointment to the cabinet, the president of the University of Indonesia. Sumantri recommended, and Soeharto approved, the creation of a single national oil company, to be known as Pertamina, and the appointment of Ibnu Sutowo as its president-director. Sumantri said later that his main purpose was to pool the country's limited manpower and capital. "This shortage of manpower was the single most important factor. I considered the concept of competition, but concluded that this would not override the other considerations."[20] It was hard not to think that among the other considerations was Soeharto's desire to see Ibnu given his head.

The new state oil corporation held a monopoly in every aspect of Indonesia's oil industry, including exploration, exploitation, refining, processing, transportation, and marketing. And it was free to negotiate agreements with any domestic or foreign party as its own management saw fit. The Indonesian oil push was now on in earnest, and Ibnu Sutowo was at the center of it. "Production sharing" contracts were signed with foreign oil firms in a continuing flurry of activity, thirty before 1969 was out, seven more in 1970, and another five in 1971.

By early 1975 Pertamina was operating seven oil refineries with a combined capacity of 400,000 barrels a day, a network of 2,680 domestic gasoline stations, and 29 joint-ventures and subsidiaries engaged in a wide range of activities, including the marketing of oil in Japan, the operation of a tanker fleet that rivaled the Indonesian navy in tonnage, the operation of a fleet of aircraft that rivaled the national airline, and much more. Pertamina was very large and very visible; according to its annual report for 1972, it had forty thousand employees. But it was still producing only a small part of the nation's oil. In 1972, the most recent year for which data were available, it was producing some 100,000 barrels a day, less than 10 percent of total production. The lion's share was produced by Caltex, which was pumping a million barrels a day and still working under a contract that did not involve any supervision by Pertamina.[21]

Pertamina in early 1975 also was on the way to becoming even larger. Its plans, all to be financed by foreign borrowings, included: two plants, estimated at $1 billion each, to produce liquified natural gas in Aceh, north Sumatra, and in East Kalimantan; petrochemical plants, estimated at $500 million each, to produce raw material for synthetic fiber production in South and North Sumatra; a novel floating fertilizer plant in East Kalimantan; and development of a major refining and transshipment center for petroleum products on Batam island, near Singapore, designed to compete directly with Singapore's oil processing industry. In addition to these and other oil-related ventures, Pertamina also was completing the construction of a steel mill in West Java, a project left unfinished by the Soviet Union in 1966, and estimated at an additional $1 billion.[22]

Ibnu Sutowo, it was said, knew how to get things done.

The Question of Corruption

These developments were not looked on with equal favor in all quarters in Jakarta. The nationalist sentiment among young people that erupted in the anti-Japanese outburst of early 1974 was aroused not only by the influx of Japanese investors, but also by the presence of hundreds of foreign, largely Western, oil men and their families whom Pertamina had introduced into the city. In addition, liberal-minded elements in the society were deeply offended by Ibnu's flamboyant life-style and accused him of corruption in public print.

The first public attack was launched by Mochtar Lubis in the pages of his newspaper, *Indonesia Raya,* in a series of articles and editorials between November 22 and 25 of 1969. Lubis charged that Pertamina was rapidly developing into a conglomerate whose activities had little to do with either the oil business or the government's economic plans. In a November 25 editorial the paper charged:

> According to reports . . . the current Pertamina leadership is not really particularly successful. . . . No figures on this can be obtained from Pertamina, because all data on the enterprise are kept secret on the pretext that oil is a vital and strategic commodity. . . . This pretext, however, is used to cover waste, inefficiency, and all kinds of irregularities and unjustifiable expenditures.[23]

Indonesia Raya also published a photograph of Ibnu posing with a new Rolls Royce, which it alleged had been imported as a Volkswagen. Lubis later said the government had protested his charges and had threatened to arrest him; but he had invited the government to take him to court—he had copies of documents to support his charges.

Within a matter of weeks of these accusations, the government increased the official price of gasoline and kerosene. The Jakarta cost of living index rose by 10 percent in a single week. Students demonstrated protesting the increases and corruption in the government. Soeharto responded by arranging for student delegations to meet with government officials to hear more detailed explanations of government policy. But the students were not convinced by these further accounts; on the contrary, they criticized the government economists for espousing theories that were far removed from the everyday realities of Indonesian life. On January 22 the public security agency banned student demonstrations, and schools were cordoned off by government troops.[24]

Having shown firmness, Soeharto then offered the students a conciliatory gesture. On January 31 he appointed the Commission of Four headed by Wilopo, the former prime minister, which, as we have seen, was critical of a number of government agencies and figured in the Malari riots of January 1974.

The Commission was especially uncomplimentary regarding Pertamina. It began the first of two reports to Soeharto on the subject with this preamble:

Just becoming a big enterprise . . . is not too difficult if it is singled out by the Government to become the only oil enterprise controlling assets of the People and State that are extremely attractive to the international world. More important is how these assets, which are extremely large, and are not renewable, are managed so as to secure the development of the State.[25]

As to Pertamina's management, the Commission reported that it had found much neglect of and deviation from the regulations set by the Minister of Mining. If this continued, the Commission observed, "there will come about a working situation in which a person will no longer know what is permitted and what is prohibited."[26]

Specifically, the Commission said, Pertamina was obligated to pay 55 percent of its profits to the government, but this had not been done in nine of the previous eleven years. Pertamina also did not pay corporate taxes in the amounts due.[27] (A subsequent report said that Pertamina and its predecessors paid no taxes at all for the years 1958 through 1963, filed no tax return for two or three years thereafter, and owed escalating amounts of unpaid taxes since.[28])

The Commission concluded that Pertamina had to become the joint responsibility of all its senior managers, not just its executive director. And it needed to be monitored by a board of commissioners composed of independent experts like the Minister of Finance.[29]

Reflecting liberal opinion in Jakarta, J. A. C. Mackie went on to discuss aspects of the case that the Commission did not raise in its reports:

It has long been common knowledge that a large part of Pertamina's oil revenues has not been paid into the state treasury, but has remained under the control of Ibnu Sutowo who has made use of it in his own ways, either as "unconventional finance" for the armed forces and other parts of the government or for diverse purposes of Pertamina or himself. There has been no public accounting for these funds. The figures for Pertamina's unpaid taxes given in the Commission's report are the first official estimates of the magnitude involved (and these may not tell the whole story). Much of the expenditure has undoubtedly been for the business purposes of Pertamina. . . . In addition, however, large outlays have been made over the last few years by Pertamina, or Ibnu Sutowo personally, for all sorts of social welfare and semi-political purposes. . . . He has been able to maintain a high degree of independence despite the efforts of several Ministers of Mining to bring him under tighter control.[30]

The revelation of the Commission reports to the public by *Sinar Harapan* gave considerable support to those both inside and outside the government who already believed that Pertamina needed to be brought under control.

The Problem of the Controllers

The law creating Pertamina in 1968 had made its president-director responsible to the Minister of Mines, had required him to provide the Minister with extensive financial reports, and had given the Minister veto power over both operating and capital budgets. But this one-to-one relationship was not sufficient to provide any serious oversight when, as was routinely the case, Ibnu Sutowo chose to ignore the Minister. The attention given this matter by the Commission of Four obliged the government to do something, and the upshot was a new law, Law no. 8 of 1971, which brought about a real change.

Pertamina was now placed under a board of directors comprised of the ministers of mining, finance, and national planning; these at the time were three of the president's principal economic advisers, former professors Sadli, Wardhana, and Widjojo. The board was given sweeping powers to determine Pertamina's policy, supervise its management, and approve its budgets, plans, loans above an amount to be stipulated by the board, the founding of subsidiary and joint-venture companies, sales and purchase agreements, and executive salaries, among other things. In addition, the new law required Pertamina to remit to the state treasury the entire proceeds obtained under the "work contract" with Caltex and sixty percent of the net operating income obtained under its "production-sharing" contracts with other producers, sixty percent of production bonuses payable under the latter, and sixty percent of Pertamina's own net operating income.[31]

The 1971 law brought about a significant change in the government's revenues. Oil tax receipts as a share of oil exports went from 33 percent in 1969–70 to 48 percent in 1971–72; in the latter year, oil surpassed foreign aid as a source of government finance for the first time. But a still more significant change occurred in the price of oil on the world market as a result of events in the Middle East, highlighted by the Arab oil embargo of October 1973. A barrel of oil, which had been worth $2.00 at the end of 1970, reached $3.70 in mid-1973, and more than $12.00 by mid-1974. Indonesia's oil exports leapt in value from $590 million in 1971–72 to more than $3 billion in 1974–75. As a result, oil revenues in the latter year for the first time amounted to more than half the government's entire income from domestic sources.[32]

Ibnu Sutowo's strategy of actively recruiting foreign firms obviously was paying off, and the enterprise appeared to be a huge success. The argument that the spectacular rise in oil income was owing to external events seemed small-minded, and members of the Pertamina board found it impossible to veto Ibnu's plans. As one member of the new board of directors observed: "Soeharto was always ambivalent when it came to a choice between the economists and the entrepreneurs. He was strongly attracted to the clarity of macro-analysis. But he also admired people like Ibnu who could get things done. We were aware of this, and had to take it into account."[33]

Another consideration was Ibnu's standing in the international business community. In his address to Parliament in May 1975 Sadli said that the government had agreed to Pertamina's carrying out various non-oil ventures "so as to take advantage of Pertamina's potential and the confidence that is held in Pertamina in the business world—especially the foreign business world—in order to attract overseas capital to Indonesia."[34]

Ibnu, confident of the president's support and that of the international business community, continued to keep his board at arm's length. The Minister of Finance was said to have difficulty learning what the foreign oil companies were paying to Pertamina. And what Pertamina was able to count as its share, it spent. Sadli reported in mid-1974 that Pertamina's budget for fiscal year 1974–75 was Rp. 777 billion ($1.9 billion), a sum equal to about half the government budget. Yet, its taxable net profits were not expected to exceed Rp. 2 billion ($5 million).[35]

If events had gone no further than this, Ibnu might have survived at the head of Pertamina for a long time. But it was exactly in these circumstances, with everything going his way, that Ibnu overreached himself. According to the Sadli report to Parliament, Ibnu secretly took on two large financial commitments. One was to increase the planned capacity of the steel plant from 500,000 tons to 2 million tons. The other was to enter contracts for the hire-purchase of oceangoing tankers.[36]

The Role of Foreign Banks

Foreign banks began to be a political factor in Jakarta as early as 1970, and they became a powerful force with the arrival of the oil companies. The editor of a leading Jakarta daily newspaper later recalled: "In 1972 or 1973, if Ibnu wanted a loan, the banks would rush to provide it, even if the Minister of Finance did not approve." The center of power began to shift away from the government economists dealing with foreign governments and their aid agencies. "When the foreign oil companies came in," said the editor, "Ibnu Sutowo quickly became a major power, able to ignore Widjojo and the rest."[37]

Erland Heginbotham, who was the economic counselor of the U.S. embassy in Jakarta during these years, said in later testimony before a U.S. Senate subcommittee:

> I think it is fair to say that General Ibnu was clearly an international glamor stock in his early days. The appeal that his operations had to an immense diversity of interests was very great. Lined up at his door were not only bankers but suppliers and a variety of other financial institutions. . . . There was a developing fever pitch of interest in Pertamina's activities and what opportunities that might have for the banking sector.[38]

Heginbotham attributed the foreign interest in part to Ibnu Sutowo's personal style. "Ibnu relied on very rapid decision making, and on his personal contacts with international financial and government officials. He moved quickly. He put projects into being rapidly and got a rapid payback, generally in self-liquidating activities." These qualities earned him the respect of his own president and of the international oil and banking communities. Indeed, Ibnu "acquired . . . a considerable international status and had ready access to heads of government in a variety of major industrial countries."[39]

Starting in about 1971 Ibnu was assigned a number of development projects and was left to find the money to finance them. "It was the tendency of the President to turn to General Ibnu, in whom he had great confidence, and say, General, here is an important project, we would like you to get it done, and nobody discussed where the money was to come from."[40] By early 1972 it was known in banking circles that Pertamina was borrowing substantially in Europe, and in some cases on unfavorable terms. The U.S. embassy was approached by U.S. banks for advice about lending to Pertamina, but had great difficulty in "getting any kind of indication of the volume of the credit that was being acquired."[41] The International Monetary Fund (IMF) also was concerned, but had equal difficulty in obtaining information. "They could not find Indonesian Government officials who were willing to take on inquiring of General Ibnu as to exactly what he was doing."[42]

In these circumstances the IMF pressed for and obtained an agreement with the Indonesian government in March 1972 setting a limit on the volume of medium-term loans that the government and its agencies could make—loans with a maturity of between one and fifteen years. The Fund monitored Indonesian performance by requesting information from the governments of countries whose banks were believed to be lending considerable amounts to Pertamina, and from these sources learned that Pertamina was breaching the ceiling. Under further pressure from the Fund, Soeharto signed a decree in October 1972 requiring all state enterprises to obtain the approval of the Minister of Finance and the governor of Bank Indonesia before negotiating any medium-term loans from international sources.[43]

Bankers found two ways to skirt the IMF agreement and the Soeharto decree. One was to make a loan for more than fifteen years, but provide for the bulk of it to be repaid in five to ten years. Another was to lend money for less than a year and when it fell due, simply "roll it over"—lend it again for less than a year. The U.S. embassy made representations to U.S. bankers, at least from early 1973 on, Heginbotham said, to cooperate with government authorities by avoiding these circumventions. But these efforts were not effective. With oil prices rising, bankers saw Pertamina as a good credit risk. If they did not agree to circumvent the IMF ceiling, their competitors would. And it seemed inconceivable that the Indonesian government would permit a Pertamina default.[44]

The result was unrestrained Pertamina borrowing, until, that is, a series of events altered the entire situation in the latter part of 1974. Toward the end of the year the rise in oil prices was causing a recession in such industrial economies as those of the United States, Germany, and Japan. The demand for oil was slackening. Some major banks collapsed, including Franklin National in the United States and Herstadt in Germany. And in the wave of caution that swept the financial community, liquidity tightened in the international markets. Some of the smaller banks among Pertamina's international creditors decided it was time to get their money out.

This situation found Pertamina in a highly exposed position. Sadli said in his May 20 statement that, from 1973 on, Pertamina "always exceeded the ceiling that had been laid down by a wide margin." Rachmat Saleh said that Pertamina was borrowing so heavily in foreign capital markets that it was preempting the government's ability to raise money for itself.[45]

Ibnu told a local reporter in January 1976 that the only real trouble was the failure of a major long-term loan from foreign sources to materialize:

> The problem was that in 1974 we made an agreement for a twenty-year loan. The total involved was $1.7 billion. We regarded the loan as secured—the loan agreement had already been signed. Because the money had to be taken in a lump sum—this was part of the agreement—we took steps to use the funds to initiate projects, including Krakatau Steel and Batam Island. We obtained short-term loans which were essentially bridging finance. Well, the long-term credit did not come, and that was the problem. I still don't understand why the loan disappeared, just like that.[46]

Ibnu said that the loan was to come from a source in the Middle East, offered by letter from a London bank. Sadli said later that the government had assented to the deal. A number of commentators have since suggested that Ibnu—and the Indonesian government with him—probably were the victims of confidence men. A remarkably similar experience, at almost the same time, befell the Australian Minister for Mines and Energy, R. F. X. Connor, leading to his resignation and a series of difficulties that eventuated in the fall of Prime Minister Gough Whitlam's government.

That Ibnu did not resign was owing in part to his character. He believed that the technocrats were exaggerating the default. Equally important was Soeharto's continued confidence in him. That confidence was shaken only later, with the uncovering of Ibnu's dealings in the international tanker business.

The Tanker Deals

Pertamina was responsible for the entire domestic distribution of oil and oil products, and, in an island nation, that meant that Pertamina was immersed in the shipping business. A government planning document projected the size of Pertamina's tanker fleet for 1974–75 at 114 ships, representing 1.87 million DWT, more than half of which was on hire-purchase.[47] Another source put the fleet at almost 3.0 million tons at the end of 1974. This was more tonnage than the Indonesian navy.[48]

A mutual interest in tankers brought Ibnu Sutowo into contact with Bruce Rappaport, a Geneva businessman, in 1966. Several press accounts have described Rappaport as having started out in the business of providing ships with supplies in ports around the world, and having gone on to become a ship broker, arranging deals between ship owners and people who wanted to use them. Ibnu Sutowo and Rappaport developed close relations, and Ibnu sent a considerable share of Pertamina's tanker business his way. Rappaport named one of the tankers he chartered to Pertamina the "Ibnu," and named one of his firms "Rasu Maritima," an acronym from the first letters of his and Ibnu's names.

Rappaport was said to be secretive, and this may have accounted for Ibnu's behavior in his dealings with him. Some Pertamina agreements with Rappaport firms were unknown even to senior Pertamina staff, and it was these that became a center of controversy as the veils were removed from Ibnu's activities in the course of 1975. The agreements concerned large, oceangoing tankers, and it was not clear what Pertamina intended to do with them. One guess was that they were to be used for "spot charter" in the Middle East.[49]

Contracts for these tankers were written at different times between September 1970 and July 1974. The agreements provided for Pertamina to acquire the tankers on a hire-purchase basis. Thirteen ships were involved, at a total cost of $1.4 billion, payable over a period of ten to twelve years.[50] All but the first of these agreements were signed after the 1971 legislation requiring Ibnu to obtain his board of directors' approval for such transactions; Sadli told the Indonesian Parliament in May 1975 that no such approval had ever been given or even sought.

Ibnu had made a huge and imprudent gamble. The high price of oil after the 1973 embargo led to decreased demand, oil shipments around the world declined in the course of 1974, and the bottom fell out of the tanker market.

In January 1975, when the Pertamina loan from the Middle East evaporated and the corporation was approaching default, Ibnu and

Rappaport met in New York and London to discuss their situation. Rappaport was being pressed by his creditors, who wanted reassurance that their contracts with him would hold. Rappaport pressed Ibnu for assurance that Pertamina would stand by its contracts with him. On one of these occasions, according to an affidavit later executed by Ibnu and submitted to a court in New York, Ibnu signed "approximately 1,600" promissory notes without reading them.[51]

Although Ibnu said in his affidavit that the notes were merely intended for Rappaport to show to worried ship owners, that seems highly improbable. Rappaport had a reputation for being highly attentive to the legal aspects of the shipping trade. His agreements with Pertamina were made in the name of four different corporations, all registered in different countries. One team of reporters who investigated the case concluded that if the whole truth were ever to be uncovered, "it would probably be necessary to ransack lawyers' offices from New York to Jakarta, Panama, London, Hongkong, Monrovia, Oslo, Bermuda, Geneva and Singapore."[52] Rappaport himself told a visiting reporter early in 1977 that he had "fought in courts around the world" to get his money ahead of other creditors when another shipping empire ran into financial trouble in the early 1960s.[53] With large amounts of money at stake in a volatile market, contract disputes were common in the shipping trade, and the notes gave Rappaport a stronger hand in the event the Pertamina deals went sour and he had to go to court to recover the ships.

When Pertamina defaulted on its repayment of the bank loan in February 1975, payments to various creditors, including Rappaport's firms, were reduced. When Major General Haryono was installed as director of Pertamina's financial affairs in May, the payments reportedly stopped altogether. That same month, according to Ibnu's affidavit, a Rappaport associate flew to Jakarta, met with Ibnu, and gave him a check for $2.5 million. The purpose of the payment is not known; presumably it was intended to enlist Ibnu's cooperation, either to get the payments renewed, or to help in the legal contest that would ensue if they were not. Ibnu said in his affidavit that the money was a personal loan, but he conceded that he had not repaid it a year-and-a-half later.[54]

Both sides had incentives to reach a settlement. The Indonesian government could not have wished to produce Ibnu Sutowo in a foreign court of law; under cross-examination on a witness stand, he might well make statements even more embarrassing to the government than what was already publicly known. In addition, Pertamina was now technically in default to Rappaport's companies, and the government had to work energetically to keep its foreign bankers from breaking ranks. Rappaport, meanwhile, was under pressure from the ship owners. Sanko Steamship Co. of Japan, for example, was suing one of Rappaport's companies for $10 million that it claimed it was owed for tankers it had chartered to Rappaport for rechartering to Pertamina.[55]

Ibnu Sutowo, interviewed in February 1977—on a golf course in Palm Springs, California, where he and his son were playing in the Bob Hope Desert Classic—did not find fault with Rappaport. Government restrictions had caused the problems with Pertamina's loans, he said, because they hampered his former ability to bargain. The "unexpected seriousness" of the world recession added to the problem. But he still thought Pertamina might have weathered the storm had the Indonesian government not stepped in. He also criticized the government's effort to renege on his agreements with Rappaport. That was just bad business practice, he said. It would have made more sense to talk the problem out.[56]

Three weeks later it was disclosed in Jakarta that Ibnu and at least twenty of his associates were under house arrest. The tanker case was said to be one of the reasons, but another was a broadening of the government inquiry into Ibnu's private business interests. It was reported that Pertamina was believed to have done hundreds of millions of dollars worth of business with thirty-five private corporations owned in whole or in part by Ibnu and his associates.[57]

Finally, in August 1977, more than two years after the unauthorized tanker deals were discovered, it was reported that an out-of-court settlement had been reached in the case. It was probably the only decision the Indonesians could have reached. Remaining in the ocean-tanker market was too risky a business for the Indonesian government—probably too risky for any government—to be in. But the cost of Ibnu's gamble was a high one to come out of a poor country's treasury.

A government minister later said that the case was the worst example of Ibnu's mismanagement. "The tanker deals alone involved $3.3 billion, and it cost us $300 million, and cases in 14 courts all over the world, to terminate them. . . . It took us two or three years to clean up the mess."[58]

7. The Pertamina Crisis

The Future of Pertamina

The Pertamina crisis had widespread implications for the Indonesian government and economy. The crisis had an immediate impact on the government's foreign debt, although the full dimensions did not become clear for a year or more, and on the foreign oil companies under contract to Pertamina. The crisis also had consequences for Ibnu Sutowo and for the expansive approach to industrialization that he represented. The first task, in addition to getting control of the financial situation, was deciding what to do with Pertamina.

The state of affairs inside Pertamina was revealed only layer by layer in the course of 1975. The organization had twenty separate units reporting directly to the president-director, and six separate systems of accounts.

One official suggested that the initial problem was simply one of getting an accurate picture of the financial situation in the face of Pertamina's disorderly bookkeeping. "It wasn't a matter of trying to hide anything. There was no secrecy. They themselves did not know the details."[59]

The economic ministers were openly contemptuous of Ibnu's performance as head of the enterprise. "The scale of mismanagement in Pertamina was enormous," said one. "When we reviewed the contracts, we found that less than half the dollar total could be justified as proper investments."[60]

One of the principal sources of Pertamina's internal disarray was the speed with which the enterprise had grown. Most of its subsidiaries and joint ventures were created in a single eighteen-month period in 1973 and 1974. The growing volume and complexity of Pertamina's business overwhelmed the staff. "They just signed anything that came through the mail."[61]

The difficulty was also structural. With so many lines of authority leading to the president-director, no one could possibly have managed the enterprise efficiently. What is surprising is that it took Soeharto until December 1975, acting on the army investigators' recommendation, to issue a decree streamlining Pertamina's internal structure.[62]

Pertamina's problems were compounded by its expansion into fields unrelated to oil. The steel mill was the most obvious case, but there were numerous others as well. As the organization became increasingly active in fields in which its staff had no experience, the odds favoring misjudgment and mischance increased.

With Ibnu heavily engaged in arranging international deals, and with the staff unsupervised, venturing beyond their expertise, and handling increasingly large flows of funds, corruption flourished. In October it was reported that some forty top officials in Pertamina had been fired.[63] Indeed, the trail of corruption seemed unending. In 1977 a court case in Singapore revealed that a former Sutowo associate, Achmad Thahir, whom Sutowo had put in charge of the Krakatau Steelworks, died leaving $35 million in Singapore bank accounts; a schedule of payments suggested that he had been receiving kickbacks of 5 percent on Krakatau's payments to West German firms.[64] His widow argued that the funds were rightly part of Thahir's estate because such commissions were "an ordinary thing" in Indonesia, and she later charged that an equal amount of commission was shared by Ibnu Sutowo and others.[65]

The government had decided as early as May 1976 to reduce Pertamina's scale of operations, although the actual process of deciding what to do in individual cases extended into the following year. Some projects were canceled altogether, such as the controversial floating fertilizer plant. Others were deferred indefinitely, including the petrochemical projects planned for Sumatra and the proposed development of Batam island. Still others were scaled down and transferred to government departments. The largest of all, the Krakatau Steelworks, which was found to be a victim of large-scale overpricing by its contractors and large-scale corruption by its managing director, was reorganized, its plans reduced to their original size, and the project returned to the department of industries.

The only active major projects that remained with Pertamina were the LNG plants. These were, however, the most lucrative of all. The Intergovernmental Group on Indonesia (IGGI) had already cleared loans for these projects as exceptions to the debt ceiling, in view of Japanese readiness to provide the extra capital needed to develop them—and to buy the LNG that resulted. The East Kalimantan plant, a joint venture with Huffco, went into production in 1977; the Arun plant in Sumatra, a joint venture with Mobil, in 1978. Their joint earnings exceeded $1 billion in 1979.[66]

The net result of these decisions was not to reduce the size of Pertamina appreciably; it remained a very large organization, almost certainly the largest employer in the country after the government itself. No public reports were made for a decade. A veil was drawn firmly over its affairs and was not lifted until 1985. In May of that year, Minister of Mines and Energy Subroto declared that Pertamina was accountable and auditable for the first time, and that its debt to the central bank had finally been paid. As of March 30, he said, Pertamina had assets of $11.7 billion, income of $9.59 billion, expenditures of $6.65 billion, and a profit before taxes of $2.9 billion. No figures were given for prior years.[67]

In these circumstances, whether Pertamina was any more efficient than it had been a decade before was impossible to say.

The Dismissal of Ibnu

Soeharto distanced himself from Pertamina's problems. Any political leader would have done the same, but it bespeaks his style, and the strength of his position, that he maintained a majestic silence on the subject for all of 1975. In January 1976 he was scheduled to give his annual budget message to the Parliament, and Pertamina could no longer be ignored. He reviewed the financial history that had first been officially described by Sadli the previous May, although without reference to the government's lack of knowledge of some of Pertamina's undertakings. He acknowledged that the "difficulties" Pertamina experienced would have "serious consequences for national development." They involved "huge amounts of money." The amount needed simply to meet Pertamina's domestic obligations was "enormous."[68]

These admissions could not have come easily for Soeharto, and by this time it was rumored in Jakarta that Ibnu was to be replaced. A dignified departure was said to be planned for some time in the first half of the year.[69] The findings of the army and civilian investigators, who had been poring over Pertamina's affairs for more than six months, left Soeharto no other choice. An army officer involved in the investigation said that Ibnu's venture into the international tanker trade was the final straw.[70] According to a friend of the president-director: "They laid out the situation, and it was clear that Ibnu had to go."[71]

The decision was long in coming, and several factors seem to have been responsible for Soeharto's delay.

Some saw the delay as a classic example of Soeharto's traditional leadership style. A historian said: "The problem of confronting a close friend with damaging information, the concern to avoid reducing a man's status in public—this is why the process was so prolonged. No Western, and no modern Asian, leader would have failed to act expeditiously in such a case."[72]

The editor of a major daily newspaper observed:

> It took Soeharto a long time to change his mind about Ibnu Sutowo. That decision came very late, after Widjojo and Ali Wardhana had submitted a whole series of reports about what they were finding out about the situation in Pertamina. Ibnu gave money to many people; he supplied the extra-budgetary fund of the president. Also, Ibnu was seen as a balance to the Western-trained economists. Ibnu was seen as a nationalist by comparison. The president has always looked for balance.[73]

Ibnu helped to prolong the process by his own behavior; a graceful departure was not going to be easy to arrange. He was not cooperative with the men appointed to look into his activities. According to a friend:

> As the investigations widened—for example, into the tanker deals—Ibnu was interviewed at home. At one point he blew up, threw the investigators out, and complained to (General) Panggabean (the army chief of staff) that they had been rude. Soeharto ordered a three-star general to be present on all future occasions. But Ibnu also was asked to stay near his phone and avoid company for a while.[74]

Ibnu's free-handed patronage had won him many friends. It is known that he helped provincial governors with projects that were locally significant in the late 1960s. He sat on the Golkar board and was reliably reported to have been the main source of its funds for the 1971 election campaign.

"There was hardly an army commander in the regions who didn't get help for some local project," according to an associate. When Soeharto began to face up to the task of dropping Ibnu in late December, according to this source, he turned to the army chief of staff.

> Soeharto called in Panggabean . . . and laid out the situation to him. Panggabean said he wanted to clear the plan to drop Ibnu with his commanders, with the heads of 10 or so major units. . . . They agreed, on the understanding that Ibnu would never go to jail. Soeharto accepted these terms but added another of his own: "provided he never talks."[75]

Up to this point the two men had avoided a personal break, but one seems to have occurred in February, at the time of the first meeting of the heads of government of ASEAN on the island of Bali. Having read the foreign press accounts of his rumored departure, Ibnu issued an announcement through Pertamina early in the month that he was taking "a long leave of absence" in the United States; no date was set for his return. On February 23, as the leaders gathered in Bali—at a Pertamina resort complex—Ibnu unexpectedly appeared on the scene and took Ferdinand Marcos, the president of the Philippines, off in a helicopter to play golf. "Soeharto was really upset by that," according to a friend. "He realized the issue was who was running the country."[76]

The final act came swiftly after this. It was said that Minister Sadli, who was chairman of the Pertamina board, had never called Ibnu to his office. Now he did: "He told Ibnu he had three alternatives: remain as a figurehead, resign, or be fired. Ibnu couldn't believe it. He didn't think Sadli would dare to do this. It took him some time to realize that the message was from Soeharto."[77]

Soeharto avoided a personal confrontation to the very end. It was announced that Ibnu was being dismissed "with honor." Major General Harjono was named as "acting" in his place. Only later, with Ibnu again abroad, did Soeharto install Harjono as president-director at a ceremony attended by the entire cabinet.

Ibnu never went to jail. He also did not talk, except once, to the reporter on the golf course in Palm Springs. Three weeks later it was disclosed that Ibnu and twenty associates were being detained in the widening government inquiry into their personal business affairs. He was not in the news again until July 1978, when the attorney general, Ali Said, announced that all investigations were at an end and that Ibnu had been found "not involved" in any criminal activity.[78]

The Foreign Oil Companies

The principal means the government used to recoup the Pertamina losses was to take more money from the foreign oil companies.

In May 1975, in his address on oil problems to the Parliament, Sadli charged that the foreign firms were making excessive profits. It was no more than "just," he said, that they should be taxed more heavily. This was only in accordance with the aspirations of all developing countries as expressed in their calls for a New International Economic Order.[79] According to one industry source, the basis for Sadli's charge was a memorandum by members of the IMF staff that compared the share of oil profits being received by the Indonesian government with those being received by governments in the Persian Gulf.[80]

In his budget speech of January 1976 Soeharto announced that the government planned an increase in oil revenues to a new total of $4 billion. This would require "the reduction of the profits gained by oil companies on each barrel of crude they produce," effective January 1. The government, he said, "sincerely seeks the understanding of the oil companies concerned."[81]

Sadli elaborated on the government proposal. Pertamina had contracts at the time with forty-eight foreign oil companies, which had invested a total of more than $1.2 billion and were producing more than 90 percent of Indonesia's crude output, estimated at 1.3 million barrels a day. The two long-time American producers now accounted for about 70 percent of total production, and the other forty-six foreign firms for about 20 percent. The government proposed to renegotiate the contracts with all these firms. The basic split had been 65:35 in the government's favor. The split was now to be 85:15.[82]

The two American firms were still operating outside the production-sharing system, and Caltex Pacific Indonesia was by far the largest company in the industry, producing 900,000 barrels a day. The government proposed to collect an extra $1.00 out of Caltex's estimated $2.00 to $2.30 profit per barrel. That meant taking about $300 million of Caltex's estimated $600 to $700 million annual earnings.

The oil firms were understandably angry. They argued that Indonesia's oil profits could not be compared directly with those of the Middle East. Indonesia had only one large oil reservoir, the Minas field of Caltex, and that was an old field requiring increasingly costly methods of recovery. Otherwise, Indonesia had a large number of widely scattered small fields, and these required a high level of continuing exploration. Pertamina officials also were opposed to the government proposal. The implication was that they had been receiving payoffs to let the foreign firms get away with excess profits.[83]

The first payment was due April 15, and by late March Soeharto was personally involved in meetings with Caltex officials. The ultimatum stuck. On April 15 Julius Tahija, president-director of the firm, called on Soeharto to inform him that the corporation had acquiesced.[84]

The principal lesson drawn from the experience has been the obvious one, that the sovereign government of a poor country will take what opportunities it can to assert itself in dealing with foreign firms extracting a nonrenewable natural resource. But two other observations are worth recording. One was that a negative attitude toward foreign oil companies could not be sustained without inhibiting further foreign investment in the industry, and thus jeopardizing Indonesia's long-term oil prospects. Oil rigs were already down by about a third from the boom years of 1973 and 1974, and there were doubts about how far into the 1990s Indonesia's proven reserves would last. The other was that oil income, even with the recent increase, was not going to solve the government's long-term problem of meeting its increased foreign debt.[85]

The Foreign Debt

The IGGI was scheduled to meet in March 1976, and at the center of the agenda was the state of Indonesian monetary affairs in the wake of the Pertamina crisis. Donor governments already had received a report from the World Bank that was described as "somber" and was said to suggest that Indonesia faced a "staggering" need for $3.4 billion in foreign loans in the coming year and heavy debt-servicing requirements for the next decade. The impact of Pertamina's spending spree in 1974 was evident. Earlier figures had shown that service of the foreign debt would peak in 1976 at $348 million and remain below that level until 1985. The new projection was that debt service would rise annually through this entire period, starting at $813 million in 1976 and rising annually to $3.1 billion in 1985.[86]

The Indonesian economic ministers were reasonably well prepared for this occasion. Ibnu Sutowo had been removed from Pertamina (the timing perhaps influenced by the IGGI date), commercial loans syndicated by American and Japanese banks had replenished the central bank's holdings of foreign exchange, and the "lumpy" investment cases of the Krakatau Steelworks and the LNG plants were under discussion with the German and Japanese governments. With the exception of possible losses in the case of the oceangoing tanker fleet, the financial hemorrhage had been brought to a halt. It did require a buoyant view of export earnings, and a national economic growth rate of about 7.5 percent a year for the next decade. But, given these, the government would manage to keep the servicing of its foreign debt just under the danger level of 20 percent of export earnings.[87]

The governments of the industrial democracies did not disappoint the Indonesian government. The request for about $1.4 billion in concessional and semiconcessional financing was accepted. So was the proposal for about $1 billion more in export credit and related financing. In addition, in a break with past practice, the IGGI members pledged themselves to helping raise an additional $1 billion in emergency finance to help meet cost overruns on several large Pertamina projects, later identified as the Krakatau Steelworks and the LNG complexes.[88]

Even so, while the short-term problem had been met, the long-term one was awesome. Before the Indonesian government assumed responsibility for Pertamina's foreign obligations, its foreign debt was estimated at $5.6 billion. The size of Pertamina's obligations was still not firmly established; estimates of the total varied between $6.2 and $11 billion, a substantial portion of which would, in the ordinary course of events, be repaid from operating profits. Pertamina's short-term debts alone, however, was on the order of $1.0 billion, and that was enough to increase the government's indebtedness by 18 percent. The larger problem was that another $4.3 billion of Pertamina's obligations had been transferred to other agencies, including prominently the central bank. Altogether, the government's decision to "bail out" its state oil enterprise had more or less doubled its foreign debt.[89]

The final cost of the Pertamina spending spree probably will never be known. Too many of its obligations were moved to too many other entities, and merged there with much else—" swept under the rug," as one not unsympathetic observer remarked.[90] The net result, however, was to increase the government's long-term foreign debt substantially, and to narrow its freedom of action in many years to come. When oil prices were on the rise in the international market, as in 1979, there was even, for a brief period, a new round of fevered interest in large-scale projects. But when oil prices fell, as they did from late 1981 on, debt management was again a major preoccupation, and government options were seriously limited. Thus, one result of the Ibnu era at Pertamina was not to free the Indonesian economy from foreign interests at all, but to anchor it even more deeply in interdependence with the rest of the world.

Oil and National Development

The Pertamina crisis inevitably focused attention at the time on its more lurid aspects, the unrestrained foreign borrowing that provoked it, the billion-dollar projects at stake, the multimillion-dollar corruption that came to light, and the fate of the personalities involved. But larger questions were at issue. These had to do with the role of oil and oil money in the economy, with the sort of development strategy the government was to pursue with its newfound wealth.

One consequence of the early expansion of exploration and production pressed by Ibnu Sutowo was to enable Indonesia to capitalize more fully than would otherwise have been the case on the oil "booms" of the 1970s. World oil prices quadrupled following the Yom Kippur War of 1973, and tripled again following the fall of the Shah of Iran in 1979. Indonesia received an initial windfall of $4.2 billion in 1974, the equivalent of a bonus of 16.5 percent of its nonmining Gross Domestic Product (GDP). The bonus continued at about 16 percent through 1978. Then the earlier "boom" was repeated, increasing the size of the windfall to 26 percent by 1980. As early as 1981, however, the second boom ended, and Indonesia lost oil exports worth almost 9 percent of its nonmining GDP.[91] Prices remained depressed until August 1990, when Iraq occupied Kuwait.

The oil windfall was in most respects worth less to Indonesia than to any other oil-exporting country in the developing world. In dollars per capita, because of its large population, Indonesia's windfall was extremely modest by comparison with all the rest. Even in total dollars the Indonesian windfall was much smaller than that of countries with better established oil industries, such as Nigeria and Venezuela. And as a percentage of GDP, because of the rich diversity of its other resources, Indonesia's oil windfall was smaller than in these countries or in, for example, Algeria.[92]

The oil windfall in Indonesia was similar to many others in one respect: most of the windfall accrued to the government. As Indonesia's net energy exports increased from about $1 billion in 1973 to $13.3 billion in 1980, the share of energy in total exports went from 45 percent to 70 percent, and the government's reliance on oil taxes reached 70 percent of domestic revenues in the 1981–82 budget.[93] The oil boom thus greatly enhanced a process already begun with foreign aid. The government's need to develop a broader tax base, which would have required that it give more weight to the views of a tax-paying citizenry, was postponed. Ideas about decentralization were stillborn as the new financial resources of "the center" were translated into political reality. Hopes of deregulating the economy also were dashed as, in the wake of the Pertamina crisis, controls over state corporations were expanded. And incentives to promote other products for export, which would have brought income into the hands of at least some of the population without direct government involvement, especially in the long-suffering "outer islands," ceased to be a matter of high public priority. Much the same happened in other countries that also experienced an oil windfall.[94]

One of the costs of easy oil money was that the Indonesian public came to view oil products as more or less free goods. The protest that greeted the domestic oil price increase in 1970 was not an isolated incident, and the government continued to find extreme difficulty in eliminating the subsidy. Pertamina sold its refined products domestically at far below the world market price; they were the lowest in Southeast Asia at least into the early 1980s. At first, the cost was hidden in the Pertamina budget. From 1977–78 on, as part of the process of accounting for Pertamina's profits and losses in a businesslike way, the subsidy was made an item in the government budget, and, within a few years, ballooned to such a size that it came to rival the entire government payroll. This artificial pricing of oil at home had several negative results. It absorbed government revenues that might have been put to better use. It encouraged rapid domestic consumption of oil products, threatening the share of oil available for export. And it skewed the prices of other goods and services, including electricity, transport, and cement, and this, in turn, had the effect of encouraging capital-intensive investment.[95] An increase in electricity charges in 1989 was greeted with outrage by parliamentarians, who were not consulted, and oil products were still being sold in Indonesia at subsidized prices in 1990.[96] There is evidence from other countries that a more open political system might well have produced even larger consumer subsidies.[97]

The largest share of the windfall in Indonesia, as in many other countries, was allocated to public investment. It has been calculated that 49 percent of the first price rise and 36 percent of the second one went to domestic investment in Indonesia. What is unusual and perhaps unique in the Indonesian case is the portion of this investment that went into agriculture and rural development. Bruce Glassburner has estimated that 13 percent of development spending in 1973–74 to 1977–78 went into agriculture, including irrigation; fertilizer subsidies averaged another 11 percent. In addition, much of the spending on physical infrastructure—which was 43 percent of development spending— went to rural public works. In Nigeria, by comparison, agriculture received 2.5 percent of federal capital outlays, and public works did not extend beyond trunk roads.[98]

A final outcome of the oil windfall in all oil exporting countries was enhanced public investment in industry. This often took the form of large, capital-intensive projects, usually designed to increase the indigenous role in the oil industry or to promote the development of non-oil sectors. It is in this respect that, as some in Jakarta like to say, the Pertamina crisis was "a blessing in disguise." Because of the crisis, many large projects, including projects in petrochemicals, were delayed in starting; when the slump occurred in the early 1980s it was still possible to cancel or reschedule them. Also, because of the losses attributable to the Krakatau Steel venture, and the cost overruns on the LNG projects, the government was cautious about commitments to other large undertakings, and foreign funding was arranged to cover most of the costs of later projects, such as the Asahan aluminum complex in Aceh. As a result, Indonesia's behavior was more conservative with respect to industrial development than was that of many other oil-exporters, and the international involvement helped to ensure foreign market access and a favorable rate of return.[99]

Nevertheless, the appeal of heavy industry did not disappear from the Indonesian scene. Ibnu Sutowo articulated the proponents' view in an article published in February 1976, when his departure from Pertamina was already imminent. Ibnu presented the argument in language that was characteristically direct. Equality of income, he said, was a utopian vision. It had never happened anywhere in the world, no matter what the system of government. Realistically, the best one could hope for was equality in the distribution of benefits. But that required production first. The means of production had to be acquired, and production had to yield increased results. Only then could the benefits be distributed, to the producers of the new wealth, and to everyone else. This task had to begin with the acquisition of technology, and with the development of large organizations to use it. In the Indonesian case, Pertamina was a good example of how this was to be accomplished. Pertamina did not work for a profit, as large organizations did in some other countries. Because the oil industry needed them, Pertamina built physical infrastructure and service industries—ports, highways, communications facilities, hospitals, schools, houses, and much else. In the process of developing the oil industry, Pertamina was developing the country.[100]

Ibnu had his successors in the Indonesian government, and, like him, they were not willing to wait. The economists argued rates of return. With the ambivalence of many of his compatriots, Soeharto supported the one, then the other.

Oil money was not responsible for this lack of direction on the part of Soeharto and his government. But oil money did make a bifurcated vision possible. Particularly in the years when oil money was flush, as in 1973–74 and again in 1979–80, it seemed that one could have one's cake and eat it too. The circumstances were ultimately corrosive. Oil money came too easily. The money was paid by foreign consumers, for oil largely produced by foreign firms, and it flowed into the Indonesian political and economic system at the very top. As Sumitro Djojohadikusumo, the dean of Indonesian economists, mused in 1980, the Indonesians had become rich "without really trying."[101]

EIGHT

The Petition of Fifty

The Pertamina affair left the government highly vulnerable to criticism. Students slowly mounted demonstrations against the government's economic policies, against corruption, and against the authoritarian nature of the regime. Islamic groups defeated the government in an election in Jakarta and mobilized a mass rally in support of human rights. Retired military officers made public addresses in which they criticized the government harshly.

These signs of political rejuvenation became focused on the reelection of Soeharto to the presidency in 1978. After some initial hesitation the armed forces announced that they stood solidly behind Soeharto, and, on the day of the election, they put on a massive display of armed might.

This display of force, and the government's apparent need to rely on it, touched off an extraordinary process of public soul-searching on the part of numerous prominent personalities in the civil and military elite. The issues had to do with army support of the government party, Golkar; with the identification of the army with the Soeharto government; and, inevitably, with the future of the presidency.

Soeharto brought this process to an eventual halt. But not before fifty prominent citizens, former Islamic party leaders and former army commanders, an unlikely coalition, issued a public statement demanding an end to the Soeharto presidency.

Islam and the 1977 Elections

The first parliamentary elections of the New Order in 1971 had been marked by the smooth and effective functioning of the bureaucracy as an electoral machine. Golkar obtained 62.8 percent of the national vote in a contest against nine parties. In 1973 the government amalgamated these parties—simplified them, in the official terminology—into two new groups as part of an effort to reduce the number of contending ideologies on the national political scene. One of these new groupings, designated the Indonesian Democracy Party, and commonly known as the PDI, combined the remnants of the secular National Party, two smaller nationalist parties, and the Protestant and Catholic parties; it was an awkward marriage, and the group was to struggle for years to establish an identity for itself. The second new grouping was initially more fortunate. The Development Unity Party, or PPP, combined four Islamic parties, of which the largest was the traditionalist Nahdatul Ulama, or NU, which had been alone among the parties in holding its mass base against the Golkar onslaught in 1971.

Numerous disagreements between the government and the leaders of the new Islamic grouping preceded the 1977 parliamentary elections. Government-sponsored legislation in 1975 and 1976 had laid down rules that imposed considerable constraints on political parties contesting future elections. For example, the 1975 law on political parties and Golkar provided that civil servants holding certain positions could not become members of political parties or Golkar unless their superiors gave them written permission. A later government regulation provided that those certain positions included all civil service posts down to village chief, all senior and branch managers of state-owned corporations and banks, all defense ministry employees, and all government teachers.[1]

The PPP emerged from this process with only one signal victory: freedom to use the Ka'abah, the most sacred building in Islam, which stands in the court of the Great Mosque in Mecca, as its symbol on the ballot. But the group also had the advantage of a united slate of Islamic-minded candidates for the first time, and the well-organized presence of the Nahdatul Ulama, especially in heavily populated rural Java. From the very beginning of the campaign, the government acted on the assumption that the PPP was the only possible threat to a Golkar victory.[2]

Three months before the elections, in early February, Admiral Soedomo, who was both the armed forces' deputy chief and the head of internal security, as well as a Javanese convert to Christianity at the time of his marriage, announced the uncovering of an antigovernment conspiracy calling itself the Komando Jihad, or Holy War Command.

Although Soedomo said there was no connection between the conspiracy and the PPP, leaders of the PPP saw the announcement as an ill-disguised attempt to undermine their candidates' appeal among moderate voters. The alleged leader of the plot was later acknowledged to have had undercover ties with Gen. Ali Moertopo, and it was widely believed that the plot had been manufactured. Laboring under such inhibitions, the Islamic party nevertheless had reason to expect to do well.

The Islamic party defeated Golkar in the capital city, but it encountered a plethora of irregularities in other provinces. In East and Central Java, the most heavily populated provinces in the country, and in South Sulawesi, the instances of fraud were so widespread that Islamic party representatives refused to sign the official tallies. When the national totals were announced in early June, showing Golkar with 62.11 percent of the vote, an Islamic party witness refused to sign the official tabulation.[3]

Later in the year, in October, Islamic activists were given a new issue when the government released the draft of its proposed "Broad Outlines of State Policy," a document designed to guide government policy for the 1978–83 period. The draft gave equal weight in several passages to the words *belief* and *religion*. Islamic leaders saw this as yet another attempt on the part of the army leadership to reduce the influence of Islam in public life.

Long-time army associates of Soeharto had for some years wanted to obtain official recognition of Javanese mystical beliefs, equivalent to that given to world religions. The principal proponent was Gen. Soedjono Humardhani, a noted adept in Javanese mysticism and reputedly an adviser to the president in spiritual matters. For such men the issue was significant not only because the army had been obliged on several occasions since independence to put down efforts to establish an Islamic state, efforts that they and other army leaders feared would split the nation. Soedjono also found it personally objectionable to be compelled to list Islam as his religion. Before the 1970 census, he had campaigned behind the scenes to have the census offer the populace the choice of identifying their religion as "Islam-abangan," a designation that suggested one adhered to Islamic principles and Javanese mystical beliefs as well. It was thought that this would dramatically reduce the recorded number of adherents to an unadulterated Islam, and would make possible a reduction in the scale of government subsidies to mosques, Islamic schools, and other Islamic institutions.

8. The Petition of Fifty

When the issue was raised again in the latter part of 1977, it evoked reactions at several levels. General Nasution, who had been quiescent for almost a decade, and who had done his part in putting down Islamic insurgencies during his own long tenure as army chief of staff, was stimulated to renewed activity; he was soon making frequent speeches critical of the government's economic policies and of its commitment to democracy. Student leaders quickly picked up the mood of opposition.[4]

Students in Opposition

Student protests spread rapidly after the 1977 parliamentary elections. These were focused initially on government economic policies, and in August a team of cabinet-level economists, headed by the redoubtable Professor Sumitro, was sent on a tour of major campuses to establish a dialogue with the student critics. This effort was no more successful than a similar effort had been four years before. At the University of Indonesia in the capital city, and at Gadjah Mada University in Yogyakarta, Central Java, the students began by challenging the cabinet ministers on economic issues, but went on to raise questions about the role of the armed forces in politics and in the government. In Bandung, the capital of West Java, the reception was hostile. Student leaders took control of the meeting from the outset, announced a number of "conditions" for discussion that the cabinet officers could not possibly meet, and declared the meeting closed before any discussion could take place. The cabinet officers were flown back to the capital by helicopter, and the rest of the campus "safari" was canceled.[5] The lesson to be drawn from this experience was not lost on Soeharto. His academic advisers had again been unable to control their own constituency, and that failure was to contribute to a reduction in their influence in his government.

In October members of the student councils from universities throughout Indonesia met in Bandung and agreed on an "Indonesian Students' Vow" to take every opportunity to express their opposition to the government.

Student parades were held in various cities on November 10, which was Heroes' Day, a commemoration of the thousands who had died in the Battle of Surabaya which began on that date in 1945 between British and republican Indonesian forces.

December 10 was Human Rights Day, and the student council of the

University of Indonesia decided to make this day the start of a "Human Rights Month." The students were moved, in part, by the plight of farmers from the nearby Krawang area who had sought refuge on the University campus. Krawang, ordinarily a rice-surplus area, had experienced a major drought and the farmers were said to be reduced to eating animal feed. The villagers also were said to have fled because authorities were pressing them to repay their rice production loans, which they could not do because the harvest had failed.[6]

On January 16, 1978, the student council of the Bandung Institute of Technology, the country's leading center of training in science and engineering, published a *White Book of the 1978 Students' Struggle*, which argued, in sum, that the people's lives were still far from the ideals of independence. This was a result of a lack of "political will" on the part of the government, of "deviations and abuses of power by government officials," and an "erosion of the authority of government institutions." It was essential that the presidency not be occupied by the same person for more than two successive terms if a dynamic political life was to develop, in which all social groups could participate in selecting the national leadership. The students of the Bandung Institute of Technology, the *White Book* said, "Do not trust and do not want Soeharto to be President of the Republic of Indonesia again." They called on all factions of the People's Consultative Assembly to nominate "prestigious figures, whose integrity is beyond any doubt," as candidates for president, and called on the armed forces to "stand above all groups in the interest of the nation and the state."[7]

Heri Akhmadi, the general chairman of the student council at the Institute, at his later trial on a charge of insulting the head of state, spent four days reading a statement in his own defense. Running to 172 pages in a later English-language translation, and containing numerous tables and charts, quotations from scholars, and citations from the Indonesian press, the statement argued that the student criticisms of the government and the president were well founded. The New Order was a bureaucratic dictatorship, he said, in which elections were a parody of democracy, state institutions other than the presidency had become mere ornaments, and the press had been "castrated" by government controls. The consequence of this concentration of power was, he argued, that Indonesia had become a nation of beggars and embezzlers, begging for foreign loans and investment, and permitting government "stooges," Chinese businessmen, and foreigners to drain the nation of its wealth. He appended a "partial" list of the Soeharto family's wealth and a comparison of the foreign debt of the Old and New Orders.[8]

The Armed Forces' Response

The widening criticism of the president and his government found resonance in army circles. An article in the army daily newspaper in November suggested that army leaders of the 1945 generation should "cleanse" themselves before handing over the leadership to their successors. The article offered as a parable the Javanese legend of a king whose actions were founded in greed and who was killed by his cousins.[9] Two days later a retired three-star general, Alamsjah Ratu Perwiranegara, who had served in Soeharto's personal staff in 1966 and was now deputy chairman of the Supreme Advisory Council, an honorific council of elders, made some unusual admissions in an address before a national conference of the Association of Indonesian Social Scientists. Alamsjah acknowledged that many of the aims of the New Order had not been achieved. The gap was growing between the rich and the poor, between the cities and the villages, and between the capital and the provinces. The general also acknowledged the existence of a long list of problems, including food shortages, crime, scandals, smuggling, bribery, abuse of authority, lack of equality before the law, and neglect of political education. It was not surprising, he said, that students, youth, the political parties, and community leaders were discontent.[10] At about the same time, an intelligence report was said to have reached Soeharto that some army brigades were ready to support Nasution and the student cause.[11] A Jakarta newspaper reported that at a November meeting of military commanders in Java special attention was given to the danger of a split in the armed forces caused by groups seeking support for their political ideas.[12]

On December 12, at a rally of twenty-thousand Muslims in Jakarta, Nasution spoke forcefully against the government on human rights and other grounds. The rally was attended by Alamsjah and by another retired three-star general, Ali Sadikin, the popular ex-governor of Jakarta.[13]

The possibility of a repetition of 1974—of a split within the armed forces over how to deal with student militants—could no longer be ignored. With his own planned reelection to the presidency only three months away, and the political temperature rising, Soeharto is said to have called Gen. Maraden Panggabean, the army chief of staff, and other senior officers to a meeting at which he let them know of his concern. Panggabean called an emergency meeting at the defense ministry on December 13. The nation's senior serving officers attended, and were later joined by fellow generals now in nonmilitary roles in the cabinet, including Amir Machmud and Mohammad Jusuf, the two surviving "kingmakers" from 1966. After two days of discussion, which at one time or another involved a total of twenty-five generals, Panggabean called a press conference and announced that the armed forces would take strong action against anyone threatening the "national leadership." That this display of army unity had taken two days to achieve indeed suggested there had been some substance to the rumors of disunity in army ranks.[14]

Within weeks another critical address was delivered by yet another retired lieutenant general. H. R. Dharsono, the former commander of the Siliwangi Division, who in 1969 had attempted to create by fiat a two-party system in the province of West Java, was now the secretary general of the Association of Southeast Asian Nations, which after a decade of existence had agreed to the establishment of a modest secretariat in Jakarta. In mid-January 1978 Dharsono addressed a gathering in Bandung of the "generation of 1966," veterans of the student movement of that year who had helped bring down Sukarno. Dharsono used the occasion to say that it was now time for the leaders of the armed forces to pay attention to public opinion. If the armed forces continued to rely on military power, they would be obeyed only out of fear. Recent events indicated that the people were growing restive and that something was seriously wrong. Civil-military relations were troubled; the New Order had moved away from its original ideals, and the government needed redirecting.[15]

In February the government moved decisively against the more vulnerable of its critics. Troops moved into the campus of the Institute of Technology in Bandung, and more than a hundred student leaders were arrested there and in other cities. Newspapers were closed for a week until their editors again agreed that they would not publish news that would threaten public security.[16]

(The government later brought charges against at least thirty student leaders in Bandung, Jakarta, Yogyakarta, Surabaya, Palembang, and Medan. The students were initially detained by army security forces on charges of subversion, but the charges were subsequently reduced to the lesser one of "insulting the Head of State," an offense dating to the Dutch colonial period. Nevertheless, Lukman Hakim, president of the student council of the University of Indonesia, argued in court that the arrests were carried out with considerable violence, and that the students jailed with him, including even high school students, were subjected to beatings, electric shocks, and solitary confinement, and that they were further abused by being pent up for months with criminals who also subjected them to beatings and other forms of violence.)[17]

At this point it was announced that the Sultan of Yogyakarta, for reasons of health, would not stand for reelection as vice president. The Sultan was known to be disenchanted with Soeharto. An aide said later that a chief source of the Sultan's disenchantment was his constantly encountering a lineup of Chinese businessmen outside the president's office when he went there to pay a call. As the 1978 election to the presidency and vice presidency neared, the Sultan also found himself increasingly hemmed in. One morning, when he was expecting to receive a delegation of students, he woke to find that his personal security guard had been changed without notice. The new officer of the guard informed him that the student visit had been canceled. That was the moment, the aide said, when the Sultan realized the time had come to bow out.

In March 1978 the People's Consultative Assembly convened to reelect Soeharto to the presidency. There was no question about the outcome. It was calculated that three generals in the Assembly, all appointees of Soeharto, spoke for 86.1 percent of the 920 votes. Nevertheless, from the time the session began on March 11, Jakarta resembled an armed camp. David Jenkins, one of the few resident foreign correspondents, described the scene:

> Soldiers with bamboo riot-sticks lounged at every major intersection in the city and armored cars and troop carriers were parked in side streets ready for action. Helicopters scudded across the city, keeping a weather eye for trouble. Combat-ready troops were stationed every 10 ft. along the back perimeter of the [Assembly] grounds. At the front, there were guard dogs and anti-riot trucks.[18]

While these precautions seemed extravagant, the government had reason for apprehension. When the "Broad Outlines of State Policy," with its controversial references to "beliefs," came up for a vote in the Assembly, PPP members staged a dramatic walkout. Mohammed

Natsir, a former prime minister and leader of the banned Masyumi Party, accused the government of trying to divide the Muslim community: "Step by step, they are trying to raise [Javanese mystical beliefs] to the level of a religion. The direct consequence will be that people who now regard themselves as Muslims, who practice Islam and who are married and buried according to Islamic law, will become a special group practicing their own ceremonies and having their own graveyards."[19]

In this environment, on March 23, 1978, Soeharto was reelected president.

Reservations about the Army's Role

The circumstances surrounding Soeharto's reelection sparked an immediate reaction from a group of retired army leaders. In a letter to General Widodo, the new army chief of staff, on March 28, they observed that Soeharto had been reelected "in an atmosphere of war." It was essential, they said, that the climate of confrontation should end and the country return to a state of normalcy.[20]

The retired army officers had met under the auspices of a new Forum for Study and Communication, the leadership of which included six former lieutenant generals and six former major generals. The chairman of the Forum's executive committee was Lt. Gen. G. P. H. Djatikusumo, a son of the Susuhunan or traditional princely ruler of Solo, a distinguished revolutionary era commander, and a former army chief of staff. The secretary general of the Forum was Lt. Gen. H. R. Dharsono, who by this time had been removed from his position as secretary general of ASEAN in reprisal for his public criticism of the government (and for his refusal to apologize). The group as a whole was a disparate collection; included were not only men of distinction and some with reason to be disaffected, but also a goodly number who had been autocratic themselves when they were on active duty. They were not the most credible of critics of government high-handedness, but they also were not unrepresentative of the retired generation of officers on whose behalf they proposed to speak.[21]

In the months that followed, the Forum sent five papers in all to Widodo. The general thrust of their observations was that an unacceptable gap existed between the army and the people. It was essential that civil-military relations be repaired. This required that the army be freed from involvement in politics, that it return to its original position of "standing above" parties and groups. This meant, among other things, abandoning the army's active support for Golkar. The government party depended too much on the armed forces, and, as a result, was insensitive and unresponsive to public opinion.[22]

These views found further expression in an official army document before the year was out. On October 17, at a meeting of the army general staff, which also was attended by a number of other senior officers, both active and retired, including the executive committee of the Forum, Widodo approved the publication of a seventy-five-page paper on the "dual function" of the armed forces. Drawing on earlier Staff College documents and the Forum papers, and revised in the course of a series of meetings in which Forum leaders participated, the document dealt both with the army's relations with other social and political groups, and with the involvement of military officers in civilian roles in government. As to the first, the paper stressed, the army must never ally itself with any one group in society, as this would endanger its unity and identity. As to the second, now that stability and dynamism had been returned to the executive branch of government, the role of armed forces personnel in civilian posts could be reduced.[23]

By this time others were publicly expressing the same view. Maj. Gen. Mas Isman, who as a twenty-one-year-old in 1945 had led the student army in East Java, and who was chairman of one of the founding units of Golkar, said at a national conference in July that it was time that relations between Golkar and the military were altered. Golkar needed to generate its own ideas, or it would be a mere bureaucratic tool. He went on to say that future elections should not be won by "abnormal" means; it would be better to win as a political force that truly obtained a mandate from the people.[24]

An independent army view continued to emerge during much of 1979. Gen. Mohammad Jusuf, now the Minister of Defense, took a broadly populist approach to his duties. He traveled incessantly, visiting camps and barracks, inspecting living conditions, and promising improvements in salaries and benefits.[25] He also was quoted frequently in the press as saying that the army had to identify itself with the whole of the Indonesian people. In speeches in Sumatra and Irian in February, in East Java in April, and in South Sulawesi in August, he repeated the theme. The army was not the instrument of a group, a political party, or an individual, he said, but an instrument of the nation and the state.

8. The Petition of Fifty

And he went further. It was time for Golkar and the parties to be freer in electing their own leaders, he said; it was time for them to function "from below."[26]

In May 1979 General Soemitro, the former deputy commander of the armed forces and former chief of internal security, joined this public discussion, breaking a public silence he had maintained since his departure from government five years earlier. In a signed article published in a major Jakarta daily newspaper on May 11, Soemitro said that while there was some continued restlessness the political situation was "relatively calm." This was so, he suggested, because of the government's willingness to allow "constructive criticism and correction," and also because of "the attitude of the public itself which is apparently aware that the way of force . . . will not reach goals or solve problems." Soemitro then proceeded to raise the issue of presidential succession:

> If in the pre-New Order era, talk about the succession was said to be "taboo," in this New Order the matter of succession is a necessity for a sound democratic life. . . . It is clear that the succession must be prepared and conducted in accordance with the existing rules of the game. . . . In fact, the election process must be begun as early as possible. Exposing the candidates earlier is a necessity to get them known nationwide.[27]

Soemitro's article created a sensation. General Nasution, in a letter to *Tempo* magazine, praised Soemitro for his initiative in raising the succession issue publicly, observing that the subject "has been discussed quite frequently in army circles when they met outside official forums."[28] Sumiskum, the former Golkar deputy speaker of Parliament, also praised Soemitro for bringing a breath of "fresh air" to Indonesian politics. It was time, he said, to decide the number of terms an individual could be president.[29]

On June 1 Adam Malik, elected vice president the year before, after the Sultan declined to stand again for the post, added fuel to the fire. The occasion was the closing session of a ten-day program in commemoration of National Awakening Day. The commemoration had been planned by twenty-one organizations, including the Forum of retired army leaders, to reflect on the state of national political life. A wide range of New Order figures, including Maj. Gen. Ali Moertopo, had already spoken in the course of the commemoration. Malik could be counted on to strike sparks. A native of Sumatra, he was a man who liked to speak his mind. A few weeks earlier he had remarked that if things continued as they were, government leaders might well be hanged. On this occasion, speaking without notes, Malik began by suggesting that the country's recent experience of a series of calamities—floods, pests, earthquakes, volcanic eruptions, and epidemics—"are really a warning from God to us." He continued:

> We have all sinned. We all have pledged to be loyal, to be imbued with and to practice Pancasila and the 1945 Constitution. But often the utterances are only on the lips without being followed by concrete action. This is our sin. This is the fundamental issue today. This is the main cause of stagnation, so that the government machinery does not run properly. . . . No matter how wrong the present situation is, no matter what the wrongs of the New Order are, there is still a way to make corrections. Not by being angry, not by vituperation or demonstrations, but by properly formulated ideas to calm the situation. . . . Our people are not fond of coups. Our people are not that stupid. There are no coups in the history of Indonesia.[30]

Soeharto and His Critics

These intimations of disaffection in elite army and civilian circles came to a head some months later.

The government sent Parliament a draft amendment to the general election law in October, and disaffected elements in the elite quickly focused on it. A central issue was the number of seats in Parliament to be filled by election, and the number to be filled by presidential appointment. Critics wanted to see more seats filled by election, and this would have been at least a step toward a more representative legislature. On February 20, 1980, twenty-six prominent public figures, including Islamic political leaders, former National Party leaders, and retired military officers, submitted a petition to Parliament concerning the general elections. "The transition period that has been going on from the birth of the New Order in 1965 up to 1980 is long enough," their petition said. A general election held sincerely, honestly, and clearly "is the one and only legal way [to elect] a legitimate government."[31]

Soeharto was adamant. Using its overwhelming majority in Parliament, the government pushed the bill to a vote on March 2. The event split the Islamic PPP; fifty members from the Nahdatul Ulama, unwilling to join in the usual unanimous approval of a government bill, and also wishing to avoid a confrontation by voting against it, absented themselves from the session.[32]

On March 27 Soeharto addressed the regional commanders of the armed forces at their annual conference in Pakanbaru. After reading his prepared text, Soeharto proceeded to get his feelings off his chest. Members of the armed forces, he said, were bound by oath to uphold the Pancasila and the constitution, and to resist any change in them. If necessary, the armed forces would take up arms in this cause. A consensus had been reached at the beginning of the New Order, involving all the political forces at the time, that the armed forces would be given the opportunity to hold one-third of the seats in Parliament by appointment, in return for their giving up the right to vote or be candidates for election. The constitution could be changed by those who held the other two-thirds of the seats. But he had told the political parties at the time that if there were ever an effort to do this, "it would be better if we kidnapped someone from the two-thirds majority to keep that from happening."[33]

He had thought at the time that a real consensus also existed in support of the Pancasila as the national ideology. It was a consensus he had fought for, that all the political parties and Golkar would be based on this one ideology. But, in reality, the consensus was still not complete. There was still a political party that said, "Beside the principles of the Pancasila, there are others." There had been many examples of this, most recently in the amending of the election law. At the very least this called for "all of us" to be vigilant. So, the president told the commanders, "choose partners, friends, companions who will really safeguard the Pancasila and who have not the least hesitation about the Pancasila."[34]

The criticism of recent months continued to rankle. On April 16 Soeharto addressed the army's paratroopers, the "red berets," on the occasion of their twenty-eighth anniversary. He used the occasion to deny various charges that had been leveled against him and his family. It was said, he observed, that his wife received commissions, decided the award of government tenders, and had made their home into "a headquarters for tender awards, commissions, and the like." This was simply not true. Another charge, making the rounds of students and housewives, "who are easily led in one direction or another," was that he had a mistress who was a well-known movie actress. It was an old story, he said, and also not true.

8. The Petition of Fifty

"Maybe," Soeharto said, "they think I am their major political obstacle. So I must be eliminated." But they forget that "if anything were to happen to me, there would arise other citizens, other soldiers, who will always oppose their politics, even more surely if they aim to change the Pancasila and the Constitution with another ideology."[35]

In early May 1980 another petition to Parliament—a "Statement of Concern"—was signed by fifty prominent citizens. The petition said that the Soeharto speeches raised serious questions about the way the government was using its power and the way it intended to carry out the next elections. The president appeared to conceive the society as being polarized between one group that viewed the Pancasila as "eternal" and another that wanted to replace the Pancasila, raising the prospect of new controversies within the society. He "misunderstood" the Pancasila, however, the petition said; whereas the five principles were intended to serve as a basis for unity, the president was using them "as a means to threaten political enemies." He approved of dishonorable action by the armed forces, on the subterfuge of honoring the soldier's oath, whereas this pledge could not possibly be given precedence over the constitution. He urged the armed forces "not to stand above all social groups, but to choose friends and enemies based solely on his own assessment." The president seemed, the petition said, to see himself as the "personification" of the Pancasila, so that even every rumor about him was taken as a sign of being against the Pancasila. The petition asked the members of Parliament to consider these issues.[36]

The "Statement of Concern" was signed by five former military leaders: A. H. Nasution; Mokoginta, his one-time chief of staff; Ali Sadikin, a retired marine general, the former governor of Jakarta, and at one time regarded as a possible presidential candidate; Hoegeng, former commander of the national police and for many years a popular television personality; and Mohammad Jasin, a former commander of the Brawidjaja Division in East Java, and by this time a noted critic of corruption in government. The principal civilian signers were three senior figures from the old Masyumi party, all active in the rebellion of 1957–58: Sjafruddin Prawiranegara, who had been head of the emergency republican government in 1948–49 when Sukarno, Hatta, and others were prisoners of the Dutch; Mohammad Natsir, who had been prime minister in 1950–51; and Burhanuddin Harahap, who had been prime minister in 1955–56 and had overseen the first national general elections.

8. The Petition of Fifty

On June 3 Admiral Sudomo and General Yoga Sugama, chief of intelligence, reportedly called the chief editors of the Jakarta news media to a briefing. The government, they said, had found evidence of a plot to assassinate a large number of people, beginning with Soeharto, and to take over the government. The charge appears not to have been meant to be taken seriously; it was never pursued. Indeed, Yoga said that the government did not intend to arrest any of the signers of the "Statement of Concern"; that would give them the martyrdom they sought. It would strike back in other ways. Expired work permits and business licenses would not be renewed; lines of bank credit would be cut off; bids on government projects would not be accepted; and exit permits to leave the country would not be granted.[37]

In early July nineteen members of Parliament, two from the PDI and the rest from the Islamic PPP, signed a letter to Soeharto. The recent petition to Parliament by fifty citizens, they said, although it was not reported by the Indonesian media, had been reported widely abroad. In addition, several senior government officials had discussed the petition at various briefings. The parliamentarians said the petition had raised important issues that demanded the attention of Parliament and the government. The authors therefore asked Soeharto for a "complete and detailed" explanation of his position on the issues the statement raised. They appended a copy of the petition for his information. The letter, dated July 5, along with the full text of the petition, finally appeared in a single Jakarta newspaper on July 16.[38]

This was followed by a debate, which took place in public as well as in private, over whether it was necessary or desirable for Soeharto to respond. He did so in early August to the extent of sending a letter to the speaker of Parliament with copies of the speeches that had given rise to the petition. He suggested that any questions about the speeches might be taken up by the appropriate committee of Parliament according to the standing procedures.[39] Since the government controlled all committees of Parliament, that was the end of the exchange.

Soeharto did respond indirectly to the criticisms of his government on August 17, in his annual address to Parliament on the eve of Independence Day. He offered a classic defense: "To materialize the progress and prosperity that is our ideal, the one and only way for us to take is to implement development; in order to implement development, we must all be able to maintain dynamic national stability."[40]

8. The Petition of Fifty

He later returned to the topic with a statement with which many of his listeners might have agreed:

> Political development is a very difficult part of the development of the nation in its entirety. Therefore it calls for the determination and patience of us all. We need to understand that we do not possess a stable tradition yet for giving substance to and for determining the forms of all the important aspects of the practice of the political life. We are still trying to find the right balance between freedom and responsibility, between the interests of the individual and those of the group on the one hand and on the other of public interests and national interests.[41]

Patience was not everywhere in adequate supply, as an outbreak of anti-Chinese violence demonstrated the following November. On November 19 a fight occurred between an Indonesian student and the son of a wealthy Chinese businessman in the old royal capital of Solo in Central Java. This led to rioting that lasted three days; thousands of young Javanese rampaged through the Chinese business district, terrorizing the population and wrecking shops, homes, and cars. Troops had to be brought in to bring the rioting under control, and one youth was killed. Although the authorities tried to keep news of the disturbance out of the mass media, the rioting spread. By November 24 there was rioting in Semarang, the port city where Soeharto had had his Diponegoro headquarters, and which was home to one of the oldest Chinese communities in Indonesia. Again troops were brought in, much property was damaged, and two rioters were shot. Rioting also spread to other towns in Central Java, including Pekalongan, Kudus, and Magalang. Troops were flown in by C130 Hercules transport planes, and nightly curfews were enforced until early December. On December 3 Gen. Yoga Sugama, the intelligence agency head, briefed a committee of Parliament in a closed session. He reportedly told them that a total of eight Javanese youths, but no Chinese, had been killed, and fourteen had been wounded. More than 240 Chinese shops, 230 homes, 23 factories, 32 office buildings, and 1 school had been damaged. More than 680 persons had been arrested.[42]

Although tensions thus remained high for a time following the confrontation between Soeharto and his critics, they did eventually subside. While Soeharto was vulnerable to criticism, the bases of his critics were diffuse. The students had a vision of a modern, democratic Indonesia, a view not widely shared among their elders. The Muslim leaders had a vision of a devout Islamic Indonesia, a view not shared by all Muslims, and especially not by many of the Javanese officers who in 1980 constituted almost 80 percent of the armed forces high command.[43] The retired army generals had a vision of an incorruptible Indonesian army presiding over the development of a grateful nation. Only rarely, as in the Petition of Fifty, did members of these disparate groups find common ground.

In addition, the armed forces establishment had yet to agree on the choice of a successor from within its own ranks. This would have to have been a Javanese, but no Javanese general had been permitted to occupy the position of Minister of Defense, and there was no obvious heir apparent. A number of other key positions had long been held by some of Soeharto's most trusted confidantes; such units as the public security apparatus and the paratroop command were under the control of long-time loyalists.[44] In these circumstances it might well have been true, as Ali Moertopo warned, that an effort to remove Soeharto from office "would lead to civil war."[45]

The pressures had nevertheless been real. Had Soeharto faced his critics of 1979 and 1980 in conditions of falling oil prices, the outcome might have been different. As it was, his run of good luck continued, and the economic trade-off he offered the elite was real. Oil prices rose continuously during both 1979 and 1980, reaching the highest levels ever experienced. Before the latter year was out, following an OPEC meeting in Bali, the base price of Indonesia's most popular grade of oil, Minas crude, was increased to $35 a barrel. Ten years earlier the same oil had sold for $1.70 a barrel. Indonesia was again awash with money.

Thus buoyed by the inertia of the situation, or, as Juwono Sudarsono put it, by the nation's lack of effective power to bring about concerted change, Soeharto remained. He lacked style and charisma, but, as Sudarsono wrote, "he is a supreme tactician who puts great premium on 'orderly change on his own terms."[46] And so the critics were dealt with, most of them gently. General Jusuf was appointed chairman of the Supreme Advisory Council. Widodo was retired. The Forum of retired army men was disbanded. Generals Soemitro, Alamsjah, and other former army leaders made their peace with the president and went on to further careers in government or business. Adam Malik retreated into relative public silence, at least until he was gone from the vice presidency. The chairman of the PDI resigned, leaving the leadership of the party in progovernment hands. The factions within the PPP, now deeply divided over support of the government, decided to go their separate ways, although this took some time to work itself out. Concern about the army's role in politics fell dormant, or at least silent, and public interest in the issue of presidential succession did not come alive again until the late 1980s. Those who had signed the "Statement of Concern" kept up their critique, petitioning Parliament on pending legislation and protesting the handling of elections, but their petitions were effectively kept out of the domestic press, and they had no audience.

The Economic Trade-Off

The economic trade-off was indeed real. The budget for fiscal year 1979–80 included subsidies of Rupiah 350 billion for kerosene and diesel fuel, Rupiah 82.6 billion for fertilizers, and Rupiah 82 billion for rice; at the then-current rate of exchange, these subsidies came to the equivalent of $823 million, which was 7.3 percent of the total government budget and 1.9 percent of Gross Domestic Product. Some of these budget decisions were reportedly arrived at only after considerable agonizing by Soeharto and his cabinet. The sharpest debate appears to have taken place over fuel price subsidies, the cost of which had escalated with the international market in oil; the rice and fertilizer subsidies were more modest and also central to the whole strategy for agriculture. A scheduled increase in domestic fuel prices had been put off in 1978 in the heated atmosphere of Soeharto's reelection, reportedly on the urging of internal security officials. An increase of 40 percent was finally carried out in March and April of 1979. After much internal debate, a further increase of 50 percent took place in May 1980.

There was less debate about salaries. During calendar year 1979, as oil prices were rising, all government employees, civil and military, received an increase of 16.6 percent in basic salaries.[47] In announcing the 1980–81 budget, Sumarlin told the press that the equivalent of $3.2 billion was budgeted for the salaries of 2.5 million civil servants. He added that this would provide for the livelihood of a total of 12.5 million people, although it was noted at the time that if this were so, civil servant families would have a per capita income that was less than 70 percent of the national average.

The 1980–81 budget also included the equivalent of $2 billion for the Department of Defense, most of which was earmarked for further pay increases and allowances.[48] The official defense budget thus came to about 12.8 percent of the budget. While this was modest by international standards, it was believed that the government was still meeting only part of the defense department's needs. One foreign embassy estimated the share as being in the range of 60–70 percent, which, if accurate, was a considerable improvement over the semiofficial estimates of 1969–70, but still left a substantial gap to be filled.[49]

The remainder of the armed forces needs were reportedly being met by a large number of companies, cooperatives, and foundations that, in turn, were engaged in a wide range of business activities. These were reported in 1980 to include ventures sponsored by the Department of Defense, the four major services, the sixteen regional commands, and such special commands as the strategic reserve. A holding company sponsored by the defense ministry held shares in at least thirty-eight companies, eleven of which had joint ventures with foreign investors. Some twenty-four of the thirty-four local companies engaged in the timber business were said to involve military interests.[50] Other military ventures, especially in construction, had benefited from Pertamina contracts during the 1974–75 oil boom, and languished following the Pertamina default.[51] Many such firms stood to benefit from the economic expansion fueled by the boom of 1979–80.

Thus, the second oil boom was already well advanced when Soeharto confronted his critics in early 1980, and the economic trade-off of which Soeharto himself spoke was in full flower. It took the form of substantial, though still inadequate, pay increases for the civil and military services, substantial fuel subsidies for urban consumers, and an economic expansion that promised benefits to a wide swath of elite interests, including firms owned by the armed forces.

The Policy Issues

There were larger issues at hand. The student protests surrounding Soeharto's reelection in 1978 obliged the government to show new resolve in addressing problems of social justice. Soeharto himself, in his first address to Parliament after that election, said the government recognized that "the people's feelings require development to take a greater depth and not just to touch upon the surface," and that "we are increasingly pressed by the necessity to make development even more equitable in the direction of social justice."[52] The "Broad Outlines of State Policy" thus gave first priority to a more equitable distribution of the benefits of development. But the Third Plan period beginning in 1978 also had been seen as the period when the government, following major investments in support of agriculture, would begin to shift its investment priorities toward manufacturing. The question was what sort of manufacturing was to be financed. The Third Plan was ambivalent. It talked about an emphasis on industries that would expand employment opportunities. But it also spoke of "industries which would process (domestic) raw materials into manufactured goods" so that "most of the country's needs could be met by locally-made products."[53]

These goals were not necessarily the same. The issue was posed sharply in a confidential World Bank report, a massive two-volume study delivered to the government in May 1978. Whatever the official plans had said about priorities, the report noted, the bulk of Indonesian investment in industry was heavily skewed toward large-scale projects that contributed little to employment. Pertamina investments in mining added to this general picture, but large-scale projects also were under way in steel, fertilizer, and petrochemicals. The largest projects, according to a project-by-project count, would generate only 8,000 jobs a year at a cost of $14,000 per job. Meanwhile, the small-scale sector was expected to generate 110,000 jobs a year at only $1,000 per job. These figures, the Bank study suggested, should be compared to the annual increase in the labor force, which exceeded one million.[54]

A. R. Soehoed, the new Minister of Industry, acknowledged that the government's Third Plan contained "two seemingly conflicting objectives." One was "a larger spread of progress," and this called for "more and smaller size operations with larger inputs in manpower." The second objective was to sustain the current rate of growth, and this could be accomplished only by investment in "bigger and more efficient, high-technology operations, obviously less labour intensive."[55] The government would search intensively for new employment opportunities, especially in agroindustries and in small- and medium-scale manufacturing. But where the market required high precision and sustained quality standards, Soehoed said, the labor-intensive priority would have to be breached.[56]

As the oil money rolled in, the breaches mounted. The government in fact had no plan for industrial development, and Soeharto's new cabinet, appointed after his reelection in 1978, included not only more army officers but several prominent supporters of an essentially physical approach to development. The civilian economists who remained in the cabinet had no experience in industry, failed to produce a reasoned plan for industrial development, and spent the next few years arguing the inefficiency of one proposed massive industrial project after another. By mid-1981 the U.S. foreign commercial service reported that the Indonesian government, in addition to planning a development budget of $10 billion for fiscal year 1981–82, and price subsidies of $3 billion for the year, was expected to spend more than $12 billion over the next several years on a long list of major industrial projects. These included refinery expansions, liquified natural gas expansions, petrochemical projects, power plants, mining ventures, cement plants, and pulp, paper, and wood industries.[57]

With Ibnu Sutowo gone from government, the role of chief protagonist of a high-technology, capital-intensive approach to development was filled by B. J. Habibie, a German-trained aeronautical engineer, a former vice president of Messerschmitt, and one of the bright young men recruited back to Indonesia by Ibnu Sutowo in the earlier oil boom. Habibie was now Minister of Research, and he exhibited an impatience with economic thinking to a striking degree.

If Indonesia was to develop a modern industry, Habibie said, scientific and technological training was essential but not sufficient. Technologies could truly be learned and developed only by being applied to concrete problems. And the problems might require advanced technologies. "They may indeed in many cases be the most advanced in the world. The only criterion for the appropriateness of technologies for any particular country, including technologically less-developed countries, is their utility in solving actual problems in that particular country." Given Indonesia's situation, the industries that appeared to be "the natural vehicles for Indonesia's transformation" were in transportation (hence calling for the manufacture of aircraft, ships, automotives, and rolling stock); electronics and telecommunications; the energy industry (including the generation and transmission of electric power); facilities for processing the country's agricultural products and its mineral and energy resources (including the production of petrochemicals); equipment for the increased mechanization of agriculture; and, finally, a domestic defense industry (which should be capable of producing patrol boats, frigates, minesweepers, helicopters, jet trainers, fighter aircraft, torpedoes, rockets, rifles, mortars, grenades, and nonguided missiles).[58]

This did not leave much out. What it did omit was any concern about employment and the limits of state power. All the large-scale industrial projects were to be undertaken by state enterprises, often in joint ventures with foreign firms capable of mobilizing the necessary technology and satisfying the requirements of international sources of funding. Soehoed believed that only state enterprises were large enough to deal with the kind of multinational corporations that were involved; Fluor, Bechtel, Thyssen, Exxon, and Marubeni were among the potential partners mentioned in reports at the time. Private domestic investors were limited in capacity and experience, he said, and unable to take the risks of pioneering in new fields.[59]

Indonesian economists were at a loss in knowing how to deal with this onslaught. Sadli, now out of government, reflected toward the end of 1980 that "the idea of using state power to 'correct' things" was so deeply ingrained in Indonesian political and administrative culture as to be irremovable. The "liberal" policies of the first years of the New Order had been "alien to an Indonesian government" and probably had been accepted at the time only "out of desperation." Using the power of the state was at other times the "natural way of seeing things." The result was that the public sector of state enterprises was now "a big sector," while private business was, by any standard of measurement, only very "minor."[60]

But the state sector also had its limits. Emil Salim observed that the government bureaucracy was already unable to absorb the funds available in the budget. There was "a piling up of unspent budget items," he said, and the government apparatus could not possibly absorb the "additional burden" of the "huge" budget increases taking place by late 1980. The private sector was still an alternative, and a number of government programs were designed to help by limiting certain government procurement to "weak" business groups and by promoting a system of subcontracting, in which "larger-scale enterprises . . . contract out certain jobs and operations to small-scale and medium-scale native industries."[61] But the indigenous business sector was still small in scale. "There is a great number of entrepreneurs and enterprises," as Sadli pointed out, "but they have a small turnover and a very small capital." The government could promote a "hot-house type of growth" among these businessmen, but it might not make much difference in the total scheme of things.[62]

An alternative source of help to the private sector might have been foreign private investment, but widening government restrictions, and ambivalence on the part of many government officials, had caused such investment to decline after 1974. Approved foreign investments, which totaled about $4 billion in the five years of 1970 through 1974, came to less than $0.9 billion in the subsequent five years of 1975 through 1979. Realized foreign investments also peaked in 1974, and most of the private foreign investment realized after that year was for the expansion of existing firms rather than the entry of new enterprises.[63] In any case, according to a spokesman for the Japanese Chamber of Commerce in Jakarta, most of the private partners available to foreign investors continued to be Chinese.[64]

Thus, as the oil money flowed in, the list of massive government projects continued to grow. A World Bank report of 1981 was harshly critical. The government was engaged in "an ambitious program to develop a heavy industry base which will lay a large claim on public resources; one estimate indicates the total cost to be around $20 billion over the next five years." While the Third Plan and recent policy pronouncements indicated that the government intended to place considerable emphasis on the promotion of labor-intensive industries, on manufacture for export, and on stimulation of the private sector, other evidence suggested a very different picture. In reality, the Bank report said, the government was engaged in a wide variety of policies and practices that were inhibiting any advance in these directions.[65]

The 1981 Bank report provided a particularly revealing portrait of the problems of private business in oil-rich Indonesia. "The private sector is controlled through an extensive system of regulations which, as a whole, has a substantial disincentive effect and which restricts the expansion of industrial output," the report said. Almost every form of manufacturing required "a wide range of licenses and permits." Even the Investment Coordinating Board, which had responsibility for promoting investment, was also expected to control it, with the result that this agency also set requirements—for detailed evaluations, licenses, allowances, reports, and reapprovals—the costs of which, except for foreign investors undertaking very large projects, appeared to exceed any benefits that could be obtained.[66]

Government financial policies worked in the same direction. About 85 percent of the credit outstanding to the industrial sector came from the state banks. But for a variety of reasons, which the Bank report laid out in some detail, the state banks, in practice, earmarked lines of credit to state enterprises and to other "prime" customers.[67] These were, presumably, local firms with good connections to the office of the president, the military establishment, and senior civil officials.

The government did not like this Bank report. According to the final document itself, the draft was discussed with government representatives from January to June of 1981. The document was reportedly stricken from the agenda for the May 1981 meeting of the thirteen-nation Intergovernmental Group on Indonesia, at the request of Indonesia's economic ministers. J. B. Sumarlin, deputy chairman of the state planning agency, was quoted as complaining, "They talk as if all we have done in the past is wrong. . . . We do not like their attitude or their analysis."[68]

But the criticism was not altogether misdirected, and thus there was a certain irony in the selection of Minister Sumarlin to make the eventual announcement that the party was over. In May 1983, after the second oil boom had led to a recession in the industrial economies, after this in turn had led to falling oil prices, and after the government had experienced difficulties in raising funds from commercial sources abroad, the government was obliged to announce that it would "rephase"—meaning it would postpone or scale down—a number of major industrial projects. In June, in an interview, Sumarlin put the list of projects at forty-seven and their value at $21 billion. Among them were a $1.6 billion petrochemical complex, a $1.5 billion aromatics center, a $1.39 billion oil refinery, a $600 million alumina plant, and a $4.9 billion electricity generation program.[69]

But the era of big spending had given Soeharto valuable breathing space. Numerous firms had had a role in start-up activities associated with the big projects. Land had been purchased, commissions paid, and contracts let for design and construction. The World Bank, aware of how popular the projects were among elements of the Indonesian elite, congratulated Soeharto on his "courageous" response to economic necessity.[70] And by now the timing was propitious. The massive retreat from heavy industrial development was announced just weeks after Soeharto's ceremonial reelection to another five-year term.

NINE

The Tanjung Priok Incident

Devout Muslims and their organizations were a prominent force in the anticommunist and anti-Sukarno actions of the mid-1960s. The Nahdatul Ulama, and particularly its youth wing, Ansor, played a major role in the killings of Communists in East Java in 1965. And the Association of Islamic Students provided most of the manpower for the demonstrations against Sukarno in Jakarta in 1966. These were, in addition, national organizations of consequence, with histories dating from the 1920s. Their support lent considerable legitimacy to the transfer of power to Soeharto, and their leaders expected to be offered significant roles in the New Order. This did not occur, and Muslim leaders were deeply disillusioned well before the long haggling over the rehabilitation of the Masyumi.

Successive Soeharto cabinets consistently failed to include any prominent member of the *santri* community of devout Muslims. The government projected an image of distance from the self-consciously Muslim element in the society. A series of policy initiatives by the government, moreover, persuaded many notable figures in the country's major Islamic organizations and institutions that the government was intent on co-opting and controlling them. The manipulation of parties, the constraints on elections, and a series of bills pressed in the Parliament all seemed designed to push Islam to the margins of public life.

A radical fringe was less accepting of these circumstances, and was able to draw on a tradition of political violence. Anti-Chinese riots erupted with some frequency from late 1965 on. National elections continued to be marred by violence. Such violence often had an Islamic coloration, and on certain occasions Islam was central. The Komando Jihad of 1977 might well have been trumped up, but it enhanced the image of Islam as a violent government opponent. That image was further strengthened when a small group of Muslim activists hijacked an airliner in 1981.

The violence involved in these events was on a limited scale, however, compared with that which occurred on the night of September 12, 1984, in the port district of Jakarta known as Tanjung Priok. A crowd of some fifteen hundred Muslims, intent on freeing several local leaders from a nearby police station, was fired on by government troops. Estimates of dead or wounded were widely divergent, but all were sufficient to establish the incident as the bloodiest confrontation between the Indonesian army and the Muslim community since the 1950s.

Violence did not end with this single late-night outburst. The following months saw a whole series of fires and bombings across the island of Java and elsewhere around the archipelago; among those later traced to the Tanjung Priok incident was the spectacular bombing of the ancient Buddhist stupa of Borobudur in Central Java. Angry criticism of the government also continued in the form of sermons, cassette tapes, and leaflets, the discovery of which led in turn to a seemingly endless series of arrests and trials. Among the trials was that of retired Lt. Gen. Rekso Hartono Dharsono, former commander of the Siliwangi Division and, though not a member of the original Petition of Fifty group, a highly active figure in the dissident community from shortly after the launching of that attack on the Soeharto presidency.

The Tanjung Priok incident raised several questions. Why was the violence occurring? Was radicalism on the rise in Indonesia's Muslim community? And how were moderate Muslims responding to a government that many viewed as being opposed to fundamental Muslim values?

The Environment in Tanjung Priok

Like most port areas in the world's poorer countries, Tanjung Priok in 1984 was still in an early stage of modernization. The port's day-to-day operation was predominantly a labor-intensive activity, and the district contained a disproportionately large number of men, many of them young, out of school, and looking for work. They comprised a polyglot population, drawn from many disparate parts of the Indonesian archipelago: Muslims from other port towns, including Bantenese from the Java coast west of Jakarta and Bugis from the coast of Sulawesi; Christians from Flores and other eastern islands; all attracted to the capital in the hope of earning a better living than could be earned at home. But for those who got no further than Tanjung Priok, life could be exceedingly harsh. Work was often no more than brute labor, wages for many were barely sufficient for survival, and living conditions could be as mean as anywhere in the nation. Drunkenness and gambling were common, and ethnic gang fights frequent. The national police chief said that the area was unique in the nation for the extent of its labor disputes, narcotics, smuggling, counterfeiting, thievery, arson, and violent crime.[1]

In the latter months of 1984 the economic situation in the port district was more than usually depressed. The recession in the industrialized nations, which had led to the cancellation or postponement of numerous industrial projects in Indonesia the year before, was now being felt in the prices of ordinary commodities. With oil revenues down, the government had slashed its subsidies of rice, sugar, and domestic fuel prices. In addition, a government program to modernize the port had led to the closure of a large number of small stevedoring firms. Gen. L. B. Moerdani, commander of the armed forces, described Priok at this time as "a poor, overcrowded area with high unemployment."[2] That was an understatement.

If this were not enough, Islamic preachers had recently been offered an ideological issue to be added to the list already available for their denunciation. The government had sent to the Assembly five draft bills on political matters, one of which would require all social organizations to declare their adherence to the five principles of Pancasila as their "sole basis." What this meant or was intended to mean was itself a matter of dispute. On August 17, 1984, National Independence Day, the Petition of Fifty group issued a pamphlet strongly protesting that the bill would mean the permanent control or suppression of all Islamic and other independent organizations.

At around the end of August a lay preacher by the name of M. Nasir or Natsir (not to be confused with the former Indonesian prime minister, Mohammad Natsir) came to Sindang Road in Priok to address what was described as a large gathering of Islamic young men. In a long and rambling sermon, Nasir derided the government for recently "inviting" him to appear at the Office of Religious Affairs, presumably to explain some of his recent sermons.[3] "If you want to invite [me]," he said, "invite me to the mosque. We can have a discussion in the mosque and provide many people to be witnesses. If a person invites only one other," he said, "one of them does not return home." Then, more ominously, he continued: "Brothers, buy and change [your] cars every day. . . . Nowadays, this is the way people [must] act. If not, they will kill. The way they [will] kill is easy. . . . [They will] send people, wait until [you] come out of a house, bring a car and use a sack. Or to make it [even easier] . . . [they will] lift [an] M-16 from afar—[and] that's it, preacher."

Nasir went on to denounce the local Chinese as "the scoundrels of Indonesia," and their non-Chinese friends as no better than the dogs that guarded the houses of rich Chinese. He also denounced the Javanese for being no better than ducks that could be herded, in large numbers, by a single person. Nasir also attacked the Christians. "Nowadays the brains of Muslims who hold power have been poisoned by Christians," he said, through schools financed by the Chinese. He denounced Muslim women for going to work in factories—usually for Christian employers, he said—and for going to the hospital to have their private parts examined, and plastic spirals inserted as contraceptives, "like so many goats." As to government corruption, Nasir observed, if Islamic law were observed, and stealing were punished by the cutting off of hands, "officials . . . would be without hands and feet and would roll like a ball."

Without mentioning Pancasila, Nasir also addressed the imputation that if the government treated all religions equally before the law, they were all of equal merit. If religions were all the same, he said, and someone died, angels would come from every "faction"—Islamic, Catholic, Protestant, Buddhist, Hindu and Javanist—to fight over the corpse. "People who die will [have to] carry a whistle so that when the angels fight, [they can whistle] *priiiit*—[and call] offside!"

Other speakers were less crude but equally provocative. Abdul Qadir Djaelani, who was later sentenced to seventeen years in prison for involvement in several bombings, gave a talk in Tanjung Priok in late August or early September. According to a cassette recording that circulated subsequently, he called on his listeners "to continue this struggle until you die the noblest death, the death of a martyr!"[4] Another talk in Priok in late August or early September, by Syarifin Maloko, who also was later jailed, was followed by a prayer:

> Oh Allah, oh our God. If indeed you are going to take away Islam from the face of the earth, in particular from our beloved Indonesia, we appeal, oh Allah, that it is much better for us who have suffered so much to be taken away before you take away Islam . . .
>
> Bring down your curses on those who will not confess that this earth is your creation, oh Allah. Shut the mouths of those who say that this earth is the creation of the Pancasila eagle.
>
> Inspire us to rise up all together in protest against those tyrannical people, oh Allah. If we rise to protest, it will no longer be through words, but we will go to them with our daggers and cutlasses, oh Allah.[5]

It was in this environment that notices were posted on a prayerhouse wall located on Alley No. 4 of the port area's Koja district.

Events of September 8 to 12

A wholly reliable account of what followed is not yet possible. General Moerdani issued a statement and answered questions at a press conference on September 13.[6] Twenty-two people, sixteen of them members of the Petition of Fifty group, issued a *White Paper* on September 18.[7] The signers included retired Lt. Gen. Hartono Rekso Dharsono, the one-time Siliwangi Division commander; Ali Sadikin, the retired marine general and former governor of Jakarta; and Sjafruddin Prawiranegara, who had served as head of the republican government in the 1940s and was now general chairman of the Muslim Preachers Korps (*Korps Muballigh Indonesia*). Underground leaflets offered further alternative versions of what happened; a highly detailed account appeared in a document apparently completed at the Al Araf Mosque in Tanjung Priok on September 20.[8] Comparing information from these sources suggests that what happened was as follows:

On September 8 two security officers came to the As Sa'adah prayerhouse. They tried to remove posters they believed might incite hostility; one officer was said to have entered the prayerhouse without taking off his shoes, the other to have smeared gutter water on the posters.

These events were reported to a number of civil and military officials in the area. They also were reported to Amir Biki, a student activist of 1966, who was now a prominent figure in the Islamic community of

Tanjung Priok and a financial supporter of Islamic missionary activities there. He telephoned local military officers to protest the incident and to ask that something be done about it immediately. On Saturday evening several religious teachers, including M. Nasir, preached on the street to a crowd that was larger than ever before.

On Monday, September 10, a group of people from the prayerhouse community confronted the two officers and demanded an apology. The men denied the accusations made against them, and some in the crowd, becoming impatient, began to push and shove. An officer was slapped. Sand and stones were thrown. The officers managed to extricate themselves from this situation, but a motorcycle belonging to one of them was set afire. Reinforcements arrived and four local people were arrested, including the head of the prayerhouse.

On Tuesday evening members of the prayerhouse community met with a number of civil officials. They protested the behavior of the security men and demanded the release of the four detainees. The officials seemed sympathetic, but the four were not released.

On Wednesday evening, September 12, the usual local teachers were joined by Amir Biki, and the theme of freeing the detainees dominated their talks. Amir Biki seems to have been particularly frustrated by his inability to have the men released. Speaking before a large crowd, he proposed that if the four detainees were not released by 11:00 P.M., he and the people should go to the place where they were held and set them free. Thus, at about 11:00 P.M., Amir Biki and the crowd set out, chanting "God is great," and carrying the national flag, as well as a green banner proclaiming in Arabic, "There is no God but Allah."

Soon the crowd found its way blocked. A line of armed soldiers stood across the roadway, while to the rear of the crowd, armored vehicles and military trucks appeared, blocking the crowd's retreat. The *White Paper* observes that these armed men were not antiriot police; another source identified them as members of an air defense regiment based in Tanjung Priok. In addition, the *White Paper* noted, the crowd did not encounter fire hoses or tear gas, but automatic weapons. One source said they were M-16s.

The crowd could not be deterred. It surged forward, and the soldiers fired into the crowd. Amir Biki was shot; at least two accounts say he tried to get up but was bayoneted. In not more than thirty minutes it was all over. Estimates ran to as many as 63 killed and more than 100 severely wounded. Families subsequently reported 171 as missing. In the melee, a pharmacy and a shop were burned down.

One of the first questions General Moerdani was asked by local journalists was how such an event could have happened without security authorities having anticipated it. Moerdani pleaded ignorance. "We didn't plan anything," he told the press. "We were trapped."[9] He later told Reuters that there was no time to call in the riot police because there had been only twenty-seven minutes' warning.[10] It is possible, of course, that senior security officials were caught by surprise. This should not have been the case, however. Testimony at later trials made it evident that public security officers had mounted a considerable surveillance of Muslim preachers in the Jakarta area prior to the Tanjung Priok incident, including widespread taping of their sermons, and calling many of them in for interrogation. Moreover, the crowd of fifteen hundred grew in the course of several evenings, as well as over the course of the evening of the twelfth. So the use of air defense troops to deal with the crowd was a case of either serious misjudgment or serious lack of preparedness. The defense in one later trial charged that the security forces knew the situation was explosive and let it explode—as an object lesson to government critics. The truth has not been established. Appeals for an independent investigation were not acted on, and no official inquiry has been made public.

Interpreting the Violence

The larger meaning of the violence also could not be ignored. According to the *White Paper*, "The greater and more basic calamity [was] the political system and social conditions which brought about the September 12, 1984, incident." Tensions had been smoldering for a long time "below the surface of pseudo-stability." Events had been adversely affecting public opinion and creating a restless atmosphere, as a number of the people's former leaders, including the late Mohammad Hatta and the late Adam Malik, had brought to the attention of those in power.

> The causes of the unrest come back to one source, namely, deviations in the execution of authority by the national government from the letter and spirit of the 1945 Constitution, which peak[ed] in the five bills concerning the 'ordering' of political life, and above all the provisions concerning Pancasila as the 'sole basis.' Meanwhile, the people did not have

the power to change the situation through democratic means. Thus, the calamity of September 1984 in Tanjungpriok is not an incident which stands on its own. It is a consequence of the existing system.[11]

The Al Araf statement that came a few days later, by which time the scale of the violence was increasingly clear in the Muslim community, contained no such cool analysis. After an extended day-by-day account, the statement concluded:

> This TRAGEDY will be seen by other sides at the surface from the statements of government supporters, public officials, and groups in society. It is certain that the actual expressions of feeling of the Islamic community and the Indonesian people still are BURIED deep in their hearts.
>
> THEN what will be the impact of this tragedy in the coming days? Is this tragedy a sign of the END of a tyranny and the BEGINNING of the coming of JUSTICE? What is certain is that from this tragedy WILL ARISE NEW BIKIs AND NEW AMIRs FROM THE YOUNG GEN-ERATION OF INDONESIAN MUSLIMS![12]

Twenty-eight young men were arrested by the end of September on charges of assault, of damaging a Chinese house before the riot began, and of setting fire to Chinese homes and shops after the confrontation with the military. In the early months of 1985 they were tried and sentenced to one to three years.[13] But that was not to be the end of it.

Underground leaflets began circulating within a few days of the incident. (Arrests for possession of these were made by year's end not only in Jakarta, but also in Bogor, Bandung, Tasikmalaya, and Cirebon in West Java; in Yogyakarta in Central Java; in Surabaya in East Java; and as far away as distant Ternate.)[14]

On September 18 the *White Paper* was signed at a meeting at Ali Sadikin's house. That evening another meeting was held at a prayer-house adjoining the house of A. M. Fatwa, where the Tanjung Priok incident also was discussed. On September 19 Fatwa was arrested on charges of subversion.

On October 2 General Moerdani gave another public account of the incident at a combined meeting of four committees of Parliament. Accompanied by senior officers of the three armed services and the national police, he charged that an effort was being made to discredit the government. Illegal leaflets were being circulated, he said, that endangered national unity.

9. The Tanjung Priok Incident

On October 4 bombs exploded in two Jakarta branches of Bank Central Asia and at a shopping center in Glodok, the old Chinese business quarter. The bank was owned by Liem Sioe Liong, the Chinese businessman well known as a financial associate of President Soeharto and his family. Two people were killed.

General Moerdani made a public statement to the effect that the armed forces were responsible for the protection of everyone—Chinese, Arabs, and every other ethnic group. The following day, Armed Forces Day, Soeharto urged all sides to avoid being provoked by destructive elements who wanted to separate the armed forces from the people. In the next day or so many military and civilian political figures made similar public comments.[15]

On October 9, H. Mohamad Sanusi, a former cabinet member, former parliamentarian, and a signer of the Petition of Fifty, was arrested in connection with the bombings.[16]

Spiraling Reactions

In the last half of the month a series of fires and explosions occurred in various parts of Jakarta. A fire burned down a noodle factory on October 17.[17] The largest fire experienced in Jakarta in years destroyed the government-owned Sarinah Jaya department store in suburban Kebajoran on October 22.[18] On October 29 fire destroyed a Chinese-owned restaurant and adjoining theater that featured a strip-tease show. Bomb threats were received at many large buildings in Jakarta, including those housing the central telephone exchange, several foreign banks, and a hospital sponsored by Mrs. Soeharto.[19] None of these events was ever traced to the Tanjung Priok incident, although they certainly heightened the sense that the situation was rapidly getting beyond the government's control.

The sense of crisis became even more acute when, on the evening of October 29, a munitions dump at a marine corps base on the outskirts of Jakarta began exploding. Huge columns of flames rose into the sky. Shells fell and other damage occurred within a radius of six kilometers from the center of the blast. Radio and television bulletins warned residents to leave the area; windows and doors were blown out of homes in an expensive residential district in the vicinity; a nearby hospital evacuated its patients. It was later announced that more than 20 tons of munitions had exploded, fifteen hundred houses had been damaged, fifteen persons had been killed, and twenty-six more had been wounded; hospital sources indicated that casualties were greater.[20] It did not escape comment that the explosions might have been set off deliberately by members of the marine corps itself. It was recalled that the marines had been counted as strong supporters of Sukarno, and that Ali Sadikin was a former three-star marine general, and A. M. Fatwa a former marine chaplain.[21]

On November 8 General Dharsono was arrested and on the following day was charged with subversion in connection with the September 18 meetings.[22] He was the seniormost retired army officer arrested by the Soeharto government up to this time.

At this point General Moerdani began a rapid personal campaign to assure friendly Islamic leaders that the government harbored no ill-will toward them. In Kediri in East Java he told eighteen hundred Muslim preachers that he was just an official who happened to be Catholic and that the government had no interest in putting the Islamic community at large "into a corner." In Demak in Central Java he told a similar audience of four thousand that those arrested had been disturbers of the peace who just "happened" to be Muslim. "It was not because they were Muslims that they were arrested." In Bandung in West Java he told a meeting of some two thousand Muslim preachers that religion was being used, as were houses of worship, to promote issues that had nothing to do with Islam.[23] No such effort, however, was made to open a dialogue with the critics.

Fires of unknown origin continued to occur. On November 11 a fire burned out two floors of a centrally located hotel in Jakarta. On the night of November 13 a fire destroyed the sixth through fourteenth floors of one of the largest buildings in the modern center of the city. On the following day bomb threats against a number of large buildings led to massive evacuations. An expensive office building belonging to the family of Liem Sioe Liong was evacuated for the second time in a week. Two nights later six separate fires broke out in the capital.[24]

Government Prosecutions

On November 19 and 20 officials of the attorney general's office began, in a series of briefings for the national press, to outline the cases they intended to prosecute in connection with the Tanjung Priok incident and the Bank Central Asia bombings.

9. The Tanjung Priok Incident

It was said that General Dharsono participated in the meeting at Ali Sadikin's house and that ways of capitalizing on the Tanjung Priok incident were discussed. Some who attended allegedly urged selective bombings and threats of other terrorist acts through anonymous telephone calls. Mention was made of blowing up facilities of Pertamina, the state oil company; Perumtel, the state telephone company; and other vital facilities. Dharsono also was accused of inciting people present at the meeting at A. M. Fatwa's house to participate in the bombings that occurred later.[25]

A. M. Fatwa also was being held on charges of subversion. Fatwa, in addition to being a former marine chaplain, had been secretary to Ali Sadikin when Sadikin was governor of Jakarta, was one of the signers of the Petition of Fifty, and was secretary of its continuing Working Group. He also was at this time Chairman II of the Indonesian Muslim Preachers Corps. He was said to have been frequently arrested from 1979 on for sermons critical of the government.[26]

H. Muhammad Sanusi, who was not present at these meetings, was alleged to have provided some of the funds for the Bank Central Asia bombings. It was reported independently that money was borrowed from Sanusi by one of the bombing suspects, reportedly to buy a motor scooter.[27]

Eventually, all three major figures were found guilty and sentenced: Sanusi to nineteen years, Fatwa to eighteen years, and Dharsono to ten, later reduced to seven. Dharsono's principal counsel, the courageous and controversial Buyung Nasution, an early supporter of the New Order, was found guilty of unethical conduct. Sanusi was later charged also with involvement in a plot to assassinate President Soeharto, and one man reportedly died in custody after refusing to implicate him.[28]

Three "extremist lecturers" who spoke in Priok on the night of September 12, including M. Nasir, were reportedly detained. At least five other "extremist lecturers" were said to be in detention. An official of the attorney general's office was reported as estimating that altogether about two hundred people had been arrested in connection with the Priok incident.[29]

Further Reactions

There was relatively little serious effort made at the time to interpret these events.

9. The Tanjung Priok Incident

The head of the National Intelligence Coordinating Board Gen. (ret.) Yoga Sugama said that recent terrorist acts had been carried out by extremist groups. He identified four such groups: remnants of the Communist Party of Indonesia; Muslims who still hoped to establish an Islamic state in Indonesia; "movements sponsored by certain groups aimed at replacing the present government under the pretext of implementing Pancasila in a genuine and consistent manner," which presumably referred to the Petition of Fifty group; and those influenced by liberal democratic ideas who were "pretending to be human rights advocates" in order to undermine the authority of the government, an apparent reference to the capital's courageous civil rights lawyers.[30]

Kompas, Indonesia's largest and most influential daily newspaper, which was widely seen to be the voice of Roman Catholics from Central Java, commented on these developments in an editorial on November 23:

> Dharsono is a quite well-known figure as the first Secretary-General of ASEAN, Indonesian Ambassador to Cambodia and Thailand, and Commander of the Siliwangi Division. In this last capacity, his role in establishing the New Order was more than just marginal. . . . If it is true as charged that he participated in a secret meeting that masterminded the violent acts of bombing after the Tanjung Priok incident, then clearly he must be held responsible for his involvement. For an act with a political background with a figure of his reputation, the question does not stop there. One of the questions that immediately emerges is why he might have gone so far. He has no extreme left and no extreme right background. . . . The achievement of stability is not without sacrifice. What has been sacrificed is democratic expression by society and groups within it. There has been a curtailment of criticism. . . . Peripheral criticism is tolerated, but criticism which touches the heart of problems is not recommended. Not all people can accept and adapt themselves to such a development. A group of people who feel that they, too, rendered their contribution in 1945 and in 1966 have shown consistent opposition and have tried various means to get themselves noticed and heard. The more narrow the room for maneuver, the more varied are the means sought. The question is to what extent the case of H. R. Dharsono can be placed in this context. . . . The government is expected to be far-seeing. . . . What we must build is a political system and culture which makes it possible for anybody to express his opinion and have it listened to and considered.[31]

9. The Tanjung Priok Incident

Merdeka, a daily newspaper with a strong nationalist orientation, published an editorial on November 26 that said:

> The government is faced with something without precedent in the experience of the New Order and which could have been foreseen by those prepared to assist the country. . . . The situation is worrisome. The political front is not calm any more and is all stirred up. . . . We can sense that the government itself is finally aware that its political demolition strategy aiming at a New Order has serious weaknesses. . . . From historical experience we can determine that the greatest danger to the unity and union of Indonesia occurs when political forces each consider themselves most able and most competent to control national developments. . . . We suggest that if disorder and anarchy are not to result from further developments, there must be an attitude of introspection on all sides.[32]

But confrontation continued to be the principal means of expression. The government produced a continuing stream of actions and statements designed to demonstrate its control. Muslim activists repeatedly struck back with violence.

On December 22 the Parliament passed two draft bills into law, one requiring all political parties, and the government quasi-party Golkar, to accept Pancasila as their "sole basis." On Christmas Eve bombs damaged a Protestant church and a Roman Catholic church in East Java. These bombings were eventually tied to Tanjung Priok.

On January 2, 1985, President Soeharto made his first pronouncement on the recent violence. In a radio and television address, he said:

> We fully regret and feel concerned about violent incidents carried out by irresponsible people motivated by deep fanaticism. . . . We will never bow to extremist threats or terrorism. . . . We will wipe out terrorism before it develops into a national disaster. . . . We are all responsible for resolving differences of opinion through democratic and constitutional procedures.

In regard to Pancasila he offered the view that after Parliament passed all five political bills a strong legal foundation would exist for strengthening national unity. With Pancasila as their sole principle, political and social organizations would focus on their "real programs" in implementing national development. Organizations would no longer suffer the bitter factional and ideological frictions of the past, and all extreme activities and crises would be avoided.[33]

9. The Tanjung Priok Incident

The first trials in the Bank Central Asia bombing case began on January 7. Testimony in the Tanjung Priok case began on January 10.

Continued Confrontation

Even with all the fires and bombings that had so far followed the Tanjung Priok incident, public opinion was unprepared for the violent event that occurred on January 22. In the early morning hours time bombs exploded on an upper level of Borobudur, a Buddhist monument dating to the eighth century and reckoned to be the world's largest Buddhist monument after Angkor Wat. Nine stone stupas, or bell-shaped, lattice-worked shrines, and two stone statues of the Buddha were damaged. The monument was one of Indonesia's most cherished national symbols. In a single stroke Muslim activists, later tied to Tanjung Priok, had struck out at a major symbol of pre-Islamic values; at the Chinese, who were the principal practitioners of Buddhism; at the military and civilian elite, which was still decidedly Javanese and Java-centric; and at Soeharto himself because of his association with all of these, and because Borobudur rises up majestically from the plains of Central Java, the president's own home province.[34]

As 1985 wore on, the pattern of confrontation continued with the predictability of a *wayang* performance. The Assembly passed into law the controversial bill regulating social organizations. No voting took place; the bill was passed by acclamation in a session attended by only 55 percent of the membership—hardly an enthusiastic turnout for a bill that involved considerable government prestige.[35] By June subversion trials against Islamic teachers and students accused of speaking and writing against the government were occurring across the island of Java.[36] Fires of unknown origin continued to occur sporadically. In July alone, fires in Jakarta destroyed a major shopping complex, a nine-story office building, and the building that housed the state radio and television stations.[37]

The conflict between the government and elements of the Islamic community, some bent on violence, others expressing only dissent, seemed never ending. Arrests of Muslim activists in Central Java continued during 1987 and 1988. Many of those arrested came from towns or villages that had been centers of Muslim dissent in the past, and several had been imprisoned before for suspected subversion in the late

1970s.[38] As late as 1989 violent clashes between army troops and aroused Muslim groups took place in the south Sumatran province of Lampung, in which the death toll was variously estimated between forty-one and more than a hundred, and in the small island of Bima in West Nusatenggara. Although authorities initially characterized these incidents as further manifestations of Islamic extremism, it became clear in time that the issues were not primarily ideological. Poor people, who had been treated with extreme severity in land disputes, had looked to Islam as a vehicle for the expression of their frustration and anger. It was, to some extent, Tanjung Priok revisited in a rural setting.[39]

Islam and the Indonesian State

Islam played an important role in the development of political awareness in preindependent Indonesia. The first patently political indigenous organization in the Indies was the Islamic Union (*Serikat Islam*), founded in 1913, initially to promote the interests of indigenous traders in competition with the Chinese. But the incipient divisions within Islamic society led to an early split of the Union. In 1923 a radical group spun off, providing the nucleus for the later founding of the Communist Party of Indonesia; a strictly Islamic wing never developed into more than a minor Islamic political party.

This fissiparous tendency persisted. The first all-encompassing Islamic organization, the Masyumi (an acronym for *Madjelis Sjuriah Muslimin Indonesia,* or the Advisory Council of Indonesian Muslims) was created by the Japanese occupation authorities in 1943 to facilitate their own political control. The Masyumi hardly survived independence in its original form. The largest component organization, the Nahdatul Ulama (NU) (Revival of the Ulama), took an early opportunity to pull out. The NU had been founded initially, in 1926, as a result of divisions within the Muslim community. It was founded by traditionally oriented Islamic leaders, predominantly leaders of *pesantren* (Koranic boarding schools) in Java; they were reacting against the efforts of other Muslims to propagate a literal interpretation of the Koran, holding out instead for their long existing tradition of cultural compromise and adaptation.[40]

The pluralism of ideas among Indonesian Muslims came to a sharp focus with the need to write a constitution, which began under Japanese auspices in May 1945. With such a culturally varied society one might have thought that Indonesia was ready made for a national federal state, along the lines of India or Nigeria. But it seems not to have been seriously considered in 1945. The experience of political organizations from the 1920s on was one of constant divisions and rivalries, cliques and factions, even in the face of the Japanese occupation. Moreover, the spirit of "one people, one nation" was a major element in the thinking of such figures as Sukarno. The Indonesian nation was not comprised only of individuals living in their varied ethnic provinces, he said; it was also "all the human beings who, according to geopolitics ordained by God Almighty live throughout the entire archipelago of Indonesia from the northern tip of Sumatra to Papua!" Traditional Hindu ideas of the state were present as well; only twice, Sukarno said, had the Indonesian people experienced a national state—"in the time of Sriwidjaja and in the time of Madjopahit." The Indonesian state was to be a unitary state.[41]

But if it was to be a unitary state, could it be an Islamic state? Mohammad Hatta, who was both a Sumatran and a devout Muslim, and who in August 1945 was to become the first vice president of independent Indonesia, said at the first meeting of the constitutional drafting committee that the new unitary state would have to be separate from Islam. A Javanese member of the drafting committee agreed, observing that an Islamic state would create problems with Christians and other minorities, but adding that this did not mean the state had to be a secular one.[42]

Sukarno took up this latter theme also in his speech to the committee on June 1. He argued that the state should be committed to the five principles of Pancasila—belief in one God, nationalism, humanism, social justice, and democracy—which had meaning for all the religious elements within the society. His speech has since been seen as marking "the birth of Pancasila."[43]

This was not enough to satisfy some Islamic interests represented in the committee. The issue was referred to a subcommittee, which produced a restatement. It was hoped that the restatement would serve as a preamble to the constitution. It read as follows:

> The constitution of the Indonesian state which is to exist in the form of the Republic of Indonesia, and to be based upon the sovereignty of the people, is founded on the following principles: Belief in God, with the obligation for adherents of Islam to practice Islamic law, the principle of

righteous and moral humanitarianism; the unity of Indonesia, and democracy led by the mutual deliberations of a representative body which will lead to social justice for the entire people.[44]

The statement did not produce a consensus. The key phrase was: "with the obligation for adherents of Islam to practice Islamic law." Some committee members thought this provision went too far in conceding the power of the state to Muslim ideological interests. That is where things stood when the Japanese suddenly surrendered, and Sukarno and Hatta were obliged quickly to proclaim Indonesian independence. In these new circumstances of uncertainty, the nation's unity became an overpowering concern. The preparatory committee dropped the controversial phrase. It was a bitter defeat for those Muslim groups that had pressed for its inclusion. The original statement came to be known as "the Jakarta Charter"—and as a symbol of Islamic disillusionment.[45]

The disillusionment first took the form of insurrections committed to the founding of an Islamic state. These broke out in the late 1940s and early 1950s in West Java, South Sulawesi, and Aceh, and continued into the early 1960s. They were followed by Masyumi support for the larger revolts that broke out in parts of Sumatra and Sulawesi in 1958, aimed at replacing the Sukarno government with a pro-Western, anti-communist one. None of these movements attracted widespread popular support, further weakening the political position of the Muslim parties and their leaders that remained.[46]

Islam and the New Order

Muslims played such an important role in helping to bring down Sukarno and the Communist party that from the beginning they assumed they would receive seats in the government that followed. This did not happen, and thus much Muslim opinion was disaffected even before Soeharto refused to renew legalization of the Masyumi Party prior to the 1971 elections. Golkar's overwhelming victory at the polls, and the subsequent merger of all the Islamic parties into a single Party for Unity and Development (*Partai Persatuan Pembangunan,* or PPP) had the effect of making political Islam the principal opposition force. The term *opposition,* however, was neither conferred by the government, which did not officially recognize the existence of any opposition, nor sought by the party, which depended almost entirely on the government for its existence.

Not all Muslims saw Islam and the New Order as unalterably opposed. Mintaredja, who was Soeharto's selection to chair the some-what-less-than-reborn Masyumi under the name of Parmusi in 1970, represented a new breed of Islamic leadership that was prepared to work more cooperatively with the New Order. Mintaredja himself, before the 1971 elections, published a lengthy rationale for accommodation to the new sociopolitical realities of the New Order and for aiming at material victories.[47]

This view, almost certainly a minority one at the time, also was championed by the general chairman from 1970 to 1972 of the Islamic Students Association (*Himpunan Mahasiswa Islam,* or HMI). Nurcholish Madjid argued that the time had come for the Muslim community to turn away from the leaders of the past and their tendency to regard all aspects of human life as governed by religious norms and values. It was time to give more weight to human knowledge, to be more open to other groups in society, and to take more seriously the need for economic and social justice—in effect, the need for development.[48]

Any hope of a new era of good feeling between the government and Islam was dashed in 1973 by the government's submission of a bill to Parliament to create a single system of laws regarding marriage and divorce. The proposal produced a massive Muslim reaction; members of Parliament walked out, and Muslim youths at one point occupied the floor of the Parliament. The government capitulated, and a compromise bill was passed the following year.[49] Some writers have seen the outcome as a partial victory for the Muslims; but not all Muslims agreed. One Muslim intellectual saw it this way:

> The new marriage law was a real victory for the government, and a way-station on the road to getting control over the Muslim community. The problem of conflicts between the national law and religious law was a long-term issue. The Muslims wanted to see their aspirations reflected in the national law, and the nationalists wanted to see a single legal system for all Indonesians. There were demonstrations, of course. And the Muslims walked out of the Parliament at one point. So there were some concessions. But the Muslim community saw the outcome as a victory for the government. They saw it as a step that put the religious law under the national law.[50]

9. The Tanjung Priok Incident

Islamic dissatisfaction erupted again over the conduct of the 1977 elections, as we have seen, leading to Soeharto's Pancasila speeches, with their thinly veiled accusations of Muslim disloyalty.

Islam's image as a violent opponent of the government was considerably enhanced on March 28, 1981, when a small group of Muslims hijacked a Garuda Airlines DC-8. (They got as far as Bangkok, where Indonesian commandos, with the permission of Thai authorities, stormed the plane, in the course of which seven people died). Imran bin Mohammad Zein, thirty-three years old, was found guilty of stirring up his followers with sermons at the Istiqamah Mosque in Bandung, attacking a police post to obtain weapons which resulted in the deaths of three police officers, murdering one of his followers accused of being a turncoat, and, finally, carrying out the hijacking. He had returned from Mecca five years earlier and, according to his widow, had "indeed been eager that the teachings of Islam should be fully put into practice here."[51]

The 1982 election campaign degenerated into serious violence. About a million people turned out for a PPP rally in Jakarta. When Golkar attempted to match this performance, some PPP supporters attempted to disrupt the motorcade. According to one report:

> In some parts of the capital the procession met with hostility. Stones were thrown, banners were torn down and some people were attacked. Security forces reacted sharply, particularly after some policemen and troops were injured. Although it was claimed that guns were fired only as a warning and then into the air, there were reports that in some instances security forces fired into the crowd. As the campaign drew to a close, security forces were told to shoot at the legs of demonstrators and, if this failed, to shoot to kill.[52]

Admiral Sudomo, the head of national security, said that 7 people were killed and 97 injured, 20 by gunfire. He said 130 people had been arrested.[53] The news magazine *Tempo,* which broke an unofficial ban by reporting the event, was closed by the government for two months.[54]

The violence of the electoral campaign, and the fact that the PPP attracted more votes in Jakarta than Golkar did, undoubtedly were major considerations in moving Soeharto to renew his efforts to reduce Muslim influence in social and political life. He had sent a draft bill to the Provisional Parliament in 1969 that would have required social organizations of every sort to accept Pancasila as their ideology, as a condition of their continued legal existence. He had sent a draft bill to Parliament that would have imposed the same requirement on political parties in 1973. Neither of these efforts succeeded, mainly because of Muslim resistance. On August 17, 1982, Soeharto renewed both initiatives in his Independence Day address before a plenary session of the Assembly.

The proposals generated immediate objections. Perhaps the most serious came from the leaders of the religious communities. In December official spokesmen for the national Muslim scholars council, the Protestant council of churches, the Catholic bishops, and the national councils of Hindus and Buddhists issued a joint statement. They did not disregard Pancasila, they said. On the contrary, their aim was "to guide their respective communities to become faithful followers of their religion while simultaneously being citizens of a Pancasilaist state." At the same time, they said:

> The respective religions have their own religious basis which is universal in character, holds for all places and times, and which may not be incremented by any other thinking beyond the authentic basis. Therefore, social organizations which are inspired by or are religious in nature remain based on their religion and respective religious beliefs.[55]

When the People's Consultative Assembly met in April 1983 to elect him to another five-year term, Soeharto returned to the topic. He rejected charges that his government was suppressing dissent. He said, however, that the country "is not going to journey backwards." The multiparty system of politics "was a failure." It was time, he said, for Indonesia to consolidate politically and accept the national ideology. "We must remove the remnants of conflicts, disunity and suspicion."[56] The division of opinion was well represented by the statements of spokesmen for the opposing sides in July 1983. On July 7 Sjafruddin Prawiranegara, the long-time Islamic leader, addressed a letter to Soeharto. He said, in part:

> If Muslims are no longer allowed to establish Islamic associations—whether political organizations or social organizations—then Islam will come to be regarded as a private matter, which is completely contrary to Islamic teachings. The Islamic religion is not merely a private matter, but is also, and primarily, a matter of the "Ummat" (Community). . . . If the Indonesian Muslim Community is to be prohibited from establishing and maintaining Islamic associations, whether in the political field or

in other social fields, this is not only in contravention of the 1945 Constitution—and thus in contravention of the Pancasila itself, but, in practice means an attempt to kill Islam—through the Pancasila! For the Pancasila, being a creation of men, can be interpreted and applied according to the wishes and thoughts of men, namely those men who hold power, the power-holders controlling the Armed Forces! And in the long run, the teaching of religion—particularly the Islamic religion will—so I fear—be suffocated by Pancasila Morality, Pancasila Economy, Pancasila Law, and all other such Pancasila offspring.[57]

That same month the following statement was made by Soedjono Humardhani, the retired army general and long-time confidant of Soeharto who was well known for his championing of Javanese mysticism as a system of beliefs that should have equal standing with Islam before the law:

Maybe it is only wishful thinking on their part, but the idea of an Islamic state is still there. The moderates want a state that at least "smells" Islamic. And there are always extremists who want more. They haven't changed. The Constitutional Convention was stalled in 1957–58 because of Islamic ideology. The MPRS (*Majelis Permusyawaratan Rakyat Sementara,* or Provisional People's Consultative Assembly) in 1966 failed to reach an agreement on anything but economic policy. It was discussed again in 1968. And they walked out of the MPR (*Majelis Permusyawaratan Rakyat,* or People's Consultative Assembly) in 1978. Now the issue is being pursued outside the MPR. Islamic organizations like the HMI don't want to follow the government. They will have to take responsibility for the war that will take place.[58]

Opinion was undoubtedly hardening, and the legislation proceeded at a pace that can only be characterized as studied. On May 30, 1984, the government finally conveyed a draft bill on social organizations to the Assembly. It provided that all voluntary associations in the country must recognize Pancasila as their sole basis. They were given two years to bring themselves into line with the new rule by inserting the necessary language in their statutes. But the bill aimed to do more than control the ideology of private organizations. It also empowered the government to provide "guidance" to every social organization in the country, to control all foreign aid to them, and to dissolve any social organization that "carries out activities which disturb security and public order."[59]

In August senior members of the Petition of Fifty group sent all members of the cabinet and the Assembly a booklet, entitled *Save Democracy* (*Selamatkan Demokrasi*), that offered a critique of all five political bills before the Assembly. It contained a statement by Gen. A. H. Nasution that said, in part:

> Pancasila actually carries within itself harmony between diversity and unity. One cannot occur without the other. Stressing only diversity could damage unity. On the other hand, stressing only unity by making diversity disappear will bring us to the regimentation of state, national, and social life, narrowing the room for initiative, creativity, and dynamism. . . . So long as diversity of motivations and aspirations is not aimed at changing the principles and nature of the Republican state proclaimed in 1945, then the parties involved have to be given the freedom of association, assembly, and expression guaranteed by the 1945 Constitution.[60]

Such protestations notwithstanding, the Assembly passed the social organizations bill as expected. Passage was delayed by the Tanjung Priok incident. Hearings had already been held, but, as was common in parliamentary affairs in this period, only the bill's supporters had been heard. Now the hearings were extended to permit testimony from moderate critics. The final draft also included cosmetic changes. In such fashion it became law in mid-1985.[61]

A leader of the Nahdatul Ulama reflected on the whole experience:

> What happened at Tanjung Priok was a tragedy. All those men killed and maimed. It did not need to happen, and it would not have happened if the two sides were communicating with each other. These people had real economic grievances. They work in the port, and they see Mercedes automobiles being unloaded, while they are lacking even clean water in their homes. But they are poor and unorganized, and the government doesn't pay any attention to them. They also are very devout, and they believe they have great power when God is on their side. Many of them believed that Pancasila was a threat to Islam. Of course that was not true. Pancasila is a matter of the law, and the law has to be one that is acceptable to all our people, while Islam is a matter of ethics, and speaks to all of us who accept it. But the government tried to move quickly, and did not think about people like these; it did nothing to help them understand its intentions. They did believe the government was acting to harm Islam, and some of them did have the idea of raising a holy war against the government. But none of this would have happened if there had been communications between the two sides.[62]

9. The Tanjung Priok Incident

Whither Islam?

In 1985 the Nahdatul Ulama voted at a national congress to leave the PPP. One of the leaders of the Nahdatul Ulama discussed his plans to bring this about:

> I want to disassociate NU from the PPP. I want NU to have minimal contact with politics. The political choice now is either the status quo or revolution. So it is important for us to pull out.
>
> Initially NU had the right to distribute fertilizer, and this helped the Islamic scholars to become rich and powerful. Then Golkar took all the patronage, and the scholars lost power and became radicalized. NU politicians always included some close to the scholars and others who were really closer to the government. The ones like ——, who were close to the government still got some patronage; for example, —— has a timber concession in Kalimantan. But NU has much less patronage than before, and it can't meet the expectations of the *pesantren*. So the politicians who speak for them in the NU now oppose nearly everything the government does.[63]

He later reflected on how the departure was accomplished:

> It had to be handled in a way that was not threatening to the government. Ideally an organization like NU would not need the government, and would be able to raise the funds it needed for its programs from its members at the grassroots. But that is not possible in this economy; the government is too important, and if it feels threatened, it can cut off everything. . . .
>
> I reached an agreement with the government. They agreed that all NU people who had been civil servants, and left the civil service to take political posts with PPP would be reinstated. They also agreed they would give preference to NU people in making new appointments to the civil service, assuming they met the necessary requirements. The government also agreed that NU would receive licenses for economic activities, so we can support ourselves by our own efforts. We have gotten government approval to develop 1,000 hectares in Sumatra to produce spices for export to India and the Middle East, and a bank loan to begin to develop the area. I am advising our local branches to do the same thing.[64]

The departure of NU meant the end of the PPP as a significant political force. When elections for parliamentary seats were next held, in 1987, a substantial number of NU members would shift their vote to Golkar. But this decline of Islam in politics also might have been possible because Islam was growing stronger. It was not a strength that came from increased numbers, but rather one that came from an increased awareness within the existing Muslim community of its "Muslim-ness."

That an Islamic revival was occurring in Indonesia at the time of the Tanjung Priok incident seems undeniable. One daily newspaper reported that the revival was occurring in the country's other major religions as well, but the evidence in the case of Islam was particularly impressive. The paper's reporters found that mosques were packed for the five obligatory daily prayers in Jakarta, Bandung, Yogyakarta, and Surabaya in Java, and in Padang and Medan in Sumatra. On Fridays one major mosque in Jakarta was regularly filled to capacity an hour before prayer time, and one in Bandung erected tents to accommodate the overflow crowds. In addition, places of worship were alive with many new activities—missionary corps, Koran recitals, and youth groups. Moreover, new study groups were meeting in people's homes.[65]

The Muslim revival was attributed, in part, to the rapid social change that people of all religions were experiencing, particularly in urban areas. There was "a need for a set of guidelines that can order, explain, and give meaning to an otherwise confusing set of events." Proselytizing increased, through radio and television, organized efforts by Islamic universities and social organizations, and personal efforts by individual scholars. But orthodox Islam also seemed to be increasing in popularity because it was fulfilling social needs, more or less along the same lines as the urban Christian churches. "Nearly every local mosque has its volleyball team, its scout troops, its kindergarten, and its women's association."[66]

Several international factors contributed to the increasing tendency for Muslims to think of themselves in Islamic terms. Sidney Jones observed:

> The triumph of Khomeini and the Soviet invasion of Afghanistan have evoked feelings of solidarity with the world Islamic community. Furthermore, the exchange of people and ideas between Indonesia and the rest of the Muslim world has been steadily expanding. The number of pilgrims to Mecca, where Indonesians constitute the largest foreign community, continues to grow. Each year, scores of Indonesian students leave to study at Muslim universities in Cairo, Medina, Baghdad, Damascus, and Qum. Increased contact with other Muslims has brought with it a new prestige in being Muslim, a sense of identity and belonging.[67]

Thus a prominent oppositionist, a member of the Petition of Fifty, but himself not particularly identified with Islam, reported at the same time:

> Islam is attracting more and more of the interest of young people. They are thirsty for something to believe in. And it isn't any longer a matter of sitting on a dirt floor listening to an old man wearing a sarong. The other night my son wanted to borrow the car. I asked where he was going. He said he was going to the house of the president of Bank ——, a brigadier general, for a meeting of an Islamic study group.[68]

Other evidence emerged that a new sort of Muslim was entering the national elite in the mid-1980s. Former leaders of the Muslim Students Association were working for multinational corporations, in the oil industry, for example, and in banking. Eight ministers and junior ministers in the cabinet formed in 1988 were former Muslim activists. These were men engaged in activities that lay wholly outside the traditional world of Islam, familiar with the management of large secular institutions, and enjoying economic benefits undreamed of by the founders of Serikat Islam.

These new elite Muslims were nevertheless still a small minority. That members of this group should have made their peace with the secular establishment was hardly surprising. That their values should be shared by many Islamic teachers and intellectuals, who also were increasing in number in the faculties of universities and in such professions as journalism, also was to be expected. It did seem that, with their upward mobility in secular society, a shift was occurring in the pattern of Islamic leadership, that while the role of Islamic teachers was narrowing to "religious" affairs, that of middle class Muslims with university educations was expanding in social and economic life.[69]

This was occurring as inequality was increasing in urban Indonesia, most markedly in Jakarta. If the urban poor were most likely to look to Islam as a vehicle to express their economic and social demands, the question of who would represent their interests to the authorities was becoming increasingly urgent—not, presumably, the highly educated Muslims entering the upper ranks of the bureaucracy. Nor does it seem conceivable that the government could, or would wish to try, to police all the mosques, prayerhouses, and study groups of urban Indonesia to prevent future Tanjung Prioks from occurring.

One would like to think that the spirit of Pancasila might prevail.

9. The Tanjung Priok Incident

Preaching and teaching about Pancasila is a large enterprise in Indonesia. Senior government people have been obliged to go through a hundred hours of officially prescribed lectures and discussion. Almost everyone, at least in what economists would call the organized or modern sector, has had to go through a Pancasila "upgrading" course of some length, right down to drivers and others who perform the most simple tasks in government agencies, and an ever-widening circle of people in the private sector. Yet, it was difficult to find support in private conversation for what foreign scholars have seen as a civil religion, or even as a cult "complete with rites and commentaries."[70]

One major figure in the teaching program, Javanese by birth, a lifelong civil servant, politically well connected at the very start of the Soeharto regime, and still a senior official in it, assessed his experience with Pancasila:

> The whole experience with Pancasila has been extremely frustrating. I am a "manggala" or "super guru" in the program, which really got started in 1978. We have to have an ideology, of course; we have to have a basis for unity. We have rejected communism. We have rejected capitalism. We need a set of values, of ideas, that we stand for as a people. And Pancasila has the potential to be that. . . .
>
> The trouble is that there is a huge gap between the ideals laid down in Pancasila and what is really going on in the society. People want to talk about the real problems that concern them—about corruption, the lack of social equity, things like that. But it's not allowed. The leader has a script to follow, and that's that. Most people feel it's just indoctrination. They feel that all you can say is that the program tells them how the present government interprets Pancasila. The whole thing is gone about in a mindless way. There is no preparation, no selection, and no follow-up. Everybody just has to do it.[71]

At the University of Indonesia in 1983 students who were accepted for admission were obliged to attend a Pancasila indoctrination program at the start of the academic year. At the opening ceremony they drowned out the official speakers with a spontaneous outbreak of hoots and handclapping. One of the young university lecturers, a former student leader assigned to help run the indoctrination program at the time, reflected on the students' behavior:

> Ideological indoctrination is a risky business. If there is too big a gap between a regime's ideals and the actual situation that people are experiencing, they are going to express their frustration and disbelief. All the

demonstrators in Eastern Europe have been indoctrinated in Stalinism. The 1966 generation of students here were all indoctrinated in Nasakom. The students who are being indoctrinated in Pancasila will be the first to turn against it. And their criticisms will be all the more serious because they will be based on a good understanding of it, of all its strengths and weaknesses.[72]

Thus a half century after Indonesia's declaration of independence and its first grappling with the writing of a constitution, relations between Islam and the state remain a fundamental problem for the Indonesian nation. Yet, it is not this alone that confounds Indonesian political life. There has been a paucity of political ideas to deal with the place of Islam, one acceptable, that is, to at least the major groups on each side of the issue, and an absence of institutions in which these ideas could be expressed and tested. The Soeharto government's record in dealing with Islam has been one of attempts to deny Islam a political role, and yet Islam remains a political force. It is not the case that the institutions of the Indonesian state have been "cleansed" of politics. It is rather that they have been made irrelevant to much of the political life that has sought expression, narrowed down to reflecting only the factional struggles within the military and civilian elite.

TEN

Deregulating Industry

The outbreak of protest in Tanjung Priok in 1984 was not unrelated to the insecurity created among the urban poor as a result of recession in the world economy. Indonesia's economic growth slowed, government resources declined, consumer subsidies were reduced, and prices of daily commodities increased. In a port district where many were already living close to the margin, the situation was ripe for calls to action.

The economic situation pressed not only on the urban poor and the government budget; it presented an unaccustomed set of problems for private and state enterprises as well. In the early 1970s manufacturing was still dominated by traditional light consumer goods that were relatively impervious to economic slumps—principally processed food, beverages, tobacco, and weaving. A decade later the intermediate and capital goods industries were much more important, mainly as a result of the rapid growth in production of fertilizer, pharmaceuticals, motor vehicles, rubber tires, electronic goods, and plywood.[1] By 1982 domestic markets for most of these latter products were shrinking rapidly.

A vigorous program was begun to protect Indonesian manufacturers from adversity. A campaign was launched to "buy Indonesian." Imports were placed under physical controls. New investment was subjected to elaborate "guidelines." The manufacturing sector of the Indonesian economy was wrapped in an elaborate protective cocoon.

Then in the late 1980s, with foreign exchange in short supply, and even manufacturers disillusioned with the way the government's protection was impinging on prices, steps were taken to reverse the direction of government policy. The financial services industry was opened further than ever before to private interests, domestic and foreign. A large portion of the nation's imports of manufactured goods was freed of physical controls. Foreign investment was encouraged as it had not been since 1974. The result by the early 1990s was a rapid improvement in investments, exports, and government revenues.

The process of regulation and deregulation was clearly one that involved conflicting interests. And it left behind continuing debate about the future of the public sector, about the dominant position of Chinese Indonesians in the private sector, and about the favored positions being acquired by the president's relatives and friends. The process and the debate went to the heart of money and power at the peak of the Indonesian political economy as the nation entered the 1990s.

Controlling Imports

Control of key imports was an established feature of Indonesia's trade regime. The Dutch had controlled imports to protect domestic industry during the depression of the 1930s. From early on in the New Order, the Logistics Agency had had the sole right to import rice and later a variety of other foods, and Pertamina had the sole right to import petroleum products. Some manufactured goods also were banned, such as fully assembled motor vehicles, in order to protect domestic manufacturers. Most other goods, however, could be imported by any general trading company holding a license from the Ministry of Trade, and manufacturers could import the raw materials and intermediate goods they needed for their own production.

This freedom ended with the introduction of an "approved traders" system in November 1982. The system established a list of categories of raw materials, components, and products that could be imported only by specified agencies. Initially the categories included a large number of agricultural products: cotton, wheat flour, milk and milk products, soybeans and soy flour, cloves, and sugar. The list also included industrial materials and products, and over time the number of these expanded greatly to include a wide array of iron and steel goods, plastics, chemicals, textiles, pharmaceuticals, paints, fertilizers, rubber goods, leather goods, wood pulp, paper, glass, vehicles, machinery, electrical equipment, and minerals. It was estimated in early 1986 that 1,484 items were by this time under import license controls, of which 1,360 were in the manufacturing sector, and that 296 items were under physical import quotas, of which 231 were in manufacturing. These items amounted to $2.7 billion worth of imports in 1985, more than half the value of Indonesia's total imports.[2]

Import licenses were sometimes granted for an entire category, leaving the "approved trader" free to import any amount or type of item in the category. Other licenses were granted only for goods of a specified type and quantity, and were subject to periodic renewal or amendment. Still other licenses established sole agents for the importation of particular brands. The "approved traders" were often state trading companies, but not always. Some were state enterprises that were themselves manufacturers or users of the goods they were to control; thus Krakatau Steel was given control of eighty-two types of iron and steel. In addition, some "approved traders" were private firms.[3]

Several explanations were offered for this elaborate system of controls.

The fundamental problem was that the economy was already highly protected by the time the recession of the early 1980s began, and in the conditions of recession still more protection was needed than before. An economic minister of the time recalled: "They all needed protection. An inward industrialization policy does that. It creates a situation that requires it. Everyone was yelling for help."[4]

Another factor was disarray in the cabinet. The same economic minister said:

> The strongest pressure came from the private sector, including foreign investors. . . . We fought it but . . . the minister of industry . . . believed in building plants . . . and . . . the minister of trade said he was under orders from the president.
>
> There was a big debate over the merits of import-substitution versus export-promotion. Some members of the cabinet didn't even believe in exporting. It is unfortunate, but we had no alternative plan.[5]

Mohammad Sadli has said that the government turned to physical quotas because it felt constrained by the General Agreement on Tariffs and Trade from imposing high tariffs, and, in addition, feared that high tariffs would only encourage smuggling.[6] Another consideration was that the "approved traders" could accumulate capital for further industrial expansion. According to Sadli:

The argument of the government is that there is no better way to establish the needed industry because under competitive conditions no investor would want to come in; also the capital requirements are too high for the degree of risk. This protection solves the problem of competition and capitalization.[7]

How the system of "approved traders" worked in practice may be seen from the cases of plastics and steel.

The Case of Plastics

A decree of the Minister of Trade on October 24, 1984, placed the importation of a variety of basic materials for the plastics industry under government control. The decree was concerned with polyethylene, which was widely used in making plastic bowls, buckets, and pans for household use; polypropylene, used in making plastic bags for marketing food and other products; polystyrene, the hard, clear plastic often used in place of glass; polyvinyl chloride, used in making pipes and tubing; acetate; and acrylic. These materials were henceforth to be imported solely by three state trading corporations—P. T. Panca Niaga, P. T. Cipta Niaga, and P. T. Mega Eltra—in effect, by subsidiaries of the trade ministry. Each was given an approximately equal quota, stated in tons for each type of material. According to the decree, the purpose of the new policy was "to give operating assurance to the domestic plastics industry . . . and to assure the continuous availability of its basic materials."[8]

The bulk of plastics imports was in two of the six categories. Total imports in all six categories were valued at $361 million in 1984, and polyethylene and polypropylene alone accounted for more than $300 million. Neither polyethylene nor polypropylene was manufactured in Indonesia, however. At the time two Japanese joint ventures were producing polyvinyl chloride, and a third company was producing polystyrene. This last was P. T. Polychem Lindo, part of the Bimantara Citra Group, led by Bambang Trihatmodjo, one of President Soeharto's sons.[9]

The decision by the Minister of Trade was followed by a further announcement in March 1985 at a meeting of plastics industry executives in Jakarta, that the three state trading companies were appointing a single private company as their sole agent for all plastics imports. The agent was Panca Holding Ltd., based in Hong Kong. A prominent businessman and relative of the president, Sudwikatmono, was introduced as a director of the firm. Steven Jones of the *Asian Wall Street Journal* later reported that records in Hong Kong showed Panca Holding was owned by two corporations registered in Vanuatu, a small South Pacific tax haven, and that two of President Soeharto's sons, Bambang and Sigit, were members of the board of directors.[10]

The state trading companies charged a fee equivalent to $23 a ton. Panca Holding charged an additional $20 a ton, later raised to $70 a ton, plus 2 percent of the value of the transaction. In 1986, with polyethylene selling at about $500 a ton, these markups added 21 percent to the cost of importing polyethylene. A survey of industry executives found other objections to the system. Big users continued to work directly with their long-term foreign suppliers, and no function was performed by the state trading houses or by Panca Holding other than passing the orders along. Even this was not done efficiently; about a month was added to the lead time on orders, and goods often arrived before the documents that were needed to clear them through customs, which meant added costs for storage. It was estimated that Panca Holding earned $30 million for its role in handling the paperwork in 1985.[11]

Industry unhappiness grew when the government announced in August 1986 that only a single state trading company, P. T. Mega Eltra, would manage the plastics quotas, still retaining Panca Holding as its agent. Industry sources were reported as saying that the waiting time for goods had been lengthened. In late 1986, following a devaluation that meant higher domestic prices for imports, the state trading company and Panca Holding did lower their fees, reducing the markup by about half, "to help the industry."[12]

In short, the plastics monopoly was a transparent scheme that had little to do with protecting local industry and a lot to do with making money for the president's family and friends.

The Case of Steel

The state-owned steel corporation, P. T. Krakatau Steel, had been given control of the import of steel and steel products by presidential decree in 1979. It was said that, in addition to protecting the domestic market for Krakatau Steel, the controls were needed because importers were engaging in "statistical smuggling"—bringing steel into the country with documents identifying it as something else with a lower tariff. It was also said that the big domestic steel users, the automobile assemblers, had tie-ins with auto manufacturers in Japan and their steel suppliers, so that the Indonesian monopoly was not expected to lead to any price advantage. A series of decrees by trade officials designated one or another of several trading companies as agents of Krakatau Steel in importing steel and steel products and distributing them domestically.[13] In April 1984 a private company, P. T. Giwang Selogam, formed earlier that year, was named to carry out the import of cold-rolled steel on behalf of Krakatau Steel. From 1985 the trading companies were removed from the steel trade altogether, and the entire field was reserved for Krakatau Steel and Giwang Selogam. Krakatau controlled the importation of hot-rolled steel in a variety of forms, which is what it was producing itself. Giwang Selogam was given control of the import of cold-rolled steel and its products, which is what a sister company to Krakatau was to begin producing in 1987. The import monopolies collected a commission of $20 per ton and a "handling fee" of 2.5 percent of the value. In 1984 and 1985, with Indonesia importing more than $400 million in cold-rolled steel, the private monopoly was roughly comparable in value to that in plastics.[14]

The key figures in P. T. Giwang Selogam were familiar ones. The chairman of the board was Liem Sioe Liong, who held a 20 percent interest in the firm. The executive director was the president's relative, Sudwikatmono, who held 6.7 percent of the shares. Most of the rest were held by relatives and business associates of Liem. Liem had a substantial interest in cold-rolled steel. P. T. Cold Rolling Mill Indonesia Utama, a joint venture between Krakatau Steel and Liem Sioe Liong, was scheduled to begin production in 1987.[15]

The World Bank, in its 1986 report on Indonesia, estimated that these import arrangements raised domestic steel prices 25 to 45 percent above international levels.[16] A domestic study found that users of every type of steel reported that prices increased significantly. Users also reported that the majority of steel was being imported by both monopolies exclusively from Japan, whereas much lower prices were being quoted by suppliers in other countries. Lead time on orders through Krakatau was up to seven months, twice the time required when producers could import on their own.[17]

The steel import monopoly thus worked badly for all parties but the monopolists: a large and costly state enterprise and a group of private investors associated with the president, who were earning easy money without performing any economic services.

Controls on Private Investment

The control of imports was only one strand to the government's program. Another was control of new investments. Foreign investment had been closely controlled from 1974 on. Domestic investment also required some form of government approval. The means of control grew more elaborate with the passing of years.

In October 1981 the head of the Capital Investment Coordinating Agency, Suhartoyo, announced at a news conference that the annual priority lists he had just issued for the year were "the most comprehensive guidelines ever issued" by his organization. The lists included 56 "top-priority" areas in which the government would permit domestic or foreign investment under certain conditions, and more than 275 specific ventures for which the government was seeking investors. Some ventures were highly specific as to location, capacity, and ownership. For example, a pulp and paper mill was listed that was to be established at Sesayap in East Kalimantan, was to be based on mixed tropical hardwood, was to have a capacity of 62,000 cubic meters of sawn timber, 81,500 cubic meters of plywood, and 165,000 tons of pulp a year, and was to be a joint venture with equity participation by an Indonesian state-owned corporation.[18]

This approach continued under the leadership of Ginandjar Kartasasmita, who was named head of the investment agency in 1985 and retained his leadership of the "buy Indonesia" program. The 1985 investment priority list included four hundred projects open to foreign investors, others restricted to domestic investors, and areas closed to investment altogether. The 1986 list included nine hundred projects open to foreign investment. By 1988 the list ran to 238 pages.[19]

Private investment in manufacturing fell off considerably. Approvals by the Capital Investment Coordinating Agency did increase in 1983, reflecting a rush of applications to beat the new tax deadlines. Otherwise, domestic and foreign investment approvals remained down and well below 1982 levels through the mid-1980s. Domestic investment approvals in 1986 were still 15 percent below 1982 in real terms. Foreign investment approvals remained below 1982 levels even in nominal terms.[20]

Government approvals also did not translate into a comparable flow of investment capital. Hal Hill has estimated that the flow of foreign capital into Indonesia in the form of direct investment, realized and in real terms, peaked in 1975 and remained at around a fourth of that level through at least 1985. The impact on Indonesian manufacturing was substantial; of all realized foreign investment from 1967 through 1985, 59 percent was in manufacturing.[21]

In comparative terms, foreign investment in Indonesia from 1970 through 1984 was dwarfed by foreign investment in Malaysia and Singapore, and also by foreign investment in such oil-producing countries as Mexico and Nigeria. The totals in billions of U.S. dollars were: Mexico, 13.2; Singapore, 12.9; Malaysia, 9.0; Nigeria, 4.0; and Indonesia, 3.0. Even Thailand, which lagged behind Indonesia in the 1975–79 period, ran some 30 percent ahead in the period of 1980–84. Only the Philippines, of the ASEAN economies, ran behind Indonesia throughout.[22]

The critical element in so far as foreign investment in manufacturing in Indonesia was concerned was Japan. When petroleum was excluded, private investment from Japan amounted to 68 percent of all foreign investment.[23] Japanese assessments, however, were turning increasingly negative. Japanese trade representatives in Jakarta issued statements to the effect that only 60 percent of Japanese joint ventures in Indonesia were operating profitably and that Indonesia's attractiveness for Japanese investors was rapidly falling below that of other countries in Southeast Asia.[24] In January 1987 a Japanese survey found this latter opinion widespread among Japanese corporations.[25]

Several reasons accounted for the decline in investments. Private economists judged that the devaluations of 1978 and 1983 were a significant cause, especially in their impact on Japanese investment. Also, import substitution was reaching a saturation point in some sectors, especially with the decline of domestic demand beginning in 1982. In the face of these obstacles the investment policy was ineffective. Indeed, it is difficult to avoid the impression that the bureaucracy's effort to give detailed direction to private investment was counterproductive.

The State Sector

A powerful lobby for government protection from foreign manufacturers was the state sector itself. The Economic Census of 1986 counted 589 large and medium-sized state enterprises operating in 1985, owned by the national government, local governments, and a variety of joint ventures among these and the private sector. Data on 215 enterprises owned and operated by the national government at the end of March 1986 provided further information. By sector, the total included thirty-eight in manufacturing, thirty-eight in agriculture, twenty-two in banking and finance, nineteen in public works, seventeen in transportation, and eight in mining and energy. Still others were involved in a variety of other activities ranging from international trade to hotels and printing.[26]

The state enterprise sector experienced massive expansion during the years from 1979 to 1985. The total assets of the 215 enterprises grew at an annual rate of 25 percent, and their sales grew from 20 to 30 percent of Gross Domestic Product (GDP).[27] Much of this was accomplished as a result of government infusions of capital. The state enterprises as a group consistently showed a significant deficit in their operations, averaging the equivalent of 4.8 percent of GDP in the 1980 to 1983 period, declining in subsequent years to become 2.8 percent in 1986. Investment in the state enterprises was not financed from their own savings for the most part; savings provided only 28 percent of investment in the enterprises in 1980 to 1983, and rose to only 40 percent in 1986. The deficit being run by the state sector enterprises was among the most important factors contributing to the resource gap of the public sector as a whole.[28]

This swelling of the role of state enterprises in the heyday of oil price rises flowed from several sources. One of these was undoubtedly ideological. The 1945 Constitution, reflecting the broadly socialist views of most national leaders at the time, provided for government ownership of mineral resources and other "important" sectors of the economy. Another source of support for the state sector was political. The state enterprises were the uncontested terrain of indigenous Indonesians, and so provided an essential counterweight to the Chinese firms that tended to dominate the private sector. In addition, the state enterprises enjoyed significant bureaucratic support. Almost every government department had one or more enterprises under its supervision, and these were sources of various perquisites, including posts for senior bureaucrats long in the department's service. We have seen that the trade ministry assigned lucrative monopolies to its own enterprises, until these were lost to more powerful interests. The armed forces also had a strong bureaucratic interest in the state sector. The great majority of state enterprises were widely believed to be headed by military personnel and retired military personnel in the mid-1980s. The expansion of the state enterprises thus served the interests of a wide swath of the political elite.

For all these reasons, when resources narrowed, the state enterprises and their managers and patrons came to constitute a powerful lobby for maintaining the status quo.[29]

The Private Sector

In comparison with the state sector, private enterprise became a significant consideration in public policy only at a relatively late date. Indigenous enterprise was all along an interest after Indonesia's independence, for the reason that the indigenous population was poorly represented in businesses beyond those small in scale, and the government tried to promote indigenous firms through a variety of public programs. But private enterprise as such was not given much attention, and, when it was, it was usually seen as a kind of activity that needed to be "guided."

The Fourth Five-Year Plan, announced in early 1984, introduced a view of the private sector that represented a sharp departure from the previously prevailing official attitude. The Fourth Plan estimated that the economy would have to create 9.0 million new jobs over the five-year period, and calculated that the economy would have to grow at a rate of 5 percent a year in order to do that. This, in turn, would require the investment of Rupiah 145.2 trillion, and the central government budget would be able to provide from oil revenue, taxes, and foreign aid only a little more than half that amount. The remainder—Rupiah 67.5 trillion—would have to come from the private sector and state enterprises. The announcement of this conclusion created something of a sensation in Jakarta. Who in the private sector would be able to invest so much? Surely, said *Tempo* magazine, the bulk would have to come from the business "giants" like Liem Sioe Liong, William Soeryadjaya, Lie Siong Thay, The Nin King, and Agus Nursalim, all well-known figures in the ethnic Chinese business community.[30]

The Indonesian Chamber of Commerce and Industry sponsored a meeting in late March 1984, attended by about four hundred of the country's leading indigenous and ethnic Chinese businessmen, to discuss the government plan. The conference was addressed by General Moerdani, commander of the armed forces, and by Lieutenant General

Sudharmono, then the state secretary and chairman of Golkar, both of whom appealed for an end to racial discrimination in the interest of harmony and continued economic growth. The conference ended with the issuance of a joint statement calling for the "mobilization of all national business resources, irrespective of racial origin, to make the fourth five-year plan a success."[31]

Relations between the government and the ethnic Chinese business community were already controversial. The government had, by this time, encouraged private investment, sometimes jointly with government investment, in cement, flour, basic chemicals, paper, petrochemicals, fertilizers, pharmaceuticals, shipbuilding, electric power generation, and coal production.[32] It was estimated that three-fourths of government bank loans were going to ethnic Chinese firms. And it was widely believed that ethnic Chinese businessmen were secretly in partnership with numerous high military and civilian officials.

Feelings were mixed on both sides at the prospect of the Chinese playing a larger role. Speaking of his fellow Chinese-Indonesians, Sofyan Wanandi said, "They really have the capital for expansion. But they are still afraid, whether the society will accept them."[33] Mohammad Sadli, now an official of the Chamber of Commerce, which was a preserve of indigenous businessmen, said the problem was "the tendency for capital and ownership to become centered in a small group of Chinese firms." It would help if there were incentives for them to "go public"; if the public was not ready, the government could establish a trust fund to buy and hold the shares temporarily. It also was time, Sadli said, to think about antimonopoly or antitrust legislation.[34]

Of a total Indonesian population of 147 million in 1981, 4.1 million, or 2.8 percent, were estimated to be ethnic Chinese. Although this was the smallest proportion of ethnic Chinese in any ASEAN state other than the Philippines, their integration with the rest of the national society was still limited. Some Chinese families had been in Indonesia for generations and had prospered under Dutch rule. Others had arrived after World War II, and some 1.0 million were still not Indonesian citizens as late as 1970. Added to the separateness these circumstances implied was an undercurrent of resentment over the phenomenon of alliances between Chinese businessmen and high officials. It was even said that some Chinese businessmen had settled their families abroad so as to make it easy to leave themselves should that become necessary.[35]

10. Deregulating Industry

The sensitivity of the subject could be judged from the absence of systematic data on Chinese-owned business, and from the government's efforts to suppress attention to the topic in the press. The magazine *Expo* undertook in early 1984 to compile and publish brief biographies of Indonesia's one hundred "millionaire" businessmen, the great majority of whom, it said, were of Chinese descent. After two issues and having gotten no further than millionaire number 44, *Expo* was banned from publication. The topic was then taken up by the magazine *Fokus*, which published a list of two hundred millionaires in April and May of 1984 and analyzed some of the country's largest business conglomerates. *Fokus* then also was banned.[36] Despite their brief existence, these sources did begin to reveal the increasing scale, complexity, and maturity of the Indonesian private sector.

Many private corporations were established from the late 1960s on by individuals who already owned one or more corporations. More than half the private equity capital invested between 1970 and 1986 was found by one study to be in 125 corporate groups owned by single individuals or families. Most were owned by Chinese Indonesians (thirty-nine of the top forty-seven). Most of these had gotten started on a small scale in the colonial period (thirty-six of thirty-nine). Most indigenous Indonesian owners (eight of the top forty-seven) had gotten started only in the 1950s.[37]

The development of these large family concerns in the late 1960s and early 1970s was made possible, at least in part, by alliances with foreign partners in fields where technology was crucial, mainly textiles, chemicals, metals, paper products, electrical appliances, and transportation equipment. Families went into several unrelated fields at the same time, perhaps seeking safety in diversity. Military and bureaucratic favoritism also was thought to be a significant factor in the start-up period by way of government licenses, contracts, and loans.[38]

The oil boom years were highly favorable to the prosperity and further expansion of these new manufacturing ventures, in part because of the January 15 "disaster" of 1974. The nationalistic policy regime—the effort to keep new foreign investment out, and the encouragement of local business by means of tax holidays and subsidized bank loans—during a period of expanded government spending was generating increased demand. One conglomerate, the Astra group, owned by William Suryadjaya and his family, had 197 companies under its control by 1986.[39]

By the 1980s many of the new conglomerates were thus well established in the manufacture of intermediate and consumer goods. And
when the boom ended they were hard hit. Auto sales peaked at 208,000
units in 1981 and fell to 150,000 after 1983. Electric appliances fell 35 percent from 1980 to 1986.[40] Thus the calls for help, and the step-up of government protection beginning in 1982.

That the bulk of these firms were Chinese ensured that, whatever the
quality of their management and whatever the justification for government protection, an undercurrent of dissent from the government program of protection would exist, both in and out of government, and this
was to be a factor in bringing the program to an eventual end.

The President's Family and Friends

There was, in addition to the state and private sectors, a growing third
sector usually referred to as "the palace group" or, simply, "the family."
Stories about the financial interests of the president's family and friends
were long a staple of Jakarta gossip. It was left largely to the foreign
press, however, to deal directly with the topic.

The first foreign press account to receive major attention in Jakarta
appeared in the *Sydney Morning Herald* on April 10, 1986, only days after
the flight of Ferdinand Marcos from the Philippines. The article, by
David Jenkins, the author of a well-known book on the Indonesian military, began: "As Philippine investigators peel back the covers on the
hidden Marcos millions, Indonesians are asking new questions about
assets of between $2 and $3 billion piled up by the family and business
associates of President Soeharto."[41] The article went on to describe a
number of cases involving two of the president's sons, one of his daugh-
ters, his half-brother, his foster brother, and another relative, all of
whom in only a few years had acquired major interests in a wide range
of businesses, including banking, the spot oil market, the clove trade,
flour milling, cement, logging, hotels, textiles, and fertilizer distribution, often in collaboration with the president's long-time associate,
Liem Sioe Liong.[42]

Photocopies of this report proliferated rapidly in Jakarta. The
Indonesian government lodged a formal protest with the Australian
government and banned all Australian journalists from Indonesia.
When President Ronald Reagan of the United States visited Indonesia
briefly in early May, two Australian correspondents accompanying him

as part of the White House press corps were turned back at the airport.[43]

The story was thus kept alive for some weeks. It was as if security officers had overreacted as a way of warning the president, of trying to protect him from himself. In June retired Brigadier General Suhardiman, the head of the army-sponsored Soksi labor union since 1962, and at this point a leading survivor of the Nasution era in the Golkar group in Parliament, said it was time to start thinking about the presidency and how long any one person should serve in it.[44]

Reaction apparently had reached a point at which the military leadership was concerned. In early July Soeharto met for three hours with the senior officers of the armed forces. At a press conference immediately following the meeting, General L. B. Moerdani said that many issues had arisen lately and that the meeting had been called to review them. One issue, he said, was the impression that the president and his wife were engaging in business. According to Moerdani, Soeharto told the service commanders that this was simply not true. He did receive many gifts, and he accepted all that were offered. Possibly foreigners thought the gifts went into his own pocket, but that was not so; they all went into foundations for humanitarian purposes. General Moerdani said the meeting also dealt with a number of other current issues, including the office of the presidency. He did not say what the president had had to say on this topic, nor did he commit the armed forces on the succession issue.[45]

Many in the Jakarta elite, in and out of government, were more depressed than angry. The facts had long been known to them. One of Soeharto's principal advisers had earlier reflected on the situation with foreboding:

> The involvement of members of the president's family in all sorts of business deals has been the great weakness of his administration. It is an easy target, and the one eventuality that can't be predicted is the possibility that some army colonel, or group of colonels, will use that weakness as the basis for a take-over. If you count all the changes of government in the Third World since World War II, the number that have taken place as a result of a coup probably easily outnumbers those that have resulted from an election. So the possibility is there.[46]

By July 1986 those in the elite were in general agreement that the situation with regard to the family had to be "cleaned up." Said a Muslim political leader: "It might be true what has happened in the Philippines could not happen in Indonesia because the two countries are very different. But we don't really know much about the Philippines, and many people think that if Marcos could fall, Soeharto could too."[47]

Those in the Chinese business community also thought Soeharto had to bring his family under control. But an economic adviser to the president said that Soeharto had not taken any action in response to the criticism, real and implied, in the mid-1986 events. "The president told his economic ministers in 1975 that he wanted his family's firms treated like any others," the adviser said. "But he hasn't done that since."[48]

Still further information about the financial interests of the Soeharto family and friends was revealed in a series of articles that appeared in the *Asian Wall Street Journal* in November 1986. According to two *Journal* correspondents, Steven Jones and Raphael Pura, those who benefited included Liem Sioe Liong; Sudwikatmono, a cousin of the president, also sometimes referred to as his foster brother; Probosutedjo, a half-brother; Sigit Harjojudanto, the president's eldest son, then age thirty-five; Bambang Trihatmodjo, the president's second son, age thirty-three; Hutomo Mandala Putera, the president's youngest son, age twenty-four; Indra Rukmana Kowara, married to the president's eldest daughter, Siti Hardijanti Hastuti; and the president's regular golfing partner, Mohamad "Bob" Hasan, an ethnic Chinese who was raised by a Muslim army officer.

These Soeharto relatives and associates, according to the two *Journal* correspondents, had substantial interests in companies that had exclusive or semiexclusive rights to import, produce, or distribute flour, cement, steel, tin plate, and plastics raw materials. They also had favored or protected positions in oil trading, LNG (liquified natural gas) shipping, insurance, and foodstuffs. Son Bambang alone, they said, had interests in more than fifty companies. Jones and Pura reported that businessmen and bankers in Jakarta estimated that the groups controlled by the president's family and friends were generating "hundreds of millions of dollars in revenue each year."[49]

(Liem Sioe Liong alone was estimated in 1989 to be the single richest private person in Southeast Asia, and one of the world's fifty billionaires, with a net worth in excess of $2 billion.[50] His operations were reported to have had a total turnover in 1990 of about $8 billion, accounting for about 5 percent of Indonesia's GDP.[51])

10. Deregulating Industry

It was undeniable that the president's family and friends had a major stake in the government's program of industrial promotion and protection.

Pressures for Deregulation

In such circumstances, why did deregulation occur at all? We have it on the authority of Ali Wardhana, who was Coordinating Minister for the Economy, Finance, and Industry from early 1983 to early 1988, and who was a major force for reform, that deregulation was a necessity. In his first public assessment after leaving public office, Wardhana said:

> Economic reform is rarely if ever undertaken for its own sake. Pressures for reform generally emerge from some crisis. . . . In Indonesia, our crisis was the slump in world prices of oil that began in 1985. Given that shock, a simple chain of economic reasoning makes it clear why economic policy makers were drawn inexorably down the path of structural adjustment.[52]

This was entirely true, but it was not the entire story. As Hadi Soesastro later observed, the negative aspects of the external environment made it possible for the government to take a "low politics" approach, focusing on resource constraints and addressing the elimination of monopoly rights, special privilege, distortions, and rent-seeking, case by case, issue by issue. This made it possible to avoid the "high politics" of normative considerations, such as distributional equity, uneasiness with increased market competition, and overall structural reform.[53]

Division within the governing elite in the mid-1980s was very much as it had been at the beginning of the decade when the second oil windfall had led to a surge of heavy industrial projects, many of which were scaled down, slowed down, or postponed when the price of oil sagged. The division was between economists, led by Wardhana and Sumarlin, and a group of ministers concerned with industrial affairs, led by Habibie, still the Minister of Research and Technology, and also head of the state aircraft industry. Others in the "engineers" camp included Ginandjar Kartasasmita, who had his early experience in Pertamina and was Junior Minister for Domestic Product Promotion, as well as head of the Capital Investment Coordination Board, and Hartarto Sastrosoenarto, with long experience in the state chemical industry, who was Minister of Industry. The issue between the "technocrats" and the "engineers" was the "high politics" of economic nationalism versus integration with the global economy, or, as the deregulators saw it, how deeply the bureaucracy was to intrude into the economy.

A principal strategist of the deregulation campaign reflected on this aspect of the matter:

> The deregulation program is in part a technical response to negative external forces. But it also is a strategic response to encroachments of the bureaucracy, not to reduce the role of the government in the economy, but to limit the government to its proper role.
>
> It isn't the government at the top that thinks it always knows best. It's the bureaucracy down the line that wants to make rules and regulations for everything. . . .
>
> Look at internal sea transport. The ministry was trying to decide what ships should be going where, and when. It was much too complicated a subject for this kind of treatment, but that's the bureaucratic mind. So we got a decision that all this detailed licensing had to stop, so the shipping companies could do their job properly. And do you know what the sea transport people said? They wanted to know, what are we supposed to do now? We said, well, you could look after the harbors, see they are dredged when needed, that sort of thing. They seemed to think that was not very interesting.
>
> Or take the case of coffee. At one time there was an international coffee agreement, Indonesia had a quota, and the quota was divided among the firms on a list of approved coffee exporters. There is no international coffee agreement anymore, but our ministry of trade still limits exports to firms on the approved list. This is really crazy. The thing to do is to let the whole thing go, to let anybody export as much coffee as he can. But the people on the approved list have become a powerful lobby, and they are tied in with officials of the ministry of trade. So they continually produce arguments why the coffee trade can't be deregulated. . . . Just think. We got rid of import monopolies held by the president's family. That was easier than getting rid of the export controls on coffee. Who would ever believe such a thing was possible?[54]

Still another element in the deregulation movement was the consideration that government protection inevitably meant protection of industry owned and operated by the Chinese minority. A cabinet officer who played a major role in the drive for deregulation said later: "People in government were giving the Chinese a lot of facilities. If they had come up as a result of fair competition, it would be all right. But they didn't. Now it's too late in some cases. They've already profited from the corruption. But it's why we need to deregulate."[55]

10. Deregulating Industry

Inexorable though the chain of reasoning might have been, the chain of action was not. It was necessary that the president himself and others at the very top of the government had to agree. No pressure was exerted on the government "from below" to act as it did. Reform had to come from the top.

Soeharto, to his credit, displayed his understanding of economic issues—and his caution in approaching change. He took his economic ministers' advice, as he had on earlier occasions when resources were constrained. He also set the pace of reform. The most controversial delay had to do, of course, with the plastics and steel industries, because of the involvement of his family and Liem Sioe Liong, but it can be assumed that many others also had to be prepared as the process of deregulation unfolded.

Cabinet ministers also counted. Wardhana and his fellow economic ministers began where they had the formal authority, bureaucratic strength, and political support to act, which was with exchange rates, interest rates, and taxes. The reelection of Soeharto in 1988, followed by new cabinet appointees, also provided opportunities for policy change. In particular, a change in the leadership of the investment coordinating agency was a signal that Soeharto saw little future in what remained of the protectionist regime.

The nature of the oil crisis also influenced the process. The oil crisis was not a single event that made "shock treatment" necessary, but rather an extended crisis that made gradualism possible. This was fortunate for two reasons. Policymakers and their staffs were able to work within their capacities to plan and execute the reforms. The long-drawn-out process also had the advantage of making it possible for each round of reforms to show results before the next round had to be pushed through the system.[56]

This incremental approach included bank reforms in 1983, a tax reform at the end of that year, reform of the customs service in 1985, a devaluation of the rupiah in 1986, and partial trade reforms in May 1986, October 1986, January 1987, and December 1987. Investment controls were eased by the opening of more areas for foreign and domestic investment in 1986 and 1987. As a result of all these measures deregulation was paying off in 1988, and that helped make possible the major actions taken at the end of that year.

On November 21, 1988, a "package" of deregulation measures was announced by Radius Prawiro, now Coordinating Minister for the

Economy, Finance, and Industry. He characterized the measures as "broader and more sweeping than any other in the area of trade and industry."[57]

There were two key decrees. One was a decree of the Minister of Trade which provided that, effective January 1, 1989, a large number of items would no longer be under the control of "approved traders" but could again be imported by any licensed trading house and by any manufacturer. Included were 82 items in the chemical industry, among them plastics, feedstocks, and pharmaceuticals; 30 types of iron and steel; 110 items used in textile production; 50 types of food and beverages; and 46 other agricultural products—318 types of imports altogether, which more than doubled the number of products freed from import controls under previous "packages" of deregulation.[58] The second key decree was one by the Minister of Finance that established revised, often higher, tariff levels for 190 of these items.[59]

The victory of the deregulators was substantial, but it was not complete. Imports of materials for the plastics industry would no longer be controlled, and that was considered a major accomplishment in light of the involvement of the president's family in the lucrative Hong Kong agency. Imports of most types of iron and steel, representing 83 percent in value of total iron and steel imports, also would no longer be controlled.[60] Some 35 percent of all imports were said to have been affected by the November decrees, but that reportedly left 16 percent still under continuing nontariff protection.[61]

Further trade deregulation measures were announced in May 1990 and June 1991. Tariffs were reduced and nontariff barriers were removed for a wide range of commodities, mostly manufactured goods. Some tariffs and tariff surcharges were increased.[62] A World Bank report, completed just before the June 1991 measures, assessed the government's performance in positive terms. The share of domestic manufacturing protected by licenses was reduced from 68 percent of production in 1986 to 33 percent in May 1990. This was seen as restoring a substantial portion of the nation's manufacturing to the marketplace, reducing the costs and uncertainties of doing business, and improving quality and the prospects for entering markets abroad.[63] At the same time the net effect of changes in tariffs between 1987 and 1990, according to World Bank staff estimates, was to reduce the effective rate of protection from 68 percent to 59 percent. The real rate of protection for manufacturing, which takes into account the effect of trade policy on general prices, fell from 50 percent to 43 percent. Indonesian industry was still protected in large measure, but the system was more transparent than before.[64]

By now it seemed the deregulation process might be running out of steam. Several of the goals of deregulation had been met in large measure. Much of the nontariff protection that remained involved the rice industry; deregulation could not go much further without touching the agricultural sector. Meanwhile, retrogression was beginning to take place, and some long-held objections to the growth of the private sector began to reemerge.

The Impact of Deregulation

As it was, by early 1992, deregulation had produced several demonstrable results. A recovery was evident in private investment, foreign as well as domestic, most of it in manufacturing. Non-oil exports increased significantly, and the economy was made dramatically less dependent on oil in other respects as well. The financial services sector was surging with new dynamism. The private sector was now, for the first time since independence, the driving force behind economic growth, which in 1990 increased at a real rate of 7.25 percent for the second consecutive year.

The rapid growth in domestic and foreign private investment was impressive. Domestic investment approvals, after sagging in the mid-1980s, doubled in 1987 and continued to rise through 1990, when they reached $30 billion. Foreign investment approvals went from a total of $1.5 billion in 1987 to $8.75 billion in 1990. Not all these projects were implemented, but it was estimated that private investment increased by more than 10 percent per annum during 1986–88 and by more than 18 percent per annum during 1989–90.[65] These developments were not wholly attributable to Indonesian government policy by any means. The same years also saw a general surge of investment into Southeast Asia as a result of the Plaza Accord of 1985 and the realignment that resulted in currency values. As elsewhere in Southeast Asia, the principal sources of foreign private investment in manufacturing in Indonesia after 1985 were Japan, Hong Kong, South Korea, and Taiwan.[66] In sheer volume, Thailand tended to attract more of this investment than Indonesia did.[67] Nevertheless, Indonesia's deregulation of investment was a significant factor; without it, it is highly doubtful Indonesia would have captured anything approaching the volume it did.

The economy became dramatically less dependent on oil between 1981 and 1990. The oil and natural gas sector grew more slowly than the economy as a whole, declined as a source of export earnings, and declined as a source of government revenues. The oil sector grew at an annual average rate of only 2.7 percent between 1983, when the world recession hit, and 1990. Oil sector exports fell from a high of 81.9 percent of total merchandise exports in 1981–82 to an estimated 44.9 percent in 1990–91. Government revenues from oil and gas fell from 70.6 percent of total revenues in 1981–82 to 44.2 percent in 1990–91.[68]

During this same period, according to World Bank staff estimates, non-oil manufacturing grew at an annual average rate of 12.2 percent, and banking and finance grew at an annual average rate of 10.7 percent. Exports other than oil also performed better than oil did in the last half of the 1980s. Non-oil exports more than doubled from $6.7 billion in 1986–87 to an estimated $14.3 billion in 1989–90, an average annual increase of about 29 percent. Much of this growth was believed to have come from a diversifying base of manufactured goods.[69]

The reform of banking and finance was possibly the most outstanding element of the deregulation program. At the start of the 1980s the financial system was dominated by banking, and banking was dominated by a handful of state banks. As a result of early deregulation of interest rates, the assets of the banking system grew at a rate of 21 percent per annum between 1982 and 1988. As a share of GDP, assets held by the banking system increased from 33 percent in 1982 to 57 percent in 1988. A second round of reforms in 1988–90 reduced the barriers to entry into the banking system and reduced the privileges of state banks. The banking system's assets grew at 26 percent per annum between 1988 and 1990, and as a share of GDP reached 66 percent. Forty new domestic banks were established in a two-year period, and fifteen new joint-venture banks. Bank branches grew from 1,640 in April 1988 to 2,842 in March 1990. The period also saw dramatic growth in the Jakarta stock exchange. A World Bank report judged the reforms to have given Indonesia "one of the most dynamic and least-distorted financial sectors in the developing world."[70]

There seemed no doubt that under the pressure of international oil prices, and in the face of unfavorable exchange rates, Indonesian policymakers had accomplished a major restructuring of the economy, reducing the role of oil and increasing that of manufacturing and finance. A dramatic example of the political consequences was

Soeharto's decision in October 1991 to postpone almost $10 billion in four major oil-related projects, including two refineries planned by Pertamina.[71] At the same time, the deregulation process was generating or reactivating a variety of countervailing forces that were beginning to define the possible limits of deregulation, raise the question of how enduring the technocrats' victory would be, and suggest that many issues still remained unsettled in government-business relations.

Government-Business Relations

One indication that the deregulation process was losing its momentum was the slowdown in plans for privatizing state-owned corporations. President Soeharto had called for reform of the state enterprises in December 1986, and public comment in early 1987 had led to widespread expectations that some would be offered for sale in whole or in part on the Jakarta stock exchange. If a policy decision had been made, however, its implementation was exceedingly slow. The finance ministry initiated an evaluation of 188 enterprises only in 1989, and announced that 52 were ready to "go public" only in 1990. Little more was then heard of the matter, and the finance minister was said to have suggested that "privatization" had perhaps not been a helpful term. This experience led two seasoned observers, Mackie and Sjahrir, to predict that there would be "no sudden and far-reaching leap towards full privatization of the vast public sector at all, but more probably a goulash of measures introducing some degree of involvement of private capital in some state enterprises."[72]

Another setback to privatization was Soeharto's decision in 1989 to place ten "strategic" state enterprises under the protection of a new Strategic Industry Administration Board headed by Habibie. The firms included not only enterprises engaged in manufacturing armaments, but such others as Krakatau Steel, a shipyard, a producer of railroad rolling stock, a telecommunications enterprise, and an electronics production unit. The president's action raised a question about the solidity of his own support of deregulation at this point.[73]

Well-publicized instances of new or renewed cases of the regulation of manufacturing also increased the ambiguity of government policy. A ban was imposed on the export of semiprocessed rattan in August 1988, following a ban on the export of raw rattan in 1986. These steps were intended to generate increased employment and export earnings by promoting the production of rattan furniture. The actions mirrored those taken early in the decade banning timber exports in order to promote plywood production. Both were seen to exemplify the power of the logging and allied industries, which were organized in a loggers association, a sawmillers association, a plywood manufacturers association, and a furniture makers association, each headed by the same individual, Bob Hasan, the president's golfing partner.[74] These associations were reportedly setting export volumes and influencing prices.

Another consortium of private traders, which included among its members a son of the president, was granted exclusive rights to trade in cloves, which were highly prized as the spice that flavored Java's distinctive clove cigarettes. This last development was enough to arouse a special critique in the World Bank's confidential annual report.[75]

While the management of public trade policy by private parties, such as the wood and clove consortia, had some precedent in Indonesian government behavior, the event that occurred on March 3, 1990, did not. In his budget address of January 1990 Soeharto had made a strong plea for cooperatives as a means of distributing the gains of development equitably. He proposed that leading companies should transfer 25 percent of their equity to cooperatives as a way of sharing their wealth. The cooperatives might be made up of their employees or of others linked to the firms in some way. As the cooperatives could not afford to buy the shares, Soeharto suggested that the firms should lend money to the cooperatives so they could buy them. On March 3, 1990, Soeharto invited the owners of thirty of the country's largest corporations, all or almost all of them Chinese-Indonesians, to his farm outside Jakarta to press the case before television cameras. In due course the company heads announced they would transfer 1 percent of their listed share capital to cooperatives.[76]

Privately, members of the economic profession and the business community in Jakarta were embarrassed by the entire episode. The assumption was that Soeharto was simply cleaning up his image in order to run for reelection in 1993. Cooperatives no longer had much support as a serious economic vehicle. The cooperative movement was heavily dependent on government patronage. Soeharto was seen as positioning himself politically more closely to the Islamic community by following the traditional Indonesian pattern of finding fault with the Chinese.[77]

In addition, anti-Chinese opinion was on the rise. The growth of the Jakarta stock exchange was probably one reason for this. With interest rates on investment credit holding steady at 21 percent from 1986 through 1990, an increasing number of large, Chinese-owned business houses were raising funds by "going public," which usually meant selling to the public a minority portion of shares of one of their better-known subsidiaries. The information being released for the first time about these firms, and the prices their shares were attracting, raised eyebrows in Jakarta; the owners of the big conglomerates were far richer than most had realized. And the exchange itself was operating increasingly in the glare of public attention. It was estimated in 1990 that some twenty thousand to thirty thousand Indonesians had invested in the stock market, and the composite share price index ran up rapidly until April 1990, when it began a sharp fall.[78]

Many signs of unease were evident. Industries minister Hartarto in early 1991 was urging large business houses, most of which were Chinese, to help smaller indigenous firms by using them as suppliers, distributors, subcontractors, and retailers. Some were of the opinion that if such voluntary schemes failed, something along the lines of Malaysia's New Economic Policy would have to be considered.[79] A Malaysia-style approach would be an improvement over the measures being rumored in Jakarta in mid-1991—that dozens of indigenous firms were obtaining credit at interest rates that were 4 to 5 percent below prevailing commercial rates, and that some seventy "giant" projects valued at a total of $70 billion were being allocated to big indigenous firms.[80]

One set of observers, which included many professional economists, believed that the system of government controls was primarily responsible for the rapid rise in the private fortunes of these "rupiah billionaires." From this perspective the "hot house" environment of the 1980s was responsible for the creation of a wide array of coalitions between senior bureaucrats and major business houses, and the remedy lay in reducing government controls. If the controls were eliminated, the coalitions would lose their reason for being. A second set of observers, which included many others in the political elite, believed that the system of deregulation itself made possible the amassing of huge fortunes. From this perspective, the structure of politics was driving the creation of coalitions between officials and entrepreneurs. No matter what the government policy might be, the government-business coalitions would be enduring.[81]

One thing was clear: since the late 1960s, when Indonesia was one of the world's least industrialized countries for its size, the nation's industrial capacity had experienced dramatic development, not only in the rapid growth of output and employment, but also in the transition to more capital-intensive and skill-intensive industries, a narrowing of the earlier large productivity differentials, and strong growth in productivity and wages.[82] The emergence of big corporate conglomerates, predominantly led by ethnic Chinese, also was almost entirely a phenomenon of the Soeharto era. Political connections were extremely important in the rise of these groups. The principal source of capital was credit from state banks, often at subsidized rates.[83] The Indonesian state had created a large private industrial sector. Now the society had to learn to live with it.

Epilogue

The Indonesian political economy in the late twentieth century was shaped by a complex array of events, personalities, institutions, interest groups, resources, ideas, and policies. It was a product of the nation's own unique history. Yet, the resulting product, in the early 1990s, was not altogether unique. Prominent features of Indonesia's political economy were quite comparable with those of the political economies of other nations. The political structure was highly authoritarian, dominated by the army, and resistant to change. The economic structure was highly productive, rooted in tropical agriculture, moving toward a new emphasis on manufacturing, fueled by oil and innovation. Social policy was relatively progressive. The very juxtaposition of such elements in a single political economy raised significant questions. Were these necessary parts of a whole? Why had they come to exist together at this time and in this place? To what extent were they the result of peculiarly Indonesian factors? To what extent were they the result of larger forces at work in Southeast Asia and beyond? Were they mutually supportive? Was the system stable? Or did it have within itself the seeds of its own destruction?

Our discussion begins with an assessment of why the Indonesian government experienced a growth in authoritarianism in the first place, and why the army became increasingly dominant; why opposition arose to this praetorian political regime; and why this opposition failed to effect any significant change up to the early 1990s. We will go on to assess the sources of Indonesia's development, its record of economic growth and social equity. We will then consider how significant the authoritarianism in government was to the economic and social policies pursued, and to what extent economic and social change was, in turn, creating pressures for political change. Finally, we will note problems that still remain for the next generation of Indonesia's elite to resolve.

Sources of Authoritarianism

It was not difficult, in the early 1960s, to see that some degree of authoritarian government was a likely prospect for Indonesia for some time to come. The country's precolonial history had been largely one of authoritarian, often autocratic, rule. The Dutch, unlike the British, had made no preparations for self-government in their East Indies colony. Indeed, by attempting to hold onto power after World War II, the Dutch left the Indonesians with no alternative but armed revolution, which, although it was a leveling experience, was hardly a prelude to successful civilian governance. Politicians and their parties did form a series of representative governments in the 1950s and eventually created an elected Parliament, but even this last did not establish a national consensus, and civil war led to its collapse. Sukarno himself pressed the attack on political parties, creating in their stead a Guided Democracy—more accurately, a soft authoritarianism, led by himself. By 1965 only three significant centers of power remained—Sukarno, the army, and the Communist party—and these last two were mutually antagonistic. Events seemed to be leading to an inevitable end.

The violence of 1965 nevertheless was unanticipated in its scale and ferocity, and it changed Indonesia's political landscape in several fundamental ways. The Indonesian elite was left even more conservative than it had been, mistrustful of what remained of the Left, and doubtful of the nation's ability to be governed by popular means. The destruction of the Communist party reduced the institutional sources of power to the presidency and the army. In March 1966, after months of uncertainty about who controlled the government, after continued harassment by student demonstrators, and eventually in the face of physical threats by army units, Sukarno conceded executive authority to General Soeharto. Although much has been made of the letter in which Sukarno made this concession, the handover was a coup d'état in the ordinary meaning of the phrase.

Epilogue

Need the transfer of power have led to a continuation of the authoritarianism already in place? Some army officers favored the rehabilitation of political parties Sukarno had banned. This would have restored to national political life at least some elements that had obtained in the mid-1950s. It was significant to the eventual outcome, however, that Sukarno had not been alone in judging the political parties a failure. The parties were in general disrepute among the elite. Leaders of the banned Socialist Party, among them some of the nation's most prominent intellectuals, did not even seek the renewed legal recognition of their organization. Soeharto and the army leadership were under no great pressure to restore the nation to the status quo ante.

The mass violence influenced this thinking. Routine life in Jakarta had been upset for months as demonstrations were mounted on behalf of the Right and the Left. Many individuals had felt themselves in genuine danger. Even before the enormity of the killings in rural areas seeped through, the elite of the capital city had reason to be shaken in its attachment to popularly based politics. As the extent of rural killings became known, civilians and military men alike urged that political parties be banned from the villages.

In these circumstances it would have required a highly self-confident successor to Sukarno, and one deeply committed to popular government, to have aimed at something other than a restoration of order. No such person existed among the potential presidential candidates. Soeharto himself was by nature a wary man, averse to taking risks, and unsure of himself among an elite that had not taken to him readily. He also seems not to have understood the thinking that lay behind the political institutions of the modern industrial democracies. Soeharto was grounded by birth and rearing in a traditional, rural Javanese view of politics. Some thought he was also heavily influenced by the Japanese occupation army, which had given him much of his military training during World War II and also had a strong sense of the army's role in a nation's preservation.

So there was little debate. The country needed a strong hand to make something positive emerge from the trauma of 1965, and it would have one.

The Increase of Militarism

The means to "a strong hand" was obviously the army. Neither Soeharto

Epilogue

nor any of the other potential presidential successors had the ability to mobilize mass opinion as Sukarno had had. Other than the presidency, the army was the sole institution that remained capable in 1966 of uniting the nation in a course of action.

The Indonesian army of 1966 was not the creature of a former colonial power; it was not an army led by men trained to serve as apolitical officers, as was the case in the Philippines, Malaysia, and Singapore. The Indonesian army was the creature of revolution; it was led by men who had joined to fight for national independence and stayed on to fight for national unity, as in Burma and Vietnam. The Indonesian army claimed a role in the management of public affairs based on its role in achieving national independence. The army claimed it had a "dual function": to defend the nation against enemies from within and without, by force of arms if necessary, and to assure wise and effective public policies. This latter claim was strengthened by the declaration of martial law during the outer island rebellion of the 1950s, and was institutionalized still further with the founding of Guided Democracy in 1959. By the time Sukarno fell, the army and the other armed services already held numerous appointed positions in the cabinet, the Parliament, the governorships of provinces, and the directorships of state economic enterprises.

Indonesia's armed forces were not large relative to the population as a whole. On the contrary, they were small by regional standards, that is, in terms of the number of armed men per thousand persons in the general population. Only the Philippines had a smaller army in the mid-1960s. But Indonesia's armed forces comprised a large part of the national elite. They appear to have outnumbered the country's central civil service at the time. And given strong central leadership, the armed forces could be overwhelmingly present in selected locations. After 1965 the "green shirts" of the Indonesian army seemed everywhere in Jakarta.

A massive infusion of military men into civil posts occurred at every level from the presidency to the villages from 1966 on. As late as 1986 the armed forces held 40 percent of the top positions in the entire central bureaucracy, and this did not include the state economic enterprises where they were believed to be almost universally in charge. This military involvement in nonmilitary affairs had more in common with the contemporary experience of Burma and Vietnam than with that of other countries of the region. Even in Thailand, where the army continued to play a significant role in the rise and fall of governments, the civil service remained separate and independent, owing perhaps to its own long history in the service of the monarchy. The result was to sustain a flexibility in Thai politics that was lost to these other countries, including Indonesia.

Taking control of the civil service was only the beginning of army expansionism in Indonesia. The eventual need to contest and win a national election occasioned a further extension of army power. It was at least possible that Soeharto might have won a free and fair election in 1971. But he and his military associates did not intend to risk a loss. The army literally overran what remained of the country's political terrain.

The Army as Government

At the outset many military officers undoubtedly thought they represented the best hope for the country. Civilian leaders had failed the nation. Politicians had quarreled ineffectually for years. Civil servants were inefficient and corrupt. Imbued with the ideology of their "dual function" and with the strong interpersonal ties that came with their years of close association, many officers had no higher loyalty than to each other. The army was not homogeneous by any means. It was divided along ethnic, divisional, generational, and other lines. But service loyalties ran deep, and in the early years after 1965 there were no stronger bonds in the nation.

Corporate and personal financial interest also was a powerful incentive for military dominance. Driven to raising funds by extralegal and illegal means to finance their own units, many armed forces officers had a strong interest in financial affairs. The state corporations, and new enterprises established after 1966 by the armed forces themselves, were the principal source of extrabudgetary subsidies. The government rice agency and the state oil corporation demonstrated amply the extent to which the armed forces, beginning with the office of the president, could divert state funds to their own corporate purposes. Nor was personal interest absent. With no external accountability functioning, some officers became deeply corrupt. An official commission said as much as early as 1970.

Over time, as the regime grew increasingly out of touch with the mood of the people, the concern for security fed on itself. A measure of paranoia already infected the security agencies at the time of the 1974 riots, when a grand conspiracy against the government was suspected, and thinly veiled charges were made against prominent citizens. Errors of judgment grew increasingly easier to make and harder to correct, as in the financial mismanagement of the state oil corporation, which reached crisis proportions before it came to light in 1975. The army had to be called in to support, in a highly visible fashion, the reelection of Soeharto in 1978. As no means of political expression remained that were permitted by law, the populace was driven increasingly to illegal acts, as when Muslim sermons and pamphlets led to arrests in 1985, and these in turn to demonstrations, and thence to firing on crowds, and eventually to acts of arson and bombing, only to be followed by more arrests and trials. The regime's political record grew exceedingly dreary, from the viewpoint of civil rights that were to be protected by the Indonesian constitution, not to mention that of human rights enshrined in international law.

The armed forces' continuing need to protect the government by force of arms raised the question of whether the Indonesian armed forces ever should have gone so far as they did in the first place in dominating public affairs, whether they should have remained in that position so long as they did, and how they were to remove themselves when that could not be avoided at an acceptable cost. These questions were not only a concern of Western liberal scholars, journalists, and politicians; some Indonesians shared the concern as well.

Sources of Opposition

The Indonesian army's domination of so many institutions of national life in the late 1960s was accomplished without much resistance at the time. But it was not accepted uncritically by three significant elements of the elite, and in time opposition arose from each of these.

Students played a role in Indonesia's history from the beginning of the national movement in the early part of the century. They were an important factor in the Indonesian revolution. Students and soldiers, working closely together, brought Sukarno down in 1966. On the other hand, students failed to attract either civilian or military support for their efforts to halt the Soeharto government in 1974, and again in 1978. They attacked the government's economic policies, official corruption, and the regime's authoritarian nature; their efforts failed, and student leaders went to jail. Many in Indonesia believe that the nation's students have since grown apathetic about national politics, that they are concerned only with their personal careers. The largest student outburst in recent years, one recalls, was aroused by a regulation requiring motor-bike riders to wear helmets. Otherwise the principal demonstrations have had to do with local abuses of power. Moreover, students have been precluded for years from organizing themselves for political action by the pervasiveness of the internal security apparatus. Nevertheless, it is still possible that students will play a role in any significant reordering of military-civilian relations in the future. Given favorable conditions, namely a socially significant issue and a divided army, the student role in Indonesia's history might well be repeated.

Islam also has been historically at the heart of Indonesian politics. The Islamic Union was the country's first significant nationalist organi-zation in the early part of the century. The Masyumi Party, the inde-pendent-minded party of outer-island Muslims, played a central role in the rebellion of the 1950s. Ansor, the youth wing of the Nahdatul Ulama, the major Muslim organization of Java, was the principal ally of the army in the killings in rural East Java in 1965. The Islamic Student Association provided the manpower for the anticommunist and anti-Sukarno demonstrations of 1965–66 in Jakarta. All these Muslim groups were considerably removed culturally from Soeharto and his chief mili-tary associates, who had strong attachments to the pre-Islamic religion of Java. (Soeharto himself finally made the *haj* only in 1991.) Yet, Islam was a major bulwark against communism, and the country's major Islamic organizations expected, after 1966, to receive Soeharto's appro-bation. All were seriously disillusioned.

The Masyumi Party, which Sukarno had banned from public life, lobbied strenuously with Soeharto for the legal right to return under its own name and leadership. Its failure to achieve its aim left a large num-ber of Muslims, especially in the islands of Sumatra, Kalimantan, and Sulawesi, disenfranchised and disaffected. The Nahdatul Ulama vigor-ously protested the official conduct of the 1978 elections; walked out of the People's Consultative Assembly over references to non-Islamic beliefs in legislation proposed just before Soeharto's reelection in the same year; walked out of Parliament over an election bill in 1980; and finally withdrew from national politics in 1985. Thus, the nation's two most prominent Islamic organizations of the last half of the twentieth century were pushed beyond the margins of official politics. But it did not mean the marginalization of Islam from Indonesian society. Indeed, Islam was enjoying something of a renaissance in Indonesia in the mid-1980s. A fundamentalist element existed, which was not insignificant among the urban poor, as the Tanjung Priok incident made clear. An elite Islamic element was becoming noticeable in the upper bureaucracy. But mainstream Islamic organizations were caught up in the *dakwah* (missionary) movement, promoting greater personal devotion among those who were Muslims from birth, recruiting a younger generation of leaders, and leaving national politics for another day.

Opposition to Soeharto's leadership also arose from time to time within the armed forces themselves and among retired military leaders. These were not a homogeneous group. Service rivalries existed between the army and the rest. The army itself was divided ethnically, between Javanese officers who comprised the majority, even though the Javanese did not comprise a majority of the population, and non-Javanese officers. The Javanese themselves were further divided between those who had served with Soeharto in the Diponegoro Division and those who traced their military service to other units. The general officer corps also was divided between those of Soeharto's generation, who had fought in the revolution, and those who were younger and had not. These latter came to be divided in time between those who had seen combat service in East Timor and those who had not. So the military was not of a piece by any means.

The protests by students and Muslim party leaders in 1978 came close to dividing the army. Soeharto asked the armed forces to give him their visible public support, and, after some hesitation, they did so; he was reelected in a city that resembled an armed camp. Many officers, both serving and retired, were deeply disturbed by these events. Had the army leadership not acted as it had, its units might well have stood for either side and found themselves in a civil war. The experience raised the question of how responsible the army must be for the protection of the government of the day, when this involved the risk of either dividing the army internally or alienating it from the population at large.

In May 1980 former national Islamic leaders and retired senior military men, including figures who had been on both sides of the civil war in the 1950s, joined together in two extraordinary petitions to the Indonesian Parliament, calling for an end to the "transition" government that had ruled since 1966; declaring that only honest general elections could provide the country with a legitimate government; and accusing Soeharto of using the armed forces dishonorably against his critics. The petitions reflected the former leaders' desire to put themselves on the historical record. The petitions had no chance of effecting any early practical change; even news of the petitions was kept out of the daily press. More than a decade later the signers of the 1980 petitions were still routinely denied their civil rights. Only in 1991 did they receive their first hearing by a parliamentary committee, and their names were permitted to appear again in the press.

Thus, significant national interest groups—students, Muslims, and retired military officers—failed to reverse the course of events in spite of their obvious desire to do so.

The Failure of Opposition

One possible reason for the opposition's failure was the small number of individuals in Jakarta and other major cities capable of independent political action. Indonesia's urban population as a whole was small in comparison with most countries in the region in 1965—half that of the Philippines, for example—and still lagged well behind most countries of the region in 1990. What might be regarded in other countries as the middle class—readers of a daily newspaper, for example, or people with access to a telephone—numbered exceedingly few in Indonesia, on the order of 2 or 3 percent of the population even in recent years, which was the lowest in the region except for Burma and Vietnam where the military also remained powerful.[1]

On the other hand, a large portion of this middle class resided in Jakarta. The situation could not be compared to Bangkok, which accounted for more than half of Thailand's entire urban population; that was unique. But a third of all the telephones in Indonesia in the late 1980s were registered in Jakarta. And while the number was low—only 300,000 in a city of nine million—each telephone probably was available to an average of no fewer than five persons. Moreover, the number of citizens on the waiting list for a telephone was larger than the number already being serviced by the inefficient state telephone company. It was thus possible that Jakarta's "middle class," defined as the portion of the population that had access to a telephone or could afford to have one, constituted about 30 percent of Jakarta's population by the beginning of the 1990s, or some 2.7 million persons. In short, by the end of the period of this study, Jakarta's "middle class" was by no means negligible in size.[2]

Many members of this middle class belonged to the civil or military service. In some Indonesian cities and towns government employment provided jobs for as much as 25 percent of the labor force. In Jakarta's case the portion might have been not much less. Soeharto reduced the size of the armed forces over time, but he vastly increased the civil service. The central bureaucracy grew faster than the national population from 1967 on as government development programs increased in number and scale. The largest increase was in the educational system; a large part of the civil service came to be composed of teachers in the primary and secondary schools. This was probably the single biggest contribution the government made to the growth of the middle class. But it was a politically dependent middle class. Even professors at the leading universities were civil servants. Independent professional people—physicians, engineers, and the like—were late to develop in Indonesia compared to those in Thailand or the Philippines, and their number was still relatively small in proportion to the population in the late 1980s; Indonesia would have had to increase its supply of physicians by 50 percent to match these neighboring countries.[3]

Most members of the newspaper-reading public, if they did not belong to the military or civil service, nevertheless depended on the regime for their economic survival. This was particularly true of private businessmen, whose ability to function depended heavily on bureaucratic patronage. Government regulation of the economy had been expanded, from independence on, by a series of nationalist politicians, martial law administrators, and leaders of the Guided Democracy period. The latter was especially favorable to the central bureaucracy, which, like the army, was heavily Javanese, and was culturally attuned to the view that the society was in need of its direction. The growth of economic regulation therefore resumed after a brief respite in the late 1960s.

Some sectors, notably oil and rice, involved high political and financial stakes, and their regulation was pursued as much for political purposes as for economic ones. These sectors involved large sums of state funds; powerful state enterprises that reported directly to the president; dealings with foreign governments and multinational corporations; and domestic armies of private suppliers and contractors. Their power was unquestioned; foreign oil companies could fire politically suspect individuals at the direction of state oil corporation officials. The manufacturing sector also was governed by a plethora of government regulations, which were increased still further in response to the recession of the early 1980s. That the vast majority of the larger private firms in all these sectors were owned by ethnic Chinese, an extremely small minority numbering less than 3 percent of the population, and one frequently harassed in times of social stress, contributed still further to the regime's ability to override its critics.

But the business environment was not static. As oil prices on the international market fell throughout the 1980s, the need for an alternate source of foreign exchange became urgent. Much of the trade regulation in manufactures was undone by the late 1980s, reducing production costs and encouraging exports. By the same time private capital was playing the major role in domestic investment, and foreign private investment was growing rapidly as well. Banking also was deregulated, spawning an explosion in the number of private money managers. All these developments increased considerably the freedom of private citizens. The very rich continued for the most part to be of Chinese descent or, by now, members of the presidential family and their circle of friends. But as their enterprises grew in size and number, the class of professional managers, engineers, accountants, and other specialists, especially in and around Jakarta, expanded broadly.

As these developments suggested, the better-off classes, especially in Jakarta, were experiencing many positive economic and social benefits as a result of the country's development. A significant urban middle class was in the process of formation during the 1970s and 1980s, especially in the capital city. A large part of this middle class was caught up in new kinds of productive activity, and was enjoying new levels of income and consumption. This was a class that was clearly benefiting from the management of the nation's affairs. It had a stake in the economic and social progress that had been achieved. It had a stake in the status quo, in continuity. It did not rush to oppose government policies and practices, even when it did not like them. But it was also a class that was growing in its economic independence of the government, and that had political implications for the future.

Sources of Development

The growth of the middle class reflected economic and social policies characteristic of the Soeharto regime. Most significant was the reorientation of economic policy toward the United States, Japan, and Western Europe. This represented a radical shift from the late Sukarno period, when the Indonesian president was declaring the founding of a new axis linking Pyongyang, Beijing, Hanoi, Phnom Penh, and Jakarta in a counter-United Nations of what he termed *the new emerging forces*. Had the leftist officers who initiated the attempted coup in 1965 succeeded, it is entirely possible they would have led Indonesia into a much more closely integrated relationship with these Marxist-Leninist regimes. Had this occurred, the Indonesian political economy probably would have become mired in the same loss of productivity and incomes that has been experienced by all these regimes in recent decades.

The Soeharto regime had another alternative. It might have chosen, like Burma's military-led regime, to turn inward, cut itself off from the rest of the world, and concentrate on consolidating its own internal control. This seems never to have been seriously considered. Many members of the elite fully expected that the industrial democracies would come to Indonesia's aid in the wake of the Communist party's destruction. The few trained economists among them had, in any case, been urging the need to reestablish ties with the country's traditional economic partners, and these were the industrial democracies. This strategic choice was made cumulatively by a small number of officials in the course of six months between March and October 1966. They included Soeharto himself; two of his subsequent vice presidents, Sultan Hamengkubuwana and Adam Malik; and the country's leading university economists, who at the time were advisers to the Sultan. Their collective decision was crucial to Indonesia's subsequent rapid development, for it committed Indonesia to an integral role in what was soon to become the world's most rapidly growing economic region. Between 1965 and 1988 Japan emerged as the second largest economy in the world, and South Korea, Taiwan, Hong Kong, and Singapore accounted for half the manufactured exports of all developing countries.

Soeharto's role in this and subsequent key economic policy decisions was substantial. He played a significant part in appointing to his personal staff, and in time to his cabinet, a group of academic economists who were to be the main source of economic policy for more than two decades. He was also the final arbiter in accepting or rejecting their advice, usually accepting it in times of financial austerity and ignoring it when resources were plentiful. In this capacity Soeharto earned much respect within the international financial community. He conducted the meetings of his economic subcabinet personally for years, and members of this group regarded him as having a good head for economic issues. He was sympathetic to every program aimed at serving the interests of the Javanese rice farmers among whom he lived as a boy. He backed the government-sponsored program to promote family planning in the face of possible religious opposition. He shared the nationalism of the army officers and civilian engineers who pressed for expansion of the state enterprises in high-technology sectors, such as petrochemicals. He was, like many other chief executives elsewhere in the world, more an arbiter than a source of economic ideas. Long-time cabinet officers tended to view Soeharto as the chairman of the board, not the chief executive. Nor was there an alter ego of this very private man. Indonesia lived under a collective leadership of technocrats during most of the Soeharto years.

The chief source of economic policy was a group of economists, initially five in number and extending over time to several times that number, most of them drawn from the Faculty of Economics of the University of Indonesia, who have filled key economic positions in the government from late 1966 until the present writing. They were the first group of Indonesian economists of any size ever to be trained to the doctorate, many at the University of California at Berkeley at least in part, most in the United States, and some elsewhere in the West. Led by a brilliant strategist, Widjojo Nitisastro, they loomed large on the Indonesian intellectual horizon, and their collective confidence in the fundamental rightness of mainstream economic theory made them a force to be reckoned with. They provided Soeharto with two essential ingredients to economic policy: the confidence of the international financial community, and policies and programs that produced demonstrable results.

The International Monetary Fund and the World Bank were consistent in their strong support of the Indonesian government from the late 1960s on. They were joined by the governments of Japan, the United States, and Western Europe, making Indonesia the principal recipient of foreign economic assistance in Southeast Asia for more than two decades. The Japanese government gave more economic aid to Indonesia than to any other country in the world between 1967 and 1990. The Indonesian economists' reputation and the support of governmental and intergovernmental agencies helped to make the Indonesian economy highly attractive to the private international banking community during the 1970s and 1980s. One result was to make Indonesia the most highly indebted economy in Asia in 1990. But that was only another way of saying that the Indonesian economy was expected to be a high-performing economy in the decade of the 1990s.

That Indonesia's ranking in terms of indebtedness had earlier been held by South Korea tended to reinforce this interpretation.

Oil also was a factor in attracting foreign grants, loans, and investments, and in boosting confidence in the performance of the Indonesian economy, from the late 1960s to the early 1990s. American oil companies were the main producers of Indonesia's oil from the 1950s on, and Japan was the chief consumer from at least the late 1960s. Oil held out the promise that Indonesia would be able to repay its foreign debts and make it possible for foreign investors to repatriate their capital. The sharp increases in the world oil price in 1973 and 1979 greatly enhanced these expectations, and even the financial crisis of the Indonesian state oil company in 1975 did not greatly alter them. Oil represented some two-thirds of Indonesia's export earnings, and financed as much of the government's spending, between 1974 and 1984.

Few nations managed the oil bonanza well. Some experienced costly inflation, as Venezuela did. Some borrowed hastily on the future, running up an unmanageable debt, as Mexico did. Still others wasted the opportunity altogether, misallocating the new resources in favor of short-term benefits, and contributing to a long-term deterioration in the economy, as Nigeria did.[4] Oil was no panacea. On the contrary, managing the windfall seems to have been much more of a challenge than an opportunity. Oil or no oil, policy mattered. In Indonesia, from the mid-1970s, oil financed a massive program of economic and social development, especially in rural Java.

From the mid-1980s, as the price of oil declined, occasionally to quite low levels, and as the growing Indonesian economy needed access to more and more foreign exchange, Indonesian policymakers were pressed to find an alternative to foreign aid and oil. The obvious alternative, in light of what was occurring in the rest of the region, was the export of manufactured goods. Manufacturing had begun late in Indonesia, relative to the other noncommunist economies of Southeast Asia. Nevertheless, it had been enjoying rapid growth under the protection of the government, which kept foreign competitors at bay until well into the 1980s. Then, with their backs to the wall, Indonesian policymakers began the painful process of deregulation. The results were highly positive. Together with traditional exports, manufactures outpaced oil exports after 1988.

If these trends continued, the Indonesian economy could complete a major restructuring before the 1990s were out.

Epilogue

The Record of Growth

The outcome of this process of decision making has been a record of growth in the Indonesian economy that has been impressive by regional and world standards. The total Gross Domestic Product (GDP) of Indonesia in 1965 has been estimated variously at $3.8 billion to $5.9 billion, compared with $6.0 billion for the Philippines, $4.3 billion for Thailand, $3.1 billion for Malaysia, and $0.9 billion for Singapore. By 1990 Indonesia's GDP was by far the largest in the region at $107.2 billion, compared with $80.1 billion for Thailand, $43.8 billion for the Philippines, $42.4 billion for Malaysia, and $34.6 billion for Singapore.[5] The GDPs of Burma, Laos, Cambodia, and Vietnam, for which data were not available, were assumed to be dramatically lower.

The Indonesian level was reached by average annual growth rates of 7.0 percent from 1965 to 1980 and 5.5 percent from 1980 to 1990. With the exception of Thailand, which grew more rapidly in both periods, Indonesia grew at a rate higher than other regional states and higher than average for low-income and middle-income economies worldwide.[6]

Indonesia's Gross National Product (GNP) also grew rapidly in per capita terms. The 1965 figure has been variously estimated at $30 to $55, which was lower than estimates for China, India, and the rest of South Asia, including Bangladesh and Nepal. The 1990 estimate was $570, which was higher than estimates for all these other nations. The average annual growth rate of GNP per capita between 1965 and 1990 was 4.5 percent, the highest in Southeast Asia and very high for low-income and middle-income countries worldwide.[7]

This was accomplished not only by the economy's high growth rate but also by the population's low growth rate. The Indonesian population grew at an average annual rate of 2.4 percent between 1965 and 1981, and 1.8 percent between 1980 and 1990. These rates were much lower than those of the Philippines, lower than those of Malaysia, lower than or equal to those of Thailand, and lower than those of most other low-income and middle-income countries worldwide. The Indonesian rates were also comparable to or lower than those of India, without involving such extreme measures as occurred in India's program at one time.[8]

The growth rate in Indonesia's agricultural production after 1965 was high by regional and global standards. The average annual rate between 1965 and 1980 was 4.3 percent, which was surpassed only by Thailand in the region, and only by a few other economies, most of them much smaller, in other parts of the world. The rate between 1980 and 1990 was 3.2 percent, which was surpassed by Thailand and Malaysia, but was again high by world standards for low-income and middle-income countries. The accomplishment was the more notable since the agricultural economy of Indonesia was by this time the third largest among the world's low-income countries, with all the technical complexities and management challenges that implied.[9]

The growth rate in manufacturing production after 1965 was also high by regional and global standards. Manufacturing contributed only 8 percent of Indonesia's Gross Domestic Product in 1965; only Nepal and Bangladesh, among Asian economies, reported a lower level than this. Indonesia's manufacturing grew between 1965 and 1980 at an average annual rate of 12.0 percent, surpassed in South and Southeast Asia only by the city-state on Singapore. Indonesia's manufacturing grew between 1980 and 1990 at 12.5 percent, which was unsurpassed in the region.[10]

A principal social benefit of this rapid economic growth was in education. In 1965 Indonesia's primary school enrollment amounted to only 72 percent of the age group, which was slightly below the level of India and well below that of China. In 1989 Indonesia had a net primary school enrollment of 99 percent, which put it one percentage point behind China and Sri Lanka among the low-income nations of Asia, and on a par with the Philippines among the middle-income nations of Asia. Secondary school enrollment meanwhile went from 12 percent to 47 percent of the age group, the latter of which was second only to Sri Lanka among all low-income Asian nations and about midway between Thailand and the Philippines among middle-income Asian nations.[11]

Indonesia was still a low-income country. It still had the lowest per capita income among the market-oriented economies of Southeast Asia or, when measured in current international dollars, shared that position with the Philippines, once its much wealthier neighbor to the north.[12] Viewed from the vantage point of the Indonesian elite, however, the record from 1965 on was justifiably a source of considerable pride. Whether compared with the country's own earlier history or with the contemporary performance of other nations, the economic and social growth registered during the successive Soeharto administrations was demonstrably of a high order. It is difficult to imagine that this growth did not contribute significantly to the stability of the political regime.

Epilogue

The Record of Equity

Equity issues were among the most persistent raised by critics of the Soeharto government. The evidence did not support the critics' more extreme charges, as reflected in statements made by student leaders in 1978 in Bandung or those made by Muslim preachers in 1985 in Tanjung Priok. On the contrary, evidence clearly indicated that the benefits of growth were reaching all social classes. At the same time disparities between Jakarta and the rest of the country, and between Jakarta's rich and poor, were becoming increasingly evident.

Consumption expenditure studies in the mid-1970s showed that the Indonesian economy was broadly more equitable at that time than the economies of Malaysia or the Philippines, and about as equitable as the economies of Thailand and Sri Lanka. Similar studies in the mid-to-late 1980s showed a pattern in Indonesia that was more equitable than those in Malaysia, the Philippines, and Sri Lanka, and similar to that of India. We should not make too much of such comparisons, but the data do not support the view that Indonesia was unusual by any means in respect to its pattern of income distribution, and, if anything, was among the more progressive in its region.[13]

That benefits have been shared by even the population's lowest income groups was also apparent. Consumption expenditure studies between 1970 and 1976 showed per capita improvements in real terms for the population as a whole, and improvements in the levels of consumption in real terms for all income groups. Moreover, by one measure, the portion of the population living in poverty declined from more than 50 percent in 1970 to about 40 percent in 1976. The rise in real consumption levels of even the poorest groups appeared to have been sufficient to bring about a decrease in absolute numbers as well.[14]

This trend appears to have continued in the 1980s. Measured by the official poverty line, a substantial decline occurred in the percentage of poor in both urban and rural areas between 1984 and 1987. The absolute number of Indonesians in poverty also declined, from 35 million in 1984 to about 30 million in 1987. Income inequality also declined between 1984 and 1987, as indicated by the increase in the share of consumption of the poorest 20 percent of the population. Other poverty measures showed the same trend.[15]

At the same time, rural-urban disparities appear to have increased in recent decades. While rural consumption was improving at real rates of

2 to 3 percent per year in the 1970s, urban consumption was improving at real rates of 4 to 7 percent. The result was a severe increase in the disparity between the bottom four-fifths of the rural population and the top fifth of the urban population. This rural-urban disparity was particularly acute on the island of Java. Java's villages contained the vast majority of the country's poor in the late 1970s—77 percent of all poor households in the nation were in rural Java. At the same time, Java's two largest cities, Jakarta and Surabaya, contained a large number of the country's citizenry who were better off; by 1971 these two cities already contained nearly 30 percent of the total urban population.[16]

Regional disparities also favored Jakarta. The capital city has consistently been the only province without minerals that has been among the richest in the nation. The exploitation of mineral resources has made several provinces with relatively small populations on the geographic periphery—Aceh, Riau, East Kalimantan, and Irian Jaya—the nation's wealthiest provinces in nominal terms. But most of the income accrued to populations elsewhere, mainly in Jakarta. Jakarta in the mid-1970s not only had 30 percent of all the telephones in Indonesia, but it also had 25 percent of all motor cars and 30 percent of all medical doctors.[17]

Per capita consumption data also pointed to a large increase in the degree of inequality within urban areas. In addition, real wage levels showed no discernible upward movement, leading analysts to conclude that business profits and property income were growing rapidly, also benefiting upper-income groups.[18]

Soeharto himself speculated on national television in early 1990 that the widening "social gap" could lead to "social disturbance."[19] It had been many years since any new antipoverty programs were undertaken; these had been a phenomenon of the 1970s. Official attention was drawn to other problems through the 1980s; the regime found itself heavily preoccupied with the orderly management of the economy in the face of uncertain and sometimes unfavorable external factors. This was an objective that appealed strongly to bureaucratic and business elements in the elite. That is not to say that a parallel concern to provide a measure of distributional relief did not exist. The government did protect its village-level programs, even in the 1980s when civil service salaries were frozen. But the rise of urban inequality did not generate a significant reponse.

Possibly the most significant progress in terms of equity in Indonesia was in regard to male and female access to social benefits. The achieve-

omplablomplseromplbiblompl# Epilogue

ment of virtually universal primary education, which was realized for females as well as males, was an extraordinary accomplishment. Female education has been regarded by some as a major factor in the reduction in the rate of population growth, and by others as a major contributor to the growth of rural incomes. The impact has been greatest in rural Java, where educational attainment had previously lagged behind other provinces.

Authoritarianism and Policy

The relationship between the political regime and its accumulated economic record was a matter of long-standing disagreement among Indonesians themselves. The regime's supporters argued that a high order of political stability was essential to the country's economic and social development—that the Indonesian people could not have enjoyed the benefits of the 1970s and 1980s had the government been as lacking in unity and discipline as, for example, that of the neighboring Philippines. Critics argued that the nature of the regime had led more or less inevitably to policies and practices that favored foreigners over Indonesians, senior officials over private citizens, and Chinese-Indonesians over indigenous people. A prima facie case could seemingly be made for both these positions. Was it possible to come to a more precise view?

What primarily linked the political regime to economic policy was Soeharto's long survival in the presidency and that of the university economists around him in positions of political significance. The appointment of men of such expertise did not in itself depend on the nature of the regime. Similar expertise existed in all the noncommunist capitals of the region and was represented at high levels of government in all the states neighboring Indonesia by the late 1960s. The Indonesian case differed from the others principally in the small number of economists and other highly trained personnel that existed in Indonesian society at the time, and in the lengthy period that a few of these individuals remained in positions of substantial power and influence.

The tenure in office reflected the mutual loyalty that existed between Soeharto and his chief economic advisers; it also reflected the army's long support of the economists, as well as of the president himself. It is difficult to imagine that the economists would have survived the events of 1974, or that Soeharto himself would have survived the events of 1978,

288

had the regime depended on popular support. As it was, with strong army support, the cautious pragmatism that characterized the rehabilitation of the Indonesian economy in the late 1960s continued to be exhibited in public policy through much of the 1970s and 1980s. The extraordinary continuity of this policy orientation has to be counted the single most important contribution to the Indonesian economy's record of growth and development.

Macroeconomic policy of the kind described did not directly favor any one economic interest group over another, although the general orientation tended to protect the average citizen. Policies that did directly favor specific groups were to be found in the regulatory regime and in government spending programs. The outstanding example of regulation and spending together in the interest of a specific group was in regard to Indonesia's farming population. The protection of agriculture, coupled with spending programs to reduce the cost of agricultural production and other programs to increase the provision of physical infrastructure and social services in rural areas, was highly progressive through the 1970s and 1980s; the major benefits went to small-holder farming families, especially in Java's rice-growing regions, which also held many of the nation's poor.

It is difficult to imagine that a political regime in which policy-making was shared with a popularly elected legislature would have been able to sustain this strong rural bias for more than two decades. Given the distribution of secondary and higher education in Indonesia, such a legislature in recent decades would have been dominated by elite urban interests. This is not to say that any authoritarian government would necessarily have favored the rural sector; Nigeria was a notorious case of a contrary orientation. Personalities and circumstance also mattered. The Soeharto regime favored rural Java not only for reasons of economic theory, but also because the president and his economic advisers, in spite of their very different backgrounds, understood its needs uncommonly well; and because the Indonesian army joined them in seeing the economic and social rehabilitation of rural Java as essential to rooting out the basic cause of the earlier growth of communism there. The authoritarian nature of the Soeharto regime enabled it to pursue this rural vision without urban hindrance.

The treatment of economic interests was more complex as one moved beyond the agricultural sector, where much of the technology was in the public domain. In the case of industry, much advanced technology, whether it was in the mining of oil and other minerals, or in manufacturing for domestic use or export, was owned or controlled by foreign private corporations. Especially, from the late 1960s on, U.S. oil and other mining firms, and Japanese manufacturers of consumer goods, were the primary sources of the technology Indonesia sought, of the capital necessary to its use in Indonesia, and of access to needed markets abroad. To what extent did the Indonesian government's authoritarian nature determine or influence the policies that were enacted in dealing with these foreign economic interests?

The oil industry was a state-owned industry in most countries of the world in the 1970s, and the state interest was in extracting the maximum feasible rent from the industry. In the Indonesian case, Sukarno himself had hesitated to rein in the U.S. oil firms that were earning the bulk of the nation's foreign exchange. After 1965 Soeharto was eager to encourage foreign firms to expand their exploration and production as a way of getting the economy on its feet again, but the Indonesian policy offered nothing particularly favorable to the foreign firms. After the 1973 oil embargo, Indonesia's revenues from the industry rose and fell as a result of the production levels set by the Organization of Petroleum Exporting Countries (OPEC), and changes in the global demand for oil as economies experienced growth and recession. Indonesia's oil reserves and production capacity were not sufficient to permit it to pursue an independent course. Only once, after the state oil company crisis of 1975, did the Soeharto government demand and obtain a larger share of its oil revenues from its long-time producers. New producers were always targets of opportunism, but opportunism also had its limits. Actions unfavorable to the oil companies reduced the incentives for exploration, whereas Indonesia's oil reserves tended to be found in small, scattered fields that required a constant search. As profits were squeezed, long-term production was threatened. On the whole, the Soeharto government opted for the longer term. The nature of the regime enabled it to pursue this course.

The principal relationship between the regime and the oil industry was not to be found in how the government dealt with the foreign oil firms, but in how the ready availability of oil money acted on domestic decision making. It was recorded by an official commission on corruption as early as 1970, and was revealed more fully by official sources subsequent to the state oil company crisis of 1975, that the state oil company was for many years run as an extension of the president's office. Oil money was used to finance projects more or less as the president of Indonesia or the head of the state oil company decided. These projects included the financing of the government's victory in the 1971 elections. To what extent this continued to be the case beyond 1975 was unknown; the state oil company had still to make public a financial report as of this writing in 1992. But oil money also made it possible for Soeharto and his economic advisers to fund numerous programs that were both politically popular and economically and socially desirable from the mid-1970s on. Oil money thus tended to amplify the regime's best and worst aspects. It reduced the number of decision makers who had to be involved in public policy, reinforcing the regime's authoritarian nature. It helped to finance the co-optation of interest groups, helping to perpetuate the regime. It corrupted some of the decision makers. And, at the same time, oil money helped make possible economic and social programs that were bringing about massive changes in Indonesian society.

The nature of the regime also was significant to industrial policy. Because the regime was so closed to outside opinion in the early 1970s, it did not accurately assess the level of nationalist feeling directed against foreign investors until rioters were in the streets in January 1974. Then, very much on the defensive, the government virtually closed down foreign investment for the better part of a decade. It seems reasonable to believe that if the political system had been more open to the pressure of public opinion, foreign private investment would have been placed under a greater measure of national control from the beginning. It also seems likely that more moderate action would then have been possible. This was the case with foreign investment policy in neighboring Thailand, for example, where the flow of foreign funds into the economy was carefully modulated for most of the 1970s and 1980s. On the other hand, when oil prices receded and foreign investment was again needed, the authoritarian nature of the Indonesian government enabled it, with no great difficulty, to open the door again.

As in the oil sector, the regime's authoritarian character was etched more precisely by its industrial policy in its domestic than in its foreign dimensions. Manufacturing in Indonesia in the early 1980s involved every major economic interest group in the Indonesian elite, including the civil and military bureaucracies, the state enterprises, the growing private business community, and the president's family and friends. An import-substitution orientation of policy had made possible double-

digit growth from 1968 on. As a result, in the early 1980s, as global recession set in, a large number of manufacturers were able to demand and
obtain even more substantial government protection from foreign competition. This response was not at all peculiar to the political regime;
governments throughout the region had done the same at one time or
another in similar circumstances, regardless of their domestic political
regimes. What was attributable to the Indonesian political regime was
its ability to begin to liberalize trade in manufactured goods within a
few years, and to accomplish a considerable liberalization of manufacturing by the end of the 1980s. This was a painful process, and it
required a disciplined leadership to carry it out. The liberalization of
industrial protection was the clearest example, perhaps, of Indonesia's
mirroring of Korea's and Taiwan's earlier experience. And it contrasted
sharply with the neighboring Philippines, where a more open political
system was still being used to serve the interests of a privileged few
native industrialists.

The most controversial aspect of the Indonesian case was not any of
these general policies, however, but rather the specific practices they permitted. The regime was immersed in corrupt practices in the granting
of licenses, lending of funds, letting of contracts, and every other form
of state action that had an economic value. Comparisons were necessarily imprecise, but many observers believed that Indonesian corruption
was the most pervasive in the region from the late 1960s on.
Domestically, two aspects of corruption predominated the private discussions of the elite. One was that Soeharto's family and a small circle of
their friends and associates were enjoying unfair advantage, enabling
them to amass large fortunes in a short time. The second was that
Chinese businessmen were being given unfair opportunity, enabling
many of them to create corporate conglomerates that vastly overshad-
owed in scale the firms of most of their indigenous competitors. These
allegations became increasingly public as the nation entered the 1990s
and presidential succession became a matter of increasing concern. It
was difficult to say which of these issues was more pernicious in its influence on the process of succession. Together they seriously threatened the
likelihood of an easy transition.

In sum, the authoritarian nature of Indonesia's political regime was
essential to the character of many of the policies that promoted the
country's growth and development. The nature of the regime made possible macroeconomic policies marked by moderation and continuity,

encouraging savings and investment. It also permitted policies that favored long-term development in regard to oil, agriculture, and industry, which, over time, and on balance, were beneficial economically and socially. The regime performed better than most and actually delivered most of the growth and equity it promised.

Managed Pluralism

Such a political economy might usefully be thought of as a *managed pluralism.*

To say that the Indonesian political economy is *managed* carries several connotations. In its archaic sense, the term *manage* refers to the schooling and handling of a trained riding horse. In the ordinary contemporary meaning of the term, what is *managed* is made and kept submissive or at least tractable. What is *managed* also is treated with care, directed with skill, and made successful in achieving its aims by the judicious use of limited resources. These meanings are applicable to the Indonesian political economy. The society has been relatively accepting of the leadership. With the exceptions of the 1974 "disaster" and the Tanjung Priok incident of 1985, the leadership has been able to maintain itself in power with minimal force of arms. (The current separatist movements on the political periphery, in Aceh, Timor, and Irian, are not challenges to the existence of the regime.) The economy has been directed with great skill. The welfare of the society has been greatly advanced in material terms.

In the *managed* pluralism of Indonesia, the managers have been relatively few in number, even fewer than in neighboring countries. Like many of the others, those of Indonesia have been protected in large measure from independent scrutiny or accountability, and have operated principally by way of incremental change, a minimum of public discussion, avoidance of debate of high principle, the resolution of issues on a case-by-case basis, and a style of decision making that places a high value on compromise. This is not to say that the managers exhibit no differences among themselves. There is a *pluralism* in the Indonesian case that begins with the managers themselves.

To say that the Indonesian political economy is a managed *pluralism* is to suggest that the general orientation of the managers' policies has the result of increasing the number of units in the economy and society capable of autonomous action within the confines of the existing political system. Indonesian *pluralism* has included an increase in the number of government agencies capable of autonomous action, in the levels of management within them, and in the range of economic and social tasks to which they are set. At the same time Indonesian *pluralism* also has involved an increase in the number, variety, and complexity of private groups and the economic and social tasks in which these also are engaged. These policy tendencies have been leading, in turn, to an increase in the differentiation among economic and social classes, among functional specializations, and among economic and social interest groups. Indonesian *pluralism* also has included a managed openness to foreign involvement in the economy and society in the form of aid, trade, investment, and intercultural communication.

It is evident that these characteristics of the Indonesian political economy have been in a highly dynamic phase over the past twenty-five years. This is apparent not only from the detailed examination of cases, but also from the comparative analysis of quantitative data. The dynamic aspect of contemporary Indonesia has been encountered in many sectors of the economy, including agriculture, mining, manufacturing, and finance, where production and productivity have been rising rapidly. Dynamism also has been a characteristic of social life, as seen in the declining rate of population growth and the rising levels of education. The observation leads to the question: How has this economic and social dynamism been impacting on the political system in which it is taking place?

On the one hand, the political system seems to have been reinforced by its economic and social output to date. The history of the last quarter-century has been largely one of success building on success. One has a general sense of events rushing forward, of the future as being open-ended. On the other hand, there is a question of how far it is possible to elaborate upon the complexity of the economy and society without modifying the political system. The widespread presumption among the elite seems to be that the process of change that has been underway for the past quarter-century still has some way to go before reaching a necessary turning point.

It does appear that the pluralism introduced in the past generation is now greatly complicating the process of public policy-making—of managing the far more complex economy and society that have resulted. Pressures exist for greater transparency in this process, and political institutions to ensure this will need to be considered. But there is a surprising lack of urgency about the matter. Many members of the Indonesian elite seem confident that having survived so many difficulties they will muddle through the political transition that lies ahead. That is not a formula for a smooth transition.

The Political Transition

By the year 1992 Soeharto had been Indonesia's de facto leader for more than twenty-five years, one of the longest uninterrupted tenures of a head of government in the world at the time. His tenure had much to say about the dilemma of authoritarianism in the late twentieth century, a dilemma that remained a feature of both communist and noncommunist regimes in Southeast Asia and in other regions of the world. Soeharto and his security aides had managed the nation's political life with a heavy hand, co-opting interest groups, controlling institutions, and repressing dissent. At the same time Soeharto and his economic aides had managed with uncommon skill the growth of the Indonesian economy and the distribution of social benefits. Politically Indonesia appeared to have much in common with countries such as Burma and Vietnam, and economically with Thailand and the Philippines. The question was this: Was Indonesia embedded in its attachments to the past, as Burma and Vietnam seemed to be, or was it, following Thailand and the Philippines, on the threshold of a political transition?

The question was highly consequential. Presidential succession was assumed to be assured before another decade had run its course. Soeharto in 1993, when scheduled to stand for yet another term, would be seventy-two years old, an elderly man by Indonesian standards. Sukarno's departure from the presidency occurred amid much bloodshed and involved a major change in the political regime and in the orientation of economic policy. Members of Indonesia's elite were quite concerned that violence should not accompany the succession again. Could the succession be managed peacefully, on the basis of a broad consensus among the elite?

A consideration that gave the succession added significance was the potential impact on human welfare in the fourth most populous nation in the world. It was not only hoped that violence would be avoided but that the country's record of economic growth and social development would continue. Not only did the elite have a stake in the continuity of policy, but in a nation in which average per capita income was still on the order of only $570 per annum, the welfare of millions was potentially at risk. The concern was widespread as to whether a change in the presidency could be accomplished without significant change in the character of economic and social policy.

Yet another consideration that added weight to the succession was the belief, widely evident among the elite, that it was time for some change in the political regime. It is true that public commentary tended to focus more or less exclusively on individuals who were potential successors to the presidency, and that these were invariably military figures. At the same time, however, much private commentary clearly indicated that many in the military and civilian elite felt it was time for a change in the balance of civil-military relations. A new generation of Indonesians saw the heroes of 1945 as a dwindling band of elderly men. Even the events of 1965 were no longer in the life experience of most Indonesians over the voting age of eighteen. And younger army officers were believed to be increasingly removed from political ambition and concerned for their own professional advancement. As these younger Indonesians looked outward on the world at large, they could not help but see that their country was lagging behind other nations politically.

A further reason for interest in the presidential succession was that Indonesia, after being preoccupied with its domestic development for most of the Soeharto years, was again seeking a larger place in international affairs. In helping to negotiate an international settlement in Cambodia, in normalizing its own relations with China, in campaigning successfully for leadership of the nonaligned movement, and in other ways as well, Indonesia was by 1992 again becoming an active member of the community of nations. At the same time serious separatist movements were occurring on the Indonesian periphery—in Aceh, Irian, and Timor. It did not require long memories for leaders of neighboring countries to see that Indonesia's role in the stability of Southeast Asia could be affected by the nature of its succession process and by the character and stability of the successor regime.

Soeharto himself could play a role in the succession process. He could retire voluntarily at the end of his term in 1993 at the age of seventy-two, when he would be in a position to shape the successor government in any number of ways. He was not expected to do this, however, for several reasons. He was thought to believe that he had come into the presidency as a result of supernatural forces, and, if this were so, he would have reason to leave his departure to the same authority. He was known to be convinced that his personal contribution to the accomplishments of his administration was of overwhelming importance. In an autobiography published at the end of the 1980s he claimed personal credit for a wide range of achievements, and was either neglectful or scornful of many who had assisted him along the way. It was entirely possible that Soeharto believed Indonesia needed him for as many years as he could give to the country. He also had grounds for concern about his personal security in the event he was no longer commander in chief of the armed forces. The treatment of former leaders of South Korea, East Germany, and Rumania in recent years, not to mention Sukarno's fate, would have led him to consider this possibility. Finally, he had to consider the security of his children and his friends, and their material assets. The experience of Marcos's relatives and friends in the Philippines was well known in Indonesia, and the comparison with Soeharto was often made. For these reasons Soeharto seemed unlikely to retire on his own initiative.

The army would inevitably play a role in the succession. The army, unlike any other institution, had a structure of command and communication that linked its leadership with all parts of the country. An army general was vice president and, under the constitution, would succeed to the presidency in the event of the president's death, pending a vote by the Consultative Assembly. Other army generals or former generals effectively controlled the Consultative Assembly. The army was strategically positioned to influence the succession.

The army also suffered several disabilities. One was a lack of unanimity among army leaders about whether the time had come for Soeharto to be replaced. Some senior officers strongly believed by the late 1980s that the issue of corruption had created a major gap between the government and public opinion. Were the situation allowed to continue, they held, it could lead to disorder on a scale the army might have difficulty controlling. But at least a few senior officers were thought not to hold this opinion, including several Soeharto protégés in key army positions in Jakarta.

Even if the army leadership were united in its opinion, it faced obstacles to taking a stand against the president. Army commanders had a formidable psychological obstacle in the loyalty they owed the commander in chief, and this was reinforced by the society's traditional deference to superiors and elders. Soeharto had successfully faced down the army in 1988 when army commanders were united in opposing his choice for the vice presidency. In 1990, as discussion of the succession surfaced in the mass media, Soeharto demanded that it stop, and it did. Army commanders were also hindered by their felt need to preserve the constitution and its formal requirements in the interest of legitimacy. If they could not nudge the president to take the initiative, they might not be able to press him to do so against his wishes either.

Even were the sense of a need for change strong enough to override these obstacles, army leaders faced serious difficulties in filling the presidency. The army had no alternate candidate behind whom it could unite. Since even discussion of the topic was seen as disloyal behavior, army leaders were inhibited from developing a consensus among themselves on this point. And that would still not be enough. Many members of the elite, including former army leaders, were generally of the opinion that army support alone would not be sufficient to enable the next president to govern. The army had no justification to fill the office on its own initiative as it had done in 1966. The army also had less interest in doing so; it was smaller, more professional, and less political. The civilian element in the elite was, at the same time, much larger, wealthier, and better educated. Meanwhile the world outside was also changing, and dictatorships were giving way to more open regimes in many regions of the globe. Many believed a national consensus was needed on a new formula for power sharing.

Such a change clearly would require both time and the freedom to debate alternative courses. Perhaps men would arise willing to stand against the president and launch this debate. Failing that, the fear was that a settled succession was problematic. It was not known when it would occur, in what circumstances, or by what process. The future could hardly be more unpredictable. The Indonesian elite's worst fear was that Soeharto's successor would be unable to hold the system together, with disastrous results. That fear was encapsulated in the prediction attributed to a Javanese mystic: Soeharto would be succeeded by a turtle. And the turtle would be succeeded by a crocodile, which would eat the turtle up.

Unfinished Business

Thus by a process that could not be foreseen the Soeharto era would eventually give way to a successor. When it did, the Indonesian elite would continue to face some long-standing challenges.

Epilogue

One of these was the army's role in politics and government. The challenge was assured by the high degree of army penetration of the national executive, the legislature, provincial governments, the state corporations, the government "party," and much else. The likelihood was that such a high degree of army involvement would give way only slowly with the withering away of interest on the part of army personnel themselves.

The alternate prospect, of a rapid army withdrawal, seemed undesirable. Among other reasons, a rapid diminution in army influence would run the risk of inviting continuing coups and attempted coups, as have occurred in Thailand and the Philippines in recent years, and even the danger of wholesale rejection of political change, as in Burma and Vietnam.

The army's ability to remove itself from the government even if it wished to do so would be conditioned by the environment prevailing at the time. It was widely believed that a global recession and depressed oil prices would create a situation in which such a change would be unlikely without some disorder. In an age of increasing ethnic and religious division and competition, the risk was that an army withdrawal from politics also might be hampered by controversy surrounding an Islamic minority or the Chinese minority or both.

The place of Islam in Indonesia's politics and government also remained unsettled. This did not mean that past debates had to be repeated. On the contrary, the issue of an Islamic state appeared to be of interest only to fringe elements of the Muslim community. There was also a source of optimism in the prospect that Islam and the bureaucratic elite were heading toward an amicable convergence as a result of fundamental changes within society—the raising of educational levels in devout Muslim communities and the success of Muslim missionary activities among members of the bureaucratic elite. Even so, significant problems remained.

The progressive secularization of politics, on the one hand, and the government's co-optation of Muslim functions and symbols, on the other, led to a high level of frustration within the community of devout Muslims, and to considerable unease among non-Muslim leaders. It was difficult to imagine that the next president of Indonesia could be as remote from the center of gravity of political Islam as Soeharto had been. It seemed increasingly desirable that the next president should be readily identifiable as a devout Muslim and readily understanding of

Muslim perceptions and concerns. But complex issues remained to be worked out among members of the Muslim community, who were of varying cultural and spiritual traditions themselves, and between them and the non-Muslim minorities, including adherents of Javanism, Hinduism, Buddhism, and Protestant and Catholic Christianity. These were issues of a sort that were not advisedly addressed by public authorities in the first place. The real challenge was for religious-minded intellectuals in all these minority communities—for each is a minority in the end—to contribute in their own way to the development of a new national consensus on the role of religion, including Islam, in Indonesia's public life.

Another challenge for the future was the need for a social philosophy to take account of the rising role of private capital in the Indonesian economy, including the share of this capital owned and managed by the Chinese minority. It seemed impossible in 1992 to imagine an Indonesian economy without a large and vibrant private sector. Including millions of small farms, shops, workshops, and service firms, as well as millions of individuals in the informal sector, the private economy was overwhelming in its significance to the society. The spectacular growth of the private sector in the 1980s did not take place among these small units, however. The growth of big industrial conglomerates in the protected conditions of the 1980s probably would not have impinged so dramatically on national politics had it not been for the fact that the bulk of them were owned and operated by members of the small Chinese community. This occurred in a political atmosphere in which the government, in the Broad Outlines of State Policy, continued to express severe criticism of "free-fight capitalism."

It was surely one of the failings of the Soeharto regime that neither the president nor any of his principle advisers had even begun the process of developing an alternate view of the role of private capital in the society. The responsibility was primarily Soeharto's because he had set himself up as the chief interpreter of the constitution, and also because he had to be sensitive to an issue that touched on the wealth of his family and friends. His recent efforts to build a new consensus on cooperatives—including efforts to obtain commitments from business conglomerates to sell or even give shares in their enterprises to cooperatives of uncertain membership—seemed doomed to failure. How any of these vague notions would be accomplished in practice on any significant scale was never worked out.

Meanwhile, approaches well established in other countries had gone wanting for attention. No antitrust legislation was in place that would keep the large accumulation of private wealth within socially acceptable constraints. There was no assured enforcement of tax collections from the very wealthy, whether individuals or corporations; the government depended largely on voluntarism among its taxpayers, and gave awards to those who met their legal obligations, a far cry from taking action against the dilatory. There was still only grudging acceptance of the worth of private institutions in promoting religion, welfare, education, science, or the arts, and no exemption from taxes to encourage gifts for such purposes.

One could only hope that somewhere in Indonesian society a few voices would be heard that heralded a new philosophy about the social roles of private capital in Indonesia.

A Last Word

Anyone who spends any time in studying the Indonesian political economy cannot fail to acquire a deep appreciation for the Indonesian elite's ability to define its own strengths and weaknesses, and prescribe for its own future. Although this elite has been highly introspective in the main for most of the past quarter century, it has drawn deeply on the experience of other societies in fashioning its economic policy, has managed its foreign economic relations with more than modest success, and has demonstrated an earned self-confidence in its relations with outside powers.

Indonesia's domestic political system has remained impervious to change through these same recent decades, but the elite has not been unaware of the winds of change blowing through much of the rest of the world. On the contrary, the evidence indicated that greater openness was widely desired and, within the limits of a deferential culture and a highly autocratic regime, was beginning to be demanded.

Societies must learn, as individuals must, in their own way and at their own pace. The Indonesian elite is a learning community, gaining knowledge principally from its own experience, but not inattentive to the values being advanced elsewhere. Like all great nations, Indonesia will fashion its own future, with or without the benefit of our counsel or approbation.

Still, one would like to raise some cheers for the Indonesian elite.

Epilogue

One cheer, certainly, for the economic record of growth, well conceived and impressively pursued. A half-cheer, probably, for the effort on behalf of equity, creatively shaped in the 1970s, on the defensive in the 1980s. Finally, if the Indonesian elite were able to fashion a new political consensus, providing for a measure of power sharing beyond the executive and the army, one would be very happy to raise a rousing third cheer as well.

Notes

Introduction

1. World Bank, *Social Indicators of Development: 1989* (Washington, D.C.: World Bank, 1989). Pakistan was an exception in one respect; its daily supply of calories per capita rivaled that of Indonesia in 1965.
2. Van Niel, *Modern Indonesian Elite,* passim.
3. Ibid.

1. The Coup That Failed

1. The literature on the failed coup is large and varied. Early accounts include Hughes, *Indonesian Upheaval,* and Shaplen, *Time Out of Hand.* Early analyses include Anderson and McVey, *A Preliminary Analysis;* Lev, "Indonesia 1965," pp. 103–10; Wertheim, "Indonesia Before and After the Untung Coup," pp. 115–27; Hindley, "Political Power," pp. 237–49; Notosusanto and Saleh, *The Coup Attempt;* and Van der Kroef, "Interpretations of the 1965 Indonesia Coup," pp. 557–77. Later assessments that focus their attention on one or another of the major actors include Legge, *Sukarno;* Mortimer, *Indonesian Communism;* and Crouch, *The Army and Politics in Indonesia.*
2. Mackie, *Konfrontasi.*
3. "Initial Statement of Lieutenant Colonel Untung," in Anderson and McVey, *A Preliminary Analysis,* p. 122.
4. "Decree No. 1 on the Establishment of the Indonesian Revolution Council," in Anderson and McVey, *A Preliminary Analysis,* p. 123.
5. Kayyam, "Bawuk," p. 168.
6. A rare eyewitness account of the killings in East Java, in which military personnel and Ansor youth are described as beheading a truck-load of victims, is excerpted in Jones, *Injustice, Persecution, Eviction,* p. 115.

Notes

7. A collection of short stories describing such events appears in Aveling, ed. and trans., *Gestapu*, p. 110.

8. Ibid., p. 39.

9. Crouch, *The Army and Politics in Indonesia*, p. 143.

10. Kahin, *Nationalism and Revolution in Indonesia*, pp. 290–305; see also Ann Swift, *The Road to Madiun: The Indonesian Communist Uprising of 1948* (Ithaca, N.Y.: Cornell Modern Indonesia Project, 1989), p. 116.

11. Kartodirdjo, *Agrarian Unrest*, p. 22.

12. Ladejinsky, "Land Reform in Indonesia," pp. 343–44.

13. Ibid., p. 343.

14. The *abangan* tradition is an "intricate complex of spirit beliefs, and a whole set of theories and practices of cunning, sorcery, and magic " (Geertz, *The Religion of Java*, p. 5). Also, and perhaps later, *abangan* is a "derogatory term to denote Javanese who do not take Islamic religious learning seriously"; Koentjaraningrat, *Javanese Culture*, p. 197.

15. Geertz, *The Religion of Java*, p. 6; also see Koentjaraningrat, *Javanese Culture*, p. 196.

16. Hindley, *The Communist Party of Indonesia*, pp. 160–80; Mortimer, *Indonesian Communism*, pp. 276–95.

17. Mortimer, *Indonesian Communism*.

18. A principal source on the PKI campaign is Mortimer, *Indonesian Communism*. For reactions in East Java, see Walkin, "The Moslem-Communist Confrontation," pp. 822–47. For reactions in Central Java, see Kartodirdjo, *Agrarian Unrest*. For a discussion of rural poverty, class structure, and peasant conservatism in West Java, see Aidit, *Kaum Tani Mengganjang Setan-Setan Desa* (Farmers destroy the village devils), which contains no hint of the "unilateral action" campaign that began in late 1963. Arguments that greater weight should be placed on class structure are found in Wertheim, "From Aliran to Class Struggle"; and Margot Lyon, *Bases of Conflict*.

19. Mortimer, *Indonesian Communism*, p. 300.

20. Kartodirdjo, *Agrarian Unrest*, p. 98.

21. Geertz, *The Interpretation of Cultures*, p. 167.

22. Anderson, "Idea of Power in Javanese Culture," p. 22.

23. Ibid., p. 21.

24. Ibid., p. 19.

25. Wertheim, "Suharto and the Untung days," pp. 50–51; Benedict Anderson and Ruth McVey, Letter to the Editor, *New York Review of Books*, June 1, 1978.

26. See, e.g., editorial, "Lilliputian Politics in Huge Indonesia," *New York Times*, April 25, 1987.

27. Coppel, *Indonesian Chinese*, p. 58.

28. Mozingo, *Chinese Policy Toward Indonesia*, p. 250.

29. Central Intelligence Agency, *Indonesia 1965*.

30. Kathy Kadane, "U.S. Officials' Lists Aided Indonesian Bloodbath in '60s," *Washington Post*, May 21, 1990.

31. Myrdal, *Asian Drama*, p. 378.

2. Sukarno Yields to Soeharto

1. Crouch, *The Army and Politics in Indonesia*, p. 137.

2. Ibid., pp. 138–39.

3. Ibid., p. 140.

4. Ibid., p. 162.

5. Ibid., p. 165.

6. Ibid., p. 161.

7. Ibid., p. 165.

8. Ibid., pp. 166–67.

9. Ibid., p. 167.

10. Ibid., p. 168.

11. Ibid., pp. 174–82.

12. Ibid., p. 184.

13. Ibid., pp. 184–85.

14. Ibid., p. 186, n. 10.

15. Ibid., p. 189.

16. The student role in the events of 1965–66 is treated briefly in many accounts of the period. An extended account can be found in Raillon, *Les Etudiants Indonesiens et l'Ordre Nouveau*.

17. Personal interview, June 6, 1983.

18. Ibid.

19. Personal interview, June 16, 1983.

20. Ibid.

21. Crouch, *The Army and Politics in Indonesia*, pp. 72–73.

22. *Apa & Siapa*, 1981, pp. 856–57.

23. Crouch, *The Army and Politics in Indonesia*, pp. 189–90.

24. Ibid., p. 167.

25. Ibid., pp. 189–90.

26. Ibid.

27. Hughes, *Indonesian Upheaval*, pp. 235–36; Polomka, *Indonesia Since Sukarno*, p. 89; Crouch, *The Army and Politics in Indonesia*, pp. 190–91.

28. Pauker, "Role of the Military."

29. Penders and Sundhaussen, *Abdul Haris Nasution*, pp. 232–33.

30. Personal interview, June 11, 1983.

31. Personal interview, June 13, 1983.

32. Personal interview, June 6, 1983.

33. Roeder, *The Smiling General*, p. 2.

34. Personal interview, July 20, 1983.
35. Personal interview, July 21, 1983.
36. Personal interview, June 14, 1983.
37. Schlesinger, *A Thousand Days,* p. 533.
38. Personal interview, July 16, 1983.
39. Soedjatmoko, *Indonesia: Problems and Opportunities* and *Indonesia and the World,* p. 266.
40. Personal interview, October 12, 1990.
41. Holt, *Art in Indonesia,* pp. 144–45.

3. The Rise of the Technocrats

1. Myrdal, *Asian Drama,* pp. 65–67.
2. Feith, "Indonesia's Political Symbols," p. 92. For an extended assessment of the Guided Democracy period, see Feith, "Dynamics of Guided Democracy."
3. Feith and Castles, eds., *Indonesian Political Thinking,* pp. 392–94.
4. Nitisastro, "Analisa Ekonomi dan Perencanaan Pembangunan"; and Mohammad Sadli, "Economic Stabilization as an Essential Condition for Effective Economic Development," August 31, 1963, reproduced in part in Feith and Castles, eds., *Indonesian Political Thinking,* pp. 396–400.
5. Sadli, "Masalah Ekonomi-Moneter Kita Jang Strukturil."
6. The extracts are from the English edition of *Business News* (Jakarta, April 15, 1966), and are reproduced in Arndt and Panglaykim, "Survey of Recent Developments."
7. Arndt, *The Indonesian Economy,* p. 3.
8. This section and the one following draw principally on the following sources: proceedings of a seminar held at the University of Indonesia from January 10–20, 1966, *The Leader, the Man and the Gun;* proceedings of a seminar held at the University of Indonesia from May 6–9, 1966, *Kebangkitan Semangat '66: Mendjeladjah Tracee Baru* (Jakarta: Jajasan Badan Penerbit, Fakultas Ekonomi Universitas Indonesia, 1966); Arndt, "Survey of Recent Developments"; Mackie, *Indonesian Inflation;* Newman, *Inflation in Indonesia;* and Mangkusuwondo, "Indonesia."
9. Subroto, "Menjusun Sendi-Sendi Ekonomi Berdasarkan Prinsip Ekonomi."
10. Sumiskum, "Konfrontasi dan Politik Luar Negeri Untuk Kepentingan Nasional."
11. Republic of Indonesia, Madjelis Permusjawaratan Rakjat Sementara, "Pembaharuan Kebidjaksanaan Landasan Ekonomi Keuangan dan Pembangunan."
12. Personal interview, May 26, 1983.
13. Personal interview, June 1988.

Notes

14. Personal interview, May 28, 1983.

15. *Financial Times,* September 22, 1966, cited in Arndt, "Survey of Recent Developments," pp. 3–4.

16. Mackie, *Konfrontasi.*

17. Hawkins, "Job Inflation in Indonesia."

18. Arndt, "Survey of Recent Developments."

19. Payer, "The International Monetary Fund."

20. Ransom, "Ford Country."

21. Nishihara, *The Japanese and Sukarno's Indonesia,* passim. On the last point, personal interviews, 1983 and 1989.

22. Gillis, "Episodes in Indonesian Economic Growth," p. 245.

23. Weinstein, *Indonesian Foreign Policy.*

24. Soedjatmoko, *Indonesia: Problems and Opportunities and Indonesia and the World,* p. 291.

25. On the comparative situation, see Milne, "Technocrats and Politics."

26. Gillis, "Episodes in Indonesian Economic Growth," pp. 242–43.

27. Personal interview, July 28, 1990.

28. Anderson, "The Idea of Power in Javanese Culture," pp. 33–43.

29. Personal interview, August 19, 1989.

30. Personal interview, August 14, 1989.

31. Furnivall, *Educational Progress,* p. 111.

32. See, for example, Harry Benda, "The Pattern of Administrative Reforms," *Journal of Asian Studies,* pp. 589–605.

33. Kahin, *Nationalism and Revolution in Indonesia,* pp. 37–63.

34. For a general introduction, see Rice, "Origins of Economic Ideas," pp. 141–53.

35. Translation by the author.

36. Kahin, "In Memoriam: Mohammad Hatta," pp. 113–19.

37. Hatta, *The Co-operative Movement,* pp. 8, 31.

38. Hatta, *Bung Hatta's Answers,* p. 84.

39. Djojohadikusumo, *Ekonomi Pembangunan,* pp. 117ff.

40. For a history of economic policy to 1957, and a review of other analyses of economic policy during the period, see Glassburner, "Economic Policy-Making in Indonesia." A telling fictional account of the political corruption that destroyed Sumitro's import-licensing scheme appears in Lubis, *Twilight in Djakarta.*

41. A history of the Faculty of Economics of the University of Indonesia has yet to be written. A valuable contribution can be found in Dye, "The Jakarta Faculty of Economics."

42. The origins and views of the younger economists are treated in considerable detail in MacDougall, "Technocrats as Modernizers," and in the same author's "The Technocrat's Ideology of Modernity."

Notes

43. Dye, "The Jakarta Faculty of Economics," p. 19.
44. *Apa & Siapa: sejumlah orang Indonesia, 1983–84* (Jakarta: Grafiti Pers, 1984), p. 577.
45. Nitisastro, *Population Trends*, pp. 383–84.
46. Personal interview, June 8, 1983
47. Personal interview, June 4, 1983.
48. Personal interview, June 8, 1983.
49. Nitisastro, *Population Trends*, pp. 383–84.
50. Boeke, *Structure of Netherlands Indian Economy,* and *Evolution of the Netherlands Indies Economy.*
51. Furnivall, *Netherlands India*, pp. 462–63.
52. Sadli, "Reflections on Boeke's Theory of Dualistic Economies," pp. 99–123.

4. Creating a Political Machine

1. The principal source on which this and the following four paragraphs are based is Feith, *Decline of Constitutional Democracy.*
2. The discussion in this and the following seven paragraphs draws on several published accounts of which Liddle, ed., *Political Participation in Modern Indonesia,* and Crouch, *The Army and Politics in Indonesia,* are the fullest.
3. Angkatan Darat, *Sumbangan Fikiran TNI-AD Kepada Kabinet Ampera* (1966), p. 49, cited by Crouch, *The Army and Politics in Indonesia,* p. 248.
4. A second party Sukarno banned was the Socialist Party, whose leaders were prominent in early cabinets but which performed poorly at the polls in 1955. Although one of its former leaders apparently did secretly negotiate with Soeharto's staff in an effort to have the party legally recognized again, the bulk of its leadership decided not to try to revive the organization but to work with the government as individuals and, they hoped, influence it from within.
5. The experience of the National Party during this period is described in most analyses of the 1971 elections; the fullest account appears to be that of Crouch, *The Army and Politics in Indonesia,* pp. 254–59.
6. The unsuccessful effort to rehabilitate the Masyumi Party is described in detail in Ken Ward, *The Foundation of the Partai Muslim in Indonesia.*
7. The discussion in this and the following four paragraphs draws on a number of personal interviews in Jakarta between 1983 and 1989. Other published accounts appear to draw on much the same sources.
8. Soeharto was quoted as saying the idea and the people were "PSI." The initials are those of the *Partai Sosialis Indonesia,* or Indonesian Socialist Party. The initials have come to be used to refer not only to former party members but also to anyone, civilian or military, who had a university-level education, had an intellectual turn of mind, and had some attachment to Western values.

To refer to someone as "PSI" was not necessarily pejorative, although it tended to be in Soeharto's circle.

9. The negotiations with the parties are described in Notosusanto, *Tercapainya Konsensus Nasional.*

10. The discussion in this and the following five paragraphs draws principally on Reeve, "Sukarnoism and Indonesia's 'Functional Group' State," and his *Golkar of Indonesia,* and Boileau, *Golkar.*

11. The 1971 elections are reported and analyzed in a number of publications, including Nishihara, *The Japanese and Sukarno's Indonesia;* Liddle, ed., *Political Participation in Modern Indonesia,* Ken Ward, *The 1971 Election in Indonesia;* and Crouch, *The Army and Politics in Indonesia.*

12. Nishihara, *The Japanese and Sukarno's Indonesia,* p. 13.

13. Ibid., p. 3.

14. See, e.g., Moertopo, *Some Basic Thoughts ,* pp. 85–86.

15. Republic of Indonesia, Biro Pusat Statistik, *Statistik Indonesia: 1982* (Jakarta, 1983), p. 118.

16. Republic of Indonesia, "Peraturan Pemerintah Republik Indonesia Nomor 10 Tahun 1983 tentang Izin Perkawinan dan Perceraian Bagi Pegawai Negeri Sipil," *Lembaran Negara Republik Indonesia Nomor 13,* April 21, 1983.

17. Raffles, *History of Java,* p. 267. Some might object that Raffles was a partisan observer, writing to make a case for British colonization, but his description does not conflict in any fundamental way with other accounts of the period.

18. Sutherland, *The Making of a Bureaucratic Elite,* p. 16.

19. Ibid., p. 79.

20. Benda, "Pattern of Administrative Reforms," p. 591, n. 8.

21. Van Niel, *Modern Indonesian Elite,* pp. 196–251.

22. Sjafruddin Prawiranegara, cited by Feith, *Decline of Constitutional Democracy,* p. 306.

23. Republic of Indonesia, Biro Pusat Statistik, *Statistical Pocketbook of Indonesia: 1957,* Jakarta, 1957, pp. 220–21.

24. Republic of Indonesia, Biro Pusat Statistik, *Statistical Pocketbook of Indonesia: 1968,* Jakarta, 1968, pp. 28–29.

25. Emmerson, *Indonesia's Elite,* p. 104.

26. Ibid., p. 91.

27. Mangkusuwondo, "Indonesia," pp. 52–53.

28. Unpublished data from the office of the Minister for Reform of the State Apparatus, 1986. The same source has been drawn on for civil service data in the paragraphs that follow.

29. *Indonesian Observer,* November 4, 1981, cited by MacDougall, "Patterns of Military Control," p. 101, n. 29.

30. On the comparative situation in Southeast Asia, see Girling, *The Bureaucratic Polity,* and Crouch, *Domestic Political Structures.*

31. All data are from the annual reports published under the title *World Military Expenditures and Arms Transfers* by the U.S. Arms Control and Disarmament Agency.

32. Ibid.

33. Crouch, *The Army and Politics in Indonesia,* p. 274, n. 1.

34. Business International Roundtable, "Indonesia's Prospect for Attracting Foreign Investment" (September 17, 1968), cited by Polomka, *Indonesia Since Sukarno,* p. 114.

35. For a detailed account of the corporate and personal economic interests of army officers in the late 1960s and early 1970s, see Robison, *Indonesia,* pp. 250–70, and Crouch, *The Army and Politics in Indonesia,* pp. 273–303. For views on corruption, see Smith, *The Indonesian Bureaucracy,* pp. 21–40.

36. Penders and Sundhaussen, *Abdul Haris Nasution,* p. 113.

37. Crouch, *The Army and Politics in Indonesia,* pp. 76–77.

38. Emmerson, *Indonesia's Elite,* p. 101; MacDougall, "Patterns of Military Control," p. 98.

39. Emmerson, *Indonesia's Elite,* p. 101.

40. Ibid., p. 102, n. 27.

41. MacDougall, "Patterns of Military Control," p. 98.

42. Emmerson, *Indonesia's Elite,* p. 103.

43. Ibid., p. 103.

44. Polomka, *Indonesia Since Sukarno,* p. 97.

5. Achieving Rice Self-Sufficiency

1. Neill, *Twentieth-Century Indonesia,* p. 69; Boeke, *Evolution of the Netherlands Indies Economy,* p. 109.

2. Neill, *Twentieth-Century Indonesia,* pp. 70–72; Boeke, *Evolution of the Netherlands Indies Economy,* pp. 39–80.

3. Neill, *Twentieth-Century Indonesia,* p. 56; Barker et al., *Rice Economy of Asia,* p. 98.

4. Barker et al., *Rice Economy of Asia,* pp. 57–58.

5. Boeke, *Evolution of the Netherlands Indies Economy,* pp. 112–16, 133–37; Mears and Moeljono, "Food Policy," pp. 23–24.

6. On the rice situation in Java during the Japanese occupation, see Anderson, ed., "The Problem of Rice," pp. 77–123; and Shizuo, "Jawa Shusen Shoriki."

7. Mears, *New Rice Economy of Indonesia,* p. 389; Mears and Moeljono, "Food Policy," p. 24.

8. Mears and Moeljono, "Food Policy," pp. 24–28.

9. Mackie, "Indonesian Inflation," pp. 33–36.

10. Mears and Moeljono, "Food Policy," p. 25.

11. Ibid., p. 29.

12. Chandler, *Rice in the Tropics*, pp. 32ff; Siamwalla and Haykin, *The World Rice Market*, pp. 37–39.

13. Mueller, "Observations on Rice Production," and Shaw, "Rice Research Project Evaluation"; William B. Ward, *Science and Rice in Indonesia*, p. 13.

14. Mears and Moeljono, "Food Policy," p. 29; Robison, *Indonesia*, p. 229.

15. Mears and Moeljono, "Food Policy," p. 32.

16. Ibid., pp. 26–27, Table 2.1, and p. 33.

17. Asian Development Bank, *Rural Asia*, p. 45; Timmer, "Formation of Indonesian Rice Policy," pp. 39–43.

18. Mears and Moeljono, "Food Policy," p. 34.

19. Economic Intelligence Unit, *The Economist, Quarterly Economic Review*, 1972; Mears and Moeljono, "Food Policy," p. 34.

20. Economic Intelligence Unit, *The Economist, Quarterly Economic Review*, 1972; Mears and Moeljono, "Food Policy," p. 29, Table 2.2, and pp. 34–35.

21. Chandler, Jr., *Rice in the Tropics*, pp. 97–98 and figure 12; Economic Intelligence Unit, *The Economist, Quarterly Economic Review*; Timmer, "Formation of Indonesian Rice Policy," p. 39.

22. Samson, "Indonesia," pp. 157–65.

23. Humphrey, *Hunger and Diplomacy*, pp. 10–13.

24. Personal interviews, 1983 and 1986.

25. Barker et al., *Rice Economy of Asia*, pp. 232–241; *Jakarta Post*, May 23, 1987; "Indonesia Survey," p. 11, *The Economist*, August 15, 1987.

26. Shaw, "Rice Research Project Evaluation," pp. 4, 7; William B. Ward, *Science and Rice in Indonesia*, pp. 24, 49–57; Siamwalla and Haykin, *The World Rice Market*, p. 38; Food and Agricultural Organization, May 1988; *Wall Street Journal*, April 16, 1990.

27. Mears and Moeljono, "Food Policy," p. 41; Mears, *New Rice Economy of Indonesia*, pp. 123–136; Barker et al., *Rice Economy of Asia*, pp. 86–87; Harvard Institute for International Development, unpublished data.

28. Harvard Institute for International Development, unpublished data; R. A. Richards, "The Kabupaten Program," *Indonesia*, no. 25 (April 1978), pp. 183–98.

29. Harvard Institute for International Development, unpublished data; Njoman Suwidjana, "Indonesia's Rice Policy," *Southeast Asian Affairs 1981* (Singapore: ISEAS, June 1982), p. 156.

30. Mears and Moeljono, "Food Policy," pp. 39–40; William B. Ward, *Science and Rice in Indonesia*, pp. 86–87; Harvard Institute for International Development, unpublished data; Suwidjana, "Indonesia's Rice Policy," p. 153.

Notes

31. Mears and Moeljono, "Food Policy," pp. 40–46; Barker et al., *Rice Economy of Asia*, p. 47, Table 4.13; personal interviews, 1983.

32. Mears, *New Rice Economy of Indonesia*, pp. 54–66; Siamwalla and Haykin, "Indonesia's Rice Policy," p. 18, Table 5.

33. William B. Ward, *Science and Rice in Indonesia*, p. 1; Harvard Institute for International Development, unpublished data; *Tempo*, May 11 and May 18, 1985; Raphael Pura, *Asian Wall Street Journal*, June 14–15, 1985; Booth and McCawley, "The Indonesian Economy Since the Mid-Sixties," p. 1.

34. Republic of Indonesia, *National Logistics Agency* (Jakarta: National Logistics Agency, 1982), p. iii.

35. *Sinar Harapan* (July 22, 1970), cited by Robison, *Indonesia*, p. 247, n. 39.

36. Robison, *Indonesia*, pp. 229–33.

37. Republic of Indonesia, *National Logistics Agency*, p. iii.

38. See, for example, Robison, *Indonesia*, p. 230.

39. Mears, *New Rice Economy of Indonesia*, pp. 422–24; Republic of Indonesia, *National Logistics Agency*, p. iii; personal interviews, 1983.

40. Republic of Indonesia, *National Logistics Agency*, pp. iv, v; Mears and Moeljono, "Food Policy," p. 41; personal interviews, 1983.

41. Republic of Indonesia, *National Logistics Agency*, p. v; personal observations and interviews, 1983.

42. Robison, *Indonesia*, pp. 232–33; Republic of Indonesia, *National Logistics Agency*, p. iv; *Jakarta Post*, May 23, 1987.

43. The discussion in this and the following two paragraphs is based principally on Mubyarto, "The Sugar Industry," and Mackie and O'Malley, "Productivity Decline in the Java Sugar Industry."

44. Soemardjan, *Petani Tebu*.

45. *Jakarta Post*, May 23, 1987.

46. Personal interview, 1983.

47. Personal interview, 1983.

48. *Jakarta Post*, May 23, 1987.

49. Geertz, "Religious Belief and Economic Behavior," pp. 134–58; and Geertz, *Agricultural Involution*.

50. White, " 'Agricultural Involution' and Its Critics," pp. 18–31.

51. Lyon, *Bases of Conflict*, and Wertheim, "From *Aliran* to Class Struggle," p. 17.

52. Collier, "Agricultural Evolution in Java" pp. 164–66.

53. Collier et al., "Recent Changes in Rice Harvesting Methods," pp. 36–42; Hayami and Hafid, "Rice Harvesting and Welfare," pp. 94–112.

54. Kikuchi et al., "Class Differentiation," *The Developing Economies*, pp. 45–64; White, "Population Involution," pp. 130ff; Barker et al., *Rice Economy of Asia*, pp. 135–36; Manning, *The Green Revolution*, passim.

55. Anne Booth and R. M. Sundrum, "Income Distribution," in *The Indonesian Economy*, ed. Booth and McCawley, pp. 182–90; Harvard Institute for International Development, unpublished data; Manning, *The Green Revolution*, p. 76.

56. Stoler, "Garden Use and Household Economy"; White, "Population Involution"; and Manning, *The Green Revolution*.

57. Mears and Moeljono, "Food Policy," p. 33; Timmer, "Formation of Indonesian Rice Policy," p. 43; Arndt and Sundrum, "Comments on Clive Gray's 'Civil Service Compensation in Indonesia' "; *Tempo*, August 27, 1977, cited by Leo Suryadinata, *Peranakan Chinese Politics in Java* (Singapore: Singapore University Press, 1981) p. 14; Booth and Sundrum, "Income Distribution" pp. 192, 194–195; *KOMPAS*, July 19, 1983; Keyfitz, "An East Javanese Village"; Manning, *The Green Revolution*, pp. 68–70; *Far Eastern Economic Review*, June 14, 1990.

6. The January 15 "Disaster"

1. *Time*, January 21 and 28, 1974.

2. Richard Halloran, *New York Times*, January 15, 1974; *Time*, January 28, 1974.

3. Halloran, *New York Times*, January 16 and 17, 1974; *Time*, January 28, 1974.

4. Ibid.

5. Accounts of the event differ somewhat. This one follows Crouch, *The Army and Politics in Indonesia*, p. 315.

6. Ibid.; also *Newsweek*, January 28, 1974.

7. Ibid.; also Reuters, January 17 and 19, 1974.

8. Panggabean, "Keterangan Pemerintah di depan DPR," pp. 323–45; Sudomo, "Keterangan Pers Kastaf Kopkamtib," pp. 388–91; Anthony Goldstone, *Far Eastern Economic Review* [hereafter *FEER*], March 11, 1974.

9. Goldstone, *FEER*, March 11, 1974.

10. Crouch, *The Army and Politics in Indonesia*, p. 312.

11. *Pedoman*, November 3, 1973, cited by Crouch, *The Army and Politics in Indonesia*, p. 311; see also Derek Davies, *FEER*, February 25, 1974.

12. Goldstone, *FEER*, January 21, 1974.

13. *Indonesia Raya*, November 12, 1973.

14. Hansen, "Indonesia 1974," pp. 148–56; Goldsone, *FEER*.

15. Frances Starner, *FEER*, January 28, 1974.

16. *Mahasiswa Indonesia*, no. 392, January 1974, cited by Raillon, *Les Etudiants Indonesiens et l'Ordre Nouveau*, pp. 99–100.

17. Starner, *FEER*, February 4, 1974.

18. Centre for Strategic and International Studies, "January 15 Affair," p. 9.

19. Ibid.

20. Ibid., p. 10.

21. Personal interviews, May 18, June 20, and July 23, 1983.

22. Personal interviews, May 18, 1983, and August 20, 1989.

23. Personal interview, June 8, 1983.

24. Others arrested were Subadio Sastrosatomo and Sarbini Sumawinata, former Socialist Party leaders, and the latter a professor of economics at the University of Indonesia; Adnan Buyung Nasution, a 1966 activist and at this time a young attorney much involved in civil rights cases in the courts; Dorodjatun Kuntjoro-Jakti, a young lecturer in economics at the University of Indonesia, and a principal figure in the "discussion group" movement; Rahman Tolleng, a 1966 activist who was by this time an official of Golkar; H. Princen, head of the League of Human Rights; and Sjahrir, who was, along with Siregar, a student leader at the University.

25. Robert Shaplen, "Letter from Indonesia," *The New Yorker*, April 1, 1974, p. 57.

26. Personal interview, June 13, 1983.

27. Among published accounts to this effect, see that attributed to Rahman Tolleng, a young Bandung intellectual, in Raillon, *Les Etudiants Indonesiens et l'Ordre Nouveau*, p. 103, and that attributed to "many of those who suffered in the aftermath" in McDonald, *Suharto's Indonesia*, p. 140.

28. Personal interview, May 18, 1983.

29. Ibid.

30. *Asahi Shimbun, A.M.* edition, January 17, 1970.

31. See, for example, Ryokichi, "Japan, the United States, and Development Assistance to Southeast Asia," pp. 97–98.

32. Yoshihara, *Japanese Investment*, pp. 3–4.

33. Ibid., pp. 50, 70.

34. Ibid., pp. 66–67.

35. Panglaykim, *Japanese Direct Investment in ASEAN*, pp. 70, 71.

36. Yoshihara, *Japanese Investment*, pp. 67–70, 94.

37. Ibid., pp. 104–6.

38. Matsuo, *Javanese Cotton Industry*.

39. Nelson, "Foreign Investment Regulatory Framework."

40. Net foreign direct private investment in 1984 was $227 million in Indonesia, $409 million in Thailand, $912 million in Malaysia, and $1,458 million in Singapore. (Table 14, World Bank, *World Development Report 1986* [Washington, World Bank, 1986].)

41. Indonesia Research Team, Japanese Transnational Enterprises Research Committee, AMPO, *Japan-Asia Quarterly Review*.

42. Matsuo, *Javanese Cotton Industry*, p. 47, Table 39.

43. Personal interview, June 20, 1983.

44. Kuntjoro-Jakti, *The Political Economy of Development*, pp. 218–22.

45. Budiman, "Sesudah Duakali Bertemu Pak Harto."
46. Crouch, *The Army and Politics in Indonesia*, p. 283.
47. Ibid.
48. Ibid., p. 284.
49. Ibid., p. 274, n. 1.
50. Ibid., p. 279.
51. Ibid., p. 278.
52. Ibid., pp. 286–87.
53. Ibid., pp. 287–89.
54. *Sinar Harapan*, July 24, 1970.
55. *Sinar Harapan*, July 18, 1970; see also Mackie, "Report of the Commission of Four."
56. *Sinar Harapan*, July 18, 20, and 22, 1970.
57. *Sinar Harapan*, July 24, 1970.
58. *Asahi Shimbun, Mainichi Shimbun,* and *Yomiuri Shimbun, A.M* editions, January 16, 1974.
59. Ibid., *P.M.* editions, January 16, 1974.
60. *Asahi Shimbun, A.M.* edition, January 17, 1974.
61. Jusuf, "Knowledge Economy and World Economy," pp. 41–43.
62. See, for example, Koentjaraningrat, "Apakah Kita Bisa Meniru Pola Pembangunan Jepang," (Can we copy the development model of Japan?), *Kompas* (March 25, 1974) (republished in *Mencari Bentuk Ekonomi Indonesia: Perkembangan Pemikiran 1965–1981*, ed. Redaksi Ekonomi Harian Kompas (Jakarta: Gramedia, 1982).
63. Kuntjoro-Jakti, *Political Economy of Development.*

7. *The Pertamina Crisis*

1. Personal interviews, May 22 and June 4, 1983.
2. Lipsky, "The Billion Dollar Bubble," pp. 14–15.
3. Personal interview, May 28, 1983.
4. Lipsky, "The Billion Dollar Bubble," p. 14.
5. Personal interview, May 22, 1983.
6. *Asia Research Bulletin* [hereafter *ARB*], March 31, 1975, p. 64.
7. Ibid.
8. Lipsky, "The Billion Dollar Bubble," pp. 16–17.
9. *Sinar Harapan*, May 21, 1975.
10. *ARB*, May 31, 1975, p. 83.
11. *ARB*, August 31, 1975, pp. 111–12.
12. *ARB*, December 31, 1975, p. 152.
13. Hamish McDonald, "The Pertamina Spin-Off," *Far Eastern Economic Review* [hereafter *FEER*], (April 23, 1976).
14. Personal interview, July 20, 1983.

15. Bartlett et al., *Pertamina*, pp. 133–58.
16. Personal interview, May 22, 1983.
17. Tanaka, *Post-War Japanese Resources and Strategies*, p. 85.
18. Articles 3 and 4, Law No. 44, October 26, 1960, cited by Bartlett et al., *Pertamina*, p. 181.)
19. Bartlett et al., *Pertamina*, pp. 193–94.
20. Ibid., p. 309.
21. Pertamina, *Annual Report: 1972*; Fabrikant, *Oil Discovery and Technical Change*, p. 226; Dan Coggin and Seth Lipsy, "The High Price of Pertamina's Big Dreams," *FEER* (May 30, 1975); *ARB*, May 31, 1975.
22. Ibid.
23. Cited by McCawley, "Consequences of the Pertamina Crisis," p. 6.
24. Donald Hindley, *Asian Survey*, February 1970.
25. *Sinar Harapan*, July 18, 1974.
26. *Sinar Harapan*, July 20, 1974.
27. *Sinar Harapan*, July 18, 1974.
28. *Sinar Harapan*, July 20, 1974.
29. *Sinar Harapan*, July 18, 1974.
30. Mackie, "Commission of Four Report," pp. 90–91.
31. Fabrikant, *Oil Discovery and Technical Change*, pp. 209–11.
32. Glassburner, "In the Wake of General Ibnu," p. 1102: McCawley, "Consequences of the Pertamina Crisis," pp. 34–69.
33. Personal interview, May 26, 1983.
34. *Sinar Harapan*, May 21–24, 1975.
35. Arndt, "Survey of Recent Developments," p. 75.
36. *Sinar Harapan*, May 21–24, 1975.
37. Personal interview, June 7, 1983.
38. *The Witteveen Facility and the OPEC Financial Surpluses*, Hearings before the Subcommittee on Foreign Economic Policy of the Committee on Foreign Relations, pp. 88 and 90.
39. Ibid., p. 84–85.
40. Ibid., p. 86.
41. Ibid., p. 90.
42. Ibid.
43. Ibid., p. 91; see also Sacerdoti, "Pertamina Cut Back to Size."
44. Ibid., pp. 95–98.
45. Lipsky, "The Billion Dollar Bubble," p. 8.
46. *Tempo*, January 17, 1976, cited by McCawley, "Consequences of the Pertamina Crisis," p. 14.
47. Republic of Indonesia, Badan Perentjanaan Pembangunan Nasional, pp. 12–24, Tables 12–16.

48. *FEER*, March 19, 1976, cited by McCawley, "Consequences of the Pertamina Crisis," p. 16.

49. Ibid.

50. David Jenkins, "The Tanker Men State Their Case," *FEER*, December 24, 1976, p. 93.

51. *Wall Street Journal*, December 23, 1976.

52. *FEER*, January 28, 1977, p. 51.

53. Seth Lipsky, "How Bruce Rappaport Built Shipping Fortune with Pertamina Deals," *Wall Street Journal*, February 11, 1977.

54. *Wall Street Journal*, December 23, 1976.

55. *Wall Street Journal*, February 11, 1977.

56. *Wall Street Journal*, February 14, 1977.

57. *New York Times*, April 9, 1977.

58. Personal interview, July 15, 1983.

59. Barry Wain, "Pertamina and the Incredible World of Ibnu Sutowo," *INSIGHT*, October 1976.

60. Personal interview, July 15, 1983.

61. Ibid.

62. Dan Coggin, "Letter from Jakarta," *FEER*, January 16, 1976.

63. Wain, "Pertamina and the Incredible World of Ibnu Sutowo."

64. *FEER*, April 17, 1981.

65. *Tempo*, February 25, 1989, p. 79.

66. Richard Cowper, "What LNG means to Indonesia's Economy," *Financial Times*, April 11, 1980.

67. Reuters dispatch, *Asian Wall Street Journal*, May 31, 1985.

68. *Keterangan Pemerintah tentang Rancangan Anggaran Pendapatan dan Belanja Negara Tahun 1976/77*, January 7, 1976, cited by McCawley, "Recent Developments," pp. 2 and 3.

69. Dan Coggin, "Letter from Jakarta."

70. Personal interview, June 14, 1983.

71. Personal interview, May 22, 1983.

72. Personal interview, July 8, 1983.

73. Personal interview, June 7, 1983.

74. Personal interview, May 22, 1983.

75. Personal interview, May 22, 1983.

76. Personal interview, May 22, 1983.

77. Ibid.

78. *Tempo*, 29 July 1978.

79. *Sinar Harapan*, May 21, 1975.

80. Personal interview, January 13, 1992.

81. *ARB*, March 31, 1976, p. 182.

82. Ibid.

83. Personal interview, January 13, 1992.

84. Hamish McDonald, "Caltex: Indonesia Cracks the Whip," *FEER*, April 30, 1976.

85. Khong Cho Oon,1 *The Politics of Oil in Indonesia*, p. 221.

86. Hamish McDonald, "Indonesia: The Debt Pile Rises Further," *FEER*, July 2, 1976.

87. Ibid.

88. Ibid.

89. Glassburner, "In the Wake of General Ibnu," pp. 1109–10.

90. Ibid.

91. Gelb et al., *Oil Windfalls*, Tables 5–2, 5–3, and 8–1.

92. Ibid., Table 1–1 and p. 197.

93. Bank of America, *Economic Report*, January 7, 1982, pp. 3–4.

94. Gelb et al., *Oil Windfalls*, pp. 61–71.

95. Sadli, "Peranan Bahan Bakar Minyak dalam Perekonomian," and Sagir, "Peranan Minyak dalam Kehidupan Ekonomi dan Pembangunan Indonesia," *Majalah Management & Usahawan Indonesia* (January–February 1982).

96. Michael Vatikiotis, *FEER*, May 31, 1990, p. 56.

97. Gelb et al., *Oil Windfalls*, pp. 138–39.

98. Ibid., pp. 205–7, 243–45; for a more extended comparison, see Pinto, "Nigeria During and After the Oil Boom," *The World Bank Economic Review*, pp. 419–45.

99. Ibid., pp. 94–117.

100. Ibnu Sutowo, "Perataan pendapatan itu suatu utopia," pp. 51–54.

101. Richard Cowper, "How the Indonesians grew rich without really trying," *The Financial Times*, November 28, 1980.

8. The Petition of Fifty

1. Suryadinata, "Indonesia under the New Order," p. 22.

2. Liddle, "Indonesia 1977," p. 180.

3. Ibid., pp. 181–82.

4. Ibid., p. 184.

5. David Jenkins, "Stirrings on the campus," *Far Eastern Economic Review* [hereafter *FEER*] (July 15, 1977), and "Campus 'gibberish' halts dialogue," *FEER* (September 2, 1977), cited in Jenkins, *Suharto and His Generals*, pp. 75–76.

6. "Map of the Activities of the University of Indonesia's Student Council in Carrying Out Social Control," *Indonesia* 27 (April 1979), pp. 17–32.

7. "White Book of the 1978 Students' Struggle," *Indonesia* 25 (April 1978), pp. 151–52.

8. Akhmadi, *Breaking the Chains of Oppression*.

Notes

9. *Angkatan Bersenjata*, November 12, 1977, cited by Jenkins, *Suharto and His Generals*, pp. 80–81.

10. *Sinar Harapan*, November 14 (1977), cited by Jenkins, *Suharto and His Generals*, pp. 77–78.

11. Ibid., pp. 81–84.

12. *Kompas*, November 29, 1977, cited by Liddle, "Indonesia 1977," p. 184.

13. Ibid., p. 185.

14. *Kompas*, December 17, 1977, cited by Jenkins, *Suharto and His Generals*, p. 85; see also ibid., pp. 84–85; Liddle, "Indonesia 1977," p. 185; and Leo Suryadinata, "Indonesia under the New Order," p. 25.

15. *Antara*, January 17, 1978, cited by Jenkins, *Suharto and His Generals*, p. 87.

16. Suryadinata, "Indonesia under the New Order," pp. 25–26.

17. "Defense of the Student Movement," pp. 1, 2, and 7.

18. David Jenkins, "Mirror, Mirror on the Wall . . . ," *FEER*, March 31, 1978, p. 23.

19. Ibid., pp. 23 and 26.

20. Jenkins, *Suharto and His Generals*, p. 93.

21. Ibid., pp. 90–92, 109.

22. Ibid., pp. 92–97.

23. Republic of Indonesia. Markas Besar, Tentara Nasional Indonesia Angkatan Darat, Departemen Pertahanan Keamanan. *Dwifungsi ABRI* (Konsep 1979), cited by Jenkins, *Suharto and His Generals*, pp. 113–21.

24. Suryadinata, "Indonesia under the New Order," pp. 28–29.

25. "Current Data on the Indonesian Military Elite," *Indonesia* 29 (April 1980), p. 160.

26. Jenkins, *Suharto and His Generals*, pp. 137–43.

27. General Soemitro, "Stability, Democracy, and Development," *Kompas* (May 11, 1979), cited by Pauker, "Indonesia 1979," p. 129.

28. General A. H. Nasution, *Tempo*, June 9, 1979, cited by Pauker, "Indonesia 1979," p. 129.

29. *Kompas*, May 18, 1979, cited by Suryadinata, "Indonesia under the New Order," p. 31.

30. *Merdeka*, June 4, 1979, and *Tempo*, June 9, 1979, cited by Pauker, "Indonesia 1979," pp. 129-30.

31. Pauker, "Indonesia in 1980," p. 240.

32. Ibid.; see also Suryadinata, "Indonesia under the New Order," pp. 33–34.

33. *Angkatan Bersenjata*, March 28, 1980.

34. Ibid.

35. *Kompas*, April 17, 1980.

36. Petisi 50, "Pernyataan Keprihatinan," May 5, 1980; reproduced in

Kelompok Kerja Petisi 50, *Muluruskan Perjalanan Orde Baru: Pertangung-Jawaban Petisi 50 Kepada Rakyat Indonesia,* mimeo. (Jakarta, March 1, 1983).

37. Jenkins, *Suharto and His Generals,* pp. 167–69.

38. *Pelita,* July 16, 1980.

39. *Kompas,* August 2, 1980.

40. Pauker, "Indonesia in 1980," p. 241.

41. Ibid., p. 242.

42. Ibid., pp. 242–43.

43. "Current Data on the Indonesian Military Elite," *Indonesia* 29 (April 1980), p. 157.

44. Ibid., pp. 155–56.

45. *Berita Buana,* July 9, 1980.

46. Sudarsono, "Political Changes and Developments," p. 63.

47. David Jenkins, "The Military's Secret Cache," *FEER,* February 8, 1980, p. 70.

48. Ibid., pp. 70–71.

50. Ibid.; see also Barry Newman, "Profits in Indonesia Enrich Military Men—and Their Branches," *Wall Street Journal,* June 27, 1980.

51. Jenkins, "The Military's Secret Cache," p. 71; Newman, "Profits in Indonesia Enrich Military Men,"; see also Richard Robison, *Indonesia,* pp. 259–66.

52. Ibid., p. 264.

53. Suryadinata, "Indonesia under the New Order," p. 17.

54. Thee Kian Wie, "Industrial and Foreign Investment Policy in Indonesia," pp. 86–87.

55. Industrial Development and Finance Department and Industrial Projects Department, World Bank, *Problems and Prospects for Industrial Development,* vol. 1 (Report No. 1647-IND, May 25, 1978), p. ii.

56. Soehoed, "The Concept of Industrialization," pp. 5, 6.

57. Ibid., p. 9.

58. U.S. Foreign Commercial Service, "Business Outlook Abroad," pp. 20–23.

59. Habibie, "Thoughts Concerning a Strategy for the Industrial Transformation of a Developing Country," pp. 3, 4, 13, and passim.

60. Soehoed, "Industrial Development During Repelita," pp. 55–56, cited by Robison, *Indonesia,* p. 246, n. 15 and n. 16.

61. Suryadinata and Siddique, eds., *Trends in Indonesia II,* pp. 148–49, 151.

62. Ibid., pp. 149–150, 152.

63. Ibid., p. 151.

64. World Bank, East Asia and Pacific Regional Office, *Indonesia: Selected Issues of Industrial Development and Trade Strategy. The Main Report* (Washington, DC: World Bank, July 15, 1981), pp. ix–x.

65. *Business Week*, December 17, 1979, p. 44.
66. World Bank, East Asia and Pacific Regional Office, *Indonesia: Selected Issues*, pp. iii, iv.
67. Ibid., pp. iv, v.
68. Ibid., pp. vii–ix.
69. Guy Sacerdoti, "Overdraft of Inefficiency," *FEER* (May 29, 1981).
70. *Asian Wall Street Journal*, June 21, 1983.
71. Susumu Awanohara, Manggi Habir et al., "Shaking the Industrial Cocktail," *FEER*, August 18, 1983.

9. The Tanjung Priok Incident

1. *Indonesia Reports: November Log*, December 15, 1984, p. 8.
2. Ibid., *December Log*, January 15, 1985, p. 29.
3. The sermon by M. Nasir appears in English translation in Dwight King, trans., "The Last Grumbles of Brother Nasir," *Indonesia Reports: Politics Supplement*, no. 10 (August 1985).
4. *Indonesia Reports: Politics Supplement*, no. 13 (November 1985), p. 3.
5. *Indonesia Mirror*, no. 5 (March 1987).
6. The full text appears in English translation in *Indonesia Reports: December Log*, January 15, 1985.
7. Saleh et al., "White Paper."
8. "Bloody Wednesday Night in Tanjung Priok (Tragedy, background, and impact)," September 20, 1984, *Indonesia Reports: Politics Supplement*, January 15, 1985.
9. "Excerpts from Transcription of Murdani's Q and A with Reporters," *Indonesia Reports: Politics Supplement*, November 15, 1984.
10. *Indonesia Reports: December Log*, January 15, 1985, p. 29.
11. *Indonesia Reports: Politics Supplement*, November 15, 1984, p. 7.
12. "Bloody Wednesday Night in Tanjung Priok (Tragedy, background, and impact)," September 20, 1984, *Indonesia Reports*, p. 9.
13. Amnesty International, *Muslim Prisoners of Conscience* p. 9.
14. Ibid., p. 10.
15. Ibid., pp. 13–16.
16. Ibid., p. 12.
17. Ibid., p. 22.
18. Ibid., p. 26.
19. Ibid., p. 32.
20. Ibid., pp. 33–36; see also *Indonesia Reports: November Log*, December 15, 1984, p. 4.
21. Ibid., pp. 28–29.
22. Ibid., p. 18.
23. Ibid., pp. 20, 24–26.

Notes

24. Ibid., pp. 24–22, 26, 28, 30.

25. Ibid., pp. 34–35; see also Tapol, *Muslims on Trial*, p. 37.

26. Ibid., p. 35; see also Amnesty International, *Muslim Prisoners of Conscience*, pp. 27–30; Tapol, *Muslims on Trial*, pp. 62–64.

27. Ibid., p. 35; see also Tapol, *Muslims on Trial*, pp. 73–74.

28. Amnesty International, "The Torture and Death of Muhammed Djabir," cited in *Indonesia Reports: Human Rights Supplement*, no. 18 (October 1986).

29. *Indonesia Reports: November Log*, December 15, 1984, p. 37.

30. Ibid., p. 38.

31. Ibid., pp. 39–40.

32. Ibid., p. 43.

33. *Indonesia Reports: January Log*, February 20, 1985, p. 3.

34. Ibid., *February Log*, March 20, 1985, p. 46.

35. *Indonesia Reports* (July 1985), p. 2.

36. *Indonesia Reports* (July 1985) reported trials in Jakarta, Bandung, Yogyakarta, Surabaya, and Malang. Amnesty International reported the arrest of dozens of Muslim activists in Central Java alone in late 1985 and early 1986; see Amnesty International, *The Imprisonment of Usroh Activists*.

37. *Indonesia Reports* (August and September 1985).

38. See, in addition to its numerous reports concerning individual cases, Amnesty International, *The Imprisonment of Usroh Activists*.

39. Asia Watch, "Violence in Lampung, Indonesia."

40. For an excellent summary of this twentieth-century history see Johns, "Islam and Cultural Pluralism," pp. 206–9.

41. Kahin, *Nationalism and Revolution*, p. 123.

42. Johns, "Islam and Cultural Pluralism," p. 209.

43. Kahin, *Nationalism and Revolution*, pp. 122–27.

44. Johns, "Islam and Cultural Pluralism," p. 210

45. Ibid., pp. 210–11.

46. Ibid., pp. 211–15.

47. Hassan, *Muslim Intellectual Responses*, pp. 84–86.

48. Ibid., pp. 91–113.

49. For an excellent summary of relations between Islam and the New Order through this event, along with much useful analysis of the historical background, see McVey, "Faith as the Outsider," pp. 199–225.

50. Personal interview, July 21, 1986.

51. *Tempo*, April 23, 1983.

52. Susumu Awanohara, "An election-eve salvo," *Far Eastern Economic Review* [hereafter *FEER*], April 30, 1982.

53. Ibid.

54. *New York Times*, April 13, 1982.

55. Basic Thoughts of Indonesian Religious Councils in the Religious Communities Consultative Body, December 19, 1983. See *Indonesia Reports: Politics Supplement*, no. 8 (1985).

56. *Asian Wall Street Journal Weekly* (April 1983).

57. Prawiranegara, Letter to the President of the Republic of Indonesia, pp. 80–81.

58. Personal interview, July 21, 1983.

59. *Indonesia Reports: Politics Supplement*, May 25, 1985.

60. Ibid.

61. Lincoln Kaye, "Legislating harmony," *FEER*, June 13, 1985.

62. Personal interview, July 26, 1986.

63. Personal interview, May 31, 1983.

64. Personal interview, July 26, 1986.

65. Kompas, January 13, 1985, cited by *Indonesia Reports: January Log*, February 20, 1985, p. 24.

66. Jones, "'It Can't Happen Here.'"

67. Jones, "What Indonesia's Islamic Revival Means," p. 46.

68. Personal interview, May 28, 1983.

69. Samsuri and Tebba, "The Shift in Pattern of Islamic Leadership."

70. Purdy, "Legitimation of Power and Authority"; Geertz, *Interpretation of Cultures*, p. 225.

71. Personal interview, July 18, 1986.

72. Personal interview, August 1, 1983.

10. Deregulating Industry

1. Thee Kian Wie, "Industrial Restructuring in Indonesia."

2. Pangestu, "Survey of Recent Developments," p. 28; see also Wardhana, "Structural Adjustment in Indonesia," p. 13.

3. Pangestu, "Survey of Recent Developments," p. 27.

4. Personal interview, August 15, 1989.

5. Ibid.

6. Sadli, "Private and State Enterprise Sectors," pp. 217–18.

7. Ibid.

8. Republic of Indonesia, Minister of Trade, "Surat Keputusan Menteri Perdagangan nomor 1208/Kp/X/1984."

9. Steven Jones, *Asian Wall Street Journal*, November 25, 1986; unpublished data, Institute of Economic and Social Research, Faculty of Economics, University of Indonesia.

10. Jones, *Asian Wall Street Journal*, November 25, 1986.

11. Ibid.; unpublished data, Institute of Economic and Social Research, Faculty of Economics, University of Indonesia.

12. Jones, *Asian Wall Street Journal*, November 25, 1986.

13. Unpublished data, Institute of Economic and Social Research, Faculty of Economics, University of Indonesia.

14. Ibid.; Steven Jones and Raphael Pura, *Asian Wall Street Journal*, November 24, 1986.

15. Ibid.

16. World Bank, East Asia and Pacific Regional Office, *Indonesia: Adjusting to Lower Oil Revenues*, May 20, 1986, p. 73.

17. Ibid.

18. National Development Information Office, Republic of Indonesia, *Indonesia Development News*, vol. 5, no. 2 (October 1981), pp. 1 and 7. For a survey of the legal regime as regards foreign investment, see Hornick and Nelson, "Foreign Investment in Indonesia."

19. *Indonesia Development News*, vol. 8, no. 12 (August 1985); *Investment News Update* (August 1986); *Indonesia Development News*, vol. 12, no. 8 (August 1989).

20. Hobohm, "Survey of Recent Developments," pp. 18–19.

21. Hill, *Foreign Investment and Industrialization*, pp. 35–41.

22. Ibid., p. 48.

23. Ibid., p. 55.

24. Hobohm, "Survey of Recent Developments," p. 19.

25. Thee Kian Wie, "Promoting Investment into Export-oriented Industries."

26. Soesastro et al., *Report: Financing Public Sector Development Expenditure*, pp. 110–12.

27. Ibid., pp. 114–15, 119–20.

28. Ibid., pp. 121–23.

29. Ibid., p. 132.

30. *Tempo*, March 31, 1984, p. 66.

31. Ibid., p. 67.

32. Rice, "The Origins of Economic Ideas," p. 143.

33. Ibid., pp. 66–67.

34. Ibid., p. 67.

35. Tan, "The Role of Ethnic Chinese Minority," pp. 367–71; Robison, *Indonesia*, pp. 272–75.

36. *Indonesia Reports: Business & Economy Supplement*, no. 20 (February 1987); no. 21 (June 1987); no. 23 (October 1987); no. 24 (November 1987); and no. 25 (August 1988); see also *Indonesia Mirror*, no. 7 (December 1987).

37. Sato, *The Development of Business Groups*.

38. Robison, *Indonesia*, provides the most extended argument on this last point.

39. Sato, *The Development of Business Groups*, p. 85.

40. Ibid., p. 116.

41. David Jenkins, "After Marcos, Now for the Soeharto Billions: A Herald Investigation," *Sydney Morning Herald*, April 10, 1986.

42. Ibid.

43. *Tempo*, April 19, 1986, p. 17; April 26, 1986, p. 14; May 3, 1986, p. 13.

44. *Tempo*, June 28, 1986, p. 12.

45. *Tempo*, July 12, 1986, p. 23.

46. Personal interview, July 31, 1983.

47. Personal interview, July 26, 1986.

48. Personal interview, July 26, 1986.

49. Steven Jones and Raphael Pura, *Asian Wall Street Journal*, November 24, 1986. See also Steven Jones, *Asian Wall Street Journal*, November 25, 1986, and Raphael Pura, *Asian Wall Street Journal*, November 26, 1986.

50. *Forbes*, July 24, 1989, p. 210.

51. Adam Schwarz, "Empire of the son," *Far Eastern Economic Review* [hereafter *FEER*], March 14, 1991.

52. Wardhana, "Structural Adjustment in Indonesia."

53. Soesastro, "Political Economy of Deregulation," pp. 866–67; see also M. Hadi Soesastro and Peter Drysdale, "Survey of Recent Developments," *Bulletin of Indonesian Economic Studies*, vol. 26, no. 3 (December 1990), p. 33.

54. Personal interview, August 23, 1989.

55. Personal interview, August 15, 1989.

56. Wardhana, "Structural Adjustment in Indonesia," pp. 5 and 23.

57. Michael Vatikiotis, "Reform without Favor," *FEER*, December 1, 1986, p. 61.

58. Republic of Indonesia, Minister of Trade, "Keputusan Menteri Perdagangan nomor 375/Kp/XI/1988," reproduced in *Himpunan Peraturan Perundang-undangan Paket Kebijaksanaan Deregulasi 21 Nopember 1988* (Jakarta: CV Eko Jaya, n.d.), pp. 76–109.

59. Republic of Indonesia, Minister of Finance, "Keputusan Menteri Keuangan nomor 1160/KMK.00/1988," in ibid., pp. 123–38.

60. Ibid., p. 2.

61. *Asia Week*, December 9, 1988, p. 64.

62. *FEER*, June 7, 1990; Nasution, "Survey of Recent Developments," p. 8.

63. World Bank, Country Department V, Asia Regional Office, *Indonesia: Developing Private Enterprise*, Report No. 9498-IND (Washington, D.C.: World Bank, May 9, 1991), pp. 58.

64. Ibid., pp. 58–62.

65. Republic of Indonesia, National Development Information Office, *Indonesia Development News*, vol. 14, no. 3 (January/February 1991) p. 4.

66. Lim and Pang, *Foreign Direct Investment and Industrialization*.

67. Guisinger, "Foreign Direct Investment," p. 35, Table 3.

68. World Bank, *Indonesia: Developing Private Enterprise*, pp. 6–8.

69. Ibid., pp. 5–8.
70. Ibid., p. 17.
71. *The Asian Wall Street Journal Weekly*, October 21, 1991.
72. Mackie and Sjahrir, "Survey of Recent Developments," p. 27.
73. Ibid., p. 30.
74. Ibid., p. 13.
75. World Bank, *Indonesia: Developing Private Enterprise*, p. 64.
76. Pangestu and Habir, "Survey of Recent Developments," pp. 33–36.
77. MacIntyre, "Political Dimensions to Controversy," pp. 122–28.
78. Nasution, "Survey of Recent Developments," p. 25; *FEER*, April 19, 1990; Soesastro and Drysdale, "Survey of Recent Developments," pp. 22–23.
79. Adam Schwarz, "Piece of the action," *FEER*, May 2, 1991.
80. Max Wangkar et al., "Yang Mengumbar, Yang Terancam," *Tempo* (July 20, 1991).
81. Soesastro et al., *Financing Public Sector Development Expenditure*, pp. 868–69; Mackie and Sjahrir, "Survey of Recent Developments," pp. 32–33.
82. Hill, "Indonesia's Industrial Transformation," pp. 79–120.
83. Mackie, "The Indonesian Conglomerates," pp. 108–28.

Epilogue

1. World Bank. *Social Indicators of Development: 1989*.
2. Ibid.; see also Hugo et al., *Demographic Dimension in Indonesian Development*, p. 99.
3. World Bank, *Social Indicators of Development: 1989*; see also Hans-Dieter Evers, "Group Conflict and Class Formation in Southeast Asia," in *Modernization in Southeast Asia*, ed. Hans-Dieter Evers (New York: Oxford University Press, 1973), pp. 122–26.
4. Gelb, *Oil Windfalls*, relevant country chapters.
5. World Bank, *World Development Report: 1991*, Table 3, pp. 182–83, and *World Development Report: 1992*, Table 3, pp. 222–23.
6. Ibid., *World Development Report: 1992*, Table 2, pp. 220–21.
7. Ibid., Table 1, pp. 218–19; see also World Bank, *Social Indicators of Development: 1989*.
8. Ibid., Table 26, pp. 268–69.
9. Ibid., Table 2, pp. 220–21, and Table 4, pp. 224–25.
10. Ibid., Table 2, pp. 220–21, and Table 3, pp. 222–23.
11. Ibid., Table 29, pp. 274–75.
12. Ibid., Table 30, pp. 276-77.
13. Ibid., Table 30, pp. 262–63; see also World Bank, *World Development Report: 1988*, Table 26, pp. 272–73.
14. World Bank, *Indonesia: Employment and Income Distribution in Indonesia*, July, 1980, p. 75.

15. World Bank, *Indonesia: Strategy for a Sustained Reduction in Poverty,* 1990, pp. 27–47.

16. Chernichovsky and Meesook, *Poverty in Indonesia,* pp. 2, 5, and 89.

17. Republic of Indonesia, Biro Pusat Statistik, *Pendapatan Regional Propinsi—Propinsi di Indonesia, 1975–1979* (Jakarta, 1982), Table 1.2, pp. 14–15; Hugo et al., *Demographic Dimension in Indonesian Development,* pp. 98–99.

18. Chernichovsky and Meesook, *Poverty in Indonesia,* p. 91.

19. Michael Vatikiotis and Adam Schwarz, "Sharing the goodies," *Far Eastern Economic Review,* March 29, 1990, pp. 21–22.

Bibliography

Books, Articles, and Government Documents

Aidit, D. N. *Kaum Tani Mengganjang Setan-Setan Desa.* Jakarta: Jajasan "Pembaruan," 1964.

Akhmadi, Heri. *Breaking the Chains of Oppression of the Indonesian People.* Translation Series, Modern Indonesia Project, no. 59. Ithaca, N.Y.: Southeast Asia Program, Cornell University, 1981.

Amnesty International. "Indonesia: Muslim Prisoners of Conscience." Mimeographed. New York: Amnesty International, June 1986.

—— *Indonesia: The Imprisonment of Usroh Activists in Central Java.* London: Amnesty International, October 1988.

Anderson, Benedict R. O'G., ed. "The Problem of Rice: Stenographic Notes of the Fourth Session of the Sanyo Kaigi, January 8, 2605." *Indonesia* 2 (1966):77–123.

—— "The Idea of Power in Javanese Culture." In *Culture and Politics in Indonesia*, ed. Claire Holt, pp. 1–69. Ithaca, N.Y.: Cornell University Press, 1972.

Anderson, Benedict R. O'G. and Ruth McVey. *A Preliminary Analysis of the October 1, 1965, Coup in Indonesia.* Interim Report Series, Modern Indonesian Project. Ithaca, N.Y.: Southeast Asia Program, Cornell University, 1971.

—— "Letter to the Editor." *New York Review of Books*, June 1, 1978.

Apa & Siapa: sejumlah orang Indonesia, 1981–82. Compiled by the weekly news magazine *Tempo.* Jakarta: Grafiti Pers, 1981.

Apa & Siapa: sejumlah orang Indonesia, 1983–84. Compiled by the weekly news magazine *Tempo.* Jakarta: Grafiti Pers, 1984.

Bibliography

Arndt, Heinz W. *The Indonesian Economy.* Singapore: Chapmen Publishers, 1984.

—— "Survey of Recent Developments." *Bulletin of Indonesian Economic Studies* no. 5 (October 1966).

—— "Survey of Recent Developments." *Bulletin of Indonesian Economic Studies* 10, no. 2 (July 1974).

Arndt, Heinz W. and J. Panglaykim. "Survey of Recent Developments." *Bulletin of Indonesian Economic Studies* no. 4 (June 1966).

Arndt, Heinz W. and R. M. Sundrum. "Comments on Clive Gray's 'Civil Service Compensation in Indonesia.' *Bulletin of Indonesian Economic Studies* 15, no. 1 (March 1979).

Asian Development Bank. *Rural Asia: Challenge and Opportunity.* New York: Praeger, 1978.

Asia Watch. "Violence in Lampung, Indonesia." *News from Asia Watch.* Washington and New York: Asia Watch, March 16, 1989.

Aveling, Harry, ed. and trans. *Gestapu: Indonesian Short Stories on the Abortive Communist Coup of 30th September 1965.* Southeast Asian Studies Working Paper, no. 6. Honolulu: Southeast Asian Studies Program, University of Hawaii, 1975.

Bank of America. *Economic Report.* January 7, 1982.

Bant, Paul S., ed. *Remang-Remang Indonesia.* Jakarta: Yayasan Lembaga Bantuan Hukum Indonesia, 1989.

Barker, Randolph and Robert W. Herd (with Beth Rose). *The Rice Economy of Asia.* Washington, D.C.: Resources for the Future, 1985.

Bartlett, Anderson G. et al. *Pertamina, Indonesian National Oil.* Jakarta, Singapore, and Tulsa: Amerasian, 1972.

Benda, Harry J. "The Pattern of Administrative Reforms in the Closing Years of Dutch Rule in Indonesia," *Journal of Asian Studies* 25 (August 1966): 589–605.

"Bloody Wednesday Night in Tanjung Priok (Tragedy, Background, and Impact)." *Indonesia Reports: Politics Supplement* (January 15, 1985).

Boeke, J. H. *The Evolution of the Netherland Indies Economy.* New York: Institute of Pacific Relations, 1946.

—— *The Structure of Netherlands Indian Economy.* New York: Institute of Pacific Relations, 1942.

Boileau, Julian M. *Golkar: Functional Group Politics in Indonesia.* Jakarta: Centre for Strategic and International Studies, April 1983.

Booth, Anne and Peter McCawley, eds. *The Indonesian Economy During the Soeharto Era.* Kuala Lumpur: Oxford University Press, 1981.

Booth, Anne and R. M. Sundrum. "The 1973 Agricultural Census." *Bulletin of Indonesian Economic Studies* 12 (July 1976):90–105.

Bibliography

Budiman, Arief. "Sesudah Duakali Bertemu Pak Harto." *Kompas* (August 8, 1970).

Centre for Strategic and International Studies. "January 15 Affair." *Monthly Review* 4 (December 1973–January 1974):8–12.

Central Intelligence Agency. *Indonesia 1965: The Coup That Back-fired.* Washington, D.C.: Central Intelligence Agency, December 1968.

Chandler, Robert L., Jr. *Rice in the Tropics: A Guide to the Development of National Programs.* Boulder, Colo.: Westview, 1979.

Chernichovsky, Dov and Oey Astra Meesook. *Poverty in Indonesia: A Profile.* World Bank Staff Working Paper, no. 671. Washington, D.C.: World Bank, 1984.

Collier, William A. "Agricultural Evolution in Java." In *Agricultural and Rural Development in Indonesia,* ed. Gary E. Hansen, pp. 147–73. Boulder, Colo.: Westview, 1981.

Collier, William A., Gunawan Wirada, and Soentoro. "Recent Changes in Rice Harvesting Methods." *Bulletin of Concerned Asian Scholars* 9 (July 1973):36–42.

Coppel, Charles A. *Indonesian Chinese in Crisis.* Kuala Lumpur: Oxford University Press, 1983.

Crouch, Harold. *The Army and Politics in Indonesia.* Ithaca, N.Y.: Cornell University Press, 1978.

—— *Domestic Political Structures and Regional Economic Co-operation.* Singapore: Institute of Southeast Asian Studies, 1984.

"Current Data on the Indonesian Military Elite." *Indonesia* 29 (April 1980).

"Defense of the Student Movement: Documents from the Recent Trials." *Indonesia* 27 (April 1979):1, 2, and 7.

Djojohadikusumo, Sumitro. *Ekonomi Pembangunan.* Jakarta: P. T. Pembangunan, 1955.

Dye, Richard. "The Jakarta Faculty of Economics." Unpublished ms. New York: The Ford Foundation, 1964.

Emmerson, Donald K. *Indonesia's Elite: Political Culture and Cultural Politics.* Ithaca, N.Y.: Cornell University Press, 1976.

Fabrikant, Robert. *Oil Discovery and Technical Change in Southeast Asia: Legal Aspects of Production Sharing Contracts in the Indonesian Petroleum Industry.* Singapore: Institute of Southeast Asian Studies, 1973.

Feith, Herbert. *The Decline of Constitutional Democracy in Indonesia.* Ithaca, N.Y.: Cornell University Press, 1962.

—— "Dynamics of Guided Democracy." In *Indonesia,* ed. Ruth T. McVey. New Haven, Conn.: HRAF Press, 1963.

—— "Indonesia's Political Symbols and Their Wielders." *World Politics* 16 (October 1963).

Bibliography

Feith, Herbert and Lance Castles, eds. *Indonesian Political Thinking, 1945–1965*. Ithaca, N.Y. and London: Cornell University Press, 1970.

Frederick, William H., ed. *Reflections on Rebellion: Stories from the Indonesian Upheavals of 1948 and 1965*. International Studies, Southeast Asia, no. 60. Athens, Ohio: Center for International Studies, Ohio University, 1983.

Furnivall, J. S. *Educational Progress in Southeast Asia*. New York: Institute of Pacific Relations, 1943.

—— *Netherlands India: A Study of Plural Economy*. New York: MacMillan, 1944.

Geertz, Clifford. *Agricultural Involution*. Berkeley: University of California Press, 1963.

—— *The Religion of Java*. Glencoe, Ill.: The Free Press, 1960.

—— "Ritual and Social Change: A Javanese Example." In *American Anthropologist* 61 (1959). Reproduced in *The Interpretation of Cultures*. New York: Basic Books, 1973.

Gelb, Alan et al. *Oil Windfalls: Blessings or Curse?* New York: Published by Oxford University Press for the World Bank, 1988.

Gelb, Alan with Henry Bienen, "Nigeria: From Windfall Gains to Welfare Losses." In *Oil Windfalls: Blessing or Curse?*, ed. Alan Gelb and Associates. New York: Oxford University Press for the World Bank, 1988.

Gillis, Malcolm. "Episodes in Indonesiam Economic Growth." In *World Economic Growth, Case Studies of Developed and Developing Nations*, ed. Arnold C. Harberger. San Francisco, Calif.: Institute for Contemporary Studies Press, 1984.

Girling, John. *The Bureaucratic Polity in Modernizing Societies*. Singapore: The Institute for Southeast Asian Studies, 1981.

Glassburner, Bruce. "Economic Policy-Making in Indonesia, 1950–1957." In *The Economy of Indonesia: Selected Readings*, ed. Bruce Glassburner. Ithaca, N.Y.: Cornell University Press, 1971.

—— "In the Wake of General Ibnu: Crisis in the Indonesian Oil Industry." *Asian Survey* 16, no. 12 (December 1976): 1102–10.

Guisinger, Stephen. "Foreign Direct Investment Flows in East and Southeast Asia: Policy Issues." *ASEAN Economic Bulletin* 8, no. 1 (July 1991): 29–46.

Habibie, B. J. "Some Thoughts Concerning a Strategy for the Industrial Transformation of a Developing Country." Bonn: Address delivered to the Deutsche Gesellschaft fur Luft und Raumfahrt, June 14, 1983.

Hansen, Gary. "Indonesia 1974: A Momentous Year." *Asian Survey* 15, no. 2 (February 1975): 148–56.

Hardjono, Joan. "Transmigration: Looking to the Future." *Bulletin of Indonesian Economic Studies* 22, no. 2.

Hassan, Muhammad Kamal. *Muslim Intellectual Responses to "New Order"*

Bibliography

Modernization in Indonesia. Kuala Lumpur: Dewan Bahasa dan Pustaka, 1982.

Hatta, Mohammad. *The Co-operative Movement in Indonesia.* Ithaca, N.Y.: Cornell University Press, 1957.

—— *Bung Hatta's Answers.* Singapore: Gunung Agung, 1981.

Hawkins, E. D. "Job Inflation in Indonesia." *Asian Survey* (May 1966).

Hayami, Yujiro and Anwar Hafid. "Rice Harvesting and Welfare in Rural Java." *Bulletin of Concerned Asian Scholars* 15, no. 2 (July 1979):94–112.

Hill, Hal. *Foreign Investment and Industrialization in Indonesia.* Singapore: Oxford University Press, 1988.

—— "Indonesia's Industrial Transformation: Part I." *Bulletin of Indonesian Economic Studies* 26, no. 2 (August 1990):79–120.

—— "Indonesia's Industrial Transformation: Part II." *Bulletin of Indonesian Economic Studies* 26, no. 3 (December 1990):75–109.

Hill, Hal and Terry Hull, eds. *Indonesia Assessment: 1990.* Political and Social Change Monograph 2. Canberra: Department of Political and Social Change, Research School of Pacific Studies, Australian National University, 1990.

Hindley, Donald. *The Communist Party of Indonesia, 1951–1963.* Berkely and Los Angeles: University of California Press, 1964.

—— "Political Power and the October 1965 Coup in Indonesia." *Journal of Asian Studies* 26 (February 1967):237–49.

Hobohm, Sarwar O. H. "Survey of Recent Developments." *Bulletin of Indonesian Economic Studies* 23, no. 2 (August 1987):1–37.

Holt, Claire. *Art in Indonesia: Continuities and Change.* Ithaca, N.Y.: Cornell University Press, 1967.

Holt, Claire et al., eds. *Culture and Politics in Indonesia.* Ithaca, N.Y.: Cornell University Press, 1972.

Hornick, Robert N. and Mark A. Nelson. "Foreign Investment in Indonesia." *Fordham International Law Journal* 11, no. 4 (Summer 1988).

Hughes, John. *Indonesian Upheaval.* New York: David McKay, 1967.

Hugo, Graeme J. et al. *The Demographic Dimension in Indonesian Development.* East Asian Social Science Monograph 25. Singapore: Oxford University Press, 1987.

Humphrey, Hubert. *Hunger and Diplomacy: A Perspective on the U.S. Role at the World Food Conference.* Washington, D.C.: U.S. Government Printing Office, 1975.

Indonesia, Republic of. Badan Perentjanaan Pembangunan Nasional. *Replita II.* Vol. 2A. Jakarta: 1974.

—— Biro Pusat Statistik. *Indikator Kesejahteraan Rakyat.* Jakarta, 1982.

—— Biro Pusat Statistik. *Pendapatan Regional Propinsi-Propinsi di Indonesia: 1975–1979.* Jakarta, 1982.

Bibliography

—— Central Bureau of Statistics. *Statistical Pocketbook of Indonesia: 1957.* Jakarta, 1957.

—— Central Bureau of Statistics. *Statistical Pocketbook of Indonesia: 1968.* Jakarta, 1968.

—— Central Bureau of Statistics. *Statistik Indonesia: 1982.* Jakarta, 1983.

—— Madjelis Permusjawaratan Rakjat Sementara. "Pembaharuan Kebidjaksanaan Landasan Ekonomi, Keuangan dan Pembangunan." *Ketetapan* no. 23 (July 5, 1966). In *Ketetapan-Ketetapan dan Keputusan-Keputusan Sidang Umum Ke-IV MPRS.* Jakarta: Departemen Penerangan (1966):54–63.

—— Minister of Finance. "Keputusan Menteri Keuangan nomor: 1160/KMK.00/1988." Reproduced in *Himpunan Peraturan Perundang-undangan Paket Kebijaksanaan Deregulasi.* Jakarta: CV Eko Jaya (November 21, 1988):123–38.

—— Minister of Trade. "Surat Keputusan Menteri Perdagangan nomor 1208/Kp/X/1984."

—— Minister of Trade. "Keputusan Menteri Perdagangan 375/Kp/XI/1988." Reproduced in *Himpunan Peraturan Perundang-undangan Paket Kebijaksanaan Deregulasi.* Jakarta: CV Eko Jaya (November 21, 1988):76–109.

—— Minister of Trade, "Keputusan Menteri Keuangan nomor: 1160/KMK.00/1988." In ibid., 123–38.

—— National Development Information Office. *Indonesia Development News* 5, no. 2 (October 1981); 8, no. 12 (August 1985); 12, no. 8 (August 1989); 14, no. 3 (January/February 1991).

—— National Logistics Agency. *National Logistics Agency.* Jakarta: National Logistics Agency, 1982.

—— "Peraturan Pemerintah Republik Indonesia Nomor 10 Tahun 1983 tentang Izin Perkawinan dan Perceraian Bagi Pegawai Negeri Sipil." *Lembaran Negara Republik Indonesia Nomor 13.* (April 21, 1983).

Indonesia Research Team, Japanese Transnational Enterprises Research Committee, AMPO. *Japan-Asia Quarterly Review, Special Issue on Japanese Transnational Enterprises in Indonesia* 12, no. 5 (1980).

International Bank for Reconstruction and Development (World Bank). Country Department V. Asia Regional Office. *Indonesia: Developing Private Enterprise.* Report no. 9498-IND. Washington, D.C.: World Bank, May 9, 1991.

—— Country Department V. Asia Regional Office. *Indonesia: Foundations for Sustained Growth.* Report no. 8455-IND. Washington, D.C.: World Bank, May 4, 1990.

—— Country Department V. Asia Regional Office. *Indonesia: Poverty Assessment and Strategy Report.* Report no. 8034-IND. Washington, D.C.: World Bank, May 11, 1990.

Bibliography

—— East Asia and Pacific Regional Office. *Indonesia: Adjusting to Lower Oil Revenues.* Washington, D.C.: World Bank, May 20, 1986.

—— East Asia and Pacific Regional Office. *Indonesia: Selected Issues of Industrial Development and Trade Strategy. The Main Report.* Washington, D.C.: World Bank, July 15, 1981.

—— East Asia and Pacific Regional Office. *Indonesia: Strategy for a Sustained Reduction in Poverty.* Washington, D.C.: World Bank, 1990.

—— *Employment and Income Distribution in Indonesia.* Washington, D.C., 1984.

—— Industrial Development and Finance Department and Industrial Projects Department. *Problems and Prospects for Industrial Development.* Report no. 1647-IND (May 25, 1978).

—— *Social Indicators of Development: 1989.* Washinton, D.C., 1989.

—— *World Development Report: 1984.* Washington, D.C., 1984.

—— *World Development Report: 1986.* Washington, D.C., 1986.

—— *World Development Report: 1989.* Washington, D.C., 1989.

—— *World Development Report: 1991.* Washington, D.C., 1991.

—— *World Development Report: 1992.* Washington, D.C., 1992.

Jenkins, David. *Suharto and His Generals: Indonesian Military Politics, 1975–1983.* Cornell Modern Indonesia Project, no. 64. Ithaca, N.Y.: Cornell University Press, 1984.

Johns, Anthony H. "Indonesia: Islam and Cultural Pluralism." In *Islam in Asia: Religion, Politics, & Society,* ed. John L. Esposito. New York: Oxford University Press, 1987.

Jones, Sidney. "'It Can't Happen Here': A Post-Khomeini Look at Indonesian Islam." *Asian Survey* 20, no. 3 (1980):311–23.

—— "What Indonesia's Islamic Revival Means." *ASIA* (September/October 1981).

—— *Injustice, Persecution, Eviction: A Human Rights Update on Indonesia and East Timor.* New York: The Asia Watch Committee, 1990.

Jusuf, Daud. "Knowledge Economy and World Economy." *The Indonesian Quarterly* 2, no. 2 (January 1974):41–43.

Kahin, George McT. "In Memoriam: Mohammad Hatta," *Indonesia* (1980):113–19.

—— *Nationalism and Revolution in Indonesia.* Ithaca, N.Y.: Cornell University Press, 1970.

Kartodirdjo, Sartono. *Agrarian Unrest and Peasant Mobilization of Java in the Nineteen Sixties: A Study of Configurations and Conditions.* Occasional Paper Series, no. O.P. 8. Yogyakarta: Centre for Rural and Regional Research and Studies, Gadjah Mada University, 1977.

Kayyam, Umar. "Bawuk." In *Reflections and Rebellion: Stories from the*

Indonesian Upheavals of 1948 and 1965, ed. W. H. Frederick. Athens, Ohio: Center for International Studies, Ohio University, 1983.

Kebangkitan Semangat '66: Mendjeladjah Tracee Baru. Proceedings of a seminar held at the University of Indonesia from May 6 to 9, 1966. Jakarta: Jajasan Badan Penerbit, Fakultas Ekonomi Universitas Indonesia, 1966.

Kesatuan Aksi Mahasiswa Indonesia, Fakultas Ekonomi Universitas Indonesia, ed. *The Leader, the Man and the Gun.* Jakarta: Jajasan Badan Penerbit, Fakultas Ekonomi Universitas Indonesia, 1966.

Keyfitz, Nathan. "An East Javanese Village in 1953 and 1985: Observations on Development." *Population and Development Review* 11, no. 4 (1985):695–719.

Khong Cho Oon. *The Politics of Oil in Indonesia: Foreign Company-Host Government Relations.* Cambridge: Cambridge University Press, 1986.

Kikuchi, Masao et al. "Class Differentiation, Labor Employment, and Income Distribution in a West Java Village," In *The Developing Economies* 17, no. 1 (March 1980):45–64.

King, Dwight, trans. "The Last Grumbles of Brother Nasir." *Indonesia Reports: Politics Supplement*, no. 10 (August 1985).

Koentjaraningrat. "Apakah Kita Bisa Meniru Pola Pembangunan Jepang." *Kompas* (March 25, 1974).

—— *Javanese Culture.* Singapore: Oxford University Press, 1985.

Kuntjoro-Jakti, Dorodjatun. *The Political Economy of Development: The Case of Indonesia under the New Order Government, 1966–1978.* Doctoral dissertation. Berkeley: University of California, 1980.

Ladejinsky, Wolf. "Land Reform in Indonesia." Letter to Dr. Sudjarwo, Minister of Agriculture and Agrarian Affairs, February 27, 1964. In *Agrarian Reform as Unfinished Business*, ed. Louis J. Walinsky. New York: Oxford University Press, 1977.

Legge, J. D. *Sukarno: A Political Biography.* Sydney: Allen and Univen Australia Party, 1972.

Lev, Daniel S. "Indonesia 1965: The Year of the Coup." *Asian Survey* 6, no. 2 (1966):103–10.

Liddle, William, ed. *Political Participation in Modern Indonesia, Monograph Series No. 19.* Vol. 8. New Haven, Conn.: Yale University Southeast Asian Studies, 1973.

—— "Indonesia 1977: The New Order's Second Parliamentary Election." *Asian Survey* 18, no. 2.

Lim, Linda Y. C. and Pang Eng Fong. *Foreign Direct Investment and Industrialization in Malaysia, Singapore, Taiwan and Thailand.* Paris: OECD, 1991.

Lipsky, Seth. "The Billion Dollar Bubble." In *The Billion Dollar Bubble ... and other stories from the Asian Wall Street Journal.* Hong Kong: Dow Jones Publishing Company (Asia), 1978.

Lubis, Mochtar. *Twilight in Djakarta.* London: Hutchinson, 1963.

Lyon, Margo L. *Bases of Conflict in Rural Java.* Berkeley: Center for South and Southeast Asian Studies, University of California, December 1970.

McCawley, Peter. "Recent Developments." *Bulletin of Indonesian Economic Studies* 12, no. 1 (March 1976).

—— "The Growth of the Industrial Sector." In *The Indonesian Economy During the Soeharto Era,* ed. Anne Booth and Peter McCawley. Kuala Lumpur: Oxford University Press, 1981.

—— "Some Consequences of the Pertamina Crisis in Indonesia," *Journal of Southeast Asian Studies* 9, no. 1 (March 1978):6.

McDonald, Hamish. *Suharto's Indonesia.* Honolulu: The University Press of Hawaii, 1981.

McVey, Ruth. "Faith as the Outsider: Islam in Indonesian Politics." In *Islam in the Political Process,* ed. James P. Piscatori, pp. 199–25. New York: Cambridge University Press, 1983.

MacDougal, John A. "Patterns of Military Control in the Indonesian Higher Central Bureaucracy." *Indonesia* 33 (April 1982):89–121.

MacDougall, John James. "Technocrats as Modernizers: The Economists of Indonesia's New Order." Dissertation. Ann Arbor: University of Michigan, 1975.

—— "The Technocrat's Ideology of Modernity." In *What is Modern Indonesian Culture?,* ed. Gloria Davis. Southeast Asia Series No. 52. Athens, Ohio: Ohio University Press, 1979.

Mackie, J. A. C. *Problems of the Indonesian Inflation.* Monograph Series. Modern Indonesia Project, Southeast Asia Program, Department of Asian Studies. Ithaca, N.Y.: Cornell University, 1967.

—— *Konfrontasi: The Indonesia-Malaysia Dispute, 1963–66.* New York: Published for the Australian Institute of International Affairs by Oxford University Press, 1974.

—— "The Indonesian Conglomerates in Regional Perspective." In *Indonesia Assessment: 1990,* ed. Hal Hill and Terry Hull. Political and Social Change Monograph 2. Canberra: Department of Political and Social Change, Research School of Pacific Studies, Australian National University, 1990.

—— "The Report of the Commission of Four on Corruption." *Bulletin of Indonesian Economic Studies* 6, no. 2 (November 1970).

Mackie, J. A. C. and W. J. O'Malley. *Productivity Decline in the Java Sugar Industry from an Olsonian Perspective.* Unpublished ms., 1987.

Mackie, J. A. C. and Sjahrir. "Survey of Recent Developments." *Bulletin of Indonesian Economic Studies* 25, no. 3 (December 1989):3–34.

MacIntyre, Andrew. "Political Dimensions to Controversy over Business Conglomerates." In *Indonesia Assessment:* 1990, ed. Hal Hill and Terry Hull. Canberra: Research School of Pacific Studies, Australian National University, 1990.

Mangkusuwondo, Suhadi. "Indonesia." In *The Economic Development of East and Southeast Asia*, ed. Shinichi Ichimura. Honolulu: The University Press of Hawaii, 1975.

Manning, Chris. *The Green Revolution, Employment and Economic Change in Rural Java: A Reassessment of Trends under the New Order.* Occasional Paper, no. 84. Singapore: Institute of Southeast Asian Studies, 1988.

"Map of the Activities of the University of Indonesia's Student Council in Carrying Out Social Control." *Indonesia* 27 (April 1979):17–32.

Matsuo, Hiroshi. *The Development of Javanese Cotton Industry.* Tokyo: Institute of Developing Economies, 1970.

Mears, Leon A. *The New Rice Economy of Indonesia.* Yogyakarta: Gadjah Mada University Press, 1981.

Mears, Leon A. and Sidik Moeljono. "Food Policy." In *The Indonesian Economy During the Soeharto Era*, ed. Anne Booth and Peter McCawley. Kuala Lumpur: Oxford University Press, 1981.

Milne, R. S. "Technocrats and Politics in the ASEAN Countries." *Pacific Affairs* 55, no. 3 (1982).

Moerdani, L. B. "Excerpts from Transcription of Moerdani's Q and A with Reporters." *Indonesia Reports: Politics Supplement* (November 1985).

Moertopo, Ali. *Some Basic Thoughts on the Acceleration and Modernization of Twenty-five Years' Development.* Jakarta: CSIS, 1972.

Mortimer, Rex. *Indonesian Communism under Sukarno.* Ithaca, N.Y.: Cornell University, 1974.

—— *The Indonesian Communist Party and Land Reform, 1959–1965.* Clayton, Victoria: Centre of Southeast Asian Studies, Monash University, 1972.

Mozingo, David. *Chinese Policy Toward Indonesia, 1949–1967.* Ithaca, N.Y.: Cornell University Press, 1976.

Mubyarto, "The Sugar Industry." *Bulletin of Indonesian Economic Studies* 12, no. 2 (July 1977).

Mueller, Kenneth. "Observations on Rice Production in Indonesia." Jakarta: The Ford Foundationa, June 1968.

Myrdal, Gunnar. *Asian Drama: An Inquiry into the Poverty of Nations.* New York: Pantheon, 1968.

Nasution, Anwar. "Survey of Recent Developments." *Bulletin of Indonesian Economic Studies* 27, no. 2 (August 1991).

Neill, Wilfred T. *Twentieth Century Indonesia.* New York and London: Columbia University Press, 1973.

Bibliography

Nelson, Mark. "The Foreign Investment Regulatory Framework under the New Order Government of Indonesia." Unpublished paper. New York: East Asian Institute, Columbia University, April 1986.

Newman, John M. *Inflation in Indonesia: A Case Study of Causes, Stabilization Policies and Implementation.* Doctoral dissertation. Tufts University, 1974.

Nishihara, Masashi. *The Japanese and Sukarno's Indonesia: Tokyo-Jakarta Relations 1951–1966.* Honolulu: The University Press of Hawaii, 1976.

Nitisastro, Widjojo. "Analisa Ekonomi dan Perencanaan Pembanguanan." August 10, 1963, 27 pp. mimeo.

—— *Population Trends in Indonesia.* Ithaca, N.Y.: Cornell University Press, 1970.

Notosusanto, Nugroho. *Tercapainya Konsensus Nasional, 1966–1969.* Jakarta: PN Balai Pustaka, 1985.

Notosusanto, Nugroho and Ismail Saleh. *The Coup Attempt of the "September 30 Movement" in Indonesia.* Jakarta: PN Balai Pustaka, 1968.

Pangestu, Mari. "Survey of Recent Developments." *Bulletin of Indonesian Economic Studies* 23, no. 1 (April 1987):1–39.

Pangestu, Mari and Manggi Habir. "Survey of Recent Developments." *Bulletin of Indonesian Economic Studies* 26, no. 1 (1990):33–36.

Panggabean, M. "Keterangan Pemerintah di depan DPR: Tentang kegiatan mahasiswa Indonesia serta peristiwa-peristiwa demonstran pada tanggal 14–15–16 Januari 1974." In *Peristiwa 15 Januari,* ed. Marzuki Arifin. Jakarta: Publishing House Indonesia, 1974.

Panglaykim. *Japanese Direct Investment in ASEAN: The Indonesian Experience.* Singapore: Maruzen Asia, 1983.

Pauker, Guy J. "The Role of the Military in Indonesia." In *The Role of the Military in Underdeveloped Countries,* ed. John J. Johnson. Princeton, N.J.: Princeton University Press, 1962.

—— "Indonesia 1979: The Record of Three Decades." *Asian Survey* 20, no. 2 (February 1980).

—— "Indonesia in 1980: Regime Fatigue?" *Asian Survey* 21, no. 2 (February 1981).

Payer, Cheryl. "The International Monetary Fund and Indonesian Debt Slavery." In *Remaking Asia: Essays on the American Uses of Power,* ed. Mark Selden. New York: Pantheon, 1974.

Penders, C. L. M. and Ulf Sundhaussen. *Abdul Haris Nasution, A Political Biography.* St. Lucia, Queensland: University of Queensland Press, 1985.

Petisi 50. "Pernyataan Keprihatinan." May 5, 1980 (reproduced in Kelompok Kerja Petisi 50, *Muluruskan Perjalanan Orde Baru: Pertanyaan-Jawaban Petisi 50 Kepada Rakyat Indonesia,* Jakarta, mimeo., March 1, 1983).

Pinto, Brian. "Nigeria During and After the Oil Boom: A Policy Comparison with Indonesia." *The World Bank Economic Review* 1, no. 3 (1987):419–45.

Polomka, Peter. *Indonesia Since Sukarno*. Harmondsworth, Middlesex, England: Penguin Books, 1971.

Prawiranegara, Sjafruddin. Letter to the President of the Republic of Indonesia, July 7, 1983. "Pancasila as the Sole Foundation." *Indonesia*, no. 38 (1984):80–81.

Purdy, Susan Selden. "Legitimation of Power and Authority in a Pluralistic State: Pancasila and Civil Religion in Indonesia." Doctoral dissertation. New York: Columbia University, 1984.

Raffles, Thomas Stamford. *The History of Java*. London: Black, Parbury and Allen, 1817.

Raillon, Francois. *Les Etudiants Indonesiens et l'Ordre Nouveau: Politique et Ideologie du Mahasiswa Indonesia (1966–1974)*. Paris: Editions de la Maison des sciences de l'homme, 1984.

Ransom, David. "Ford Country: Building an Elite for Indonesia." In *The Trojan Horse, A Radical Look at Foreign Aid*, ed., Steve Weissman et al. Palo Alto, Calif.: Ramparts, 1974.

Reeve, David. "Sukarnoism and Indonesia's 'Functional Group' State. Part 2: 'Implementing Indonesian Democracy.' "*Review of Indonesian and Malaysian Affairs* 13, no. 1 (1979):115.

—— *Golkar of Indonesia: An Alternative to the Party System*. Singapore: Oxford University Press, 1985.

Republic of Indonesia. See Indonesia, Republic of.

Rice, Robert C. "The Origins of Economic Ideas and Their Impact on Economic Development in Indonesia." *Masyarakat Indonesia* 9, no. 2 (1982):141–53.

Robison, Richard. *Indonesia: The Rise of Capital*. Sidney: Allen & Unwin, 1986.

Roeder, O. G. *The Smiling General: President Soeharto of Indonesia*. Djakarta: Gunung Agung, 1970.

Ryokichi, Hirono. "Japan, the United States, and Development Assistance to Southeast Asia." In *Development Assistance to Southeast Asia: The U.S. and Japanese Approaches*, ed. Michael Blaker. New York: East Asian Institute, Columbia University, 1983.

Sacerdoti, Guy. "Pertamina Cut Back to Size." *Far Eastern Economic Review*, December 23, 1977.

Sadli, Mohammad. "Masalah Ekonomi-Moneter Kita Jang Strukturil." In *The Leader, the Man and the Gun*, ed. Kesatuan Aksi Mahasiswa Indonesia, Fakultas Ekonomi Universitas Indonesia. Jakarta: Jajasan Badan Penerbit, Fakultas Ekonomi Universitas Indonesia, 1966.

—— "Reflections on Boeke's Theory of Dualistic Economies." *Ekonomi dan Keuangan Indonesia* (June 1957). Reprinted in *The Economy of Indonesia:*

Bibliography

Selected Readings, ed. Bruce Glassburner. Ithaca, N.Y.: Cornell University Press, 1971.

—— "Peranan Bahan Bakar Minyak dalam Perekonomian," *Majalah Management dan Usahawan Indonesia* (January–February 1982).

—— "The Private and State Enterprise Sectors in Indonesia." *The Indonesian Quarterly* 16, no. 2 (1988):153–57.

Sagir, Soeharsono. "Peranan Minyak dalam Kehidupan Ekonomi dan Pembangunan Indonesia." *Majalah Management dan Usahawan Indonesia* (January–February 1982).

Saleh, Azis et al. "White Paper: The September 84 Incident in Tanjungpriok!" *Indonesia Reports: December Log* (January 15, 1985).

Samson, Allan A. "Army and Islam in Indonesia." *Pacific Affairs* 54 (Winter 1971/72):545–65.

—— "Indonesia 1973: A Climate of Concern." *Asian Affairs* 14, no. 2 (1974):157–65.

Samsuri, Oemar and Sudirman Tebba. "The Shift in Pattern of Islamic Leadership in Indonesia." *Kompas* (January 14, 1987). Reproduced in English translation in *Indonesia Reports: Culture and Society Supplement*, no. 20 (February 1987).

Sato, Yuri. "The Development of Business Groups in Indonesia: 1967–1989." Dissertation. Fakultas Pascasarjana: Universitas Indonesia, 1989.

Schlesinger, Arthur M. *A Thousand Days*. Boston: Houghton Mifflin, 1965.

Shaplen, Robert. *Time Out of Hand*. New York: Harper and Row, 1969.

Shaw, Robert d'A. "Rice Research Project Evaluation." Unpublished memorandum. Jakarta: The Ford Foundation, December 19, 1974.

Shizuo, Miyamoto. "Jawa Shusen Shoriki." In *The Japanese Experience in Indonesia: Selected Memoirs of 1942–45*, ed. Anthony Reid and Oki Akira. Athens, Ohio: Ohio University Center for International Studies, 1986.

Siamwalla, Ammar and Stephen Haykin. *The World Rice Market: Structure, Conduct, and Performance*. Washington, D.C.: International Food Policy Research Institute, 1983.

Smith, Theodore M. "The Indonesian Bureaucracy: Stability, Change and Productivity." Unpublished ms., 1971.

Soedjatmoko. *Indonesia: Problems and Opportunities (I)* and *Indonesia and the World (II)*, Dyason Memorial Lectures. Melbourne: The Australian Institute of International Affairs, 1967.

—— "Perceptions of Social Justice in Southeast Asia." In *Questioning Development in Southeast Asia*, ed. Nancy Chang. Singapore: Select Books, 1977.

Soeharto. *Soeharto: Pikiran, Ucapan dan Tindakan Saya* (Seperti dipaparkan kepada G. Dwipayana dan Ramadhan K. H.) Jakarta: PT Citra Lamtoro Gung Persada, 1988.

Bibliography

Soehoed, A. R. "The Concept of Industrialization in the Third Five Year Plan of Indonesia." *The Indonesian Quarterly* 7 (January 1979).

—— "Industrial Development During Repelita III." *Indonesian Quarterly* 10, no. 4 (1982).

—— "Reflections on Industrialization and Industrial Policy in Indonesia." *Bulletin of Indonesian Economic Studies* 24, no. 2 (August 1988):43–57.

Soemardjan, Selo. *Petani Tebu: Laporan Penelitian tentang Masalah-Masalah dalam Pelaksanaan Program TJI di Jawa Timur, Jawa Tengah dan Jawah Barat.* Jakarta: Yayasan Ilmu-Ilmu Sosial dan Dewan Gula, 1983.

Soesastro, M. Hadi. "The Political Economy of Deregulation in Indonesia." *Asian Survey* 29, no. 9 (September 1989).

Soesastro, M. Hadi, Djisman S. Simandjuntak, and Pande R. Silalahi. *Report: Financing Public Sector Development Expenditures in Indonesia.* Jakarta: Centre for Strategic and International Studies, 1988.

Stoler, Anne L. "Garden Use and Household Economy in Java." In *Agricultural and Rural Development in Indonesia,* ed. Gary E. Hansen. Boulder, Colo.: Westview Press, 1981.

Subroto. "Menjusun Sendi-Sendi Ekonomi Berdasarkan Prinsip Ekonomi." In *Kebangkitan Semangat '66: Mendjeladjah Tracee Baru,* Diselenggarakan oleh Universitas Indonesia, 6 Mei 1966–9 Mei 1966, Buku II. Djakarta: Jajasan Badan Penerbit, Fakultas Ekonomi Universitas Indonesia, 1966.

Sudarsono, Juwono. "Political Changes and Developments in Indonesia." In *Trends in Indonesia II,* ed. Leo Suryadinata and Sharon Siddique. Singapore: Institute of Southeast Asian Studies, 1981.

Sudomo. "Keterangan Pers Kastaf Kopkamtib, 21 February 1974." In *Peristiwa 15 Januari,* ed. Marzuki Arifin. Jakarta: Publishing House Indonesia, 1974.

Suhadi, Mangkusuwondo. "Indonesia." In *The Economic Development of East and Southeast Asia,* ed. Shinichi Ichimura. Honolulu: University of Hawaii Press, 1975.

Sumiskum. "Konfrontasi dan Politik Luar Negeri Untuk Kepentingan Nasional." In *Kebangkitan Semangat '66: Mendjeladjah Tracee Baru,* Diselenggarakan oleh Universitas Indonesia, 6 Mei 1966–69 Mei 1966, Buku II. Djakarta: Jajasan Badan Penerbit, Fakultas Ekonomi Universitas Indonesia, 1966.

Suryadinata, Leo. "Indonesia under the New Order: Problems of Growth, Equity, and Stability." In *Trends in Indonesia II,* ed. Leo Suryandinata and Sharon Siddique. Singapore: Institute of Southeast Asian Studies, 1981.

Suryadinata, Leo and Sharon Siddique, eds. *Trends in Indonesia II.* Singapore: Institute of Southeast Asian Studies, 1981.

Sutherland, Heather. *The Making of a Bureaucratic Elite: The Colonial Transformation of the Javanese Priyayi.* Singapore, Kuala Lumpur, Hong Kong: Heineman Educational Books, 1979.

Bibliography

Sutowo, Ibnu. "Perataan pendapatan itu suatu utopia." *Prisma* 5, no. 1 (February 1976):51–54.

Tan, Mely G. "The Role of Ethnic Chinese Minority in Development." *Southeast Asian Studies* 25, no. 3 (December 1989):367–71.

Tanaka, Shoko. *Post-War Japanese Resources and Strategies: The Case of Southeast Asia.* Cornell University East Asia Papers. Ithaca, N.Y.: China-Japan Program, Cornell University, 1986.

Tapol. *Indonesia: Muslims on Trial.* London: Tapol, 1987.

Thee Kian Wie. "Promoting Investment into Export-oriented Industries." Paper prepared for a meeting organized by the Indonesian Financial Executives Association. Jakarta: October 22, 1987.

—— "Industrial and Foreign Investment Policy in Indonesia Since 1967." *Southeast Asian Studies* 25, no. 3 (December 1987):83–96.

—— "Industrial Restructuring in Indonesia: Some Problems." Paper prepared for the First Convention of the East Asia Economic Association. Kyoto, Japan: October 29–30, 1988.

—— "The Investment Surge from Asia NICs into Indonesia." In *Indonesia Assessment: 1990,* ed. Hal Hill and Terry Hull. Political and Social Change Monograph II. Canberra: Department of Political and Social Change, Research School of Pacific Studies, Australian National University, 1990.

Timmer, C. Peter. "The Formation of Indonesian Rice Policy: A Historical Perspective. In *Agricultural and Rural Development in Indonesia,* ed. Gary E. Hansen. Boulder, Colo.: Westview Press, 1981.

U.S. Arms Control and Disarmament Agency. *World Military Expenditures and Arms Transfers.* Annual, various years.

U.S. Foreign Commercial Service, "Business Outlook Abroad: Indonesia," *Business America* (July 13, 1981).

Van Niel, Robert. *The Emergence of the Modern Indonesian Elite.* Dordrecht, Holland: Foris Publications, 1984.

Van der Kroef, Justus M. "Interpretations of the 1965 Indonesia Coup: A Review of the Literature." *Pacific Affairs* 43, no. 4 (1970–71):557–77.

Wain, Barry. "Pertamina and the Incredible World of Ibnu Sutowo." *INSIGHT* (October 1976).

Walkin, Jacob. "The Moslem-Communist Confrontation in East Java, 1964–1965." *Orbis* 13, no. 3 (Fall 1969): 822–47.

Ward, Ken. *The Foundation of the Partai Muslim in Indonesia.* Ithaca, N.Y.: Cornell University Press, 1970.

—— *The 1971 Election in Indonesia: An East Java Case Study.* Clayton, Victoria: Centre of Southeast Asian Studies, Monash University, 1974.

Ward, William B. *Science and Rice in Indonesia.* Boston: Allgeschlager, Gunn and Hain, 1985.

Bibliography

Wardhana, Ali. "Structural Adjustment in Indonesia: Export and the 'High-Cost Economy.' " Keynote address at the twenty-fourth conference of the Southeast Asian Central Bank Governors. Bangkok: January 25, 1989.

Weinstein, Franklin B. *Indonesian Foreign Policy and the Dilemma of Dependence: From Sukarno to Soeharto.* Ithaca, N.Y.: Cornell University Press, 1976.

Wertheim, W. F. "Indonesia Before and After the Untung Coup." *Pacific Affairs* 39, nos. 1–2 (1966):115–27.

—— "From *Aliran* to Class Struggle in the Countryside of Java," *Pacific Viewpoint*, no. 10 (1969).

—— "Suharto and the Untung Days—the Missing Link." *Journal of Contemporary Asia* 1, no. 2 (Winter 1970):50–51.

White, Benjamin. "Population, Involution, and Employment in Rural Java." In *Agricultural and Rural Development in Indonesia*, ed. Gary E. Hansen. Boulder, Colo.: Westview Press, 1981.

—— "'Agricultural Involution' and Its Critics: Twenty Years After." *Bulletin of Concerned Asian Scholars*, no. 2 (1983):18–31.

"White Book of the 1978 Students' Struggle." *Indonesia* 25 (April 1978):151–52.

The Witteveen Facility and the OPEC Financial Surpluses, Hearings before the Subcommittee on Foreign Economic Policy of the Committee on Foreign Relations, United States Senate, Ninety-fifth Congress, First Session (September 21, 23, October 6, 7, 10, 1977). Washington, D.C.: USGPO, 1978.

Yoshihara, Kunio. *Japanese Investment in Southeast Asia.* Honolulu: The University of Hawaii Press, 1978.

Newspapers and Magazines

Angkatan Bersenjata, March 28, 1980.

Asahi Shimbun, January 17, 1970; January 16, 1974; January 17, 1974.

Asia Research Bulletin. March 31, 1975; May 31, 1975; August 31, 1975; December 31, 1975; March 31, 1976.

Asia Week, December 9, 1988.

Asian Wall Street Journal, June 21, 1983; May 31, 1985; June 14–15, 1985; November 24, 1986; November 25, 1986; November 26, 1986.

Berita Buana, July 9, 1980.

Business Week, December 17, 1979.

Economist, August 15, 1987.

Far Eastern Economic Review, January 28, 1974; February 4, 1974; February 25, 1974; March 11, 1974; May 30, 1975; January 16, 1976; April 23, 1976; April 30, 1976; July 2, 1976; December 24, 1976; January 28, 1977; July 15, 1977;

Bibliography

September 2, 1977; December 23, 1977; February 8, 1980; April 17, 1981; May 29, 1981; August 18, 1983; December 1, 1986; February 9, 1989; June 29, 1989; November 16, 1989; March 29, 1990; May 30, 1990; June 14, 1990.

Financial Times, April 11, 1980; November 28, 1980.

Forbes, July 24, 1989.

Jakarta Post, May 23, 1987.

Kompas, August 8, 1970; April 17, 1980; July 16, 1980; July 19, 1983.

Mainichi Shimbun, January 16, 1974.

New York Times, January 15, 1974; January 16, 1974; January 17, 1974; April 9, 1977; April 25, 1987.

New Yorker, April 1, 1974.

Newsweek, January 28, 1974.

Pelita, July 16, 1980.

Sinar Harapan, July 18, 1970; July 20, 1970; July 22, 1970; July 24, 1970; July 18, 1974; July 20, 1974; May 21, 1975.

Sydney Morning Herald, April 10, 1986.

Tempo, August 27, 1977; July 29, 1978; March 31, 1984; May 11, 1985; May 18, 1985; March 15, 1986; April 19, 1986; April 26, 1986; May 3, 1986; June 28, 1986; July 12, 1986; February 25, 1989.

Time, January 21, 1974; January 28, 1974.

Wall Street Journal, December 23, 1976; February 11, 1977; February 14, 1977; June 27, 1980; April 16, 1990.

Washington Post, May 21, 1990.

Yomiuri Shimbun, January 16, 1974.

Index

Index

Antigovernment movements, and terrorism, 229

Antipoverty programs, 287

Anti-Sukarno activists: army officers, 34, 38–40; student leaders, 38

Anti-Sukarno demonstrations, Muslim groups and, 276

Antitrust legislation, lack of, 301

Approved traders import system, 246–48, 263; plastics industry, 248–49; steel industry, 249–51

Arifin, Bustanil, 126, 127, 129

Armed forces, 1, 9, 28, 96, 104; corruption and, 155–57; and criticisms of government, 199–205; and electoral campaign, 98; electoral reforms and, 90; funding for, 212; Islamic protests and, 277; and Malaysia campaign, 9–10; opposition to Soeharto, 277; and presidential succession, 210; reduction of, 106–8; and reelection of Soeharto, 194, 201; Soeharto and, 206; and state enterprises, 253–54; strength of, 273. *See also* Army

Army, 96, 270, 271, 273–75, 299; business enterprises, 155–56, 168–69; and communists, 8, 10, 12–15; ethnic divisions, 277; and manufacturing, 291; reorganization of, 162; Soeharto and, 45–48; student leaders and, 38; and Sukarno, 31–32, 33; support of Soeharto regime, 288–89; and violence, 23, 30. *See also* Armed forces; Army officers

Army officers, 8–9, 46, 274–75, 296; abuse of power, 107; and civilian government, 42–43; and civil service, 106; control of Java enterprises, 18; and coup attempt, 11–12; and criticisms of government, 199, 203; education for, 81; and election campaign, 97–98, 100; and electoral reform, 89, 91; and functional groups, 96; and January 15 riots, 146; and National Party, 92; and Pertamina crisis, 165; and political parties, 94; and presidential succession, 297–98; and reelection of Soeharto, 200; and students, 34, 38, 142; and Sukarno, 34, 35, 38–40; and university economists, 80–82

Army Staff and Command School, 81

Arndt, Heinz, 56

Arrests: after coup attempt, 27; of government critics, 219; of Muslim activists, 231, 322–36; of student leaders, 200–201; after Tanjung Priok incident, 228

Arthur Young & Co., 167

Asahan aluminum complex, 192

Asian governments, and rice, 121

Asian Wall Street Journal, and Soeharto family finances, 259

As Sa'adah prayerhouse, 222–23

Association of Indonesian Social Scientists, 199

Association of Islamic Students, 218

Association of Southeast Asian Nations, 200

Astra group, 256

Audit of Pertamina operations, 167

Australia, 63; trade with, 68

Australian journalists, banning of, 257–58

Autarchy, and economy, Daud's view, 159

Authoritarian government, 72, 270–75, 295; and economic policy, 288–93; university economists and, 82

Authority, government source, 99

Automobiles, 257, 287

Average annual growth rates, 284–85

Badan Urusan Logistik, 117. *See also* Bulog

Balance of budget, economic reforms and, 65–67

Bali 7, 19; purge of Communists, 13, 14, 15

Bambang Trihatmodjo, 248–49, 259

Bandung, textile industry, 150

Bandung Institute of Technology: arrests, 200; protests, 197, 198

Bangkok, 278; student protests, 135, 138, 148

Bangladesh, 285

Bank Central Asia, bombings, 226, 228

Bank credit, economic reform and, 67

Bank Indonesia, and Pertamina crisis, 166, 167

Banking industry: deregulation, 280; growth after deregulation, 265; inflation and, 58; reforms, 262; state enterprises, 253

Banks: Chinese, bombings of, 226; collapse of, 177

Bank Windhu Kencana, 155

Index

Index

Index

Index

imports, 246; and rice economy, 113–15; and self- government, 271
Dutch-owned properties, takeover of, 57

Eastern Europe, university economists and, 81–82
East Java: military personnel in government, 110; peasant uprisings, 19; purge of Communists, 13–15; terrorist bombings, 230
East Kalimantan: mineral resources, 287; Pertamina operations, 171, 183
Economic advisers of Soeharto, 52, 73–74
Economic analysis, 53
Economic decision making, 161
Economic development, 280–83; authoritarian government and, 293; and civil service expansion, 106; conglomerates and, 160–61; corruption in government and, 155; oil income and, 164–65, 283; Soedjatmoko's view, 144; student protests, 140; Sumitro's theories, 77; Widjojo's views, 80
Economic factors in militarization of government, 109
Economic inequality, urban, 242
Economic planning agencies, Southeast Asia, 72
Economic policy: authoritarianism and, 288–93; new, 63–67; political transition and, 296; Soeharto regime, 280–83; student protests, 197
Economic reform, pressures for, 260–64
Economic situation, Tanjung Priok, 220
Economic theories, 83–84; of Hatta, 76–77; of Sumitro, 77
Economic trade-off, 211–12
Economists, 72–79; and army officers, 80–81; and authoritarian regime, 288–89; and Chinese-Indonesians, 84–85; and communism, 81–82; decline of influence, 161; and economic policy, 281–82; and economic reform, 260; Ibnu Sutowo and, 176; and industrial development, 213–15; and Pertamina debts, 165–66; and Soeharto, 62–63; statement on the economy, 61–62; and Sukarno, 75–76

Economy of Indonesia, 1–2; army involvement, 46; after coup attempt, 32; and fall of Sukarno, 51; government regulation, 279; and January 15 riots, 138; Malaysian campaign and, 9; oil prices and, 210; perceptions of, 53–56; Provisional People's Consultative Assembly and, 61; Soeharto and, 51–52
Education, 2; for army officers, 81; and civil service, 105, 279; economic growth and, 285; gender equality, 287–88; Southeast Asia, before World War II, 75
Elections: control of, 97–98; fraudulent practices, 196; Indonesian experience, 87–89; Islamic violence, 218–19; Soeharto and, 86–87; West Irian, 94
Electoral campaigns: army and, 274, 275; Muslims and, 236; 1977, 194–202; 1993, 267
Electoral laws, 87, 89–90; draft amendment, 205; reform of, 89–91, 95
Electric appliance sales, 257
Elite classes, 2–4, 285, 301–2; and anti-communist violence, 271; and armed forces, 273; and army support of Soeharto, 194; Bulog officials, 127; bureaucratic, Muslims and, 299; and civil service, 103; conservatism of, 28; and corruption in armed forces, 107–8; and corruption in government, 292; criticisms of government, 205; and economic change, 52, 62, 63, 71, 260; educated, leadership from, 75–76; elections viewed by, 88; Islamic, 242, 277; managerial, 280; and manufacturing, 291; and Pertamina crisis, 165; Pertamina viewed by, 167; and political change, 294–96; and political parties, 272; and presidential succession, 298; rural landowners, 132; and Soeharto family finances, 258–59; and state enterprises, 254; and Sukarno's government, 35; technocrats, 72–73
Employees Association, 97
Employees of government, and budget deficit, 56. See also Civil service
Employment, by government, 66–67, 279; Habibie's ideas and, 215; industrial devel-

Index

opment and, 213; local public works and, 123; in rural areas, 132–33. *See also* Civil service

Energy, state enterprises, 253

Entrepreneurs: indigenous, government programs and, 153; Sumitro's views of, 77

Equality of income, Ibnu Sutowo's view, 192

Equity, economic development and, 286–88

Essential commodities, government import of, 65

Ethics, traditional, of Javanese politics, 74

Ethnic groups, student leaders from, 37. *See also* Chinese business community; Chinese-Indonesians; Chinese people

Expansion of civil service, 105

Expo magazine, and Chinese businessmen, 256

Exports: agricultural crops, 113–15; control of, 266–67; deregulation and, 264, 265; earnings from, 57, 68, 283; economic reforms and, 65; Malaysian campaign and, 9; manufactured goods, 283; non-oil, growth after deregulation, 265; oil, 164, 175, 283; university economists and, 83

Expropriation of foreign-owned plantations, 16

Extraconstitutional means of expression, 163. *See also* Terrorism

Extremist groups, terrorist acts, 229

Extremist lecturers, detention of, 228

Factionalism: and political stability, 162; in Soeharto regime, 100

Faculty of Economics, 77–78, 282; and Army Staff and Command School, 81; conferences on economy, 33, 54, 60

Family background of Soeharto, 45. *See also* Relatives of Soeharto

Family businesses, Chinese, 256

Family planning, Soeharto and, 282

Farmers: government protection of, 289; and rice program, 117–18, 123; and sugar program, 128; and new rice varieties, 129–30

Farming, Java, 16

Fate, Soeharto's belief in, 50

Fatwa, A. M., 225, 227, 228

Feith, Herbert, 52

Female education, and population growth, 288

Fertilizer for rice, 113, 117–18, 122, 213; distribution by government, 116; Pertamina project, 171, 183; subsidies of, 191, 211

Fifth force, Communist proposal, 10

Financial consortium, national, Daud's idea, 160

Financial crisis, international, Pertamina and, 164–65

Financial interests, and military dominance, 274

Financial policies, governmental, 216–17

Financial services industry, 246; deregulation and, 264

Financing for domestic industry, 150–51

Fires, after Tanjung Priok incident, 226, 227

First Five-Year Plan, and civil service, 104–5

Floating fertilizer plant, Pertamina project, 171, 183

"Floating mass" concept, 98

Fokus magazine, and millionaires, 256

Food crops, Java, 113

Food supply, 1965, 1, 2, 28

Ford Foundation, 146

Foreign aid, 70–71, 282; and balanced budget, 67; and civil service expansion, 106; criticisms of, 135; economic reform and, 64, 68; from Japan, 148; rice shipments, 126; Soeharto and, 74; student protests, 139; university economists and, 83

Foreign banks, and Pertamina crisis, 176–78

Foreign debt, 57, 282–83; economic reform and, 67–68; moratorium on payments, 70; Pertamina crisis and, 182, 188–89

Foreign exchange, 57, 169, 280, 283; fradulent use, 157

Foreign exploration for oil, 164

Foreign investment, 192, 215–16, 246; authoritarianism and, 291; criticisms of, 135; deregulation, 262, 264; and funding for armed forces, 212; government control, 151, 154, 251–52; and January 15 riots, 147; Japanese, 148–49; protests against, 139

Foreign investors, and economic policy, 247

Index

Index

Index

Impact of deregulation, 264–66

Imperialism, views of, 72

Imports, 57; Bulog and, 127; control of, 245, 246–51; deregulation of, 263; economic reforms and, 65; sugar, 128; tax revenues, 66
—rice, 58, 112–13, 115; Bulog and, 126; 1972 crisis, 119; oil prices and, 124

Imprisonment of journalists, 143

Income: distribution of, 286–88; per capita, 28, 285; in rural areas, 132–33
—governmental, from oil, 174–75; and foreign debt, 188; Soeharto regime and, 290–91

Independence, national: achievement of, 2–3; and civil service, 103–5; students and, 36; Sukarno and, 27

Independence Day address, 1963, 53

Independent group, progovernment, 93–94

Independent political action, limitations of, 278

India, 286; population growth, 284

Indigenous businessmen, 153–54; Chinese and, 152

Indigenous enterprise, 256; government control, 254

Indochina, rice surplus, 117

Indoctrination programs, 163, 243–44

Indonesia: colonial, education in, 75; foreign investment, 252, 314–40; Japan and, 147–52; political economy, 270; urban population, 278; windfall oil profits, 190 *See also* Government, Indonesia
—economy of, 1–2; growth, 284–85; Orientalist view, 83–84

Indonesian Chamber of Commerce and Industry, 254–55

Indonesian Communist Party. *See* Communist Party of Indonesia

Indonesian Democracy Party (PDI), 195, 210

Indonesian flag, first raising, 29

Indonesian Muslim Party, 93

Indonesian National Army (Tentara Nasional Indonesia, TNI), 8–9, 273; and purge of Communists, 13–15. *See also* Armed forces; Army

Indonesia Raya (newspaper), 143; attack on Pertamina, 172

Indonesians, interviews with, 3–4

Indonesian Socialist Party, 308–8

Indonesian society, differing views, 209–10

Indonesian Student Action Front (Kesatuan Aksi Mahasiswa Indonesia, KAMI), 32, 33, 34, 87; election laws and, 89, 90; and symposium on economy, 60

Indonesian Student Movement Center, 81

"Indonesian Student's Vow," 197

Indonesian University Graduates Action Front, and symposium on economy, 60

Indra Rukmana Kowara, 259

Industrial development, 213–17

Industrial materials, control of imports, 246–47

Industry, 279, 283; authoritarianism and, 289–92; concentration of, 160; deregulation of, 260–69, 280; government protection, 245–48, 263–64; Ibnu Sutowo's views, 192; Muslims in, 242; public investment, 192

Inefficiency of import control system, 249–51

Inequality, in urban society, 242

Inflation, 32, 51, 68; causes of, 56–58; civil service and, 104; consequences of, 58–60; control of, 64; economic reforms and, 65, 67, 71; government corruption and, 172; and January 15 riots, 138; and rice economy, 115, 116, 119; student protests, 140

Information, availability of, 3, 4

Infrastructure: decline of, and export earnings, 57; development spending, 191; rural, and rice production, 122–23

Inner perfection, Javanese idea, 48

Institutional sources of power, 271

Institutions of government, criticisms of function, 162–63

Intellectuals, employment of, 4

Interest groups: and economic policy, 289; and manufacturing, 291

Interest rates, economic reform and, 67

Intergovernmental Group on Indonesia (IGGI), 139, 148; and Pertamina, 183,

354

Index

188–89; and World Bank report, 217
International business community, Ibnu's
standing, 175
International economy, national economy and,
Daud's view, 159–60
International factors in Islamic revival, 241
International grain reserve, 120
International investment bankers, and Perta-
mina crisis, 166
International Monetary Fund (IMF), 68, 282;
and Indonesian economic policies, 63,
69–70; and Pertamina, 177
International relations, and political transition,
296
International Rice Research Institute, 122
International trade, economic reforms and,
64–65, 68
Interviews with Indonesian elites, 3–4
Invasion of Malaysia, Communist party and, 9
Investment Coordinating Board, 216
Investments: government control, 245, 262; in
state enterprises, 253
Irian Jaya province, mineral resources, 287
Irrigation of crops, 113, 114, 191; improve-
ment of canals, 122–23
Islam, 244, 276–77; divisions in, 232; and
political transition, 299–300; and unitary
state, 233–34; revival of, 241–42, 276–77.
See also Muslims
Islamic groups: Communists and, 19–20;
human rights protest, 194; Java, 17
—political parties, 232; and election laws,
205–6; merger of, 195–96, 234. *See also*
Nahdatul Ulama
Islamic leaders, 209–10, 235, 242; and 1977
elections, 194–97; and peasant uprisings,
19; protests against government, 138
Islamic pilgrimage, corrupt practices, 158
Islamic Student Association (*Himpunan Maha-
siswa Islam*, HMI), 36, 37, 81, 235, 276
Islamic Union (*Serikat Islam*), 232, 276
Islamic values, Hatta and, 76–77
Islamic youth organization, massacre of Com-
munists, 13, 14
Isman, Mas, 80, 203

Isolation of Indonesia, 2–3; Communist party
and, 10
Istana Merdeka, Jakarta, 29
Italy, and Indonesian economic policies, 63

Jakarta, 7–11, 242, 278, 280, 287; anti-
Chinese demonstrations, 154; attacks on
Chinese property, 25, 226; Koningsplein,
29; stock exchange, 265, 268; student
protests, 139; Tanaka visit, 135–36;
Tanjung Priok incident, 219; terrorism,
after Tanjung Priok incident, 226–27
Jakarta Charter, 234
January 15 riots, 135–38; background of,
138–40; and Chinese businessmen, 152–54;
and corruption in government, 154–57; and
Japanese investments, 147–52; lessons from,
159–63; as plot to overthrow government,
141–47
Japan, 281; agreement with Permina, 168–69;
aid to Indonesia, 70, 282; economic policy
toward, 63, 68, 69, 280; and Indonesian oil,
283; investment in Indonesia, 252, 264;
involvement in Indonesian economy,
147–52; and January 15 riots, 159; rice
from, 126; student protests against, 135–36,
139; trade with, 68; World War II, 115
Japan Economic Cooperation Fund, 159
Jasin, Mohammad, "Statement of Concern,"
207
Java, 19, 21, 74, 102; agriculture, 113–14;
anticommunist reaction, 27; Communist
party, 8, 9, 17–18; land ownership, 16–17;
oil-financed development, 283; per capita
income, 133; political conflict, 15; purge of
Communists, 14; rice production, 124,
129–30; rural-urban disparity, 287; violence, 7
Javanese army officers, 277
Javanese culture, Soeharto and, 48–50
Javanese mysticism, 196; and presidential succession, 298
Javanese people: in bureaucracy, 279; Nasir's
attack, 221
Jenkins, David, 201, 257

Index

Index

Logistics Agency. *See* Bulog
Long-term development policies, authoritarian government and, 293
Lubis, Mochtar, 143, 149; attack on Pertamina, 172

Machmud, Amir, 35, 40–42, 97, 101, 200
Mackie, J. A. C., 66, 173–74, 266
MacNamara, Robert, 83
Macroeconomic policy, 289; authoritarian government and, 292–93
Madiun, revolutionary government, 15
Madjid, Nurcholish, 235
Malari, 137–38
Malaya, education, pre-WWII, 75
Malaysia: agricultural production, 285; equity of economy, 286; foreign investment, 151, 252, 314*n*40; Gross Domestic Product, 284; New Economic Policy, 268; population growth, 284; student protests, 135
—Indonesian campaign against, 9–10, 70; armed forces and, 104; and budget deficit, 56; economy and, 61, 66; and decline in export earnings, 57; and foreign debt, 68; Kemal Idris and, 39; Soeharto and, 47
Malik, Adam, 51–52, 70, 210; and economic policy, 281; and political situation, 204–5; and social unrest, 224; and student protests, 136
Maloko, Syarifin, 222
Managed pluralism, 293–95
Management of Indonesian economy, 293
Manipulation of elections, 99
Manufactured goods, banned imports, 246–47
Manufacturing, 213, 245–48, 253, 279, 283; authoritarianism and, 291–92; deregulation, 263–64, 280; foreign investment, 252; growth of, 265, 285; renewed regulation, 266
Marcos, Ferdinand, 186, 257; Soeharto and, 297
Marine corps, and munitions dump explosion, 227
Market information service, rice economy, 126
Markets: Japanese search for, 148; local, 123

Marriage laws, 101; Muslims and, 138, 235
Marriage of Soeharto, 45–46
Mashuri, and coup attempt, 24
Massacre of communists, 13; Muslims and, 218
Mass guidance, agriculture program, 123
Mass violence, and rise of authoritarianism, 272
Masyumi (*Madjelis Sjuriah Muslimin Indonesia*), 92, 232, 276; army officers and, 89; revolts supported by, 234; Soeharto and, 93, 234
Mayors, military men as, 97, 110
Mechanical improvements, village society and, 131–32
Medan, Chinese-Indonesian refugees, 25–26
Medan Merdeka, Jakarta, 29
Membership: of Consultative Assembly, 86–87; of representative institutions, electoral reform and, 90
Members of Parliament, and Consultative Assembly, 86
Merdeka, and political unrest, 230
Mexico, 283; foreign investment, 252
Middle class, 161, 278–80
Militarism, increase of, 272–74
Militarization of government, 108–11
Military dictatorships, Nasution and, 108
Military expenditures, foreign debts, 68
Military officers, 4; abuse of power, 107; and coup attempt, 12; politics of, 8–10; and Soeharto family finances, 258. *See also* Army officers
Military spending, 106–7
Millenarianism, 21
Mills: for imported wheat, 127; sugar, 128
Mineral resources, 169–70, 287; exports, 57; U.S. investments, 148
Mining operations: nationalization of, 169–70; state enterprises, 253
Minister of Mines, responsibility for Pertamina, 174
Ministry of Finance, budget control, 67
Ministry of Trade: easing of controls, 263; import licenses, 246; and plastics industry, 248–49

357

Index

Minority communities, religious, and presidential succession, 300

Mintaredja, 235

Mistrust between armed forces, 9

Mixed economy, Hatta's view, 76

Mobil Oil Co., Pertamina project, 183

Mochtar Lubis, 143, 149, 172

Modernization of civil service, 101–3

Moerdani, L. B., 220, 227, 254; and anti-Chinese bombings, 226; and Soeharto family finances, 58; and Tanjung Priok incident, 222, 224, 225

Moertopo, Ali, 40, 47, 93, 136, 196; and electoral campaign, 95, 96–98; and January 15 riots, 145–47; and National Party, 92; Soemitro and, 140; and student leaders, 34, 38; and successor to Soeharto, 210

Mokoginta, "Statement of Concern," 207

Money supply, increase in, 56–57

Monopolies: import controls and, 246–51; oil industry, 170–71

Monthly Review, and January 15 riots, 141–42

Moratorium on debt payments, 70

Muhamad, Mar'ie, 36

Muhammadiyah (Islamic social organization), 81

Munitions dump explosion, 226–27

Muslim leaders, view of society, 209–10

Muslims, 218; and Communists, 15–16; Moerdani and, 227; opposition to government, 231–44, 276–77; and Pancasila legislation, 237–38; and presidential succession, 299–300; and Tanjung Priok incident, 225
—activists, 196, 229, 230, 275; airline hijacking, 236; arrests of, 231, 322n36; industrial careers, 242

Muslim students, 37; protests, 138

Muslim youth groups, massacre of Communists, 13, 14

Myrdal, Gunnar, 26, 52, 72

Mysticism, Javanese, 27, 196

Nahdatul Ulama (NU), 33, 36, 92, 93, 195, 218, 232, 276; and election laws, 205–6; and massacre of Communists, 15; and peasant uprisings, 19; separation from PPP, 240

Nahdatul Ulama leader, and Tanjung Priok incident, 239

Nasakom, 21

Nasir, M., 220–21, 223, 228

Nasution, Abdul Haris, 11, 33, 43–44, 61, 135; and army role in politics, 96; criticism of government, 199; and electoral reform, 91; and government, 88; and Ibnu Sutowo, 168; and Letter of Instruction, 42; and massacre of Communists, 14–15; and militarization of government, 108; and Pancasila legislation, 239; plans for armed forces, 106; and presidential succession, 204; and radical unionists, 46; and religious policy, 197; and Soeharto, 46–47; "Statement of Concern," 207; youth groups and, 37

Nasution, Adnan Buyung, 228, 314n24

National Awakening Day, 204

National economy, and global economy, Daud's view, 159–60

National Food Research Institute, 122

National Independence Day, 1984, 220

National independence movement, and social solidarity, 82

Nationalism, 71–72; and anti-Chinese sentiment, 84; Islamic, 276; and Pertamina operations, 171; of Soeharto, 282

National Logistics Agency. *See* Bulog

National Party (Partai Nasional Indonesia, PNI), 15, 19, 92, 195; Communist Party and, 17; Soeharto and, 46; Sukarno and, 33, 95

National Peasants Conference, 18

National policy, university economists and, 72

National stability, Soeharto and, 208

National unity, 21, 233–34; Pancasila legislation and, 230; Soeharto and, 162–63; Sukarno and, 27

National Youth Federation, 36–37

Native rulers, Dutch colonialism and, 102

Natsir, Mohammed, 201–2; "Statement of Concern," 207

Natural resources, 53; nationalization of, 169–70

Navy, 9; arrest of officers, 51; and foreign debt, 68; Soeharto and, 47

Index

Nepal, 285

Netherlands: and Indonesian economic policies, 63; trade with, 68

Netherlands Indies, education, pre-WWII, 75

New economic policies, 1966, 63–72

New hybrid rice varieties, 112–13, 116–18, 122–25

New Order: armed forces and, 206; and control of imports, 246; criticisms of, 198–200; Muslims and, 218, 235

Newspapers: reactions to Tanjung Priok incident, 229–30; report of peasant uprisings, 19; report of religious revivals, 241; repression of, 137, 143, 200

New Zealand, and Indonesian economic policies, 63

Nigeria, 283, 289; development spending, 191–92; foreign investment, 252; windfall oil profits, 190

Nishihara, Masashi 97, 98

Nitisastro, Widjojo, *See* Widjojo Nitisastro

Noncommunist nations, 72; trade with, 68

Nonmilitary role of army, 62

Non-Muslim minorities, and presidential succession, 300

Non-oil exports, deregulation and, 264

Nontariff protection, 264

North Sumatra, purge of Communists, 14

NU. *See* Nahdatul Ulama

Oil: and Indonesian economy, 190–93, 283; U.S. investments, 148

—exports, 57, 68; decline of, 265; to Japan, 147; price increases, 161

—income from, 174–75; and civil service expansion, 105; and foreign debt, 188; and industrial development, 216; and rice consumption, 120–21, 124; Soeharto regime and, 290–91

—prices: decline of, 217, 280; rise in, 164, 177, 190, 210

Oil boom: and growth of conglomerates, 256–57; management of, 283

Oil crisis, and reform of economy, 262

Oil industry: government control, 279, 290; Pertamina monopoly, 170–71

Oil palm, as export crop, 114

Okita, Saburo, 159

OPEC (Organization of Petroleum Exporting Countries), 290

Opposition to government, 270, 278–80; Islam and, 234–35; sources of, 275–78; students and, 197–98

Oratory of Sukarno, 29–30

Organization of Petroleum Exporting Countries (OPEC), 290

Organization of students, 36

Orientalist view of Indonesian economy, 83–84

Outer islands, 22

—rebellion of, 27, 79, 273; armed forces and, 104; and budget deficit, 56; Masyumi Party and, 92, 276

Ownership of land, 16–17, 132

Palace, Dutch colonial government, 29

"Palace group," financial interests, 257–60

Panca Holding Ltd., plastics imports, 248–49

Pancasila, 162–63, 233–34; armed forces and, 89, 206; Islamic groups and, 220; legislative enforcement, 230, 236–39; and social unrest, 224–25; "Statement of Concern" and, 207; teaching of principles, 243

Panggabean, Maraden, 200; and Ibnu Sutowo, 185

Panglaykim, 159

Pangreh Praja, 102

Paracommando Regiment, 39

Parliament, 86, 89–90, 95–96, 194–95; armed forces representatives, 108, 110; and elections, 87–88, 90–91, 95, 99, 205–6; government control, 99; land laws, 16–17; Pancasila laws, 230, 236–39; and Pertamina crisis, 166–67; petitions to, 277–78; and "Statement of Concern," 207–8; and Tanjung Priok incident, 225

Parmusi, 235

Partai Komunis Indonesia. *See* Communist Party of Indonesia

Partai Nasional Indonesia. *See* National Party

Partnerships with Japanese investors, 149

Index

Party for Unity and Development. *See* Development Unity Party

Party leaders, power of, 90

Party politics, and religion, 21

Pasar Senen shopping center, student protests, 136

Pauker, Guy, 144

PDI. *See* Indonesian Democracy Party

Peasants: arming of, Communist proposal, 10; uprisings, Communist inspired, 19

Pedoman (newspaper), 143

People's Bank, rural credit program, 134

People's Consultative Assembly, 86–87, 90–91, 95; armed forces representatives, 108; and presidential candidates, 198; reelection of Soeharto, 201

People's Republic of China, Jakarta embassy, 25

Per capita income, 28, 133, 285, 296–97

Permina, 170; Ibnu Sutowo and, 168–69

Personal style of Ibnu Sutowo, 176

Pertamina, 107, 160, 170–71, 174–75, 182–84; and armed forces business ventures, 212; control of imports, 246; corrupt practices, 147, 158, 164, 171–74, 183; distribution of fertilizer, 122; and electoral campaign, 98; financial collapse, 165–67; and foreign debt, 188–89; Ibnu Sutowo's view, 192; January 15 riots and, 147; loan default, 180–81; mining investments, 213; mismanagement of, 275; postponement of projects, 266

Peta (rice variety), 114, 116–17

Petition of Fifty, 207–8

Petition of Fifty group: Fatwa and, 228; and Pancasila bill, 220, 238–39; and Tanjung Priok incident, 222; and terrorism, 229

Petition of Fifty group member, and Islamic revival, 242

Petitions to Parliament, 277–78

Petrochemical projects, 213; Pertamina operations, 183

Petroleum products: importation rights, 246; Pertamina operations, 171

Philippines, 284, 286, 295; coups, 299; education, 75, 285; foreign investment, 252; per capita income, 285

Physical import quotas, 247

Physicians, 279, 287

PKI. *See* Communist Party of Indonesia

Plastics industry: deregulation of imports, 263; government control, 248–49

Plaza Accord, and investment in Southeast Asia, 264

Plot to overthrow government, student demonstration as, 141–47

Pluralism, managed, 293–95

PNI. *See* National Party

Poesponegoro, Djuned, 78, 81

Police, 104

Political consequences of inflation, 58

Political culture of Java, 74

Political development, Soeharto and, 209

Political economy, 3–4, 270; as managed pluralism, 293

Political expression, terrorism as, 275

Political factors in state enterprises, 253–54

Political history, popular ideas, 21

Political ideology, and Indonesian violence, 26

Political leaders, and economic reforms, 71

Political machine, creation of, 96–111

Political parties, 76, 272; election laws and, 90–91; elections and, 87, 99; government groupings, 195; Islamic, 232; Pancasila requirement, 230, 237–39; Provisional People's Consultative Assembly and, 61; Soeharto and, 91–94; Sukarno and, 33, 95–96, 271

Political regime, and economic policy, 288–93

Political stability: and economy, 285, 288; and expansion of civil service, 106; factionalism and, 162

Political transition, 295–98; army and, 299

Politicians, elite class, 28

Politics: army officers and, 8–10, 43; Muslims and, 276–77

Popular representation, Indonesian government and, 27

Population of Indonesia, 3; Chinese people in, 255; Tanjung Priok, 220; urban, 278

Index

—growth of, 284; and fragmentation of land-holdings, 16; female education and, 288; university economists and, 83

Poverty of Indonesia, 1, 28, 52; decline of, 133, 286; education and, 75

Power, 1, 21–22, 27; Guided Democracy and, 52; Javanese culture and, 48; 1965 centers, 271

PPP. See Development Unity Party

Prawiranegara, Sjafruddin, 54; and Pancasila legislation, 237–38; "Statement of Concern," 207; and Tanjung Priok incident, 222

Precolonial Indonesia, 271

Presidency, 271–72; Consultative Assembly and, 86; student protests and, 142, 198; reelection of Soeharto, 194–202

—succession to, 43–45, 91, 100, 295–98; corrupt practices and, 292; Soemitro's view, 204

Presidential assistants, student protests, 140

Press: and financial interests of palace group, 257–58; and student protests, 135, 141–42; and Tanjung Priok incident, 224

—suppression of, 163, 200, 236, 256; after January 15 riots, 136–37, 142–43

Pressures for economic reform, 260–64

Price supports for rice, 118, 123–25

Primary education, 2, 123, 285; gender equality, 288; universal, 105

Princen, H., 314n24

Private business firms, 4, 256; import monopolies, 247; and manufacturing, 291; political dependence, 279

Private enterprise, Widjojo's views, 80

Private institutions, acceptance of, 301

Private investments, 280; deregulation and, 264; government control, 251–52

—foreign, 161; and industrial development, 215–16; Japanese, 148

Private organizations: governmental control, 238–39; Pancasila legislation and, 236–39

Private sector, 254–57; deregulation and, 264; and economic policy, 247; and industrial development, 215–16; social philosophy and, 300–301

Privatization: of elite classes, 4; of state-owned corporations, 266

Probosutedjo, 156, 259

Production: decline in, and inflation, 58; of fertilizer, 122; of rice, new hybrids and, 112–13

Professionals, independent, 279

Progovernment political party, Soeharto and, 93–94

Pronk, J. J., 139

Proportional representation, 87, 89

Prosecutions after Tanjung Priok incident, 227–28

Protestant party, 195

Provincial governors, military men as, 97, 108, 109–10

Provisional People's Consultative Assembly, 42, 61; economic statement, 61–63, 82. See also People's Consultative Assembly

PSI (Socialist Party), youth leaders, 37

"PSI" officers, 144, 308–9n8

Public dissidence, Soeharto and, 162–63

Public expenditures, and inflation, 58

Public investment of oil windfall, 191

Public persona of Soeharto, 49

Public trade policy, private influences, 267

Public works, 253; rural, 191

Publishing industry, 65

Pupuk Sriwijaya (fertilizer corporation), 122

Pura, Raphael, 259

Pusri, 122

Rachmat, Basuki, 35, 41–42

Racial conflicts, and January 15 riots, 138

Racism, 152; anti-Chinese, 84; Muslims and, 218–19; Nasir and, 221

Radical fringe, Islamic, 218–22

Radical social movements, 21

Radio Indonesia, coup announcement, 11

Radius Prawiro, 262–63

Raffles, Stamford, 102

Ransom, David, 146

Rappaport, Bruce, 179–81

Rattan, export controls, 266–67

Raw materials, importation of, 246

Index

Reagan, Ronald, visit to Indonesia, 257–58

Rebellion, Madiun, 15

Recession, international: oil prices and, 177, 217; and Tanjung Priok incident, 220, 245

Recivilianization of government, 111

Record of growth, 284–85

Redistribution of income, Widjojo's views, 80

Reelection of Soeharto, 194–202; armed forces and, 277; 1978, 275; 1988, 262; 1993, 267

Reforestation, 123

Reforms: economic, Soeharto and, 64; electoral, 89–91; after January 15 riots, 137

Refugees, Chinese-Indonesian, 25–26

Relatives of Soeharto: corrupt practices, 156, 206, 292; favored positions, 246; financial interests, 257–60; industry advantages, 248–50, 291; trade benefits, 267

Religion: need for national consensus, 300; party politics and, 21; revivals of, 241–42

Religious conflicts, 196–97; and January 15 riots, 138; Muslims and, 230, 231, 234; and reelection of Soeharto, 201–2

Religious conversions, 27

Religious intolerence, and violence, 26

Religious law, Islamic, and national law, 235

Religious leaders, and Pancasila legislation, 237

Remoteness of Indonesia, 2–3

Representative institutions, electoral reform and, 90

Republic National Bank of Dallas, 165

Republic of Indonesia, 29

Research, in rice cultivation, 122

Res Publica University, 31

Retaliation for "Statement of Concern," 208

Retired military officers: criticism of government, 194, 202–5; opposition to Soeharto, 277; and reelection of Soeharto, 194, 202; "Statement of Concern," 207; view of society, 210

Retirement: of armed services personnel, 107; of Soeharto, likelihood of, 296–97

Reuters, reports of drought, 19

Revival of religions, 241–42

Revolts, Muslim-supported, 234

Revolutionary Council, 1; anticommunist youth groups and, 37; coup attempt, 11–12

Riau province, mineral resources, 287

Rice: government programs, 115–18, 279; importation rights, 246; land ownership limitations, 16; protection of industry, 264; subsidies, 211

—economy of, 58; colonial period, 113–15; social inequities, 59

—shortage of, 112, 118–21; and January 15 riots, 138

Riots, racial conflicts, 138, 209. See also Student protests

Ritual purification, Soeharto and, 48–49

Roads, improvement of, 122–23

Roeslan Abdulgani, 39

Rosihan Anwar, 143, 146

Royal Dutch Shell, 169–70

Rubber exports, 57, 68

Rulers: native, Dutch colonialism and, 102; as personification of unity, 21–22

Rural areas, 17, 122–23, 272, 286–87; communist campaign, 8, 18–20; government spending, 289; public works, 191; radical politics, 26; social changes, 129–34

—credit, 134; for rice production, 113, 117–18

—Java, 283; female education, 288; government favoritism, 289

—population, 20–21; elections and, 98, 99

Rural communist stronghold, army attack, 12–13

Rural development, oil windfall and, 191

Rural elite, land ownership, 16

Rural-urban disparities, 286–87

Sadikin, Ali, 199, 225, 226, 227; "Statement of Concern," 207; and Tanjung Priok incident, 222

Sadli, Mohammad, 54, 61, 73; and Chinese investments, 255; and control of imports, 247–48; and dismissal of Ibnu Sutowo, 186; economic theory, 84; and foreign aid, 68; and foreign oil companies, 186–87; and industrial development, 215; oversight of Pertamina, 174–75, 177, 179; and Pertamina crisis, 166–67

Said, Ali, 186

Index

Index

Soedjono Humardhani, 48, 146, 157, 196; and Muslims, 238

Soedomo, and antigovernment plot, 195–96

Soeharto, 45–46, 272, 276; accession to power, 271–72; and anticommunist protests, 34; and anti-Sukarno officers, 39–40; appointment as president, 42; and armed forces, 30, 45–48, 106, 206, 297–98; and Bulog, 125–26, 129; and capitalism, 300; and Chinese Communists, 25; and civil service, 279; Consultative Assembly and, 87; control of press, 143; cooperatives proposal, 267; and corruption in government, 157–58; and coup attempt, 7, 11, 24; criticisms of, 205–11; and criticisms of government, 162–63; and deregulation, 262, 266; and development, 193; economic advisers, 62–63, 73–75; and economic inequities, 287; and economy, 51–52, 281–82; and elections, 86–87, 99, 94–95, 100; and electoral reform, 90–91, 205; and foreign loans, 177; and foreign oil companies, 164, 187; and functional groups, 96; and Ibnu Sutowo, 170, 175, 176, 178, 184–86; and industrial development, 217; and Islam, 299; and January 15 riots, 161–62; Japan and, 69; and Javanese culture, 48–50; and Letter of Instruction, 42; and massacre of Communists, 14–15; and militarization of government, 109, 111; military officers and, 258; Moertopo and, 145; and Muslims, 218, 234; Nasution and, 44; and new economic policies, 63–64; and oil industry, 290; opposition to, 277; and Pancasila legislation, 230, 236–37; and Pertamina, 165, 167, 182, 184; and political parties, 91–94; and presidential succession, 296–97; and privatization, 266; Provisional People's Consultative Assembly and, 61; reelection to presidency, 194–202, 262, 275; relatives of, benefits to, 156, 248–50, 257–60, 267, 292; and rice shortage, 112, 116–18, 119, 121; and Soedjatmoko, 143; and "Statement of Concern," 208; State of the Nation Report, 1977, 133; student leaders and, 37–38; and student protests, 136–37, 140, 172, 197, 275; and succession to presidency, 43, 45; Sukarno and, 31–36; Sultan of Yogyakarta and, 201; and Tanjung Priok incident, 226; tenure of office, 288, 295; and terrorism, 230; transfer of authority from Suharto, 40–43; youth leaders and, 37

Soeharto, Mrs. Tien, 156

Soeharto regime, 280–83; corrupt practices, 154–57

Soehoed, A. R., 213; and industrial development, 215

Soemitro, 136, 137, 139, 210; and Ali Moertopo, 140; and Chinese issue, 152; and January 15 riots, 144–45, 147; and presidential succession, 204

Soesastro, Hadi, 260

Solo, anti-Chinese riots, 209

Southeast Asia, 72, 75; civil service patterns, 106; foreign investment in manufacturing, 264; and Indonesian political transition, 296

South Korea, 281, 283; investment in Indonesia, 264

Soviet Union, 9, 67–68; and Indonesian economic policies, 63

Specificity of government investment lists, 251

Sri Lanka, 286; education, 285

Stability of government: and civil service expansion, 106; and economy, 285, 288; elections and, 87; factionalism and, 162

Stabilization program, 1963, 71

Staff and Command School, Bandung, 47; and electoral reform, 89–90; seminar on economy, 62

Standard Vacuum, 169–70

State banks: deregulation and, 265; and industrial development, 216–17

State enterprises, 57, 100, 160, 252–54, 266; communists and, 13; import monopolies, 247, 248; manufacturing, 291; military and, 274; mismanagement of, 275. See also Pertamina

"Statement of Concern," 207–8

State power, and industrial development, 214–15

Index

Index

Sutowo, Ibnu. *See* Ibnu Sutowo

Suwarto, 81; and economic seminar, 62; and electoral reform, 89–90; Soemitro and, 144

Switzerland, and Indonesian economic policies, 63

Syarifin Maloko, 222

Sydney Morning Herald, 257

Synthetic fibers: Japanese production, 150; Pertamina production, 171

Tahija, Julius, 187

Taiwan, 281; investment in Indonesia, 264

Tanaka, Kakuei, 135–36, 147–48

Tanjung Priok, 219–24; government prosecutions, 227–28; interpretations of incident, 224–26; and Pancasila legislation, 239; reactions to violence, 226–27, 229–31

Tankers, Pertamina contracts, 175, 178–81

Tariffs, and trade deregulation, 263

Taxes, 66, 71; collection of, 301; on international trade, 56; Pertamina and, 173; reforms, 262

Tea, as export crop, 113

Teaching of Pancasila ideology, 243

Technocrats, 72–79, 109, 281–82; and rice crisis, 121; election and, 100

Technological advances, village society and, 131–32

Technology, 290; Habibie's view, 214; Ibnu Sutowo's view, 192; for rice production, 113

Teijin (Japanese synthetic fiber producer), 150

Telecommunications, corrupt practices, 158

Telephones, 278, 287

Tempo magazine: and private sector investments, 254; report of electoral campaign violence, 236

Tenancy laws, 17

Tentara Nasional Indonesia. *See* Indonesian National Army

Tenure in office, of Indonesian economists, 73

Tenure of regime, and economic policy, 288

Territorial administration, military personnel and, 110

Territorial army commanders, 46

Terrorism, 275; airline hijacking, 236; anti-Chinese, 226; Borobudur bombing, 231; charges against Dharsono, 228; extremist groups and, 229; reactions to, 229–31; Soeharto and, 230; after Tanjung Priok incident, 226–27

Textile industry: Chinese involvement, 153; Japanese investment, 149–52

Thahir, Achmad, 183

Thailand, 295; agricultural production, 284–85; civil service, 273–74; coups, 299; education, pre-WWII, 75; equity of economy, 286; fall of military government, 138, 161–62; foreign investment, 252, 264, 291, 314n40; Gross Domestic Product, 284; growth rate, 284; Japanese investment, 149, 151–52; population growth, 284; rice surplus, 117; student protests, 135, 148; urban population, 278

Thajeb, Sjarif, 31, 32

Thanom Kittikachorn, 138; fall of, 161–62

Third Plan, 213, 216

"Three Demands of the People," 33, 140

"Three togethers," 18

Timber exports, control of, 267

Tin, Tun, 70

Tin mining, 57

Tirtosudiro, Achmad, 117; Soeharto and, 125–26

Tjan, Harry, 36

Tjokroaminoto, Anwar, 158

TNI. *See* Indonesian National Army

Tokyo conference on Indonesian economy, 63–64

Tolleng, Rahman, 314n24

Toray Industries, 150

Toronto Dominion Bank, 166

Trade: economic reforms and, 68; policy reforms, 262

Traditional government, Java, 102

Transition, political, 295–98

Transportation, state enterprises, 253

Trihatmodjo, Bambang, 248–49, 259

Tri Usaha Bhakti (Army holding company), 155

Index

Index

Studies of the East Asian Institute

The Ladder of Success in Imperial China, by Ping-ti Ho. New York: Columbia University Press, 1962.

The Chinese Inflation, 1937–1949, by Shun-hsin Chou. New York: Columbia University Press, 1963.

Reformer in Modern China: Chang Chien, 1853–1926, by Samuel Chu. New York: Columbia University Press, 1965.

Research in Japanese Sources: A Guide, by Herschel Webb with the assistance of Marleigh Ryan. New York: Columbia University Press, 1965.

Society and Education in Japan, by Herbert Passin. New York: Teachers College Press, 1965.

Agricultural Production and Economic Development in Japan, 1873–1922, by James I. Nakamura. Princeton: Princeton University Press, 1967.

Japan's First Modern Novel: Ukigumo of Futabatei Shimei, by Marleigh Ryan. New York: Columbia University Press, 1967.

The Korean Communist Movement, 1918–1948 by Dae-Sook Suh. Princeton: Princeton University Press, 1967.

The First Vietnam Crisis, by Melvin Gurtov. New York: Columbia Univeristy Press, 1967.

Cadres, Bureaucracy, and Political Power in Communist China, by A. Doak Barnett. New York: Columbia University Press, 1968.

The Japanese Imperial Institution in the Tokugawa Period, by Herschel Webb. New York: Columbia University Press, 1968.

Higher Education and Business Recruitment in Japan, by Koya Azumi. New York: Teachers College Press, 1969.

The Communists and Peasant Rebellions: A Study in the Rewriting of Chinese History, by James P. Harrison, Jr. New York: Atheneum, 1969.

How the Conservatives Rule Japan, by Nathaniel B. Thayer. Princeton: Princeton University Press, 1969.

Aspects of Chinese Education, edited by C.T. Hu. New York: Teachers College Press, 1970.

Documents of Korean Communism, 1918–1948, by Dae-Sook Suh. Princeton: Princeton University Press, 1970.

Series List

Japanese Education: A Bibliography of Materials in the English Language, by Herbert Passin. New York: Teachers College Press, 1970.

Economic Development and the Labor Market in Japan, by Koji Taira. New York: Columbia University Press, 1970.

The Japanese Oligarchy and the Russo-Japanese War, by Shumpei Okamoto. New York: Columbia University Press, 1970.

Imperial Restoration in Medieval Japan, by H. Paul Varley. New York: Columbia University Press, 1971.

Japan's Postwar Defense Policy, 1947–1968, by Martin E. Weinstein. New York: Columbia University Press, 1971.

Election Campaigning Japanese Style, by Gerald L. Curtis. New York: Columbia University Press, 1971.

China and Russia: The "Great Game," by O. Edmund Clubb. New York: Columbia University Press, 1971.

Money and Monetary Policy in Communist China, by Katharin Huang Hsiao. New York: Columbia University Press, 1971.

The District Magistrate in Late Imperial China, by John R. Watt. New York: Columbia University Press, 1972.

Law and Policy in China's Foreign Relations: A Study of Attitude and Practice, by James C. Hsiung. New York: Columbia University Press, 1972.

Pearl Harbor as History: Japanese-American Relations, 1931–1941, edited by Dorothy Borg and Shumpei Okamoto, with the assestance of Dale K. A. Finlayson. New York: Columbia University Press, 1973.

Doctors in Politics: The Political Life of the Japan Medical Association, by William E. Steslicke. New York: Praeger, 1973.

Teachers and Politics in Japan, by Donald Ray Thurston. Princeton: Princeton University Press, 1973.

Japan's Foreign Policy, 1868–1941: A Research Guide, edited by James W. Morley. New York: Columbia University Press, 1974.

Palace and Politics in Prewar Japan, by David Anson Titus. New York: Columbia University Press, 1974.

The Idea of China: Essays in Geographic Myth and Theory, by Andrew March, Devon, England: David and Charles, 1974.

Origins of the Cultural Revolution: I, Contradictions Among the People, 1956–1957, by Roderick MacFarquhar. New York: Columbia University Press, 1974.

Shiba Kokan: Artist, Innovator, and Pioneer in the Westernization of Japan, by Calvin L. French. Tokyo: Weatherhill, 1974.

Insei: Abdicated Sovereigns in the Politics of Late Heian Japan, by G. Cameron Hurst. New York: Columbia University Press, 1975.

Embassy at War, by Harold Joyce Noble. Edited with an introduction by Frank Baldwin, Jr. Seattle: Univeristy of Washington Press, 1975.

Rebels and Bureaucrats: China's December 9ers, by John Israel and Donald W. Klein. Berkeleyd: University of California Press, 1976.

Deterrent Diplomacy, edited by James W. Morley. New York: Columbia University Press, 1976.

House United, House Divided: The Chinese Family in Taiwan, by Myron L. Cohen. New York: Columbia University Press, 1976.

Escape from Predicament: Neo-Confucianism and China's Evolving Political Culture, by Thomas A. Metzger. New York: Columbia University Press, 1976.

Cadres, Commanders, and Commissars: The Training of the Chinese Communist Leadership, 1920–45, by Jane L. Price. Boulder, CO: Westview Press, 1976.

Sun Yat-sen: Frustrated Patriot, by C. Martin Wilbur. New York: Columbia University Press, 1976.

Japanese International Negotiating Style, by Michael Blaker. New York: Columbia University Press, 1977.

Contemporary Japanese Budget Politics, by John Creighton Campbell. Berkeley: University of California Press, 1977.

The Medieval Chinese Oligarchy, by David Johnson. Boulder, CO: Westview Press, 1977.

The Arms of Kiangnan: Modernization in the Chinese Ordance Industry, 1860–1895, by Thomas L. Kennedy. Boulder, CO: Westview Press, 1978.

Patterns of Japanese Policymaking: Experiences from Higher Education, by T. J. Pempel. Boulder, CO: Westview Press, 1978.

The China Connection: Roger S. Greene, Thomas W. Lamont, George E. Sokolsky, and American-East Asian Relations, by Warren I. Cohen. New York: Columbia University Press, 1978.

Militarism in Modern China: The Career of Wu P'ei-fu, 1916–1939, by Odoric Y. K. Wou. Folkstone, England: Dawson, 1978.

A chinese Pioneer Family: The Lins of Wu-Feng, by Johanna Meskill. Princeton University Press, 1979.

Perspectives on a Changing China, edited by Joshua A. Fogel and William T. Rowe. Boulder, CO: Westview Press, 1979.

The Memories of Li Tsung-jen, by T. K. Tong and Li Tsung-jen. Boulder, CO: Westview Press, 1979.

Unwelcome Muse: Chinese Literature in Shanghai and Peking, 1937–1945, by Edward M. Gunn, Jr. New York: Columbia University Press, 1980.

Yenan and the Great Powers: The Origins of Chinese Communist Foreign Policy, by James Reardon-Anderson. New York: Columbia University Press, 1980.

Uncertain Years: Chinese-American Relations, 1947–1950, edited by Dorothy Borg and Waldo Heinrichs. New York: Columbia University Press, 1980.

Series List

The Fateful Choice: Japan's Advance into Southeast Asia, edited by James W. Morley. New York: Columbia University Press, 1980.

Tanaka Giichi and Japan's China Policy, by William F. Morton. Folkestone, England: Dawson, 1980; New York: St. Martin's Press, 1980.

The Origins of the Korean War: Liberation and the Emergence of Separate Regimes, 1945–1947, by Bruce Cumings. Princeton: Princeton University Press, 1981.

Class Conflict in Chinese Socialism, by Richard Curt Kraus. New York: Columbia University Press, 1981.

Education Under Mao: Class and Competition in Canton Schools, by Jonathan Unger. New York: Columbia University Press, 1982.

Private Academies of Takugawa Japan, by Richard Rubinger. Priceton: Princeton University Press, 1982.

Japan and the San Francisco Peace Settlement, by Michael M. Yoshitsu. New York: Columbia University Press, 1982.

New Frontiers in American-East Asian Relations: Essays Presented to Dorothy Borg, edited by Warren I. Cohen. New York: Columbia University Press, 1983.

The Origins of the Cultural Revolution: II, The Great Leap Forward, 1958–1960, by Roderick MacFarquhar. New York: Columbia University Press, 1983.

The China Quagmire: Japan's Expansion of the Asian Continent, 1933–1941, edited by James W. Morley. New York: Columbia Unversity Press, 1983.

Fragments of Rainbows: The Life and Poetry of Saito Mokichi, 1882–1953, by Amy Vladeck Heinrich. New York: Columbia University Press, 1983.

The U.S.-South Korean Alliance: Evolving Patterns of Security Relations, edited by Gerald L. Curtis and Sung-joo Han. Lexington, MA: Lexington Books, 1983.

State and Diplomacy in Early Modern Japan, by Ronald Toby. Princeton: Princeton University Press, 1983 (he); Stanford: Stanford University Press, 1991 (pb).

Discovering History in China: American Historical Writing on the Recent Chinese Past, by Paul A. Cohen. New York: Columbia University Press, 1984.

The Foreign Policy of the Republic of Korea, edited by Youngnok Koo and Sungjoo Han. New York: Columbia University Press, 1984.

Japan and the Asian Development Bank, by Dennis Yasutomo. New York: Praeger Publishers, 1983.

Japan Erupts: The London Naval Conference and the Manchurian Incident, edited by James W. Morley. New York: Columbia University Press, 1984.

Japanese Culture, third edition, revised, by Paul Varley. Honolulu: University of Hawaii Press, 1984.

Japan's Modern Myths: Ideology in the Late Meiji Period, by Carol Gluck. Princeton: Princeton University Press, 1985.

Shamans, Housewives, and other Restless Spirits: Women in Korean Ritual Life, by Laurel Kendall. Honolulu: University of Hawaii Press, 1985.

Human Rights in Contemporary China, by R. Randle Edwards, Louis Henkin, and Andrew J. Nathan. New York: Columbia University Press, 1986.

The Pacific Basin: New Challenges for the United States, edited by James W. Morley. New York: Academy of Political Science, 1986.

The Manner of Giving: Strategic Aid and Japanes Foreign Policy, by Dennis T. Yasutomo. New York: Free Press, 1986.

Security Interdependence in the Asia Pacific Region, James W. Morley's Ed., Lexington, MA: D.C. Heath and Co., 1986.

China's Political Economy: The Quest for Development since 1949, by Carl Riskin. Oxford: Oxford University Press, 1987.

Anvil of Victory: The Communist Revolution in Manchuria, by Steven I. Levine. New York: Columbia University Press, 1987.

Urban Japanese Housewives: At Hime and in the Community, by Anne E. Imamura. Honolulu: University of Hawaii Press, 1987.

China's Satellite Parties, by James D. Seymour. Armonk, NY: M.E. Sharpe, 1987.

The Japanese Way of Politics, by Gerald L. Curtis. New York: Columbia University Press, 1988.

Border Crossings: Studies in International History, by Christopher Thorne. Oxford & New York: Basil Blackwell, 1988.

The Indochina Tangle: China's Vietnam Policy, 1975–1979, by Robert S. Ross. New York: Columbia University Press, 1988.

Remaking Japan: The American Occupation as New Deal, by Theodore Cohen, edited by Herbert Passin. New York: The Free Press, 1987.

Kim Il Sung: The North Korean Leader, by Dae-Sook Suh. New York: Columbia University Press, 1988.

Japan and the World, 1853–1952: A Bibliographic Guide to Recent Scholarship in Japanese Foreign Relations, by Sadao Asada. New York: Columbia University Press, 1988.

Contending Approaches to the Political Economy of Taiwan, edited by Edwin A. Winckler and Susan Greenhalgh. Armonk, NY: M.E. Sharpe, 1988.

Aftermath of War: Americans and the Remaking of Japan, 1945–1952, by Howard B. Schonberger, Kent, OH: Kent State University Press, 1989.

Single Sparks: China's Rural Revolutions, edited by Kathleen Hartford and Steven M. Goldstein. Armonk, NY: M.E. Sharpe, 1989.

Neighborhood Tokyo, by Theodore C. Bestor. Stanford: Standford University Press, 1989.

Missionaries of the Revolution: Soviet Advisers and Chinese Nationalism, by C. Martin Wilbur and Julie Lien-ying How. Cambridge, MA: Harvard University Press, 1989.

Education in Japan, by Richard Rubinger and Edward Beauchamp. New York: Garland Publishing, Inc., 1989.

Financial Politics in Contemporary Japan, by Frances Rosenbluth. Ithaca: Cornell University Press, 1989.

Suicidal Narrative in Modern Japan: The Case of Dazai Osamu, by Alan Wolfe. Princeton: Princeton University Press, 1990.

Thailand and the United States: Development, Security and Foreign Aid, by Robert Muscat. New York: Columbia University Press, 1990.

China's Crisis: Dilemmas of Reform and Prospects for Democracy, by Andrew J. Nathan. Columbia University Press, 1990.

Anarchism and Chinese Political Culture, by Peter Zarrow. New York: Columbia University Press, 1991.

Race to the Swift: State and Finance in Korean Industrialization, by Jung-en Woo. New York: Columbia University Press, 1991.

Competitive Ties: Subcontracting in the Japanese Automotive Industry, by Michael Smitka. New York: Columbia University Press, 1991.

The Study of Change: Chemistry in China, 1840–1949, by James Reardon-Anderson. New York: Cambridge University Press, 1991.

Explaining Economic Policy Failure: Japan and the 1969–1971 International Monetary Crisis, by Robert Angel. New York: Columbia University Press, 1991.

Pacific Basin Industries in Distress: Structural Adjustment and Trade Policy in the Nine Industrialized Economies, edited by Hugh T. Patrick with Larry Meissner. New York: Columbia University Press, 1991.

Business Associations and the New Political Economy of Thailand: From Bureaucratic Polity to Liberal Corporatism, by Anek Laothamatas. Boulder, CO: Westview Press, 1991.

Constitutional Reform and the Future of the Republic of China, edited by Harvey J. Feldman. Armonk, NY: M.E. Sharpe, 1991.

Driven by Growth: Political Change in the Asia-Pacific Region, edited by James W. Morley. Armonk, NY: M.E. Sharpe, 1992.

Schoolhouse Politicians: Locality and State during the Chinese Republic, by Helen Chauncey. Honolulu: University of Hawaii Press, 1992.

Managing Indonesia: The Modern Political Economy, by John Bresnan. New York: Columbia University Press, 1993.

Asia for the Asians: Japanese Advisors, Chinese Students, and the Quest for Modernization, 1895–1905, by Paula S. Harrell. Stanford: Stanford University Press, forthcoming.

Social Mobility in Contemporary Japan, by Hiroshi Ishida. Stanford: Stanford University Press, forthcoming.

Pollution, Politics and Foreign Investment in Taiwan: The Lukang Rebellion, by James Reardon-Anderson. Armonk, NY: M.E. Sharpe, forthcoming.

Series List

Tokyo's Marketplace: Custom and Trade in the Tsukiji Wholesale Fish Market, by
Theodore C. Bestor. Stanford: Stanford University Press, forthcoming.
Nishiwaki Junzaburo: The Poetry and Poetics of a Modernist Master, by Hosea
Hirata. Princeton University Press, forthcoming.
In the Shadow of the Father: The Writing of Koda Aya (1904–1990), by Alan
Tansman. New Haven: Yale University Press, forthcoming.
Land Ownership under Colonial Rule: Korea's Japanese Experience, 1900–1925, by
Edwin H. Gragert. Honolulu: University of Hawaii Press, forthcoming.

Designer:	Kathleen Szawiola
Text:	11/13 Adobe Garamond
Display:	Adobe Poster Bodoni Compressed
Compositor:	Impressions, a division of Edwards Brothers, Inc.
Printer:	Edwards Brothers, Inc.
Binder:	Edwards Brothers, Inc.